PROBLEMS OF SUFFERING
IN RELIGIONS OF THE WORLD

To MARGARET
from whom I received much
help in writing this book.
עזה כמות אהבה

PROBLEMS
OF SUFFERING IN
RELIGIONS OF THE
WORLD

BY

JOHN BOWKER

*Fellow of Trinity College, Cambridge, and Adjunct Professor of
Religious Studies in the University of Pennsylvania and North
Carolina State University*

CAMBRIDGE
UNIVERSITY PRESS

PUBLISHED BY THE PRESS SYNDICATE OF THE UNIVERSITY OF CAMBRIDGE
The Pitt Building, Trumpington Street, Cambridge, United Kingdom

CAMBRIDGE UNIVERSITY PRESS
The Edinburgh Building, Cambridge CB2 2RU, UK   http://www.cup.cam.ac.uk
40 West 20th Street, New York, NY 10011–4211, USA   http://www.cup.org
10 Stamford Road, Oakleigh, Melbourne 3166, Australia
Ruiz de Alarcón 13, 28014 Madrid, Spain

First published 1970
First paperback edition 1975
Reprinted 1977, 1980, 1987, 1988, 1990, 1995, 1998, 1999

Printed in the United Kingdom at the University Press, Cambridge

Library of Congress Catalogue card number: 77–93706

ISBN 0 521 07412 6 hardback
ISBN 0 521 09903 X paperback

CONTENTS

Contents

ACKNOWLEDGEMENTS

Thanks are due to the following for permission to reproduce copyright material: Darton, Longman & Todd Ltd and Doubleday & Company Inc., excerpts from *The Jerusalem Bible* © 1966; the Delegates of the Oxford University Press and the Syndics of the Cambridge University Press, excerpts from *The New English Bible*; Harper and Row Ltd, excerpt from J. N. D. Kelly, *Early Christian Doctrine*; the Rt Rev. J. L. Wilson, excerpt from *A Treasury of the Kingdom*, ed. E. A. Blackburn, Oxford University Press 1954; the SCM Press Ltd and the Fellowship of Reconciliation, excerpts from Thich Nat Hanh, *Vietnam: The Lotus in the Sea of Fire* 1967; George Allen & Unwin, Ltd, excerpt from R. C. Zaehner, *The Teachings of the Magi* (reprinted in M. Eliade, *From Primitives to Zen*, Harper & Row 1967); Columbia University Press, excerpts from W. T. de Bary (ed.), *Sources of Indian Tradition* 1958.

Thanks are also due to Professor H. D. Lewis, for permission to reproduce material in chapter 3 which was first published in *Religious Studies* IV, April 1969.

GLOSSARY

In some chapters, particularly those on Hinduism and Buddhism, a number of words and phrases are used in a transliterated form, without translation; this has been done in the case of words which have no exact English equivalent, or for which a direct translation would be more misleading than helpful. However, a proliferation of foreign terms may well be confusing for readers who are not already familiar with them. For this reason, a brief index is given here of the places where the meaning of each of the terms (which occur frequently) is discussed. For ease and simplicity of reference, this index includes *only* the places where the meaning of the terms is discussed. For other, more general, occurrences, see the General Index.

So far as transcriptions are concerned, it should be noted that an attempt has been made to give the most usual and familiar forms (though sometimes the forms have been slightly changed to give a guide to pronunciation), rather than to achieve uniform or exact precision. Those who know the languages will probably have little difficulty in recognising the forms in any case.

Glossary

ABBREVIATIONS

ad Autol. ad Autolycum
Adv. Haer. Adversus Haereses
A.H. After Hijra (see p. 107)
A.I.P.H.O.S. Annuaire de l'Institut de Philologie et d'Histoire Orientales et Slaves
B. Babylonian (Talmud)
Bar. Baruch
B.C.E. Before the Christian Era
Ber. Berakoth
Ber. Bereshith
B.I.H.R. Bulletin of the Institute of Historical Research
B.M. Baba Mezia
Cant. Canticles (Song of Songs)
C.E. Christian Era
Chron. Chronicles
Col. Colossians (Letter to)
Conf. Confessions (of Augustine)
Cor. Corinthians (Letter to)
C.W. Collected Works (of Lenin)
de Civ. Dei de Civitate Dei
de Hab. Virg. de Habitu Virginum
de Op. et Eleem. de Opere et Eleemosynis
de Resurr. Carn. de Resurrectione Carnis
de Test. An. de Testimonio Animae
de Util. Cred. de Utilitate Credendi
Deut. Deuteronomy
Eccles. Ecclesiastes
Econ. MSS. Economic and Political Manuscripts (by K. Marx)
Ep. Epistle
Eph. Ephesians (Letter to)
Exod. Exodus
Gal. Galatians (Letter to)

Gen. Genesis
Hab. Habakkuk
Heb. Hebrews (Letter to)
Isa. Isaiah
J. Jerushalmi (i.e. Palestinian Talmud)
Jas. James (Letter of)
Jer. Jeremiah
J.N.E.S. Journal of Near Eastern Studies
J.S.S. Journal of Semitic Studies
Lev. Leviticus
LXX Septuagint (Greek translation of the Old Testament)
Macc. Maccabees
Mal. Malachi
Matt. Matthew
MEGA Marx and Engels, Historisch-Kritische Gesamtausgabe
Midr. Teh. Midrash Tehillim (Midrash on Psalms)
N.E.B. New English Bible
N.T.S. New Testament Studies
Num. Numbers
Or. Oratio
Pet. Peter
Phil. Philippians (Letter to)
Prov. Proverbs
Ps. Psalm
P.T.S. Pali Text Society
Qoh. Qoheleth (Ecclesiastes)
R. Rabbah (in references to Midrash Rabbah)
R. Rabbi or Rabban (before name)
Radh. Radhakrishnan, S.
Rev. Revelation (Book of)
Rom. Romans (Letter to)
S. Sura (division of Quran)
Sam. Samuel

Abbreviations

San.   Sanhedrin
Shab.   Shabbath
Shem.   Shemoth (Exodus)
Taan.   Taanith
Tanh.   Tanhuma
Tanh. B.   Tanhuma (Buber's edn.)

Thess.   Thessalonians (Letter to)
Tim.   Timothy (Letter to)
Up.   *Upanishad*
Vay.   Vayyiqra (Leviticus)
Wisd. of Sol.   Wisdom of Solomon

INTRODUCTION

How much misery is presaged to us, when we come so generally weeping into the world, that, perchance in the whole body of history we reade but of one childe, *Zoroaster* that laughed at his birth: What miserable revolutions and changes, what down-fals, what break-necks, and precipitations may we justly think ourselves ordained to, if we consider, that in our comming into this world out of our mothers womb, we doe not make account that a child comes right, except it come with the head forward, and thereby prefigure that headlong falling into calamities which it must suffer after.[1]

John Donne, whose words those are, may well have been a man of unusually pessimistic temperament: he dwelt frequently on death, wrote his own epitaph and had his portrait painted in his shroud. And yet in that passage he is simply stating one of the most obvious facts of human existence, that suffering is the common lot of all men. It is because suffering, in one form or another, is a common experience that religions give to suffering a place of central importance or consideration—indeed, it is often said that suffering is an important *cause* of religion, since the promises held out by religion represent a way in which men can feel reassured in the face of catastrophe or death. It is, many would add, an inadequate or immature way of seeking reassurance, because it rests in illusion: it is an attempt to control the real world by means of the wish-world, and it was this insight which formed the basis of Freud's critique of religion:

The assertions made by religion that it could give protection and happiness to men, if they would only fulfil certain ethical obligations, were unworthy of belief. It seems not to be true that there is a power in the universe, which watches over the well-being of every individual with parental care and brings all his concerns to a happy ending. On the contrary, the destinies of man are incompatible with a universal principle of benevolence or with—what is to some degree contradictory—a universal principle of justice. Earthquakes, floods, and fires do not differentiate between the good and devout men, and the sinner and unbeliever. And even if we leave inanimate nature out of account and consider the destinies of individual men insofar as they depend on their relations with others of their own kind, it is by no means the rule

[1] Donne, *Sermon III*, Nonesuch edn. (ed. J. Hayward), London, 1962, p. 588.

I

that virtue is rewarded and wickedness punished, but it happens often enough that the violent, the crafty, and the unprincipled seize the desirable goods of the earth for themselves, while the pious go empty away.[1]

That passage, as an account of religion, is vastly over-simplified, not least because religions tend to start, not end, with exactly those observations of Freud. But it does effectively isolate the crucial importance in any religion of the account it gives of suffering. There is nothing theoretical or abstract about it. To talk of suffering is to talk not of an academic problem but of the sheer bloody agonies of existence, of which all men are aware and most have direct experience. All religions take account of this; some, indeed, make it the basis of all they have to say. Whatever theoretical constructions may be built, the foundations are laid in the apparent realities of what it is like to be alive. Thus what a religion has to say about suffering reveals, in many ways more than anything else, what it believes the nature and purpose of existence to be.

This to a great extent explains the purpose of this book. There are few better ways of coming to understand the religions of the world than by studying what response they make to the common experience of suffering. Obviously, a book which deals with several of the major religions at once cannot hope to be comprehensive. It would be possible, as indeed it has been done, to write a book on each of the religions on its own. But there is a quite separate value in studying religions in conjunction with each other. It brings out very clearly the extent to which they have contributed to each other, but even more than that, the extent to which they remain inescapably distinct. What has been attempted in this book is the description and illustration of some of the main themes and ideas in connection with suffering in each of the religions treated.

The title of this book refers to 'problems of suffering' in the plural, because there is no single, definable 'problem-of-suffering' which appears in all religions in the same form. On the contrary, it will be seen that suffering occurs *differently* as a problem in each religion. There is, of course, considerable overlap, particularly in closely related religions of either the Western or the Eastern

[1] *New Introductory Lectures on Psycho-Analysis*, 1933, pp. 228 f.

2

Introduction

traditions. But the overlap is usually in general terms rather than in points of specific application. So, for example, it can be said that in general both Marxism[1] and Islam have an instrumental theory of suffering, but in point of detail and application the instrumental theory in Marxism is completely different from that of the Quran. If the different religions have a common factor in their treatment of suffering, it is that they start with the facts of suffering as they are, not with suffering conceived as a theoretical problem. Suffering becomes a problem when it is related to other facts or other propositions which seem to be contradicted by it. Insofar as those other facts and propositions differ in the various religions, to that extent suffering is located differently as a problem in them; insofar as the facts and propositions coincide, to that extent suffering is located as a problem similarly. Thus one of the purposes of this study is to explore in what ways and for what reasons suffering became problematical in each religion, and also to show what responses to suffering have been proposed or advocated.

In writing this book, three general principles have been kept in mind: (1) No *extensive* knowledge of other religions has been assumed; an attempt, therefore, has been made to explain the basic features of each religion as they occur, so far as they are relevant to this study.[2] (2) So far as possible, each religion has been allowed to speak for itself, hence the very large number of original quotations in the book. The intention has been to supply sufficient original material to make the arguments within each religion intelligible. The book would perhaps have been strengthened by the inclusion of additional illustrations from other sources, such as art and music, but that would have produced a work of quite unmanageable length.[3] In selecting illustrations I

[1] Marxism has been included in this study because of its derivation from a religious tradition, and because of its continuing connections with that tradition; furthermore, its ostensible repudiation of religion has an obvious bearing on religious responses to suffering. Its inclusion does not imply an answer to the disputed and usually academic question of whether Marxism is or is not a religion.

[2] A *general* knowledge is obviously necessary: many books are now available summarising the beliefs and practices of different religions; a particularly useful and readable one is *The Concise Encyclopaedia of Living Faiths*, ed. R. C. Zaehner.

[3] Limitations of length were in any case imposed on this book by the fact that its material first took shape as a course of University Lectures which, in turn, were intended to provide a basis for class or seminar work. In that context, collecting further illustrative material from musical and artistic sources is in itself a rewarding project.

Introduction

have concentrated on the sources which are of particular importance and value to each religion in the formation of the attitudes of
its adherents. (3) On those foundations I have then, more briefly,
illustrated some of the ways in which those basic and fundamental
attitudes have been developed and applied down to the present
day. It would, obviously, be quite impossible to include everything
that every religion has ever said on the subject of suffering, but it
is possible to isolate certain prevailing characteristics and give
them a reasonably detailed examination.

It is possible that such an approach may seem academic and
detached—and to some extent, in a book, it is bound to be so. For
that reason it must be emphasised that the facts and instances of
suffering occur first, not the problem, and that the many passages
quoted in this book come more often from experience than from a
desire for intellectual satisfaction. The realities of suffering are
common to us all, and it is not hard to feel a very real identification
with those who have expressed their feelings about this common
experience—no matter what their time or place or generation
may be:

I am the man, I suffer'd, I was there.
The disdain and calmness of martyrs,
The mother of old, condemn'd for a witch, burnt with dry wood, her
    children gazing on,
The hounded slave that flags in the race, leans by the fence, blowing,
    cover'd with sweat,
The twinges that sting like needles his legs and neck, the
    murderous buckshot and the bullets,
All these I feel or am...
Agonies are one of my changes of garments,
I do not ask the wounded person how he feels, I myself become the
    wounded person,
My heart turns livid upon me as I lean on a cane and observe.[1]

[1] W. Whitman, 'Song of Myself' from *Leaves of Grass*, Nonesuch edn. (ed.
E. Holloway), London, 1964, p. 63.

1

JUDAISM

You must not molest the stranger or oppress him, for you lived as strangers in the land of Egypt.[1]

There can be few sentences which express so briefly, but at the same time so clearly, the essence of Hebrew and Jewish religion: relationship with God has, in immediate terms, practical rather than speculative consequences; and the imperative (or in this case the prohibition) is based on an appeal to history, not on an appeal to authority or to revelation in abstract form. Among the many cultures and religions of the ancient world, Israel stands out as distinct and different from them all. The religion of Israel drew on many alien sources, and it often made use of foreign practices and ideas, but always it constructed out of them something distinctively its own. The distinctive genius of Israel lay in its realisation and acceptance of the possibility that God might disclose himself in the events of history. It would be absurd to say that no one else in the ancient world believed that that might be so, just as it would be absurd to say that in Israel there was no other way in which God was believed to reveal himself. In point of fact, God was believed to make himself known in a great variety of ways—in creation, for example, or in the natural order, in the lives of exemplary men, in the words and actions of inspired individuals, in carefully ordered rituals, or even in the chance occurrences and accidents of life. In a sense it could be said that God is knowable in all things since all things are his creation. Yet still the fact remains that the distinctive and controlling factor in Israelite religion was the conviction that in the past God had unmistakably shown his hand in particular events, and that consequently in the present there were good grounds for believing that he would do so again. A foundation of this belief was laid in the sequence of events known as the Exodus. Under the banner of a newly-discovered (or perhaps newly-rediscovered) god, Yahweh,

[1] Exod. 22: 21; see also 23: 9, Lev. 19: 33 f., Deut. 10: 19, 24: 17 *et al*. Note that in this chapter the words 'Scripture' and 'Biblical' refer to *Jewish* Scripture.

a tiny handful of enslaved tribes made their escape from Egypt. The success of that escape and of their subsequent efforts to establish themselves in Canaan, not only vindicated their faith in Yahweh; it vindicated Yahweh himself. It showed, to put it crudely (as it would be put crudely in those early days), that Yahweh was up to his job—he was worth trusting.

> Yahweh I sing: he has covered himself in glory,
> horse and rider he has thrown into the sea...
> Yahweh is a warrior;
> Yahweh is his name.
> The chariots and the army of Pharaoh he has hurled into the sea;
> the pick of his horsemen lie drowned in the Sea of Reeds...
> Who among the gods is your like, Yahweh?
> Who is your like, majestic in holiness,
> terrible in deeds of prowess, worker of wonders?[1]

That understanding of God's activity has given to Judaism its capacity, not simply to survive, but also to sustain and inspire people down to the present day. Its roots are planted, not in mythology, but in history, or at least in an interpretation of historical events. This is not to say that mythology is absent from Scripture: on the contrary, it plays a prominent part, but almost invariably it is as a vehicle, conveying the significance of an experience and interpretation of history. From that central core of events in the Exodus the people of Israel gradually unified history by extending it backward to creation and forward to their own time, and by seeing it all as the arena of God's activity. In that process, random elements of tradition and mythology were gathered in, but only to serve the unifying vision of faith, that God is a potential participant in the affairs of men. Frequently, in early days, this was expressed in direct and simple terms as the participation of Israel's God, Yahweh, on behalf of his people to secure their welfare. Gradually (though by no means invariably, even down to the present) the crudity of this was transformed, and it was realised that knowledge of God demands more in the way of obligation than it offers of privilege or of immediate, effortless victory:

You alone of all the families of earth, have I acknowledged, *therefore* it is for all your sins that I mean to punish you.[2]

[1] Exod. 15: 1, 3, 4, 6, 11.   [2] Amos 3: 2.

Foundations

Decisive in this development was the application by the Hebrews of the concept of Covenant to religion. Clear covenant-forms were used in the Ancient Near East, particularly by the Hittites, to govern relations between nations or states. Those covenant-forms were used by the Israelite tribes to express the relationship which they believed to exist between themselves and God.[1]

In those covenants the conditions obligatory on both sides were laid down, and at the same time a summary was usually given of the historical circumstances on which the covenant-relationship was based. The application of the covenant-form to religion gave natural rise to the integration of law and narrative which together constitute Torah,[2] and which are so characteristic of Israelite religion. The obligations expressed as Law were subsequently accepted in their own right as being the revealed will of God, but the guarantee of that revelation, the guarantee, almost, that it *is* revelation, lay in God's self-disclosure in historical events.[3]

It may seem that this brief summary of the importance of history in Israelite religion has little direct relevance to the problem of suffering, but in fact this simple belief, that God has shown his hand in history, remains the key with which the Jewish people can hope to turn the lock of suffering. Yet at the very same time it also *creates* the problem of suffering, because the more firmly it is believed that God has participated in historical events the more inevitably it is bound to be asked why he does not participate more often. Why does he not always intervene to deliver his faithful servants? Why do the innocent suffer?

This at once begins to isolate the particular way in which suffering occurs as a problem in Scripture. On the whole, there was no great anxiety about the actual occurrence of suffering, or why it should exist. Those questions were certainly raised, as particularly in the opening chapters of Genesis, but there the fundamental assertion is made that the created order is 'very good',[4] and that evil and suffering, summarised in death, are a

---

[1] For general treatments of this theme, see G. E. Mendenhall, *Law and Covenant* (Pittsburgh, 1955); D. J. McCarthy, *Treaty and Covenant* (Rome, 1963).

[2] The word Torah means, roughly, guidance for life. It is sometimes translated 'Law', but it has a more extensive reference than that. It was applied particularly to the first five books of Scripture, the Pentateuch, which includes not only the laws revealed to Moses, but also long sections of narrative which are equally regarded as revelation. See further p. 43.

[3] For a particularly good example of this interaction between history, faith and law, see Ps. 105, especially vss. 42–5. [4] Gen. 1: 31.

consequence of Man (Adam)[1] alienating himself from God. In other words, dualism[2] was excluded, and the existence of suffering and death was located in the choices of Man which open up those possibilities inherent in creation. There is no second principle or creator responsible for evil. Indeed, it might even be said that Genesis does not portray a single 'fall of man', but rather a gradual extension and exploration of the human capacity to corrupt the gifts of God. The opening chapters of Genesis are a progressive illustration of the effects of the alienation of men from God, particularly in self-centredness, rivalry and murder, exploitation and lust in sexual relationships, the abnegation of responsibility in wilful drunkenness, tension and rivalry between nations; and set against them, immediately and directly, is the covenant promise which offers the restoration of relationship, and which in itself asserts that God is in purposeful control:

Yahweh said to Abram, 'Leave your country, your family and your father's house, for the land I will show you. I will make you a great nation; I will bless you and make your name so famous that it will be used as a blessing.'[3]

Thus although the opening chapters of Genesis are aetiological, attempting to explain the origin of particular examples of suffering and evil, the explanations do not call into question the purposefulness and supremacy of God. This absence of dualism has had profound effects in the Western tradition, because although dualism, which in many ways is the most obvious explanation of evil, has at times asserted itself, it has always been as an alien element. Zoroastrianism, for example, had an important imaginative influence on Judaism and Christianity, but its direct effect was slight, and it found more congenial ground for development in the East.[4] In face of the idea that the world is a battle-ground between the forces of light and the autonomous forces of darkness, Deutero-Isaiah[5] asserted that God creates both light and

---

[1] The name Adam = Man.
[2] On the meaning of dualism see pp. 270–84, esp. p. 272.
[3] Gen. 12: 1 f.   [4] On Zoroastrianism, see pp. 270–4.
[5] Deutero-Isaiah (Isa. 40–55) was almost certainly written during the exile of many of the Jews in Babylonia, after the fall of Jerusalem to the Babylonians in 587 B.C.E. It was during this period that Cyrus rose to power at the head of the Persians and overthrew the Babylonians; and it was also at about this time that the prophet Zoroaster lived, who, although he was not himself strictly dualist, proclaimed a religious message with discernibly dualistic tendencies (see pp. 271–3). The reaction of Deutero-Isaiah against dualism is, therefore, particularly interesting.

darkness, weal and woe; and in this he is consistent with the Biblical understanding and experience of God. There is scarcely ever any question that God cares for the world he has made. As the book of Job puts it:

> His works are great, past all reckoning,
> marvels, beyond all counting.
> He sends down rain to the earth,
> pours down water on the fields.
> If his will is to rescue the downcast,
> or raise the afflicted to the heights of joy,
> he wrecks the plans of the artful,
> and brings to naught their intrigues.[1]

In the light of the many tragic experiences of the Jewish people, it might seem odd that this conviction remained credible. But it was, of course, guaranteed by precisely that understanding of historical events which saw them as the disclosure of God. If God has once delivered his people from 'the iron furnace of Egypt',[2] this remains the case, no matter how great the suffering of a particular individual or generation in subsequent times. There is no other furnace of suffering, however great, which can possibly falsify this or count against it, once that interpretation has been accepted as the only credible explanation of those original events. This explains why, in Scripture, suffering is usually accepted quite simply as one of the facts of existence. It is a part of the way things happen to be. The problem in Scripture is not why suffering exists, but why it afflicts some people and not others. The problem is not the *fact* of suffering but its *distribution*. Why do the wicked prosper, while those who try to keep faith with God suffer?

The acuteness of this problem can be seen quite easily by reading through the Psalter. There are very few Psalms which do not have something to say about it, and many of them arose as a direct response to it. Furthermore, the problem became steadily more acute, not less, as the people of Israel explored and developed the implications of their faith and trust in Yahweh. The faith of Israel, as recorded in Scripture, is remarkable for the quite extraordinary degree of integrity with which that exploration was carried out. The conviction that God had taken the initiative in

[1] Job 5: 9–12.   [2] Deut. 4: 20.

9

Judaism

creation and redemption meant that individuals could live with God in their own time in an entirely open-ended way. The implications of accepting the reality of God and of his involvement in the affairs of men were known in general but not in detail, and they had to be discovered by living with God faithfully in actual events. This is why the writings of Israel so often reveal a conflict between those who were content with a traditional or conventional idea of God, and those who searched for a deeper and more realistic understanding of what it ought to mean to live with God in their own time and generation. The Prophets, for example, often found themselves not only *contra mundum* but also *contra fidem*—against, that is, the prevailing understanding of faith amongst their contemporaries. It was in the integrity of this experimental faith that Israel came to realise the universality of God (no longer the deity of a particular group of tribes), his power in creation, his overriding justice and retribution, and his constancy.

> He lives above the circle of the earth,
> its inhabitants look like grasshoppers...
> 'To whom could you liken me
> and who could be my equal?' says the Holy One.
> Lift your eyes and look.
> Who made these stars
> if not he who drills them like an army,
> calling each one by name?
> So mighty is his power, so great his strength,
> that not one fails to answer.[1]

But the more it was believed that God was in control of the situation, the more his control in the distribution of suffering ought to have been apparent. The more profound their understanding of God became, the more acute became the problem of distribution; and it is significant that the passage quoted above, extolling the majesty and creative power of God, immediately goes on:

> How can you say, Jacob,
> how can you insist, Israel,
> 'My destiny is hidden from Yahweh,
> my rights are ignored by my God'?[2]

The doubt was bound to be expressed; but what answers could be given to it?

[1] Isa. 40: 22, 25 f.   [2] Isa. 40: 27.

The most common response was also the simplest, namely, to say that suffering was a punishment and just requital of wickedness:

> Tell them, 'Happy is the virtuous man,
> for he will feed on the fruit of his deeds;
> woe to the wicked, evil is on him,
> he will be treated as his actions deserve.'[1]

That simple, cause-and-effect explanation of suffering is written very deeply into Scripture. This is not surprising, since it is implicit in the idea of the Covenant, through which the people of Israel expressed their understanding of how, most fundamentally, they were related to God.[2] A covenant-relationship is one of promise and threat, depending on the extent to which the conditions have been observed or broken. In Scripture it is frequently held to the credit of Yahweh that although his people have repeatedly broken their side of the bargain, he has never forsaken them. But that is recognised as an act of favour and mercy, and it is clearly recognised that according to strict justice punishment is deserved.

These ideas implicit in a covenant-relationship were most fully worked out in Deuteronomy and in the Deuteronomic theory of history which provided the inspiration for the final editing of the documents of Israel's history.[3] The Deuteronomic theory of history is akin to an uncomplicated Western, where the good triumph and the evil meet their doom. Applied to Israel's history it meant that kings were evaluated according to the extent to which they exemplified the theory. Manasseh, for example, reigned for more than forty years in the sixth century B.C.E., but the narrative in 2 Kings records nothing of the achievements of his reign. It was known that he had accepted idolatrous, or at least polytheistic, observances in the Temple, and those only are recorded. Furthermore, they are made an explanation for the fall of Jerusalem to the Babylonians a century later:

He built altars to the whole array of heaven in the two courts of the Temple of Yahweh. He caused his son to pass through the fire. He

---

[1] Isa. 3: 10 f.   [2] See p. 7 above.
[3] The historical books in Scripture are the consequence of a process of editing. They contain much early material, but the material was arranged to illustrate later insights of faith and belief. This can be seen particularly in the contrasts between Kings and Chronicles.

practised soothsaying and magic and introduced necromancers and
wizards. He did very many more things displeasing to Yahweh, thus
provoking his anger...Then Yahweh spoke through his servants the
prophets, 'Since Manasseh king of Judah has done these shameful
deeds..., and has led Judah itself into sin with his idols, Yahweh, the
God of Israel, says this, "Look, I will bring such disaster as to make the
ears of all who hear of it tingle...I will scour Jerusalem as a man
scours a dish and, having scoured it, turns it upside down."'[1]

This understanding of suffering which Deuteronomy and the
Deuteronomic historians applied to history was applied also to
individuals and to individual experiences of suffering, and it
might justifiably be called the classical response—that suffering is
a punishment for sin:

> The fear of Yahweh adds length to life,
> the years of the wicked will be cut short.[2]

But unfortunately this idea was open to an important objection:
it was not true. Even the most casual observation of life makes it
apparent that the wicked do not get cut off, and that the ruthless
frequently prosper. The question was unavoidable of why this
should be so, and in Scripture the question breaks out again and
again. In its most anguished form it was raised by Jeremiah, who
lived just before the fall of Jerusalem to the Babylonians. He was a
man possessed by an overwhelming experience of God, and he
knew that he must speak as a prophet, yet he was persecuted and
his message was despised. He was brought to the edge of death for
his beliefs, without any apparent recognition from God:

> You have seduced me, Yahweh, and I have let myself be seduced;
> you have overpowered me; you were the stronger...
> The word of Yahweh has meant for me
> insult, derision, all day long.
> I used to say, 'I will not think about him,
> I will not speak in his name any more.'
> Then there seemed to be a fire burning in my heart,
> imprisoned in my bones.
> The effort to restrain it wearied me,
> I could not bear it.[3]

[1] 2 Kings 21: 5 f., 10–13.
[2] Prov. 10: 27.
[3] Jer. 20: 7–9.

Not surprisingly, when Jeremiah raised the problem of the distribution of suffering, he did so in anguished rather than in academic terms:

> You have right on your side, Yahweh,
> when I complain about you.
> But I would like to debate a point of justice with you.
> Why is it that the wicked live so prosperously?
> Why do scoundrels enjoy peace?[1]

Jeremiah found no real answer to his question. Indeed, having asked the question he then almost immediately went on to pray for the conventional, classical answer:

> Drag them off like sheep for the slaughter-house,
> reserve them for the day of butchery...
> For they say,
> 'God does not see our behaviour.'[2]

Almost all his life, Jeremiah's only answer was to hang on grimly to his conviction that God *is* in control.[3] The enormity of human wickedness and folly which Jeremiah saw all around him compelled him at times to envisage the possibility that God would bring this particular experiment in creation to an end—that God would, so to speak, draw a line and start all over again:

> I looked to the earth, to see a formless waste;
> to the heavens, and their light had gone.[4]

The words for 'formless waste' are *tohu wabohu*, the exact words which are used in Gen. 1:2 to describe the pre-created state of chaos and nothingness. Jeremiah saw God reversing the process and carrying the world back to its pre-created state.[5] It is only then that God will re-establish that relationship which he had intended all along:

See, the days are coming—it is Yahweh who speaks—when I will make a new covenant with the House of Israel (and the House of Judah),

[1] Jer. 12:1.   [2] Jer. 12:3 f.
[3] A particularly famous expression of that conviction occurs in his use of the image of God as a potter, who is entitled to do as he pleases with the clay. For this, see Jer. 18:1–6. The image occurs frequently in Scripture (see, e.g., Isa. 29:16), and important use was made of it by Paul when dealing with exactly the same question of the distribution of suffering (see pp. 69–71).   [4] Jer. 4:23.
[5] Jer. 4:23 ff. Note that the negative in v. 27*b* should be translated *interrogatively*, expecting the answer, 'Yes': 'Will I not make an end of it once and for all?'

Judaism

but not a covenant like the one I made with their ancestors on the day I took them by the hand to bring them out of the land of Egypt. They broke that covenant of mine, so I had to show them who was master. It is Yahweh who speaks. No, this is the covenant I will make with the House of Israel when those days arrive—it is Yahweh who speaks. Deep within them I will plant my Law, writing it on their hearts. Then I will be their God and they shall be my people.[1]

The point of great importance about Jeremiah is that although the agonising problem of evil and of the distribution of suffering compelled on him a vision of necessary discontinuity, there remained within the vision an equally necessary continuity which nothing could shake or disturb, since God, for him, was not defeated. Jeremiah is a supreme example of a man confronted by two sets of facts which are in conflict, but neither of which he is able to abandon or deny. The problem becomes one of reconciliation. His acceptance of God's disclosure in the past, and his experience of God's disclosure in the present, were given quantities; but so too were his experience and observation of the unequal distribution of suffering, not least in his own case. Jeremiah's tentative attempts to find a reconciliation in the future, in a new creation and a new covenant, were aspirations rather than answers. They were, of course, crucial in the development of apocalyptic: works of apocalyptic, as the name implies,[2] contain revelations of the future, and the various 'apocalypses'[3] are frequently designed to support the view that the solution to the problem of suffering lies undoubtedly with God, but that it requires a more dramatic, cataclysmic intervention on his part than has hitherto been the case. One of the purposes of apocalyptic was to unfold, or reveal, some of the details of what that intervention would be like. But although Jeremiah was of great importance in the development of apocalyptic, its full development lay in the future. Apocalyptic appears in late Biblical books, but it did not come into its own until the post-Biblical period. So far as Jeremiah was concerned, speculations about the future offered grounds for hope, but not for supposing that the problem had been solved.

[1] Jer. 31: 31-3.
[2] The word is from the Greek *apocalypsis*, meaning 'an uncovering' or 'revelation'; apocalyptic, therefore, reveals what will happen in the future, particularly at the end of days. Two Biblical examples of apocalyptic are the book of Revelation and parts of the book of Daniel. [3] I.e. works which contain such revelations.

14

Foundations

Jeremiah found few answers to his own question, 'Why do the wicked live so prosperously?' But there were other people around, both before his time and after, who were prepared to answer it for him. The commonest solution was to go on asserting that although the retribution of the wicked has been delayed, it will nevertheless take place:

> Do not be indignant about the wicked,
> do not be envious of evil men,
> since there is no morrow for the wicked man;
> the lamp of the wicked will be snuffed out.[1]

But this, again, was open to the fatal objection that it was not true—or at least, it was open to the objection that a glance round the human scene suggests the opposite. Therefore, alongside the 'classical' answer, and sometimes in conjunction with it, more realistic notes were sounded. In particular, the advice was given not to be preoccupied with the wicked, even if they seemed to be prospering. It is better to ignore them and leave them on one side, and concentrate instead on the more positive aspects of relationship with God—'Stand away, I beg you, from the tents of these perverse men, and touch nothing that belongs to them, for fear that with all their sins you too will be swept away.'[2] Sometimes this policy of dissociation was expressed even more strongly:

> In my household, I will advance
> in purity of heart;
> I will not let my eyes rest
> on any misconduct...
> Morning after morning I reduce to silence
> all who are wicked in this country,
> banishing from the city of Yahweh
> all evil men.[3]

But the inexorable fact remained that the righteous, even in their aloof dissociation, suffer. A more positive estimate of the place of suffering was needed; and the most common, from the earliest days, was the view that suffering is a test of faith. It appears in classic form in the story of Abraham's willingness to

[1] Prov. 24: 19 f. An even better example is Ps. 37, especially vss. 16 f., 25, 28 f., where the assertion that the virtuous are rewarded and the wicked punished becomes almost desperate.
[2] Num. 16: 26.   [3] Ps. 101: 2–4, 6, 8.

15

sacrifice Isaac.¹ It appears in even more familiar form in the advice of Proverbs:

> My son, do not scorn correction from Yahweh,
> do not resent his rebuke;
> for Yahweh reproves the man he loves,
> as a father checks a well-loved son.²

It is an understanding of a way in which suffering can be made purposeful that has gone deep into the Western tradition—not least in educational theory. It has been even more effective in the idea, for better and for worse, of the 'ennobling effects of suffering'. But inevitably for some people, then as now, it looked like a desperate attempt to rescue a little dignity from a hopeless situation. It comes perilously close to saying that the distribution of suffering is a problem quite beyond men's understanding, let alone their control:

And then I see the wicked brought to burial and people come from the Temple to honour them in the city for having been the men they were...Since the sentence on wrong-doing is not carried out at once, men's inmost hearts are intent on doing wrong. The sinner who does wrong a hundred times survives even so. I know very well that happiness is reserved for those who fear God, because they fear him; that there will be no happiness for the wicked man and that he will only eke out his days like a shadow, because he does not fear God. But there is a vanity found on earth; the good, I mean, receive the treatment the wicked deserve; and the wicked the treatment the good deserve.³

It is scarcely necessary to indicate the source of that quotation, particularly since it continues, 'This, too, I say is vanity.' The writer of Ecclesiastes found the problem of the distribution of suffering insoluble. The classical answer was certainly inadequate:

Just as one fate comes to all, to virtuous as to wicked, to clean and unclean, to him who sacrifices and him who does not sacrifice, so it is with the good man and the sinner, with him who takes an oath and him who shrinks from it. This is the evil that inheres in all that is done under the sun: that one fate comes to all...The race does not go to the swift, nor the battle to the strong; there is no bread for the wise, wealth for the intelligent, nor favour for the learned; all are subject to

---

¹ Gen. 22: 1–19. Cf. also the story of Joseph, Gen. 37–50.
² Prov. 3: 11.   ³ Eccles. 8: 10–14.

time and mischance. Man does not know his hour; like fish caught in
the treacherous net, like birds taken in the snare, so is man overtaken by
misfortune suddenly falling on him.[1]

Ecclesiastes, baffled by what appears to be a total mystery,
pointed out that there are at least some consolations to be found
in life, some delights and pleasures which are a consequence of
being alive:

There is no happiness for man but to eat and drink and to be content
with his work...Spend your life with the woman you love, through all
the fleeting days of the life that God has given you under the sun.[2]

Or as it is put more briefly:

A living dog is better than a dead lion.[3]

Ecclesiastes has often been considered sceptical and cynical—or
even epicurean, as being an advocate of the maxim, 'Eat, drink
and be merry, for tomorrow we die.' But that is certainly unjust.
Ecclesiastes is one of the earliest coherent expositions of the view
that life is to be evaluated in terms, not of quantity, but of
quality;[4] 'I find that man is simple; man's complex problems are
of his own devising.'[5] The passing of time is a matter of infinite,
almost angry, regret, and the irony of winter in the midst of
spring, of death at the moment of new life, is fully recognised.[6]
Yet even so, in the face of this apparent waste, the writer of
Ecclesiastes could not quite believe that the experience of living
had escaped the control of God:

There is a season for everything, a time for every occupation under
heaven:
> a time for giving birth,
> a time for dying,
> a time for planting,
> a time for uprooting what has been planted...

What does a man gain for the efforts that he makes? I contemplate the
task that God gives mankind to labour at. All that he does is apt for its
time; but though he has permitted man to consider time in its wholeness, man cannot comprehend the work of God from beginning to
end. I know there is no happiness for man except in pleasure and
enjoyment while he lives. And when man eats and drinks and finds

---

[1] Eccles. 9: 2 f., 11 f.   [2] Eccles. 2: 24, 9: 9.   [3] Eccles. 9: 4.
[4] See further pp. 89–91.   [5] Eccles. 7: 29.   [6] See especially Eccles. 12: 5.

Judaism

happiness in his work, this is a gift from God. I know that what God does he does consistently. To this nothing can be added, from this nothing taken away; yet God sees to it that men fear him.[1]

Ecclesiastes offers advice rather than solutions. The problem remains, and in many other parts of Scripture it comes again to the surface—in Habakkuk, for example, which asks how God can use an evil instrument to accomplish a necessary purpose; or in Abraham's plea for Sodom,[2] or in the Chronicler's analysis of David's census.[3] All those passages have a bearing on the theoretical problem of the distribution of suffering. But of course for many people suffering occurred, not as a theoretical problem, but as a practical experience. It is significant, therefore, that much material in Scripture engages the problem in its practical aspects. A particularly clear example is the fierce eloquence of the prophets against those who increase the burden of suffering in the world. There is scarcely a single prophet who did not denounce actual examples of inhumanity, and they reserved some of their most savage invective for those who caused suffering to others, whether they did so thoughtlessly or with deliberation: 'Then Nathan said to David, "You are the man."'[4] This is the constant prophetic accusation: you are the man, you are the one responsible and therefore accountable to God. And it is in this prophetic vigilance that the first important line of practical response to suffering emerges, a determination to contest or to diminish instances of suffering where they occur.

The second most obvious example of this practical concern lies in much of the legislation contained in Torah. It is true that the purpose of many of the laws is to regulate the ways in which Israel expresses its relationship with God, and they are concerned, therefore, with cult and ritual. But many of them are concerned with the campaign against inhumanity and injustice, which is equally a part of Israel's relationship with God. Prophetic anger and social legislation are two related elements in the Jewish response to suffering which have been profoundly influential in the Western tradition. It has meant that practical concern has always been likely to outweigh theoretical considerations, and that the visionary appeal, 'Come over and help us',[5] has always a

[1] Eccles. 3: 1 f., 9–14. [2] Gen. 18: 16–33.
[3] 1 Chron. 21: 1 ff.; cf. 2 Sam. 24: 1 ff.
[4] 2 Sam. 12: 7. [5] Acts 16: 9.

18

good chance of falling on sympathetic ears. Yet even so practical action is not a solution to the theoretical problem, and the perplexing question of the distribution of suffering remained. It remained to be brought to a head, acutely and dramatically, in the book of Job.

The book of Job is a dialogue between Job, the innocent sufferer, and his three friends, Eliphaz, Bildad and Zophar, who try to explain to him, in classical terms, the reason for his suffering. The essential point about Job is that the problem is raised in a totally artificial and isolated way. Job is defined in the Prologue as being absolutely innocent, 'a sound and honest man who feared God and shunned evil',[1] and even in the worst of his afflictions he did not waver or cry out against God. That has to be so, since otherwise it would be open to his friends to say—as in fact they do say—that no man is totally innocent, and that all without exception commit some offences, known or unknown, hidden or open, which merit punishment from God. The classical solution, therefore (that suffering is a punishment for sin), is always bound to be applicable. But Job is defined, artificially and completely, as innocent, and thence arises the great debate of Job. The variations on the classical response advanced by Job's friends prove ineffective and barren. In fact they prove to be so ineffective that a fourth speaker, Elihu, is introduced at the end of the book to put the case more strongly:

He fumed with rage against Job for thinking that he was right and God was wrong; and he was equally angry with the three friends for giving up the argument and thus admitting that God could be unjust.[2]

But Elihu has little to add to the classical response. How, then, does Job himself answer the problem—or, to put it more accurately, what other answers does the book suggest? The Prologue offers one solution, that Job's suffering was to test his faithfulness;[3] the Epilogue suggests another solution, that Job made his suffering redemptive by accepting it faithfully and by praying for his misguided friends. It certainly redeemed himself, since his fortunes were at once restored.[4] In Job, that suggestion of suffering being made redemptive is almost

[1] Job. 1: 1, 8.   [2] Job. 32: 2.   [3] Job. 1: 6–12.
[4] Job. 42: 10: 'Yahweh restored Job's fortunes, because he had prayed for his friends. More than that, Yahweh gave him double what he had before.'

accidental, and it is certainly crudely expressed. But elsewhere in Scripture it becomes central and inspiring, particularly in Deutero-Isaiah. Deutero-Isaiah was composed during the Babylonian exile, in the desolation and misery of total national defeat. With the fall of Jerusalem to the Babylonians, the faith of the people of Israel in Yahweh was in danger. He was apparently not strong enough to look after his own people. The response of Deutero-Isaiah was to say that the defeat was not a catastrophe but a moment of opportunity. If they could accept their distress as deserved, and still keep faith with Yahweh, their suffering would be the foundation of better things. In the figure of the Servant, Deutero-Isaiah represented those people of Israel who were bearing the griefs and sorrows of deserved exile:[1]

> Ours were the sufferings he bore,
> ours the sorrows he carried.
> But we, we thought of him as someone punished,
> struck by God, and brought low.
> Yet he was pierced through for our faults,
> crushed for our sins.
> On him lies a punishment that brings us peace,
> and through his wounds we are healed.
> We had all gone astray like sheep,
> each taking his own way,
> and Yahweh burdened him
> with the sins of all of us.
> Harshly dealt with, he bore it humbly,
> he never opened his mouth,
> like a lamb that is led to the slaughter-house,
> like a sheep that is dumb before its shearers
> never opening its mouth [2]

Deutero-Isaiah did not regard this patience as being an end in itself, but as a means to restoration. If the people retain their trust

---

[1] The original application of the Servant Songs is much disputed. My own view is that whatever the origin of the Servant-passages may have been, whether quoted or original, the Servant-image has been applied consistently, in the book as it now is, as a metaphor of Israel, but that the precise correspondence of the metaphor is transferred. This accounts for the shift in the application of the metaphor from the people as a whole, to the exiles in contrast to the rest, to a minority within the exiles who keep faith. It seems to me more sensible to accept a transference of metaphor than to look for a uniform application and regard as suspect those passages which do not fit it.

[2] Isa. 53: 4–7.

and confidence in Yahweh, he will restore them to their land. Deutero-Isaiah had no hesitation in making that promise because he was confident of God's self-disclosure in the past, in history and in creation. Deutero-Isaiah developed both those themes in a magnificent way. He even took the imagery of the Exodus from Egypt and applied it brilliantly to the restoration which he predicted from Babylon, as being a second Exodus. Furthermore, he believed that the very act of restoration would be a proof to the nations of the world that Yahweh is supreme. They would see a people, whom they had believed to be completely humiliated and despised, returning in triumph across the desert from Babylon to Zion; and as the Exodus from Egypt had vindicated Yahweh long ago in the eyes of his own people, so the new Exodus would vindicate him in the eyes of the whole world.[1]

Here is perhaps the supreme contribution of Israel to a human response to suffering, that suffering can be made redemptive, that it can become the foundation of better things, collectively, if not individually. Such a view cannot be, or rather ought not to be, imposed on others in their grief, but it can be accepted for oneself. 'By his sufferings shall my servant justify many, taking their faults on himself.'[2] In Job that view appears casually, almost as an afterthought; in Deutero-Isaiah it appears as a superb vision. The difference between them lies precisely in the fact that Deutero-Isaiah accepted the saving-history of Israel as relevant to the problem, Job did not—or at least, no specific appeal is made to it. But the difference between them, although great, is not absolute, because they have a *second* vital theme in common, the disclosure of God in creation.

In Job that theme is set forth in the speeches of God at the end of the book: 'Then from the heart of the tempest Yahweh gave Job his answer.'[3] In essence, the answer suggested is that the individual problem must be set in the far greater context of creation as a whole.[4] The individual is such a tiny part of the whole pattern that he cannot possibly comprehend the total design:

> Where were you when I laid the earth's foundations?
> Tell me, since you are so well-informed!
> Who decided the dimensions of it, do you know?
> Or who stretched the measuring line across it?[5]

---

[1] See, e.g., Isa. 40: 3–5, 49: 7.   [2] Isa. 53: 11.   [3] Job 38: 1.
[4] Cf. Eccles. 3: 11, quoted above, pp. 17f.   [5] Job 38: 4 f.

Complex and intricate particulars of creation are paraded in front of Job. He is shown such extraordinary creatures as the hippopotamus and the crocodile, which God is not only able to create but also to keep within his care and control. In the face of such miracles of creation and of life itself, what can Job say? 'My words have been frivolous: what can I reply?'[1] In the end he turns to God in dust and ashes:

> I know that you are all-powerful:
> what you conceive, you can perform...
> I have been holding forth on matters I cannot understand,
> on marvels beyond me and my knowledge...
> I retract all I have said,
> and in dust and ashes I repent.[2]

This, obviously, is not a solution, it is a suggestion that no solution is possible because man is too small a fragment of the universe to discern the total design. But in many ways, more important than the answers put forward in the book of Job are the answers *not* put forward. In particular, no significant concession is made to the classical response, that suffering is a punishment for sin—or as God says to Job in Robert Frost's *Masque of Reason,*

> ...I have no doubt
> You realize by now the part you played
> To stultify the Deuteronomist
> And change the tenor of religious thought.[3]

But even more remarkable is the absence of any suggestion that there might be a solution in life after death. There is no suggestion that the inequalities of suffering in this life will be put right in another. Allusions to life after death have sometimes been found in Job 19: 25 f. It is an extremely difficult passage to translate, but its most probable meaning is:

> I know that my advocate is active on my behalf,
> and as the last speaker he will stand up in court.
> I will see my witness take his place in court,
> and my defending counsel I will see to be God himself.

[1] Job 40: 4 (39: 34).   [2] Job 42: 2 f., 6.
[3] *The Collected Poems of Robert Frost* (paperback ed. London, 1967), p. 449.

In other words, it is an example of the familiar and much-repeated Biblical image of the law-court. It does not imply or require life after death. On the contrary, Job's views of death are stark and factual:

> There is always hope for a tree:
> when felled, it can start its life again;
> its shoots continue to sprout.
> Its roots may be decayed in the earth,
> its stump withering in the soil,
> but let it scent the water, and it buds,
> and puts out branches like a plant new set.
> But man? He dies, and lifeless he remains;
> man breathes his last, and then where is he?
> The waters of the seas may disappear,
> all the rivers may run dry or drain away;
> but man, once in his resting place, will never rise again.
> The heavens will wear away before he wakes,
> before he rises from his sleep.[1]

The writer of Job refused to dissolve the problem of suffering by taking refuge in life after death, and in this he is typical of much of the other material contained in Scripture. Ecclesiastes, for example, has exactly the same realistic honesty in its assessment of death and in its refusal to look for a solution in life after death:

> Naked from his mother's womb he came, as naked as he came he will depart again; nothing to take with him after all his efforts...The living know at least that they will die, the dead know nothing; no more reward for them, their memory has passed out of mind. Their loves, their hates, their jealousies, these all have perished, nor will they ever again take part in whatever is done under the sun.[2]

This is of extreme importance, not least because it casts doubt on a central point in the Marxist critique of religion, the criticism that religion is effective because it offers supernatural compensations for the natural catastrophes of men; unable to face the terrible evils of alienation, and unwilling to cut at the roots of the problem by removing the causes of alienation, religion holds out the spurious hope that all will be put right after death. Of Scripture that is not true. What must always be remembered

[1] Job 14: 7–12.   [2] Eccles. 5: 14, 9: 5 f.

Judaism

about the material contained in Scripture is that it was wrought out of an actual, open-ended experience of what it was like to live with God as real here and now, without any substantial hope that life would continue with him after death—indeed, almost the exact opposite: in view of their understanding of the composition of man it was impossible to see how such a hope could be meaningfully expressed. Man was an amalgam of the dust of the earth infused with the breath of God. When he died the body returned to dust and the breath returned to God. What could survive? At best, only a thin, filtered shadow, weak and empty, and deprived of relationship with God.[1]

The mourners are already walking to and fro in the street before the silver cord has snapped, or the golden lamp been broken, or the pitcher shattered at the spring, or the pulley cracked at the well, or before the dust returns to the earth as it once came from it, and the breath to God who gave it.[2]

It is an impressive testimony to the integrity of the Biblical material that it refused to advance beyond the evidence and yet it could not deny the experiential reality of God. It did not need a belief in life after death to recognise the disclosure of God. And yet paradoxically, at the very end of the Biblical period and increasingly after it, life after death came to play a decisively important part in the Jewish response to suffering.

Here is what has come to the surface after so many throes and convulsions.
How curious! how real![3]

THE DEVELOPMENT

In Scripture the main elements of the Jewish understanding of suffering can be found. The classical response was to say that suffering was a punishment for wrong-doing. That solution was repeatedly questioned and probed by those who found it an inadequate way of accounting for all instances of suffering. Those

[1] It was this thin shadow of the former self which went to Sheol. Sheol was defined by J. Pedersen as 'the primitive grave'. It was certainly not regarded as 'heaven'— or for that matter as hell.
[2] Eccles. 12: 5–7.
[3] W, Whitman, 'Starting from Paumanok' (*Leaves of Grass*), Nonesuch ed. pp. 14 f.

24

doubts received their most concentrated expression in Job and Ecclesiastes, and they were expressed in both those books with such realism and impassioned integrity—refusing to advance beyond the evidence of life as it is and death as it will be, and yet unable to deny the reality of God—that they became deeply influential in the Western tradition. Furthermore, they have remained influential, though not in isolation, since in later times they were reinforced by similar observations from other sources, not least from Greek and Latin literature. Even in secular responses of the present time, which assert the dignity of man in the face of his defeat, many of the elements of Ecclesiastes and Job have been fused: from Ecclesiastes, the acceptance that there are many things worth attempting, many things which provide their own intrinsic pleasure and reward; and from Job, defiance in the face of ultimate defeat in death and in the many terrible griefs and anguishes of human existence—rage against the dying of the light. In contemporary secular responses, it is not so much that Ecclesiastes and Job have had any direct influence as that they both contribute to that tradition by having expressed supremely well what many men come to recognise for themselves:

My mother encouraged one to be optimistic when, crippled with arthritis and dying, she asserted the value of each instant; but her vain tenaciousness also ripped and tore the reassuring curtain of everyday triviality. There is no such thing as a natural death: nothing that happens to a man is ever natural, since his presence calls the world into question. All men must die: but for every man his death is an accident and, even if he knows it and consents to it, an unjustifiable violation.[1]

But many Jews, including the writers of Ecclesiastes and Job, felt that they had something more to say, even though they might well have given their assent to that passage. They found that, despite the harsh and frightening realities of existence, the possibility of God was not defeated. This was not in any way an attempt to salvage God despite the evidence, but precisely because of the evidence to try to work to a more adequate understanding of God and of their relationships with him. They were able to do this—indeed, they felt compelled to do this—because of their experience of what it was like to live with God in this life. As a

[1] Simone de Beauvoir, *A Very Easy Death* (trs. P. O'Brian) (London, 1966), p. 106.

result of the sufficiency of their doctrine of creation they were able to maintain a doctrine of providence which could take into account facts which might otherwise seem to weigh decisively against it.

The foundations of that experience, and the conditions by which it could be made repeatable in one generation after another, were laid at a time when there was no serious belief that it would be continued after death. There were certainly popular views of survival or of restoration, but generally speaking death involved severance of relationship with God:

> Come back, Yahweh, rescue my soul,
> save me, if you love me;
> for in death there is no remembrance of you:
> who can sing your praises in Sheol?[1]

It is because the experience of God in this life was so real that the development of a belief in life after death was created as much by positive elements as by negative. The negative elements are the temptation to make use of life after death to reduce the dilemma of innocent suffering. The positive elements lie particularly in the strength of the experience of God here and now which makes it seem incredible that death will bring it to an end. Belief in the continuation of life with God scarcely occurs in Scripture, but it rapidly became a breakthrough:

> The souls of the virtuous are in the hands of God,
> no torment shall ever touch them.
> In the eyes of the unwise, they did appear to die,
> their going looked like a disaster,
> their leaving us, like annihilation;
> but they are in peace...
> Those who are faithful will live with him in love;
> for grace and mercy await those he has chosen.[2]

This development received great impetus when an entirely new problem of suffering emerged in the second century B.C.E. when for the first time on a large scale (in the Maccabean revolt) Jews were martyred for their faith. Some Jews refused to accept the

[1] Ps. 6: 5; on Sheol see n. 1, p. 24.
[2] Wisd. of Sol. 3: 1–5, 9. An emerging belief in life after death can be seen in the latest parts of Scripture, as, particularly, in Dan. 12: 1–4.

Development

Hellenising policy[1] of Antiochus Epiphanes, since it involved contravening various Biblical commands:

> There were many in Israel who stood firm and found the courage to refuse unclean food. They chose death rather than contamination by such fare or profanation of the holy covenant, and they were executed. It was a dreadful wrath that visited Israel.[2]

This raised the problem of the distribution of suffering in the acutest possible form. Those who are prepared to die rather than abandon or betray their faith in God must come almost as close to being a definition of undeserved suffering as the artificial definition located in the person of Job. It is not surprising, therefore, that in the later reflection on the Maccabean revolt in 2 Maccabees a stronger emphasis on life after death appears. In the famous story of the martyrdom of the mother and her seven sons in 2 Macc. 7, four of the sons and also the mother attest their faith that God, who gave them life in the first place, would, if he wished, be able to restore it to them. The mother, for example, cries out to encourage her sons:

> I do not know how you appeared in my womb; it was not I who endowed you with breath and life, I had not the shaping of your every part. It is the creator of the world, ordaining the process of man's birth and presiding over the origin of all things, who in his mercy will most surely give you back both breath and life, seeing that you now despise your own existence for the sake of his laws.[3]

Yet it is worth noting that in the analysis of suffering and persecution in 2 Macc. 6: 12–17 this element is not stressed at all, and the old teaching of discipline reappears:

> Now I urge anyone who may read this book not to be dismayed at these calamities, but to reflect that such visitations are not intended to destroy our race but to discipline it. Indeed when evil-doers are not left long to their own devices, but incur swift retribution, it is a sign of great benevolence. In the case of the other nations the Master waits patiently for them to attain the full measure of their sins before he

---

[1] Roughly speaking, this means that Antiochus encouraged a Greek way of life among the inhabitants of the Seleucid empire (of which Judaea was a part), as a means of fostering unity and common feeling. Some Jews welcomed this as a relief from the demands and restrictions of Torah. See 1 Macc. 1: 11–15.

[2] 1 Macc. 1: 62–4; cf. also 2: 29–38.   [3] 2 Macc. 7: 22 f.

punishes them, but with us he has decided to deal differently, rather than have to punish us later, when our sins come to a head. And so he never entirely withdraws his mercy from us; he may discipline us by some disaster, but he does not desert his own people.

When the same events came to be analysed later on in 4 Maccabees the atmosphere has changed sharply. In 4 Maccabees those who accept suffering and death rather than betray God are described in sacrificial terms: they die on behalf of the community to give it life by their death, and to inspire it by their example. This is another crucial development, that suffering in certain circumstances can be sacrificial. It is not in any way an innovation, since a similar understanding had long before been expressed in Deutero-Isaiah, and it is in any case an extremely natural development among those who regard ritual sacrifices as being important in religious life. But the application to martyrdom was of critical importance, since it moves on into the area of suffering voluntarily undertaken, or even sought out.

Belief in life after death was applied, not simply to the specific problem of martyrdom, but also to the more general problem of suffering, and of that 1 Enoch is a good example. 102: 6–11 poses the problem, and 103: 1 ff. suggests an answer:

> When you die the sinners speak over you:
> 'As we die, so die the righteous,
> And what benefit do they reap for their deeds?...'
> Now, therefore, I swear to you, the righteous, by the glory
> of the great and honoured and mighty One in dominion,
> and by his greatness I swear to you.
> I know a mystery,
> And have read the heavenly tablets,
> And have seen the holy books
> And have found written therein and inscribed regarding them:
> That all goodness and joy and glory are prepared for them,
> And written down for the spirits of those who have died in
>   righteousness.

In other words, the problem is dissolved, because the balance will be put right after death. That might well appear to be a blind assertion or a wild guess in the dark. It is of importance, therefore, that 1 Enoch tries to safeguard itself against that accusation, and it does so by claiming to have derived its views from revelation, albeit a secret revelation only now being disclosed: 'I know a mystery, and have read in the heavenly tablets, and have seen the holy books.'

This at once opens up another vitally important area in which the Jewish response to suffering was explored, namely, apocalyptic. The general nature of apocalyptic has already been briefly described:[1] it claims to reveal something of the unknown, particularly the details of heaven and hell, and of the end of the ages, and often the details are vivid and circumstantial. The great strength and merit of apocalyptic was that it clothed abstract assertions in meaningful images and pictures. That is to say, it gave people something practical that they could grasp in their imagination, so that their faith could be given a more concrete substance. In contrast, the great weakness of apocalyptic was that by putting emphasis on the future reward it made the present less significant. It was always in danger of dissolving the agonies of present suffering by pointing to a greater reward yet to be attained; and by reiterating constantly that God would surely act in a decisive manner one day it tended to pre-empt the question, What, then, is he up to at the moment?[2]

That question was posed in a particularly acute form by an event of major importance, the fall of Jerusalem to the Romans in 70 C.E., at the end of the first Jewish revolt. For two works, 2 Baruch and 4 Ezra, the fall of Jerusalem appeared as an epitome of the problem of the distribution of suffering. 2 Baruch, as the name implies (since Baruch was the scribe of Jeremiah), set the problem in the *first* fall of Jerusalem to the Babylonians. The problem is raised specifically and repeatedly, as, for example, in 14: 4 ff., where Baruch cries out to God:

But again I will speak in your presence: what have they profited who had knowledge before you, and have not walked in vanity as the rest of the nations...see! they have been carried off, nor on their account have you had mercy on Zion. And if others did evil, it was due to Zion, that on account of the works of those who wrought good works she should be forgiven, and should not be overwhelmed on account of the works of those who wrought unrighteousness.

---

[1] See p. 14.

[2] It is important to remember that apocalyptic was not accepted by all Jews in the post-Biblical period, and indeed some strongly opposed it as not belonging to the true and original revelation of God.

Judaism

Baruch's own answer, in vss. 8 and 9, is that of Job. The answer of God in ch. 14 is that he gave Torah to men: before that there was perhaps excuse, but with the coming of Torah there is no longer any excuse, because men know what is required of them. A similar argument was used by Paul in Romans. Certainly it is hard on just and upright men to be included in the punishment for disobedience, but they need have no fear, since a greater reward is reserved for them: 'For this world is to them a strife and a labour with much trouble; and that accordingly which is to come, a crown with great glory.'[1]

2 Baruch 20: 2 goes even further in suggesting that Jerusalem was destroyed in order to hasten the final visitation of God. This view of suffering as a necessary prelude became increasingly common, but it is unlikely to have offered much consolation, particularly if the visitation did not take place.

4 Ezra also repeats the response of Job:

The way of the Most High has been formed without measure, how, then, should it be possible for a mortal in a corruptible world to understand the ways of the Incorruptible?[2]

But 4 Ezra goes on to turn that into more positive advice, that men should not try to exceed the limits of their condition:

Once upon a time the woods of the trees of the field went forth, and took counsel, and said: 'Come, let us go and make war against the sea, that it may retire before us, and we will make us more woods.' In like manner also the waves of the sea took counsel, and said: 'Come, let us go up and wage war against the wood of the field, that there also we may win us more territory.' The counsel of the wood was in vain, for the fire came and consumed it; likewise, also, the counsel of the waves of the sea, for the sand stood up and stopped them. If you, now, had been judge between them whom would you have justified or whom condemned? I answered and said: 'Both have taken a foolish counsel; for to the wood the land has been assigned, and to the sea a place to bear its waves.'[3]

The moral is drawn:

As the earth has been assigned to the wood, and the place of the sea to bear its waves; even so the dwellers upon earth can understand only

[1] 2 Bar. 15: 8 (trs. Charles).
[2] 4 Ezra 4: 11 (trs. Box in R. H. Charles, ed. *Apocrypha and Pseudepigrapha . . .*).
[3] 4 Ezra 4: 13–19 (trs. Box).

30

what is upon the earth, and they who are above the heavens that which is above the heavenly height.[1]

All this is extremely conservative. It is not hard to pick up traces of the agony caused by the fall of Jerusalem, as, for example, in 2 Baruch 35, but the analysis is not particularly profound. It is constructed almost entirely out of Biblical elements, reinforced by apocalyptic visions of the heavenly and to a large extent compensatory Jerusalem. What this means in effect is that although the fall of Jerusalem was recognised to be an epitome of the problem of suffering, it was met in already established terms. Thus the event which might have been expected to shatter the faith of Judaism, the loss of its holy city and Temple, caused in fact scarcely a tremor. For this there are two main reasons, both of them important in connection with the problem of suffering. The first and less important reason is that a large number of Jews were already deeply dissatisfied with the state of affairs in Jerusalem and in the Temple before the Jewish revolt, and were not at all surprised to find out that God agreed with them and that he was prepared to make a clean sweep. Among those who were dissatisfied, the most organised and influential group was that of the Pharisees. Because they had been excluded from central control of the Temple for a hundred years before the Jewish revolt, and because also they disagreed radically with many of the views held by the Sadducees who *did* have the greatest authority in the Temple, they had already been constructing an interpretation of Judaism which did not depend on its being expressed absolutely and completely in the Temple. When the Temple was destroyed they were already prepared; thus in many ways the most important effect of the destruction was that it gave the Pharisaic interpretation of Judaism the opportunity to become the prevailing (and eventually the only) interpretation of what Judaism ought to be. This development was carried out by the rabbis, and is therefore known as Rabbinic Judaism. It is not that other understandings of Judaism were excluded, but that Rabbinic Judaism eventually became synonymous with orthodoxy.[2]

The second reason why the fall of Jerusalem was absorbed with

[1] 4 Ezra 4: 21 (trs. Box).
[2] For fuller details of the emergence of Rabbinic Judaism, see J. Bowker, *Targums and Rabbinic Literature: an Introduction to Jewish Interpretations of Scripture* (Cambridge 1969), pp. 36–42, 54f.

Judaism

scarcely a tremor was simply that it had happened before. Here the fundamental importance of the Jewish discovery of God in history reasserts itself. The purposefulness of God is too well-established to be destroyed by any events in this life, however agonising or catastrophic they may be. The phrase *déja vu* is usually employed in a bored or almost *blasé* sense, but for the Jews it expresses an inalienable truth.

After the fall of Jerusalem the main developments were concentrated in Rabbinic Judaism. In connection with suffering there were no startling innovations, and, as might be expected, the already familiar responses were re-employed—though frequently they were refined and extended.[1] Thus the 'classical response', that suffering is a punishment for sin, frequently reappears. It was put almost as briefly as it could be in the much-repeated dictum of R.[2] Ammi: 'R. Ammi said: "There is no death without sin, there is no suffering without sin."' It is of interest that when that saying is quoted in B. Shab. 55*a* it is at once followed by several examples which refute it, or which at least call it in question. This means that the rabbis and compilers of Babylonian Talmud were not prepared to accept it as an absolute truth. On the other hand, Vay. R. 37: 1 and Qoh. R. 5: 4.1 both record the saying in an absolute form without any refutation at all.

It is equally of interest that Maimonides, an outstanding Jewish philosopher of the Middle Ages,[3] recognised that Ammi's dictum (quoted above) represented the majority opinion of the Rabbis, although he himself extended the discussion much further.[4] In the *Guide for the Perplexed* he devoted a long section to the problems of evil and providence; his analysis of evil bears some

[1] For rabbinic assessments of the fall of Jerusalem see, e.g., B. Shab. 119*b* which collects several explanations based on the 'classical' response to suffering. A particularly interesting explanation was that of R. Johanan, who said that Jerusalem was destroyed because the authorities stuck far too rigidly to the letter of Torah, and did not try to interpret Torah to make it relevant to changed conditions (B.B.M. 30*b*). It is a typical example of Pharisaic polemic against the Sadducees, and highlights the importance of the exegetical debate in pre-Fall Judaism (see further p. 43).

[2] The initial R. stands for the title Rabbi or Rabban.

[3] 1135–1204.

[4] 'People have generally the notion that trials consist in afflictions and mishaps sent by God to man, not as punishments for past sins, but as giving opportunity for great reward...The teaching of our Sages, although some of them approve this general belief (concerning trials), is on the whole against it. For they say, "There is no death without sin, there is no suffering without sin."' *Guide for the Perplexed*, iii. 24 (trs. M. Friedlander (London, 1904), p. 304).

Development

relation to that both of Augustine and of Irenaeus,[1] but since he was more optimistic about the existing state of affairs he saw less need of radical redemption—'for it is an act of great and perfect goodness that God gave us existence':[2]

The evils that befall man are of three kinds:

(1) The first kind of evil is that which is caused to man by the circumstances that he is subject to genesis and destruction, or that he possesses a body. It is on account of the body that some persons happen to have great deformities or paralysis of some of the organs. This evil may be part of the natural constitution of these persons, or may have developed subsequently in consequence of changes in the elements, e.g. through bad air, or thunderstorms, or landslips. We have already shown that, in accordance with the divine wisdom, genesis can only take place through destruction, and without the destruction of the individual members of the species the species themselves would not exist permanently. Thus the true kindness, and beneficence, and goodness of God is clear. He who thinks that he can have flesh and bones without being subject to any external influence, or any of the accidents of matter, unconsciously wishes to reconcile two opposites, viz., to be at the same time subject and not subject to change. If man were never subject to change there could be no generation; there would be one single being, but no individuals forming a species. Galen, in the third section of his book, *The Use of the Limbs,* says correctly that it would be in vain to expect to see living beings formed of the blood of menstruous women and the semen virile, who will not die, will never feel pain, or will move perpetually, or will shine like the sun...

(2) The second class of evils comprises such evils as people cause to each other, when, e.g., some of them use their strength against others. These evils are more numerous than those of the first kind; their causes are numerous and known; they likewise originate in ourselves, though the sufferer himself cannot avert them...

(3) The third class of evils comprises those which everyone causes to himself by his own action. This is the largest class, and is far more numerous than the second class. It is especially of these evils that all men complain—only few men are found that do not sin against themselves by this kind of evil. Those that are afflicted with it are therefore justly blamed in the words of the prophet, 'This hath been by your means'[3] . . .[4]

---

[1] For Augustine and Irenaeus as representing two important tendencies in Christian thought, see pp. 84–91.
[2] *Guide for the Perplexed,* iii. 12 (trs. Friedlander, p. 272).
[3] Mal. 1: 9.   [4] *Guide for the Perplexed,* iii. 11, 12 (trs. Friedlander, pp. 267–9).

Judaism

In the rabbinic period (i.e. up to *c.* 500 C.E.), the same understanding of suffering as a punishment occurs quite frequently, as in the advice of Raba,[1] 'If a man sees that painful suffering visits him, let him examine his conduct.'[2] It is almost as though the book of Job had never been written—and indeed, rabbinic opinion about Job is very ambivalent. Along with this, in the rabbinic period, the other main line of Biblical response was reasserted, the view that suffering is a test—a test, moreover, to which all are subjected:

Happy the man who can stand when he is tested, for there is none whom the Holy One, blessed be he, does not prove. He tests the rich man to see if he will be generous to the poor, and the poor man to see if he will accept suffering without complaint.[3]

This confident assertion arises from the belief, which is so essential in Scripture, that suffering is in the control of God. Its effect in the rabbinic period was that suffering could be accepted as 'a good thing'. According to Shem. R. 30: 13, suffering was one of the four great blessings which God wished to bestow on the world, as being one of the ways in which men draw close to him:

R. Aha said: 'God wished to give men four things, Torah, suffering, sacrifice and prayer, but they were unwilling to accept them.'

By a slightly different application of this, it was quite often pointed out that few good things are produced without pain, of which birth pangs form an obvious analogy. This was particularly expressed in connection with the Messianic woes, the convulsions which will precede the final access of God's kingdom, but it was also expressed in more general ways. According to R. Simeon b. Yohai:

The Holy One, blessed be he, gave Israel three precious gifts, Torah, the land of Israel and the world to come, but none of them were given except through suffering.[4]

This leads on to a point of central importance in the rabbinic understanding of suffering, the belief that suffering purges and leads to life. On the verse in Genesis, 'And God saw everything

[1] 'Some say R. Hisda.'
[2] B. Ber. 5*a*.
[3] Shem. R. 31: 3.
[4] B. Ber. 5*a*; Tanh. Shem. 1. On Torah, see pp. 7, 43.

that he had made, and behold, it was very good', Ber. R. 9: 8 records a comment of R. Huna:

'And, behold, it was very good', refers to the distribution (lit., 'the measure') of suffering. But can suffering actually be 'very good'? Yes, because through suffering men attain to life in the world to come.

And so by an almost iron logic men are encouraged to look for suffering, almost as a kind of opportunity for advancement:

We should not simply accept evil as well as good from God, but we should in fact rejoice over sufferings more than over good, for if a man prospers all his life his sins are not forgiven him. But they are forgiven him through sufferings.[1]

Suffering, then, belongs to human nature as a necessary part of its evolution and development, a somewhat harsh expression, perhaps, of survival of the fittest. Discussing the generation that was destroyed in the Flood, R. Aibu asked:

What was the reason for their rebelling against me? Was it not because I did not bend them through sufferings? What is it that keeps a door in its place? Its hinges.[2]

This is balanced by a belief that God does not test a man more than he is able, or as R. Ishmael put it more briefly, 'According to a camel's strength, so is its load.'[3] But in such a situation it is obvious that the only sensible response is acceptance and trust:

R. Abbahu once had the misfortune to lose a young son. R. Jonah and R. Jose went to visit him... He said to them, 'In this world, where there are lies and falsehood and deceit..., Mishnah[4] says that the relatives of a criminal who has been executed must acknowledge the judges and witnesses with the words, "We have nothing against you in our hearts, your judgement was just." How much more, therefore, ought we to accept the verdict of Justice from the court above, where there is no lying or deceit, and where the Judge is the one who lives and reigns for ever?'[5]

In order to exemplify this, and perhaps to provide a kind of *imitatio sanctorum*, a great many stories were recorded of how the great rabbis reacted in occasions of suffering and particularly in

---

[1] Sifre on Dt., Waethhanan, 32.　　　　[2] Ber. R. 26: 6.
[3] Qoh. R. 1: 18. 1. Cf. the story of R. Johanan's response to suffering in Cant. R. 2: 16. 2, and cf. also R. Johanan's visit to R. Eleazar, in B. Ber. 5*b*.
[4] On the meaning of Mishnah, see *Targums and Rabbinic Literature*, pp. 40, 46f.
[5] J. San. 6: 12.

martyrdom. Of the martyrs one of the great exemplars was R. Akiba, who was executed by the Romans for his part in the Bar Kokeba revolt:[1]

While Akiba was being tortured, the time for saying the *shema*[2] came round. He said it and laughed out loud. The Roman officer in charge said to him: 'Old man are you in touch with magic powers, or are you trying to make light of your sufferings, that you laugh in your agony?' R. Akiba said, 'Neither; all my life whenever I have said the *shema*, "You shall love the Lord your God with all your heart and soul and might", I have been sad, for I wondered when I would be able to fulfil the command. I have loved God with all my heart and with all my might, but I could not see how to love him with all my soul. But now I am giving my life, and the hour for saying the *shema* has come, and I do not waver. Is it not right that I should laugh?' And as he spoke these things, his soul departed.[3]

It is not surprising that R. Akiba was one of several rabbis to whom was attributed the saying, 'Much to be loved are sufferings.' For this, in fact, is the most distinctive element in the rabbinic response to suffering, that suffering is a way of atonement.[4] Here a number of different lines of thought converge: atonement in the days of the Temple required sacrifice; the doctrine of merits (*zekuth*) meant that the faithful acceptance of suffering could effect atonement not simply for oneself, which would be selfish, but for others; it could stand by them. And again, the strength of this belief arose directly out of the rabbinic understanding of free will—that men possess two inclinations, or *yazrain*, the evil *yezer* which is the inclination to evil, and the good *yezer* which is the inclination to good. This puts the onus of responsibility ultimately on to God, who created the evil *yezer* in the first place (hence the many passages which assert that the evil *yezer* is a good thing, because without it, no one, for example, would ever build a house, marry a wife, beget a child or engage in business), yet immediately the responsibility is that of the individual, 'for God will not tempt you above that ye are able'.[5] Furthermore, he has

---

[1] 132–5 C.E.

[2] The word *shema* (*shema'*) means 'hear', and it is the first word of the fundamental command, 'Hear, O Israel, the Lord your God, the Lord is One' (Deut. 6: 4).

[3] J. Ber. 9: 7. For accounts of other Jewish martyrs in the Tannaitic (i.e. pre-220 C.E.) period see especially Ebel Rabbati (Semahot) 8: 8–16, which also includes R. Akiba's famous eulogy on his son.

[4] See, e.g., Midr. Teh. on Pss. 94: 12, 98: 18.   [5] 1 Cor. 10: 13.

created the means with which a man can resist the evil inclination, if he wishes to make use of it. He gave Torah to be an antidote, he ordained the Day of Atonement to be a means of renewed grace in the struggle, and after the destruction of the Temple he gave sufferings for the same purpose.[1]

The rabbinic discussion of suffering extended over increasingly wide fields. It gave, for example, greater consideration to the suffering of animals,[2] and it also made attempts to differentiate and distinguish between different kinds of suffering.[3] But the understanding of suffering as a potential means of grace, not only for the individual, but for the whole community of the faithful, became the key to the Jewish response to suffering and persecution. 'He who gladly bears the sufferings that befall him brings salvation to the world.'[4] Without this sense of commitment to the totality of God's creation and purpose, the tenacious survival of Jewish communities under at times intense and relentless persecution would be almost inexplicable. And it is with again an almost iron logic that the most violent and enflamed persecution of the Jews in Nazi Germany should have issued in the restoration of the Promised Land—or at least of a part of it. Moves to establish in Palestine a national home for the Jews started before and during the First World War, but the fate of European Jews under Hitler made the argument virtually irresistible in the conscience of the world. Israel rose literally on the ashes of Buchenwald and Auschwitz, and in a most tragic way the sufferings of millions of individual Jews did become a means of grace for the community at large, and not least for the community as it continues in time. But to say that, in a detached and academic way, is to say nothing about the realities of the suffering itself; and no account of the Jewish response to suffering can in any way be adequate if it does not fully recognise what has had to be endured. What happened at Dulmo in the Ukraine may stand as a typical example. It was reported by a German eye-witness, Hermann Graebe, and is summarised in this account by Malcolm Hay:

Graebe was manager of a building contractor's business at Dulmo. On October 5, 1942, he went as usual to his office and there was told by his

[1] For illustrations of the two *yazrain*, see *Targums and Rabbinic Literature*, pp. 115–17.
[2] See, e.g., Ber. R. 33: 3.
[3] See, e.g., Ber. R. 92: 1 ('punishments of reproof and punishments of love'), Tanh. B. 101*a*, *b*. Poverty is regarded as the worst suffering in Shem. R. 31: 12.
[4] B. Taan. 8*a*.

foreman of terrible doings in the neighbourhood. All the Jews in the district, about five thousand of them, were being liquidated. About fifteen hundred were shot every day, out in the open air, at a place nearby where three large pits had been dug, thirty metres long and three metres deep. Graebe and his foreman, who was intensely agitated, got into a car and drove off to the place. They saw a great mound of earth, twice the length of a cricket pitch and more than six feet high—a good shooting range. Near the mound were several trucks packed with people. Guards with whips drove the people off the trucks. The victims all had yellow patches sewn onto their garments, back and front—the Jewish badge. From behind the earth mound came the sound of rifle shots in quick succession. The people from the lorries, men, women and children of all ages, were herded together near the mound by an SS man armed with a dog whip. They were ordered to strip. They were told to put down their clothes in tidy order, boots and shoes, top clothing and underclothing.

Already there were great piles of this clothing, and a heap of eight hundred to a thousand pairs of boots and shoes. The people undressed. The mothers undressed the little children, 'without screaming or weeping,' reported Graebe, five years after. They had reached the point of human suffering where tears no longer flow and all hope has long been abandoned. 'They stood around in family groups, kissed each other, said farewells, and waited.' They were waiting for a signal from the SS man with a whip, who was standing by the pit. They stood there waiting for a quarter of an hour, waiting for their turn to come, while on the other side of the earth mound, now that the shots were no longer heard, the dead and dying were being packed into the pit. Graebe said:

'I heard no complaints, no appeal for mercy. I watched a family of about eight persons, a man and a woman about fifty, with their grown up children, about twenty to twenty-four. An old woman with snow-white hair was holding a little baby in her arms, singing to it and tickling it. The baby was cooing with delight. The couple were looking at each other with tears in their eyes. The father was holding the hand of a boy about ten years old and speaking to him softly; the boy was fighting his tears...'[1]

In a way, the outsider has no right to intrude on grief such as this—or at least, those who lived through those years find it hard to do so. Perhaps in the perspective of history it will be easier, but so close to the event there is no comment that can usefully be

---

[1] *Europe and the Jews* (paperback ed. 1960), p. 8; reprinted in *Religion from Tolstoy to Camus*, ed. W. Kaufmann (paperback ed. 1964), pp. 339 f.

made. The scale is so vast, the enormity of evil so great, that it defies comprehension. It is at least something to be able to come away from those events with a deeper sensitivity to the continuing outrages of our own world, for as Richard Bentley put it, 'It was an excellent saying of Solon's who when he was asked what would rid the world of injuries replied, "If the bystanders would have the same resentment with those that suffer wrong."'

On the day following *die Kristallnacht*, the Night of Glass, so-called because on the night of 9 November 1938, the windows of Jewish shops throughout Germany were smashed and over 200 synagogues destroyed, Lichtenberg, the Provost of Berlin, protested:

What took place yesterday, we know; what will be to-morrow, we do not know; but what happens today, that we have witnessed. Outside the walls of this Church the Synagogue is burning, and that also is a house of God.[1]

There were few others who made a similar stand, and the results are known. The Jewish response to all this could again be illustrated from many sources. One that is particularly moving is contained in the *Wolkovisk Memorial Book*.[2] Wolkovisk, in 1939, was a large Polish town close to the German border. It had a considerable Jewish population, probably then about 15,000 in number. At the end of the War about 25 were left. Moses Einhorn, who put the book together to commemorate the dead, was in America when the War began. The whole of the rest of his family was killed. 'And now,' he wrote, 'now I alone of the children of my parents survive. I know not, I understand not, the ways of the Lord.'[3] He included in his book an account by Eliezer Kovenski of a visit that he made to Wolkovisk immediately after the War:

I came back to the neighbourhood of my old home in the village of Stutchin where I was born, immediately after the freeing of the town, and found no one. I saw only graves and more graves. But when I arrived in Wolkovisk, when I came to the beloved town, where my best years were spent, where I was married, where my dear children

---

[1] G. Lewy, *The Catholic Church and Nazi Germany* (London, 1964), p. 284.
[2] *Wolkovisker Yizkor Book* (New York, 1949).
[3] *Op. cit.* II, p. 955.

39

were born, I did not even find a grave. The Wolkovisker Jews have
been transformed to ashes in the crematoria of Treblinka and
Auschwitz. I wanted to throw myself upon the ground and weep,
weep without end. A Gentile acquaintance, Bolish Shareika, met me. He
invited me to his house and asked me if I wished anything to eat. 'No',
I said, 'I am sated. Thank you'. 'Give me' I asked him, 'a bit of earth
out of friendship'. I took the earth and covered my head. So I went out
upon the Neie Gaessel where my home once stood and sat down upon
a stone. I sat *Shivah* for my wife, for my children, and for all my dear
friends, the Jews of Wolkovisk.

The Gentiles gazed upon me with sympathy, 'Now,' I said, 'Now
it is well with you. There are no more Jews here. Now, now you will
live forever'. They replied they were not responsible, they had nothing
to do with what had happened.

I found the few partisans who were in town and bade them farewell,
and placed my bag upon my shoulders and took to the road. I went
through ruined towns and villages—villages without Jews exactly as
though it were the Day of Atonement when all Jews are to be found in
the synagogue for Kol Nidre. So it appeared everywhere. I turned
Eastward upon the road that leads to the Land of Israel.[1]

In that passage there are almost all the elements of the Jewish
response to suffering: there is the utter realism, the earth and the
ashes of death; there is the refusal to invoke a supernatural
solution as though it might in some way dissolve the agonising
realities of what has happened; there are the references to the
Day of Atonement, the intense feelings of family and community
and of involvement in the sufferings of others; there are the
Biblical allusions and rhythms in his writing, which hint that
there, in the past, is the guarantee that some hope is worth
retaining; but above all, there is the turning of his face to the
East, along the road that leads to Israel. The land of Israel is not
only a place, a geographical location, but, like Trebizond or
distant Byzantium, it is, also, an abiding vision:

> Come into hiding, brother:
> The ships of destruction have scorned the anchor.
> Under bombing planes and poisonous gases
> Open the book of psalms,
> And chant a *nigun* (melody).

[1] *Op. cit.* II, p. 902.

Development

And thus shalt thou say:
'Zion!'
While all roads are polluted with blood,
I shall raise my eyes to man.
'Zion!'

Bend deep into thine own soul
And hearken:
In the fields of Jezreel and Hafer the furrow calleth...
Take sack in hand, and go forth,
And sow...[1]

[1] Sh. Shalom, quoted in R. Wallenrod, *The Literature of Modern Israel*, (New York, 1956), pp. 203 f.

2

CHRISTIANITY

The Gospels

The Jewish world into which Jesus was born was one of great diversity and variety. Geographically, the Jews were dispersed over a large part of the Mediterranean world; politically, the sources of authority in Judaea were uncertain, resting on a balance between the controlling power of Rome, the permitted rule of the family of Herod, and the traditional institutions of Israel—which in very recent times had achieved a considerable measure of independence under the Hasmonaeans; and theologically, the Jews were pursuing a quest along many different paths for the meaning and application of their faith. In fact, there is a sense in which it is true to say that at the time when Jesus was born there was no such thing as 'Judaism'; instead there were a variety of ways in which Jews sought to define what Judaism ought to become and be, in their own time and generation.[1] There was, of course, an enormous amount of common ground: there was, above all, the common acceptance of the discovery and experience of God in history, which issued in the recognition as 'scripture' of certain documents recording that discovery and experience. It is true that there was, as yet, no complete agreement on what books belonged to Scripture. The basic books, Torah[2] and the Prophets, were generally (though not universally) accepted, but there was no final agreement on the other 'Writings'. Thus a Jew in Alexandria might accept certain books as Scripture which a Jew in Jerusalem would not. The Samaritans, who were bitterly rejected by most Jews but who still regarded themselves as representing 'Judaism', probably accepted only Torah, the Pentateuch, as Scripture. Yet the fact remains that the basic idea of 'scripture' was commonly accepted, and there was considerable agreement about the books contained within it. This naturally gave

---

[1] For further details of this, see *Targums and Rabbinic Literature*, pp. 6–8.
[2] For the meaning of Torah, see p. 7.

rise to other very extensive areas of common ground, since what Scripture emphasises is not so much men discovering God as men being discovered by God, and being confronted by his demands, his assistance and his judgement. So far as the demands of God are concerned, they are often detailed and specific, particularly in the first five books of Scripture, collectively known as Torah. It has already been pointed out that Torah is not Law as such; it is, rather, guidance for life which contains, amongst many other things, legislation. The guidance may be in the form of specific laws, or it may be in the form of narratives which reveal God's dealings with men or display exemplary characteristics of life. The important fact for the Jews is that the complex of material which constitutes Torah is not only guidance, but more than that it is *God's* guidance. It is the source of the kind and quality of life which he desires for his creation. As a result, there was, at the time of Jesus, a considerable conformity among Jews in religious and ritual observances, as well as in family and daily life. Yet still the fact remains that although there was much common ground in the understanding of God's relationship with his people Israel—a relationship which was particularised and authenticated in Scripture—there was considerable *disagreement* about the detailed interpretation of Scripture in the present— what it might mean in the lives of individuals and of society.

The disagreement existed, broadly speaking, on two different levels, the actual meaning or application of particular passages in Scripture, and the methods by which the meaning was extracted— or to put it more briefly, they were disputes about substance and methodology, of which the latter was probably the more fundamental, since the methods regarded as legitimate for the exegesis of a text affect considerably the meanings discovered in it. For example, an exegete might attempt to establish the strict grammatical sense of the original words, or he might attempt to establish what the words meant to the writer, or he might attempt to derive spiritual lessons for himself and his contemporaries. What Scripture 'means' will vary according to the intention of the exegete, and according to what he hopes to find in the text. Variety in methods of exegesis certainly existed among the Jews at the time when Jesus was alive. It can be seen most obviously in the differences existing between the allegorical methods particularly favoured by Philo, the literalistic methods of the Sadducees, the hermeneutic and expository methods of the Pharisees, the narrative method of such works as Jubilees and Ps.Philo, the imitative method of such works as the Thanksgiving Hymns of Qumran, and the indirect method which was particularly favoured by Jesus.[1] Such varieties in the methodology of exegesis supported and supplied widely differing interpretations of what Judaism ought to be, leading to separate parties or even sects. They had a common foundation in Scripture, but they often had also an acute hostility towards each other. There was certainly, for example, no love lost between Pharisees and Sadducees. What, therefore, emerges from this brief survey of the context in which Jesus lived, is that any attempt to understand the teaching (and life) of Jesus and the emergence of early Christianity must take into account the extent to which they were an interpretation, one among many, of what Judaism ought to be. They belong, first and foremost, to the variety and diversity of the Jewish world, although very rapidly a different, but related, question became dominant and all-important: for what reasons should Christianity become *separate* from Judaism—or indeed, as a *de facto* question, why had that separation already taken place?[2] The writings which became for Christians the New Testament show how prominent and sometimes vexing that question was. Yet the eventual separation of Church and Synagogue does not alter the extent to which the life and teaching of Jesus appeared on the Jewish scene as a part of the diverse quest among Jews for the meaning and implications of their faith.

In connection with suffering, it means that the teaching and actions of Jesus were inevitably related to the various ways in which suffering was understood by Jews in his time. Yet at the same time it is quite apparent that Jesus' 'interpretation' of what Judaism ought to be was highly original and distinctive. It possessed an independence built on a degree and quality of direct relationship with God which is always an implicit possibility in Judaism, but which has rarely, if ever, been so explicitly asserted as it was in the life and teaching of Jesus. The security of that relationship enabled him to move with an extraordinary degree of detachment among the varied patterns of Jewish life while

[1] For a fuller discussion of the varied methods of Jewish exegesis, see *Targums and Rabbinic Literature*.
[2] See, e.g., my own article 'The Origin and Purpose of St John's Gospel', *N.T.S.* XI, pp. 398 ff.

remaining completely involved in them. It was precisely this detachment and independence which eventually, to many Jews, marked out his interpretation of Judaism as a *mis*interpretation, though to what extent that reaction took place during his life as opposed to later on (when Christianity was gaining strength) is difficult now to determine. It was precisely his detachment and independence which seemed destructive, since it called in question the collective wisdom of a community which had long since come to see itself as the people of God, and it called in question also some of the traditional ways in which that collective wisdom had risen to the surface and been applied—hence the central import-ance in the Gospels of the question of authority, of the basis on which Jesus acted.[1] From the evidence, the basis seems in fact to have been a sense of affinity with God amounting to a directly causal relationship. What is perhaps the simplest image of human relationship with God, that of Father and child, was steadily worked out by Jesus on the ground, in the circumstances of life as they occurred.[2] It was not without intense agonies of prayer and conflict, yet consistently the implications and causal possi-bilities of that relationship were asserted. The strength and reality of the relationship can be seen clearly in the extent to which the independence produced by it was regarded by many Jews as heretical and destructive—'You have learned that our forefathers were told...but what I tell you is this.'[3]

Thus the life and teaching of Jesus belong to Judaism, yet they represent an individual and independent interpretation of it. His independence was grounded in an experiential certainty of God, particularly lived with as Father, which became an overriding and all-important fact. In the light of it, other affirmations and practices could be, and were, assessed, and it provided the particular agony of the crucifixion when it seemed that it might, after all, be empty: 'My God, my God, why hast thou forsaken me?' In both Mark and Matthew those are recorded as the last words of Jesus; of the Synoptics,[4] it is only in Luke that the image is specifically

---

[1] See, e.g., Mark 11 : 27 ff. (= Matt. 21 : 23 ff. = Luke 20 : 1 ff.).
[2] There were, of course, many other 'images' of God expressed in the life and teaching of Jesus, but that of Father was particularly important and constructive.
[3] Matt. 5 : 21.
[4] The term 'synoptics' refers to the three gospels, Matthew, Mark and Luke, which contain a great deal of common material, and which are often printed in three parallel columns in order to display the exact extent of the agreements or dis-agreements between them.

retained, and the last words become, 'Father, into thy hands I commit my spirit.'[1]

Mention of the crucifixion at once isolates the focal point of the Christian understanding of suffering. To the early Christians it was a matter of plain knowledge and fact that the cross was the point to which Jesus' involvement in God had led him. But it was also a matter of plain knowledge and fact that this involvement had been vindicated by what they described as his resurrection. The 'matter-of-factness' of the resurrection as an event is emphasised repeatedly in the New Testament, both in theological reflection on its significance, and also in many of the narratives selected for the Gospels to describe it. What gave rise to that conviction has frequently been made a matter of dispute, but what cannot be disputed is the strength of the conviction and the startlingly abrupt nature of its origin and impact.

What that means, so far as the Gospels are concerned, is that they are not simply records of what Jesus said and did, but they are also interpretations of why that life and teaching are of continuing and vital importance. They lead the reader directly towards an event which in a sense epitomises the fearful agonies of human suffering—an innocent and early death of an all too typical savagery. In ordinary human terms there would be no reason for regarding this as other than the end of the story. But the Gospels know that in the case of Jesus what appeared to be the end was in fact a new beginning, and what appeared to be defeat was a victory.[2] Thus in connection with suffering the Gospels are controlled by a knowledge that Jesus met the realities of suffering in his own person and was not defeated by them. This is applied in the Gospels in two important ways: first, it is made entirely clear that Jesus knew where his life was leading, and that it would issue in his own suffering; and secondly, the conquest of suffering which took place in his own person in the crucifixion and resurrection also took place throughout his life in the way in which he met, actively and positively, the facts of suffering as he found

---

[1] Luke 23: 46.
[2] Although the word 'victory' is used, it should perhaps be pointed out that the most obvious Greek equivalents, the verb *nikao* and its derivatives, occur mostly in the so-called Johannine literature (the Gospel according to John, the 1st, 2nd and 3rd letters of John, and the Revelation to John)—though there are important references in Luke 11: 22, 1 Cor. 15: 57. But the general *sense* of 'victory' pervades the whole New Testament.

them. Those two elements have remained characteristic of the Christian response to suffering.

The first point is particularly obvious in the predictions of the Passion which occur repeatedly, in both specific and general terms, throughout the Gospels. The most detailed are the three 'Passion-predictions' which occur in all three synoptic Gospels, and which are given quite specific content.[1]

Less detailed references to the certainty, and even necessity, of his Passion also occur,[2] particularly in connection with the Last Supper and the agony in the Garden:

In the evening he came to the house with the Twelve. As they sat at supper Jesus said, 'I tell you this: one of you will betray me—one who is eating with me.' At this they were dismayed; and one by one they said to him, 'Not I, surely?' 'It is one of the Twelve', he said, 'who is dipping into the same bowl with me. The Son of Man is going the way appointed for him in the scriptures; but alas for that man by whom the Son of Man is betrayed! It would be better for that man if he had never been born.[3]

Luke added an even more specific note:

And he said to them, 'How I have longed to eat this Passover with you before my death![4] For I tell you, never again shall I eat it until the time when it finds its fulfilment in the kingdom of God.'[5]

In Gethsemane the sense of time running out becomes even stronger:

When they reached a place called Gethsemane, he said to his disciples, 'Sit here while I pray.' And he took Peter and James and John with him. Horror and dismay came over him, and he said to them, 'My heart is ready to break with grief; stop here, and stay awake.' Then he went forward a little, threw himself on the ground, and prayed that, if it were possible, this hour might pass him by. 'Abba, Father,' he said,

---

[1] Mark 8: 31 f., Matt. 16: 21 f., Luke 9: 22; Mark 9: 30–2, Matt. 17: 22 f., Luke 9: 44 f.; Mark 10: 32–4, Matt. 20: 17 f., Luke 18: 31–3.
[2] See, e.g., Mark 9: 11–13 = Matt. 17: 10–13 (there is no direct parallel in Luke, because the reference to suffering and death has been involved in the preceding narrative of the Transfiguration, Luke 9: 31); Luke 17: 25. Certain parables are given a reference to the crucifixion and vindication of Jesus, though of course it does not follow that they were originally told with that interpretation in mind. See, e.g., Matt. 21: 33 ff.
[3] Mark 14: 17–21 = Matt. 26: 20–4 = Luke 22: 14–22.
[4] The word is *pathein*, lit. 'suffer'.   [5] Luke 22: 15 f.

'all things are possible to thee. Yet not what I will, but what thou wilt.'[1]

To what extent the detailed predictions of the Passion were filled in *post eventum* has long been a matter of dispute, and it is simply one question among many about the historicity of the Gospels. What is beyond dispute is the intention of the evangelists to show that Jesus became increasingly aware of the direction in which his life was leading, and that he faced the possibility of suffering with a wish that it might be otherwise, but with an unbroken confidence in God. Whether or not every single detail is original, the general attitude seems inescapably demanded by the evidence.

The realistic confrontation with suffering epitomised in the crucifixion is seen also in the Gospels in his response to suffering during his life. It is particularly obvious in the many recorded incidents of healing. They are rarely told for their own sake but in order to exemplify some point of his teaching or some aspect of his authority and control. He is represented as actively engaged with the forces which give rise to human suffering, and those forces are frequently portrayed in personified form as devils or unclean spirits. Thus the 'engagement' is an almost literal battle. This is made entirely clear in the very first healing incident recorded in Mark:

There was a man in the synagogue possessed by an unclean spirit. He shrieked: 'What do you want with us, Jesus of Nazareth? Have you come to destroy us? I know who you are—the Holy One of God.' Jesus rebuked him: 'Be silent', he said, 'and come out of him.' And the unclean spirit threw the man into convulsions and with a loud cry left him. They were all dumbfounded and began to ask one another, 'What is this? A new kind of teaching! He speaks with authority. When he gives orders, even the unclean spirits submit.'[2]

It is perhaps the strongest and most consistent impression of the Gospels that Jesus was one whose authority and control were complete, and that they were grounded in his deliberate and self-conscious certainty of God:

[1] Mark 14: 32–6 = Matt. 26: 36–9 = Luke 22: 39–42. Some MSS of Luke immediately add the intensified description, 'And now there appeared to him an angel from heaven bringing him strength, and in anguish of spirit he prayed the more urgently; and his sweat was like clots of blood falling to the ground.'
[2] Mark 1: 23–7 = Luke 4: 33–6.

He stood up, rebuked the wind, and said to the sea, 'Hush! Be still!' The wind dropped and there was a dead calm. He said to them, 'Why are you such cowards? Have you no faith, even now?' They were awestruck and said to one another, 'Who can this be whom even the wind and the sea obey?'[1]

His authority was believed to have extended even over death, as can be seen, perhaps most graphically, in the story of the healing of Jairus' daughter.[2] Jesus was thus seen as one who engaged the griefs and sufferings of existence with authority and power. His engagement was by no means confined to instances of disease or physical deformity. He was constantly in conflict with those who increased the sufferings of others, particularly those who did so on over-scrupulously religious grounds:

'Alas for you Pharisees! You pay tithes of mint and rue and every garden-herb, but you have no care for justice and the love of God. It is these you should have practised, without neglecting the others...' In reply to this one of the lawyers said, 'Master, when you say things like this you are insulting us too.' Jesus rejoined: 'Yes, you lawyers, it is no better with you! For you load men with intolerable burdens, and you will not put a single finger to the load.'[3]

But although Jesus was seen to have engaged in active contest against conditions which give rise to suffering, in no sense at all did it mean that he was prepared to use all available methods with which to carry on the struggle. Where two of his disciples were anxious to call down fire on an inhospitable village, he turned and rebuked them;[4] where his disciples drew swords to defend him against his arrest in Gethsemane, Jesus allowed himself to be taken (and according to Matthew and Luke he healed the servant of the high priest who was wounded);[5] where the savage events of his trial and crucifixion stormed about him, he remained before his accusers silent. As an early exposition of Christianity put it, 'force is not a means of which God makes use.'[6] The refusal of Jesus to allow the end to justify the means in giving relief to

[1] Mark 4: 39–41 = Matt. 8: 26 f. = Luke 8: 24 f.
[2] Mark 5: 22–4, 35–42 = Matt. 9: 18 ff. = Luke 8: 41 ff.
[3] Luke 11: 42, 45 f.; cf. also the vehement way in which Jesus is described as having expelled the money-changers from the Temple (Mark 11: 15–17 = Matt. 21: 12 f. = Luke 19: 45 f.). That incident is often referred to as an example of Jesus' willingness to use violence in contesting evil.
[4] Luke 9: 51–6.   [5] Mark 14: 47 ff. = Matt. 26: 51 ff. = Luke 22: 49 ff.
[6] *Ep. ad Diognetum* vii. 4.

suffering can be seen in its most concentrated form in the story of the Temptations—'If you are the Son of God, tell these stones to become bread.'[1] It is abundantly clear that in Jesus' view there are no short-cuts to the kingdom. For those who have power, there are obviously great temptations to use it ruthlessly for the domination of others; but there are *equally* great dangers involved in using it for their welfare.

The effective authority with which Jesus confronted instances of suffering was in no way dispassionate. If one of the strongest impressions of Jesus emerging from the Gospels is that of his control, equally strong is that of his compassion. It is displayed as intense and unceasing:

When he came ashore, he saw a great crowd; and his heart went out to them, because they were like sheep without a shepherd.[2]

In both word and deed his sense of identity with those in need is made manifest: 'Jesus said to them, "It is not the healthy that need a doctor, but the sick; I did not come to invite virtuous people, but sinners."'[3] Jesus, therefore, is represented in the Gospels as one whose sane authority arose out of a confident and uncompromising dependence on God as the source of his activity. There was nothing remote or overbearing about the exercise of that authority, even though it sometimes issued in fierce condemnation. It was controlled and made gentle by an agonised compassion, and the two often appear in conjunction:

O Jerusalem, Jerusalem, the city that murders the prophets and stones the messengers sent to her! How often have I longed to gather your children, as a hen gathers her brood under wings; but you would not let me.[4]

The synoptic Gospels, then, represent Jesus as one who met the facts of suffering in a direct and practical way. In view of the very large amount of material in the Gospels devoted to the ways in which Jesus responded, both in word and deed, to the facts of suffering, it is perhaps surprising that there is virtually no discussion why suffering should exist. Various attitudes belonging to

[1] Matt. 4: 3 = Luke 4: 3.   [2] Mark 6: 34; cf. Matt. 9: 36.
[3] Mark 2: 17 = Matt. 9: 13 = Luke 5: 32.
[4] Luke 13: 34 = Matt. 23: 37. Many of the characteristics so far described appear in a single and revealing incident, Mark 9: 14–27 = Matt. 17: 14–21 = Luke 9: 37–43. In many ways it may be taken as an effective summary of the authority of Jesus, and of the evident source of that authority in faith.

the Jewish tradition emerge in the narratives, but they emerge by
implication rather than by way of specific discussion. Thus there
is a clear sense, particularly in the apocalyptic material incorporated in the Gospels, that suffering may well be a punishment or
retribution.[1] Equally characteristic of the Jewish understanding
of suffering is the connection between sin and suffering, which
underlies several of the Gospel narratives:

When after some days he returned to Capernaum, the news went
round that he was at home; and such a crowd collected that the space
in front of the door was not big enough to hold them. And while he
was proclaiming the message to them, a man was brought who was
paralysed. Four men were carrying him, but because of the crowd they
could not get him near. So they opened up the roof over the place where
Jesus was, and when they had broken through they lowered the
stretcher on which the paralysed man was lying. When Jesus saw their
faith, he said to the paralysed man, 'My son, your sins are forgiven.'
Now there were some lawyers sitting there and they thought to
themselves, 'Why does the fellow talk like that? This is blasphemy!
Who but God alone can forgive sins?' Jesus knew in his own mind
that this was what they were thinking, and said to them: 'Why do you
harbour thoughts like these? Is it easier to say to this paralysed man,
"Your sins are forgiven", or to say, "Stand up, take your bed, and
walk"? But to convince you that the Son of Man has the right on earth
to forgive sins'—he turned to the paralysed man—'I say to you, stand
up, take your bed, and go home.' And he got up, took his stretcher at
once, and went out in full view of them all, so that they were astounded
and praised God. 'Never before', they said, 'have we seen the like.'[2]

Still in close contact with the Jewish tradition, but further
removed from Scripture, is the view that suffering is a consequence
of the direct activity of the Devil or devils. In Scripture (*i.e.* in the
Old Testament) Satan appears only three times,[3] not as the
embodiment of evil, but as a member of the heavenly court whose
job is to test and to provoke men in order to prove whether their
faith in God is substantial or brittle. But in the post-Biblical

---

[1] See, e.g., Luke 17: 26–30 = Matt. 24: 37–41; but even here the theme of suffering
as a punishment is only implicit, because the incidents are used by the evangelists to
illustrate a different theme, the unexpectedness of the final coming of the Son of
Man.

[2] Mark 2: 1–12. It can also be seen in the stress on internal defilement as a source of
evil and suffering: see, e.g., Mark 7: 17–23 = Matt. 15: 15–20, and cf. the graphic
illustration in Matt. 12: 43–5 = Luke 11: 24–6.

[3] 1 Chron. 21: 1, Job 1: 6, Zech. 3: 1.

period the figure of Satan began to fill out, and he started to appear as a rebel against God, the prince of darkness and the ruler of evil powers. He is, therefore, to be found slipping into the Garden of Eden so as to become instrumental in the origin of all human suffering—that is to say, in the Fall. Elaborate and fantastic stories came later to be told of how Satan, the evil one, changed himself into the form of a serpent in order to come to Eve without immediately terrifying her by his undisguised appearance.[1] A major influence in the vastly increased emphasis on Satan as the opponent of God would seem to have been the dualistic tendency in Persian religion, and perhaps more particularly in Zoroastrianism.[2]

The exact influence of Persian religion on Judaism is difficult to establish, but there is no doubt that it was considerable, both by rejection as well as by assimilation. It was certainly an important factor in the increasing tendency to see dualism as a most natural explanation of the existence of evil and suffering. The personal experience of conflict between good and evil, which produced the concept of a good and evil tendency at war with each other in each human being,[3] was easily translated on to a cosmic level. Absolute dualism (that is to say, the view that the two principles of Good and Evil are eternally self-subsistent) was excluded by the belief that God was ultimately in control and that the final victory would be his, and also by the belief that the evil powers were originally good, but that they fell in an act of rebellion against God. In the meantime, the powers of evil have a wide scope and effect, and Luke even suggests that temporal authority is at the devil's disposal, by adding a sentence to the narrative of the Temptation of Jesus:

'All this dominion will I give to you,' he said, 'and the glory that goes with it; for it has been put in my hands and I can give it to anyone I choose.'[4]

That general mythological framework allowed experiences of temptation or suffering to be regarded as a part of a direct and naked struggle. Much of the New Testament interpretation of the life and work of Jesus was put within that framework, and he

[1] For examples of such stories, see *Targums and Rabbinic Literature*, pp. 105, 125f.
[2] On Zoroastrianism, see pp. 270 ff.   [3] The two *yazrain*—see pp. 36 f.
[4] Luke 4: 6; cf. Matt. 4: 8. Luke also writes of individuals being bound or imprisoned by Satan: Luke 13: 16.

Foundations

was seen as one whose conflict with the forces of evil was unceasing and ultimately successful. The working-out of the cosmic implications of that victory can be seen more prominently in the Epistles, but the Gospels also frequently represent the activity of Jesus as being a direct attack on the devil and his agents.

So far as the synoptic Gospels are concerned, the devil (or in Mark's case[1] Satan) appears on the scene at once, in the story of the three Temptations,[2] where the temptation to achieve results by means of 'miracle, mystery, and authority'[3] is rejected on scriptural grounds—that is to say, it is rejected out of the collective experience of God in the religious tradition to which Jesus belonged. In that way at least, the story of the Temptations is true to the foundation of Jesus' activity. The devil appears equally early in Mark's narrative. Apart from the brief and unexpanded note of the Temptation,[4] and apart from general references to Jesus' success in casting out devils from the very start of his ministry,[5] there is then recorded Jesus' own analysis of his activity in relation to Satan. The 'doctors of the law' suggest that Jesus must be in league with the devil, since otherwise he could not be so successful. The devils and unclean spirits indeed 'know him',[6] because he is really one of them:

The doctors of the law,...who had come down from Jerusalem, said, 'He is possessed by Beelzebub', and, 'He drives out devils by the prince of devils.' So he called them to come forward, and spoke to them in parables: 'How can Satan drive out Satan? If a kingdom is divided against itself, that kingdom cannot stand; if a household is divided against itself, that house will never stand; and if Satan is in rebellion against himself, he is divided and cannot stand; and that is the end of him.'[7]

Mark immediately goes on to record a saying which shows to what extent the activity of Jesus was regarded as a violent invasion of Satan's territory:[8]

On the other hand, no one can break into a strong man's house and make off with his goods unless he has first tied the strong man up; then he can ransack the house.[9]

[1] Mark 1: 13.   [2] Matt. 4: 1 ff. = Luke 4: 1 ff.
[3] Dostoevsky, *The Brothers Karamazov* (Penguin ed.), I, pp. 299, 301.
[4] Mark 1: 12 f.   [5] Mark 1: 26 f., 34, 39, 3: 11.   [6] Mark 1: 34.   [7] Mark 3: 22-6.
[8] The 'violence' of Jesus' onslaught on the forces of evil occurs elsewhere. See, e.g., Luke 12: 49-51 (cf. Matt. 10: 34-6): 'I have come to set fire to the earth, and how I wish it were already kindled! I have a baptism to undergo, and how hampered I am until the ordeal is over! Do you suppose I came to establish peace on earth? No indeed, I have come to bring division.'   [9] Mark 3: 27.

Although much evil and suffering was regarded as being the consequence of the personal activity of the devil and his agents, there is little evidence in the Gospels of any attempt to work out systematically the implications of that view. It appears far more as a part of the context in which Jesus lived, and through which he expressed his convictions about the overriding certainty of God. To that extent the Gospels represent him as realistic and practical, rather than theoretical. But at one point the existence of suffering is raised as a question in almost classic terms, as representing a 'problem of distribution':

At that very time there were some people present who told him about the Galileans whose blood Pilate had mixed with their sacrifices. He answered them: 'Do you imagine that, because these Galileans suffered this fate, they must have been greater sinners than anyone else in Galilee? I tell you they were not; but unless you repent, you will all of you come to the same end. Or the eighteen people who were killed when the tower fell on them at Siloam—do you imagine they were more guilty than all the other people living in Jerusalem? I tell you they were not; but unless you repent, you will all of you come to the same end.'[1]

The passage as recorded by Luke suggests a repudiation of a simple cause-and-effect understanding of suffering. At the same time there is retained a sense of suffering as an ultimate punishment—or perhaps, rather, sanction—which is emphasised by the parable that Luke immediately goes on to record of a barren fig-tree being given one last chance to bear fruit before being cut down.[2]

The problem of the distribution of suffering occurs, in the synoptic Gospels, most specifically in that passage from Luke, but it underlies many other passages, particularly in some of the material assembled in the two great Sermons in Matthew and Luke, the Sermon on the Mount and the Sermon on the Plain (Matt. 5:1 – 7:29; Luke 6: 20–49). The material in Luke is displayed in a far more 'primitive' and direct way, in the sense that it retains the note of the Siloam passage, that ultimate rewards and punishments are in mind, and that present sufferings will receive their compensation. This is clearly present in Matthew but it is stronger in Luke, since Luke stresses the reverse side of the coin, that present indulgence will be punished. It can be seen

[1] Luke 13: 1–5.   [2] Luke 13: 6–9.

most clearly in the fact that Luke adds to the Blessings the Four
Woes which do not occur in Matthew:

How blest are those who know
that they are poor; the kingdom of heaven is theirs.

How blest are the sorrowful; they
shall find consolation.

How blest are those of a gentle
spirit; they shall have the
earth for their possession.

How blest are those who hunger
and thirst to see right prevail;
they shall be satisfied.

How blest are those who show
mercy; mercy shall be shown
to them.

How blest are those whose hearts
are pure; they shall see God.

How blest are the peace-makers;
God shall call them his sons.

How blest are those who have
suffered persecution for the
cause of right; the kingdom
of heaven is theirs.

How blest you are, when you
suffer insults and persecutions
and every kind of calumny
for my sake.

Accept it with gladness and exul-
tation, for you have a rich
reward in heaven; in the same
way they persecuted the
prophets before you.[1]

How blest are you who are poor;
the kingdom of God is yours.

How blest are you who now go
hungry; your hunger shall be
satisfied.

How blest are you who weep
now; you shall laugh.

How blest you are when men hate
you, when they outlaw you
and insult you, and ban your
very name as infamous, because of the Son of Man. On
that day be glad and dance
for joy; for assuredly you
have a rich reward in heaven;
in just the same way did their
fathers treat the prophets.

But alas for you who are rich; you
have had your time of happiness.

Alas for you who are well fed
now; you shall go hungry.

Alas for you who laugh now; you
shall mourn and weep.

Alas for you when all speak well
of you; just so did their
fathers treat the false
prophets.

But although the problem of distribution is less specific in
Matthew's opening of the Sermon on the Mount, it becomes more
apparent as an underlying problem in subsequent passages:

You have learned that they were told, 'Love your neighbour, hate your
enemy.' But what I tell you is this: 'Love your enemies and pray for
your persecutors; only so can you be children of your heavenly
Father, who makes his sun rise on good and bad alike, and sends the

[1] Matt. 5: 3–12; Luke 6: 20–6.

rain on the honest and the dishonest. If you love only those who love you, what reward can you expect? Surely the tax-gatherers do as much as that. And if you greet only your brothers, what is there extraordinary about that? Even the heathen do as much. You must therefore be all goodness, just as your heavenly Father is all good.'[1]

That passage emphasises the extent to which the synoptic Gospels are more concerned with practical responses than with theoretical solutions. Indeed, they stress that the truly creative response is not to be preoccupied with theoretical problems, but to be active in expressing a quality of life which is its own sufficient solution—particularly by asserting in life the possibility that God can be known as Father, as 'our Father':[2]

Therefore I bid you put away anxious thoughts about food and drink to keep you alive, and clothes to cover your body. Surely life is more than food, the body more than clothes...No, do not ask anxiously, 'What are we to eat? What are we to drink? What shall we wear?' All these are things for the heathen to run after, not for you, because your heavenly Father knows that you need them all. Set your mind on God's kingdom and his justice before everything else, and all the rest will come to you as well. So do not be anxious about tomorrow; tomorrow will look after itself. Each day has troubles enough of its own.[3]

This is the essence of the Christian response to suffering, the realisation of God as Father, and it comes out with particular clarity in Matthew's Sermon on the Mount:

Not everyone who calls me 'Lord, Lord' will enter the kingdom of Heaven, but only those who do the will of my heavenly Father.[4]

The synoptic Gospels make it entirely clear that a disciple's response to suffering is practical and active because it is laid in the pattern of Christ. His own life demonstrated that the relationship of child and father can be sustained, even in the worst imaginable torment and suffering, as in the crucifixion—though

---

[1] Matt. 5: 43–8. Cf. the quite different emphasis in Luke 6: 35 f.: 'You must love your enemies and do good; and lend without expecting any return; and you will have a rich reward: you will be sons of the Most High, because he himself is kind to the ungrateful and wicked. Be compassionate as your Father is compassionate.'

[2] Matt. 6: 9, Luke 11: 4. [3] Matt. 6: 25–34 = Luke 12: 22–31.

[4] Matt. 7: 21; cf. the again different emphasis in the parallel in Luke 6: 46: 'Why do you keep calling me "Lord, Lord"—and never do what I tell you?'

there it was within inches of destruction. But so far as the writers of the synoptic Gospels were concerned, the factual reality of the resurrection meant that 'the theistic experiment was verified':

It cannot be doubted that Jesus had the whole fact of pain present to his mind. He lived in the midst of suffering. Yet it did not present itself to him as a problem. Certainly he made no explicit reference to the questions with which Job wrestled. His compassion flowed forth unhindered by any theory of the causes of pain. He never viewed suffering as other than a great evil. He devoted a large part of his ministry to its alleviation. But he never stood before it confounded and paralysed. If he was conscious of its challenge to theism, he never replied by arguments. He lived in unbroken communion with God, and faced all the problems of life from that position of perfect acquaintance. He knew God. He knew that God's love gathers into its company all the suffering of man and of the whole sentient creation. The goodwill of a God whom he knew as the Father cannot be impugned. The victory of his love cannot be doubted. In this faith Jesus lived and died. He revealed to men its divine object and gave theism the verification of experience.[1]

Thus the Gospels firmly declare themselves to *be* gospels—that is, to be good news, and each of the synoptic Gospels introduces Jesus on exactly that note.[2] The victory has already been won and there can be no final defeat. On that foundation of a triumph already won the lives of the first Christians and the writings of the New Testament were built. Certainly the synoptic Gospels make it clear that disciples of Jesus are expected to express the two attitudes exemplified in his life; supreme confidence that even the furthest extremes of suffering do not defeat the possibility of God; and combined with that, an active and practical response to suffering wherever it occurs. The first has already been exemplified in the advice, 'Put away anxious thoughts';[3] as for the second element—the obligation on the part of the true disciple to share

---

[1] T. P. Kilpatrick, article on 'Suffering' in Hastings' *Encyclopaedia of Religion and Ethics.*

[2] Mark 1: 1 (the title 'Christ' is the Gk. *christos* which in turn represents the Hebrew *mashiach*, or in its more familiar transliteration, Messiah. It means literally 'anointed one', and had come to refer particularly among the Jews to the figure—usually descended from David—who they believed would be sent by God to establish his reign on earth. 'Christians' were therefore seen to be those who accepted Jesus as that figure); Luke 1: 30-3; Matt. 1: 1 (in the shorthand of Judaism this implies what is spelt out in Luke 1: 30-3, but cf. also Matt. 1: 20 f.).

[3] Matt. 6: 25, quoted on p. 56; there are, of course, many other examples.

Christianity

not only Jesus' confidence but also his compassion—it appears with equal clarity. Indeed, in some passages compassion in the relief of suffering is the mark of discipleship. According to Matthew, the teaching of Jesus ends on exactly that note. The last parable, before Matthew moves on to the events of 'the final conflict',[1] is the famous one, which Matthew alone records, of the Sheep and the Goats, where the sole criterion for judgement is the plain consideration 'Anything you did (or did not do) for one of my brothers here, however humble, you did (or did not do) for me.'[2]

Comparable in its implications is a parable which only Luke records, that of the Good Samaritan[3]—indeed, there is almost no limit to the number of instances which might be given of the practical compassion of Jesus and of the obligation on the part of his disciples to follow the example of that compassion. That they can do so effectively is suggested in the many passages which state that the authority and power of Christ have been transferred to them. The final words of Matthew summarise the experience of the early Church as it appears on almost every page of the New Testament:

Full authority in heaven and on earth has been committed to me. Go forth therefore and make all nations my disciples; baptize men everywhere in the name of the Father and the Son and the Holy Spirit, and teach them to observe all that I have commanded you. And be assured, I am with you always, to the end of time.[4]

It is clear that the synoptic Gospels see the teaching and activity of Jesus in the light of a victory which he shares with his disciples. That is equally true and even more directly apparent in the fourth Gospel, that of John,[5] where the significance of Jesus is explored and penetrated on even deeper levels.[6]

In connection with suffering, the truth of this can be seen in the

1 'The Final Conflict' is the heading given by the *N.E.B.* to the last three chapters of Matthew.
2 For the whole parable, see Matt. 25: 31–46.
3 Luke 10: 30–7—ending, 'Go, and do thou likewise.'
4 Matt. 28: 18–20; cf. Mark 16: 15–20.
5 The Gospel according to St John is often referred to as 'the fourth gospel', to distinguish it from the other three (the synoptics) which are more obviously connected to each other.
6 For an effective summary of some of the differences between the synoptics and John, see C. K. Barrett, *The Gospel According to St John* (London, 1956), pp. 58 f.

fact that all the key-notes of the synoptic Gospels appear also in John, but in a different relationship to each other and often with a quite different emphasis. Particularly striking is the way in which the foundation of Jesus' activity, his sense of a completely involved relationship with God as Father, is developed in John and shown to be the essential element in understanding who and what Jesus is:

The Jews gathered round him and asked: 'How long must you keep us in suspense? If you are the Messiah say so plainly.' 'I have told you,' said Jesus, 'but you do not believe. My deeds done in my Father's name are my credentials, but because you are not sheep of my flock you do not believe. My own sheep listen to my voice; I know them and they follow me. I give them eternal life and they shall never perish; no one shall snatch them from my care. My Father who has given them to me is greater than all, and no one can snatch them out of the Father's care. My Father and I are one.'[1]

It is a theme to which the Gospel repeatedly returns, demonstrating the consequences of this relationship throughout. Indeed, the note is set in the opening words:

When all things began, the Word already was. The Word dwelt with God, and what God was, the Word was. The Word, then, was with God at the beginning, and through him all things came to be; no single thing was created without him. All that came to be was alive with his life, and that life was the light of men. The light shines on in the dark, and the darkness has never quenched it.[2]

That last sentence leads directly into the area of evil and suffering, because it means that John, like the synoptics, saw the activity of Jesus as being the initiative of God in taking direct and positive action against both—'it is he who takes away the sin of the world.'[3] But whereas in the synoptics the sense of encounter was expressed frequently in personified terms of the devil,[4] in John the devil is not prominent at all, though he does appear at certain key points—in connection with the crucifixion, as being instrumental in Judas' act of betrayal,[5] and as involved in the Jewish rejection of Jesus.[6] But otherwise the sense of encounter is transferred to a far wider scale, and it is expressed particularly as a contrast between light and darkness.

[1] John 10: 24–30.   [2] John 1: 1–5.   [3] John 1: 29.
[4] See above, pp. 51–4.   [5] John 12: 31, 13: 2, 27, cf. 6: 70 f.   [6] John 8: 44 f.

God loved the world so much that he gave his only Son, that everyone who has faith in him may not die but have eternal life. It was not to judge the world that God sent his Son into the world, but that through him the world might be saved. The man who puts his faith in him does not come under judgement; but the unbeliever has already been judged in that he has not given his allegiance to God's only Son. Here lies the test: the light has come into the world, but men preferred darkness to light because their deeds were evil. Bad men all hate the light and avoid it, for fear their practices should be shown up. The honest man comes to the light so that it may be clearly seen that God is in all he does.[1]

As E. C. Hoskyns, commenting on that passage, put it:

This is the issue raised by the historical figure of Jesus, by his words and actions, and finally by his death. The death of Jesus is the supremely good action, since it is that work which above all others makes room for the creative action of the love of God. The light which Jesus is (i. 5) penetrates every corner of human behaviour, and either lights it up or throws it into the darkness. There is no twilight in his presence, for he compels the final distinction between those who have everlasting life and those who have lost everything (vv. 15-16).[2]

John thus saw Jesus as a light and illumination showing up the things of the world for what they really are. The great insight of John was to realise that the act of illumination is at one and the same time both welcome and unwelcome—welcome, insofar as it dispels darkness so that there is no longer cause for doubt; unwelcome, insofar as it exposes things that are hideous in contrast with itself. That insight is directly relevant to John's understanding of suffering, because it is applied in its most concentrated form to the Passion.

Like the synoptics, John makes it clear that Jesus was aware, in advance, of the point to which his life was leading, and therefore (again like the synoptics) John sees the suffering of Jesus as the decisive and all-important act in relation to *all* suffering, since Jesus knew beforehand that his relationship with God would not exempt him from suffering, and yet he did not 'lose' God in the experience of it.[3] Indeed, in a vitally important sense he

---

[1] John 3: 16-21; on light and darkness in connection with Jesus see also John 12: 34-6.

[2] Hoskyns, *The Fourth Gospel* (London, 1956), p. 209. The whole passage (pp. 202-9) is an extremely clear and penetrating analysis. For reasons of space, it cannot be quoted here, but it is well-worth careful study and reflection.

[3] But John, as usual, is different from the synoptics in the way in which he handles the same theme. Whereas the synoptics make the foreknowledge of Jesus clear

established the relationship of God as Father conclusively, because by the willing acceptance of his own innocent suffering and by the vindication of that acceptance in the resurrection, he removed or transferred the relationship to an area where no further accident of suffering could threaten it:

Jesus said, 'Do not cling to me, for I have not yet ascended to the Father. But go to my brothers, and tell them that I am now ascending to my Father and your Father, my God and your God.'[1]

Not only is the relationship secured; it is also shared. It is not surprising, therefore, that John regarded the crucifixion as the supreme manifestation of light in the midst of darkness—light in the double sense of illumination and exposure. Whereas the synoptics all recorded darkness as prevailing at the time of the crucifixion—'and when the sixth hour was come, there was darkness over the whole land'[2]—John put the note of darkness right back to the moment when Judas went out to betray him: 'Judas, then, received the bread and went out. It was night.'[3] In John there is no specific mention of darkness at the time of the crucifixion as there is in the synoptics, because in John the whole Passion narrative exemplifies what he has already said, that the light shines on in the dark, and the darkness has never quenched it.[4] Consequently, since the crucifixion appears to be defeat but is in fact victory, John describes the crucifixion by the word 'glory' or 'glorify', in Greek *doxa* and *doxadzo*. It is a choice of words of almost breathtaking brilliance, as C. K. Barrett's summary of the meaning of *doxa* makes clear:

In the LXX [the Greek translation of the Old Testament], in certain other Hellenistic religious literature, and in the New Testament, the noun and verb respectively mean 'glory', 'to glorify'. In the LXX *doxa*...denotes particularly the visible manifestation (often of light) accompanying a theophany (e.g. Ex. xxxiii. 22; Dt. v. 21; 1 Kings viii. 11). It acquired in the Old Testament an eschatological significance[5]

particularly in the detailed Passion-predictions (see p. 47) and only occasionally in general terms, John makes it clear most often in general terms and only occasionally in detail. See, e.g. John 6: 64–71, 8: 37.
[1] John 20: 17.
[2] Mark 15: 33 = Matt. 27: 45 = Luke 23: 44.
[3] John 13: 30.   [4] John 1: 5.
[5] I.e. it was used to refer to the full and final revelation of God in light and glory at the end of times.

61

Christianity

(e.g. Is. lx. 1; Hab. ii. 14), which it retained in the New Testament (e.g. Mk. viii. 38, xiii. 26; Rom. viii. 18; I Peter iv. 13), though in the New Testament the eschatological *doxa* occasionally appears, by anticipation, in the present (II Cor. iii. 18, Eph. iii. 21). The clearest example of this proleptic *doxa* is the Transfiguration[1] (Mk. ix. 2–8 and parallels), an incident which is not recounted in John... John nevertheless asserts that the glory of God was manifested in Jesus (i. 14). It was shown in his miracles (ii. 11, xi. 4, 40); but in particular he enjoyed a position of glory before the Incarnation, and subsequently returned to it (xvii. 5, 24). Jesus did not enjoy this glory because he sought it for himself, but because he sought only God's glory (v. 41; vii. 18; viii. 50), whereas other men sought their own (v. 44; xii. 43). The glory of Jesus is thus dependent upon both his essential relation with God (i. 14) and his obedience. To this corresponds the special use of the verb *doxadzo* as a description of the death of Jesus (vii. 39; xii. 16, 23; xiii. 31 f.); Jesus dies as Son of God and as an obedient servant; he is thereby lifted up on the cross and exalted to heaven.[2]

What John endeavours to convey through his application of the word 'glory' to the crucifixion is that when men look at the Cross they can see not only the relentless tragedy of human suffering but also a complete victory and triumph. Unless the worst consequences of suffering, epitomised in death, have been met and overcome, then the victory is incomplete:

Then Jesus replied: 'The hour has come for the Son of Man to be glorified. In truth, in very truth, I tell you, a grain of wheat remains a solitary grain unless it falls into the ground and dies; but if it dies, it bears a rich harvest. The man who loves himself is lost, but he who hates himself in this world will be kept safe for eternal life. If anyone serves me, he must follow me; where I am, my servant will be. Whoever serves me will be honoured by my Father. Now my soul is in turmoil, and what am I to say? Father, save me from this hour. No, it was for this that I came to this hour. Father, glorify thy name.' A voice sounded from heaven: 'I have glorified it, and I will glorify it again.' The crowd standing by said it was thunder, while others said, 'An angel has spoken to him.' Jesus replied, 'This voice spoke for your sake, not mine. Now is the hour of judgement for this world; now shall the Prince of this world be driven out. And I shall draw all men to myself,

In the Transfiguration the *doxa*, or glory, of Jesus is described as visibly apparent:
1 'His clothes became dazzling white, with a whiteness no bleacher on earth could equal' (Mark 9: 3).
2 C. K. Barrett, *The Gospel According to St John* (London, 1956), pp. 138 f.

Foundations

when I am lifted up from the earth.' This he said to indicate the kind of death he was to die.[1]

Because John is assured of the victory of God in Christ over suffering *as such* there is not so much portrayal in John of Jesus dealing with individual instances of suffering. Healing incidents are recorded, but with nothing like the same repetition as in the synoptics.[2] The point is that so far as John is concerned *all* suffering is potentially destroyed in his company.[3]

This belief, that in the company of Jesus all suffering is potentially destroyed because of the all-embracing nature of his victory over death, means that in John the problem of the distribution of suffering is differently handled. The problem is raised as specifically as in Luke,[4] but it is transferred to a quite different realm of discussion:

As he went on his way Jesus saw a man blind from his birth. His disciples put the question, 'Rabbi, who sinned, this man or his parents? Why was he born blind?' 'It is not that this man or his parents sinned,' Jesus answered; 'he was born blind that God's power might be displayed in curing him. While daylight lasts we must carry on the work of him who sent me; night comes, when no one can work. While I am in the world I am the light of the world.' With these words he spat on the ground and made a paste with the spittle; he spread it on the man's eyes, and said to him, 'Go and wash in the pool of Siloam.' (The name means 'sent'.) The man went away and washed, and when he returned he could see.[5]

The contrast with Luke's 'Siloam-incident'[6] is considerable, although both agree in repudiating the theory of direct 'cause-and-effect'. John does not represent the man's blindness as being in any sense unreal, or other than tragic; but he affirms that, as a consequence of Jesus' presence, disasters even as great as this can become the place where God is to be found. Hence a Christian responds to suffering with the knowledge that there was no

---

[1] John 12: 23–33; the verb 'lifted up' is another of John's brilliantly double-edged words, because it refers not only to the lifting up of Jesus on the Cross, but also to his lifting up in the resurrection; in other words, it again emphasises that what looks like defeat is in fact a victory, and that what looks like tragedy is in fact the threshold of triumph. See especially, John 3: 13–15, and cf. 8: 28, 12: 34.
[2] See, e.g., John 4: 46–53.   [3] See, e.g., John 8: 31–6, 4: 13 f., 6: 30–6.
[4] See p. 54.   [5] John 9: 1–7.   [6] See p. 54.

63

pretence in Christ's life of the facts of suffering being unreal, but that in his life the whole matter has been taken 'beyond tragedy'. *Beyond Tragedy* is the title of a collection of 'sermonic essays'[1] by Reinhold Niebuhr, who explained the title as follows:

It is the thesis of these essays that the Christian view of history passes through the sense of the tragic to a hope and an assurance which is 'beyond tragedy'. The cross, which stands at the centre of the Christian world-view, reveals both the seriousness of human sin and the purpose and power of God to overcome it. It reveals man violating the will of God in his highest moral and spiritual achievements (in Roman law and Jewish religion) and God absorbing this evil into himself in the very moment of its most vivid expression. Christianity's view of history is tragic insofar as it recognises evil as an inevitable concomitant of even the highest spiritual enterprises. It is beyond tragedy inasfar as it does not regard evil as inherent in existence itself but as finally under the dominion of a good God.[2]

So far as the Gospels are concerned, the sense that men are taken in the company of Jesus beyond tragedy is concentrated in the view that his death was not an end but a beginning. In the synoptic Gospels it appears most clearly in the accounts of the Last Supper which point to a continuing relationship between Jesus and his friends. But it is made even more specific in John in the Last Discourses. These chapters (14–16, together with the prayer in 17) are set in the context of the Last Supper, and constantly reiterate the extent to which the death of Jesus is not a loss but a gain. This belief can be seen concentrated in a single word, the Greek *sumferei* 'it is expedient'. It exemplifies once more the extraordinary skill with which John 'placed' individual words in his Gospel: *sumferei* occurs in two completely different contexts, both of which refer to the death of Jesus. It occurs in the Last Discourses as an analysis of the importance of Jesus' death:

Now I am going away to him who sent me. None of you asks me 'Where are you going?' Yet you are plunged into grief because of what I have told you. Nevertheless, I tell you the truth: it is expedient[3] for you that I am leaving you. If I do not go, your Advocate will not come, whereas if I go, I will send him to you... When he comes who is

---

[1] Niebuhr, *Beyond Tragedy* (London, 1947), p. ix.
[2] *Op. cit.* pp. x f.   [3] *N.E.B.* 'it is for your good'.

the Spirit of truth, he will guide you into all the truth...He will glorify me, for everything that he makes known to you he will draw from what is mine.[1]

But the word *sumferei* occurs in another analysis of Jesus' death, that of Caiaphas, who also regards his death as expedient and beneficial, but in a very double-edged sense:

The chief priests and the Pharisees[2] convened a meeting of the Council. 'What action are we taking?' they said. 'This man is performing many signs. If we leave him alone like this the whole populace will believe in him. Then the Romans will come and sweep away our temple and our nation.' But one of them, Caiaphas, who was High Priest that year, said, 'You know nothing whatever; you do not use your judgement; it is more expedient[3] for you that one man should die for the people, than that the whole nation should be destroyed.'[4]

The contrast is deliberate and specific: so far as Caiaphas is concerned, the death of Jesus is beneficial in a limited sense, in that it achieves a political breathing-space. So far as John is concerned, the death of Jesus is beneficial in a far wider sense, in that it is beneficial, not simply in a particular local situation, but for all men, for all time, and for all the world. Therefore immediately in ch. 11 the analysis of Caiaphas is continued with a comment:

He did not say this of his own accord, but as the High Priest in office that year, he was prophesying that Jesus would die for the nation—die not for the nation alone but to gather together the scattered children of God.[5]

The Last Discourses draw out the implications of that comment. The relationship of Son and Father, which he has lived out and demonstrated, is now extended to embrace all those who come, by faith and trust, into his company; the assertion of such a relationship would be empty and meaningless without his having died,

[1] John 16: 5–7, 13 f.
[2] It should be remembered that in John the word 'Pharisees' is a shorthand way of talking about 'those individuals among the Jews who consistently opposed Jesus'; it has lost all reference to a whole class of people; for details of this, see 'The Origin and Purpose of St John's Gospel', pp. 399 f.
[3] N.E.B. 'it is more to your interest'.
[4] John 11: 47–50; see also the same reference in John 18: 14.
[5] John 11: 51 f.

Christianity

since otherwise death would not have been shown up as impotent to destroy it:

I will not leave you bereft; I am coming back to you. In a little while the world will see me no longer, but you will see me; because I live, you too will live; then you will know that I am in my Father, and you in me and I in you... Though you will be plunged in grief, your grief will be turned to joy. A woman in labour is in pain because her time has come; but when the child is born she forgets the anguish in her joy that a man has been born into the world. So it is with you: for the moment you are sad at heart; but I shall see you again, and then you will be joyful, and no one shall rob you of your joy.[1]

In connection with suffering, the Last Discourses assert from first to last—literally from first to last—that the victory has already been won, even though the details have not yet been worked through:

Set your troubled hearts at rest. Trust in God always; trust also in me. There are many dwelling-places in my Father's house; if it were not so I should have told you; for I am going there on purpose to prepare a place for you. And if I go and prepare a place for you, I shall come again and receive you to myself, so that where I am you may be also; and my way there is known to you... Look, the hour is coming, has indeed already come. when you are all to be scattered, each to his home, leaving me alone. Yet I am not alone, because the Father is with me. I have told you all this so that in me you may find peace. In the world you will have trouble. But courage! The victory is mine; I have conquered the world.[2]

Thus the foundations of the Christian response to suffering are laid in an experience of the risen life of Christ: for what is manifestly obvious is the fact that the Gospels in general and the Last Discourses in particular were written *after* the death of Jesus, and that someone thought it worthwhile to write them. In other words, the Gospels exist because certain people believed—and in their own experience knew—that the promises of Christ were not empty, and that for them his victory was real. The New Testament represents the first endeavours of particular individuals to share that triumphant experience with others, and to work out its implications in life:

When our mortality has been clothed with immortality, then the saying of Scripture will come true: 'Death is swallowed up; victory is

[1] John 14: 18–20, 16: 20–2. [2] John 14: 1–3, 16: 31–3.

66

won!''O Death, where is your victory? O Death, where is your sting?'
The sting of death is sin, and sin gains its power from the law; but,
God be praised, he gives us the victory through our Lord Jesus
Christ. Therefore, my beloved brothers, stand firm and immovable,
and work for the Lord always, work without limit, since you know
that in the Lord your labour cannot be lost.[1]

The New Testament

To separate the other writings in the New Testament from the
Gospels is in an important sense misleading, since both groups of
writings represent an attempt to convey and to understand the
experience of the risen life of Christ. The Gospels are based on the
narrative of Jesus' life (or on what seemed to be the significant
parts of it, since they make no attempt to be complete 'bio-
graphies'), whereas the rest of the New Testament (much of
which was written earlier than the Gospels) makes very little
reference to details of that life. To that extent the two groups
might be regarded as parallel ways of achieving the same purpose,
to draw out and explain the reasons why the life of Christ and
relationship with him are of continuing and abiding importance.
Thus in the New Testament, in connection with suffering, two
related activities appear: the first is explanatory, the second
practical. Both theory and practice depend on exactly the same
foundation, the clear and triumphant sense of being participants
in a victory that nothing can remove or destroy. It has happened.
As the crucifixion was an event, so also was the resurrection,
hence (as was pointed out in the last section)[2] there was a constant
stress on the actuality of the resurrection as an event. But the
stronger the sense of the resurrection as a— or even *the*—decisive
event, the more natural it was to try and explain how, so to speak,
it worked. In what sense was it decisive? What is the nature and
origin of evil that the death and resurrection of Christ dispel it?
How does the victory of Christ become effective in the lives of
others, and in what ways does it affect the response of men in their
continuing experience of suffering and death?

That last question leads directly into the second area, the
practical, and it shows how closely the two are related. How in
practice do people live on the basis of the risen life of Christ, and
in what ways does it affect their response to suffering? Both

[1] 1 Cor. 15: 53–8.   [2] See p. 46.

Christianity

activities, of explanatory and practical response, have been prominent in Christian history, but it is important to realise that they do not, in themselves, constitute 'the Christian understanding of suffering'. They are both derivative, in the sense that they are both derived from a more fundamental point, a knowledge and an experience of the risen life of Christ. This knowledge and experience may be either collective or individual or both—that is to say, it may first be learned by taking on trust the experience of the first Christians and the subsequent experience of others in the continuing history of the Church; or it may first be established in the experience of the individual as he lives with it as a possible reality for himself; or it may be a combination of both. One important effect of this has been (as will be seen) that Christianity has not depended for its survival on its explanations either of the origin of suffering or of the existence of evil in connection with a God who is believed to be both omnipotent and loving. Some have put it more despairingly by saying that Christians are in the irritating position of allowing nothing to falsify their beliefs.[1] In fact what appears to have happened in practice is that Christians have frequently allowed that their explanations have been shown to be inadequate, but they have not allowed that this affects the reality of what they are trying to explain, particularly insofar as it is based on the person of Christ. It has had one further important effect, that practice has often been more important than theory, and that Christians have frequently expressed their response to suffering in practical rather than theoretical terms, since that is what has seemed to be involved in the imitation of Christ.[2]

In the earliest days of Christianity some of the most striking work in the two areas of theory and practice was done by Paul. Paul, who had originally been a Pharisee, believed that he had been rescued by Christ dramatically (in the vision on the road to Damascus)[3] from bondage both to sin and to Law—Law being closely related to sin in Paul's view, since it designates and puts beyond doubt certain actions as sinful.[4]

[1] See further pp. 91 f.
[2] It is of interest that the book known most usually by that exact title, *The Imitation of Christ*, makes this point in its opening chapter: 'What shall it profit you to dispute learnedly about the Trinity, if you are lacking in humility, and are thereby displeasing to God? I would rather feel compunction than know its definition.'
[3] For the possible connections between the visions of Paul and contemporary Jewish 'mysticism', see my forthcoming 'The Visions of Paul and Merkabah Mysticism'.
[4] See, e.g., Rom. 7: 7 f.

The sense of rescue and freedom, not only for himself but for all men, dominated Paul's life; it produced a fervour of action and thought which carried him like a restless fire throughout the Mediterranean world in the service of Christ. It meant that he had an enormously strong sense of the purposefulness of God which had issued in the effective action of Christ.[1]

The purposefulness of God can be seen particularly in the way in which Christ was believed by Paul (and by others) to have consummated and fulfilled all that was foreshadowed and promised in Scripture. Individual passages were frequently applied to him, as a consequence of the general belief that, 'This gospel God announced beforehand in sacred scriptures through his prophets.'[2] There was nothing accidental about the life of Christ: it was a part of God's deliberate plan to maintain justice in the universe but to combine it with mercy.

The justice of God was for Paul extremely important, because without it the work of Christ was inexplicable. Paul believed, as he contemplated the world around him (and himself as a part of that world), that God was fully entitled to exact retribution.[3] But, by emphasising the justice of God, he was at once brought face to face with suffering as a problem, since the inequalities of the world seem to count against it. In Romans Paul took up that question in connection with the Jews, who had been chosen by God, but who had then largely rejected the promised Christ, Jesus. Did that mean that the purposes of God had been frustrated? 'Will their faithlessness cancel the faithfulness of God?'[4] Or again, to take particular instances in Scripture, can the justice of God be reconciled with such incidents as God's hardening of Pharaoh's heart (for which the people of Egypt were punished), or with the favour shown to Jacob and the hostility shown to Esau on the apparently arbitrary ground, 'Jacob I loved and Esau I hated'?[5]

What shall we say to that? Is God to be charged with injustice? By no means. For he says to Moses, 'Where I show mercy, I will show mercy, and where I pity, I will pity.'[6] Thus it does not depend on man's will or effort, but on God's mercy. For Scripture says to Pharaoh, 'I have

---

[1] See especially Eph. 1: 4–10. The Pauline authorship of Ephesians has been denied. It is not a view with which I agree, but it should be borne in mind that Ephesians may represent the continuation of Pauline thought in the early Church, rather than the thoughts of Paul himself towards the end of his life.

[2] Rom. 1: 2.   [3] See especially Rom. 1: 18, 2: 3, 5; cf. Rom. 3: 5, 25.
[4] Rom. 3: 3.   [5] Rom. 9: 13.   [6] Exod. 33: 19.

raised you up for this very purpose, to exhibit my power in my dealings with you, and to spread my fame over all the world.[1] Thus he not only shows mercy as he chooses, but also makes men stubborn as he chooses.[2]

Not surprisingly, Paul was well aware that such a view was hardly likely to commend itself:

You will say, 'Then why does God blame a man? For who can resist his will?'[3]

But Paul still found it hard to answer the question, and he reverted to the response of Jeremiah,[4] that God is best likened to a potter, who can make of the clay whatever vessels he wishes:

Who are you, sir, to answer God back? Can the pot speak to the potter and say, 'Why did you make me like this?' Surely the potter can do what he likes with the clay. Is he not free to make out of the same lump two vessels, one to be treasured, the other for common use?[5]

It can scarcely be said that that passage from Romans in isolation from its context is an attractive picture of God's activity. But the truth is, of course, that Paul was far more concerned with the tragic realities of the human situation as he knew it in the present than with explanations of how that situation had originated in the past.[6] And the reason for this is obvious: he was urgently convinced that God had met those realities effectively and decisively in the person of Christ. Therefore his knowledge of human frailty and suffering was balanced by his knowledge of a decisive event in history which can be applied to *any* circumstances to show that they are within God's control and purpose. Romans begins on precisely that note, and in that sense it is the 'context' of the whole letter:

This gospel God announced beforehand in sacred scriptures through his prophets. It is about his Son: on the human level he was born of David's stock, but on the level of the spirit—the Holy Spirit—he was declared Son of God by a mighty act in that he rose from the dead: it is about Jesus Christ our Lord.[7]

---

[1] Exod. 9: 16, cf. John 9: 1–5.   [2] Rom. 9: 14–18.
[3] Rom. 9: 19.   [4] See n. 3, p. 13.   [5] Rom. 9: 20 f.
[6] See p. 68 above.   [7] Rom. 1: 2 f.

Foundations

As Barth commented on Paul's portrayal of God in the passage in Rom. 9 on Jacob and Esau:

> According to human conceptions such a God can be described only as a 'Despot',[1] and men are bound to rebel against his tyranny. But he whom men would not naturally wish to name 'God' is, nevertheless, God. Through the knowledge of God which is in Christ, he whom men name 'Despot' (Lk. ii. 29, Acts iv. 24, etc.), is known and loved as the eternal, loving Father. The God of Esau is known to be the God of Jacob. There is no road to the knowledge of God which does not run along the precipitous edge of this contradiction.[2]

Thus the vital truth for Paul was that all men are in the same condition; the circumstances of their lives may be unequal, but essentially they are the same, aspiring to great things but unable to bring them to perfection, and therefore in need of God's assistance:

> For all alike have sinned, and are deprived of the divine splendour, and all are justified by God's free grace alone, through his act of liberation in the person of Christ Jesus. For God designed him to be the means of expiating sin by his sacrificial death, effective through faith.[3]

But equally vital for Paul was his conviction that the whole situation, in which all men are in the same case, has been transformed by Christ. He struggled to convey the urgency of this good news by employing an almost bewildering variety of illustrations and metaphors to explain how Christ has restored men to God—making peace after war (or perhaps better, after rebellion), breaking down the wall in the Temple which divided Jews from Gentiles, mediating a new covenant, ransoming prisoners, redeeming slaves and setting them free, replacing sacrifices, which had been one of the earliest ways of expressing the restored relationship between men and God (though the exact force of expiation and propitiation in Paul is extremely uncertain), securing a just verdict of acquittal in court. The range of metaphors is extremely wide and at the same time local,

---

[1] The English word 'despot' is from the Greek *despotes*, which is used as a title of God in the New Testament. 'This day, *Master*, thou givest thy servant his discharge in peace' (Luke 2: 29): '*Sovereign Lord*, maker of heaven and earth and sea and of everything in them...' (Acts 4: 24).

[2] K. Barth, *The Epistle to the Romans* (trs. E. C. Hoskyns, Oxford, 1933), p. 350.

[3] Rom. 3: 23–5; for a more 'psychological' description of the gap between aspiration and achievement see Rom. 7: 14–25.

Christianity

because Paul naturally made use of illustrations that would be known and understood in the world of his time. In a particularly eloquent symbol, Paul grasped a correlation between the first Adam and the last. The story of the first Adam[1] in Genesis summarises the human condition, with its frailty and suffering concentrated in the advent of death; but the second Adam summarises the restored potentiality of the human condition concentrated in the advent of Christ. By his conquest of suffering and death, suffering and death are exposed as limited truths.[2] It is not an isolated victory, because all men can be involved in it if they 'lay hold of' Christ by faith. Men are identified with the first Adam by the simple fact of being born: they are identified with the second Adam by being born again into his new and risen life.[3] This identification with Christ, by which men pass with him through death to life, is symbolised in baptism.[4] The condition of being identified was also expressed symbolically through the common meal.[5]

Identification with Christ and participation in his risen life were not left as a metaphor: they were intended to have entirely practical effects:

Were you not raised to life with Christ? Then aspire to the realm above, where Christ is, seated at the right hand of God, and let your thoughts dwell on that higher realm, not on this earthly life. I repeat, you died; and now your life lies hidden with Christ in God. When Christ, who is our life, is manifested, then you too will be manifested with him in glory. *Therefore*[6] put to death those parts of you which belong to the earth—fornication, indecency, lust, foul cravings, and the ruthless greed which is nothing less than idolatry... *Therefore* put on the garments that suit God's chosen people, his own, his beloved: compassion, kindness, humility, gentleness, patience. Be forbearing with one another, and forgiving, where any of you has cause for complaint: you must forgive as the Lord forgave you. To crown all, there must be love, to bind all together and complete the whole.[7]

[1] The word 'Adam' means Man.
[2] For the way in which the crucifixion 'exposes' both the condemnation of sin and at the same time the victory of God (cf. the double meanings of 'light' and 'glory' in connection with the crucifixion in John) see Rom. 3: 25 f., 8: 3, 37–9, Phil. 2: 8–11, Col. 2: 14 f.
[3] On the two Adams, see especially Rom. 5: 12–19.
[4] See especially Rom. 6: 1–11.
[5] See 1 Cor. 11: 23–34. [6] *N.E.B.* 'Then'.
[7] Col. 3: 1–5, 12–14; cf. Gal. 5: 13–25.

Foundations

That passage leads on directly to Paul's understanding of the place of suffering as it continues to be experienced, and of a Christian response to it. In personal terms, it means avoiding all behaviour that might cause suffering to others; it means taking effective action to relieve suffering; and in the experience of suffering, it means resting in the total and cosmic victory of Christ:

For I reckon that the sufferings we now endure bear no comparison with the splendour, as yet unrevealed, which is in store for us. For the created universe waits with eager expectation for God's sons to be revealed. It was made the victim of frustration, not by its own choice, but because of him who made it so; yet always there was hope, because the universe itself is to be freed from the shackles of mortality and enter upon the liberty and splendour of the children of God. Up to the present, we know, the whole created universe groans in all its parts as if in the pangs of childbirth. Not only so, but even we, to whom the Spirit is given as firstfruits of the harvest to come, are groaning inwardly while we wait for God to make us his sons and set our whole body free. For we have been saved, though only in hope. Now to see is no longer to hope: why should a man endure and wait for what he already sees? But if we hope for something we do not yet see, then, in waiting for it, we show our endurance...

With all this in mind, what are we to say? If God is on our side, who is against us? He did not spare his own Son, but surrendered him for us all; and with this gift how can he fail to lavish upon us all he has to give? Who will be the accuser of God's chosen ones? It is God who pronounces acquittal: then who can condemn? It is Christ—Christ who died, and, more than that, was raised from the dead—who is at God's right hand, and indeed pleads our cause. Then what can separate us from the love of Christ? Can affliction or hardship? Can persecution, hunger, nakedness, peril, or the sword? 'We are being done to death for thy sake all day long,' as Scripture says; 'we have been treated like sheep for slaughter'—and yet, in spite of all, overwhelming victory is ours through him who loved us. For I am convinced that there is nothing in death or life, in the realm of spirits or superhuman powers, in the world as it is or the world as it shall be, in the forces of the universe, in heights or depths—nothing in all creation that can separate us from the love of God in Christ Jesus our Lord.[1]

The sense that no suffering can separate the Christian from Christ (because his own suffering did not separate him from God)

---

[1] Rom. 8: 18–25, 31–9; cf. Col. 1: 13–20.

Christianity

is extremely strong in the New Testament.[1] Indeed, Paul valued suffering because it pointed to the effective power of Christ:

Three times I begged the Lord to rid me of it ('a sharp pain in my body'), but his answer was: 'My grace is all you need; power comes to its full strength in weakness.' I shall therefore prefer to find my joy and pride in the very things that are my weakness; and then the power of Christ will come and rest upon me. Hence I am well content, for Christ's sake, with weakness, contempt, persecution, hardship, and frustration; for when I am weak, then I am strong.[2]

In Paul's experience, as that passage implies, discipleship of Christ *involves* suffering, since although his victory is total and complete, it still has to be asserted and realised in individual cases. Thus Paul wrote to the 'congregation of Thessalonians who belong to God the Father and the Lord Jesus Christ':[3]

And you, in your turn, followed the example set by us and by the Lord; the welcome you gave the message meant grave suffering for you, yet you rejoiced in the Holy Spirit.[4]

By the time 2 Timothy was written the sense of Paul's sufferings being exemplary, as well as those of Christ, has become even stronger.[5]

Thus suffering is an important part of identification with Christ; it is a way of continually asserting and realising his victory:

It is now my happiness to suffer for you. This is my way of helping to complete, in my poor human flesh, the full tale of Christ's afflictions still to be endured, for the sake of his body which is the church.[6]

This sense of identification with the sufferings as well as the victory of Christ became for Paul the foundation of his practical response to suffering:

Praise be to the God and Father of our Lord Jesus Christ, the all-merciful Father, the God whose consolation never fails us! He comforts us in all our troubles, so that we in turn may be able to comfort others in any trouble of theirs and to share with them the consolation we ourselves receive from God. As Christ's cup of suffering overflows,

[1] See, e.g., 2 Cor. 4: 16-18, 5: 1-5.   [2] 2 Cor. 12: 8-10.
[3] 1 Thess. 1: 1.   [4] 1 Thess. 1: 6; cf. 3: 4. See also 2 Thess. 1: 4.
[5] See 2 Tim. 3: 10 f.; cf. 1: 7-10, 2: 3-13.
[6] Col. 1: 24. In 2 Cor. 11: 23-33 Paul listed some of his sufferings in dramatic terms.

and we suffer with him, so also through Christ our consolation over-flows. If distress be our lot, it is the price we pay for your consolation, for your salvation; if our lot be consolation, it is to help us to bring you comfort, and strength to face with fortitude the same sufferings we now endure. And our hope for you is firmly grounded; for we know that if you have part in the suffering, you have part also in the divine consolation.[1]

The Letters constantly urge practical action in relief of suffering. It is summarised 'in the one rule, "Love your neighbour as yourself"';[2] or indeed it can be said to be summarised in the single word 'love'—for which the early Christians developed their own distinctive word, *agapē*, in order to avoid it being confused with transient emotions or passions. The most famous description of the distinctive meaning of *agapē* is that of 1 Cor. 13, but it is also summarised as the imitation of Christ:

Be generous to one another, tender-hearted, forgiving one another as God in Christ forgave you. In a word, as God's dear children, try to be like him, and live in love (*agapē*) as Christ loved you, and gave himself up on your behalf as an offering and sacrifice whose fragrance is pleasing to God.[3]

And again, in the pattern of Christ, it is an active engagement against evil and suffering expressed in personified terms:

Finally, then, find your strength in the Lord, in his mighty power. Put on all the armour which God provides, so that you may be able to stand firm against the devices of the devil. For our fight is not against human foes, but against cosmic powers, against the authorities and potentates of this dark world, against the superhuman forces of evil in the heavens. Therefore, take up God's armour; then you will be able to stand your ground when things are at their worst, to complete every task and still to stand. Stand firm, I say. Buckle on the belt of truth; for coat of mail put on integrity; let the shoes on your feet be the gospel of peace, to give you firm footing; and, with all these, take up the great shield of faith, with which you will be able to quench all the flaming arrows of the evil one. Take salvation for helmet; for sword, take that which the Spirit gives you—the words that come from God.[4]

In the end the question 'why'—why had God allowed such a state of affairs to develop that it required the coming of Christ to

[1] 2 Cor. 1: 3–7. [2] Rom. 13: 9.
[3] Eph. 4: 32–5: 2. See also the appeal in Phil. 2: 4 ff. [4] Eph. 6: 10–17.

put it right—remained unanswered, perhaps because Paul
realised that it was unanswerable:

O depth of wealth, wisdom, and knowledge in God! How unsearchable
his judgements, how untraceable his ways! Who knows the mind of the
Lord? Who has been his counsellor? Who has ever made a gift to him,
to receive a gift in return? Source, Guide, and Goal of all that is—to
him be glory for ever! Amen.[1]

What was absolutely certain, so far as Paul was concerned, was
that however the present situation of tragic suffering and evil
arose, there have now been established unshakeable grounds for
hope—not in the realm of wishful thinking but in the hard
realities of the life and death and resurrection of Christ. It meant
that although the work of explanation was important, it was quite
outweighed by the importance of living with Christ in the practical
situations of life.[2]

The rest of the New Testament exemplifies how those two
activities, of explanation and practical response, belong together,
and how they are both derivative from a prior belief in the
resurrection. Their close relationship is certainly clear in the Book
of Acts. Acts is a collection of heterogeneous material, both early
and late, which was organised to tell the story of the founding and
expansion of the Church under the guidance of the Holy Spirit.
On the explanatory side, it records many sermons and speeches,
and it is significant how frequently they attempt to answer why it
was necessary that the Messiah should suffer—as opposed to the
view that he would come in triumph. In particular, attempts were
made to show that Scripture had in fact foreseen it:

For the next three Sabbaths he argued with them, quoting texts of
scripture which he expounded and applied to show that the Messiah had
to suffer and rise from the dead.[3]

One long speech, that of Stephen,[4] deals specifically with the
theme of rejection, pointing out from Biblical examples that God
has frequently used the most rejected servants to achieve his
greatest ends. On the practical side, Acts makes it abundantly
clear that discipleship involves suffering, particularly in persecution,

[1] Rom. 11: 33–6. [2] See especially Eph. 3: 14 ff.
[3] Acts 17: 2 f. For a particular example of the application of Scripture to the
suffering of Christ, see the story of Philip and the Ethiopian eunuch (Acts 8:
26–40). See also 2: 22–36, 13: 29. [4] Acts 7: 1–53.

and that it also involves practical activity in the relief of suffering. It is of interest that one of the few sayings of Jesus directly quoted in Acts, which is in fact not recorded in the Gospels, emphasises exactly that point:

I showed you that it is our duty to help the weak in this way, by hard work, and that we should keep in mind the words of the Lord Jesus, who himself said, 'Happiness lies more in giving than in receiving.'[1]

In view of the many notes in Acts of the persecution or suffering of individuals or of Christian communities, it is not surprising that the other writings of the New Testament frequently refer to suffering and to the Christian response to it, though to what extent those sufferings are connected with actual persecution is not always easy to determine. The First Letter of Peter, for example, has sometimes been connected with Nero's persecution of Christians, particularly 4: 12 ff. (though in view of 3: 19–22 it may perhaps, rather, be connected with the rabbinic exegesis of Gen. 6).

My dear friends, do not be bewildered by the fiery ordeal that is upon you, as though it were something extraordinary. It gives you a share in Christ's sufferings, and that is cause for joy; and when his glory is revealed, your joy will be triumphant. If Christ's name is flung in your teeth as an insult, count yourselves happy, because then that glorious Spirit which is the Spirit of God is resting upon you.[2]

Certainly there is an awareness in 1 Peter that suffering is to be endured, and again it is expressed in personified terms:

Awake! be on the alert! Your enemy the devil, like a roaring lion, prowls round looking for someone to devour. Stand up to him, firm in faith, and remember that your brother Christians are going through the same kinds of suffering while they are in the world. And the God of all grace, who called you into his eternal glory in Christ, will himself, after your brief suffering, restore, establish, and strengthen you on a firm foundation. He holds dominion for ever and ever. Amen.[3]

Not surprisingly, appeal is made to the example of Christ as the ground of endurance:

It is a fine thing if a man endure the pain of undeserved suffering because God is in his thoughts. What credit is there in fortitude when

---

[1] Acts 20: 35. It issued particularly in the famous 'Collection for the saints', which figures so prominently in Acts and the letters of Paul. See K. F. Nickle, *The Collection* (London, 1966).   [2] 1 Pet. 4: 12–14.   [3] 1 Pet. 5: 8–11.

you have done wrong and are beaten for it? But when you have behaved well and suffer for it, your fortitude is a fine thing in the sight of God. To that you were called, because Christ suffered on your behalf, and thereby left you an example; it is for you to follow in his steps. He committed no sin, he was convicted of no falsehood; when he was abused he did not retort with abuse, when he suffered he uttered no threats, but committed his cause to the One who judges justly. In his own person he carried our sins to the gallows, so that we might cease to live for sin and begin to live for righteousness. By his wounds you have been healed. You were straying like sheep, but now you have turned towards the Shepherd and Guardian of your souls.[1]

The same idea, of Christ as the 'figure-head' of suffering, occurs in the Letter to the Hebrews:

It was clearly fitting that God for whom and through whom all things exist should, in bringing many sons to glory, make the leader who delivers them perfect through sufferings.[2]

That sentence implies an instrumental view of suffering as a discipline, and that is exactly the view spelt out in detail at the end of the letter. Having listed examples of faithful endurance, mostly drawn from Scripture, the writer of Hebrews then appealed to his readers to follow that example:

Think of him who submitted to such opposition from sinners: that will help you not to lose heart and grow faint. In your struggle against sin, you have not yet resisted to the point of shedding your blood. You have forgotten the text of Scripture which addresses you as sons and appeals to you in these words:

> 'My Son, do not think lightly of the Lord's discipline,
> Nor lose heart when he corrects you;
> For the Lord disciplines those whom he loves;
> He lays the rod on every son whom he acknowledges.'[3]

You must endure it as discipline: God is treating you as sons. Can anyone be a son, who is not disciplined by his father? If you escape the discipline in which all sons share you must be bastards and no true sons. Again, we paid due respect to the earthly fathers who disciplined us; should we not submit even more readily to our spiritual Father, and so attain life? They disciplined us for this short life according to their lights; but he does so for our true welfare, so that we may share his holiness. Discipline, no doubt, is never pleasant; at the time it

---

[1] 1 Pet. 2: 19–25.   [2] Heb. 2: 10.   [3] Prov. 3: 11 f.

seems painful, but in the end it yields for those who have been trained by it the peaceful harvest of an honest life. Come, then, stiffen your drooping arms and shaking knees, and keep your steps from wavering. Then the disabled limb will not be put out of joint, but regain its former powers.[1]

Such a view is not surprising in view of the close connections that Hebrews has with a Jewish background.[2] It appears even more strikingly in the Letter of James, which is *so* Jewish, that scarcely anything distinctively Christian can be found in it; it has in fact been thought to be a Jewish work adopted into Christianity. As an example of how to endure suffering it appeals not to Jesus but to the prophets![3] It is, therefore, not surprising to find in James the instrumental view of suffering as discipline:

My brothers, whenever you have to face trials of many kinds, count yourselves supremely happy, in the knowledge that such testing of your faith breeds fortitude, and if you give fortitude full play you will go on to complete a balanced character that will fall short in nothing... Happy the man who remains steadfast under trial, for having passed that test he will receive for his prize the gift of life promised to those who love God.[4]

James envisages 'trials of many kinds', not necessarily persecution; but throughout Christian history the issue has frequently become concentrated at the point where death is preferred to life, if the continuation of life on this earth is only possible at the cost of denying the foundation of one's being. In the New Testament, the book which seems most clearly to envisage martyrdom is the Revelation of John:

...I saw underneath the altar the souls of those who had been slaughtered for God's word, and for the testimony they bore. They gave a great cry: 'How long, sovereign Lord,[5] holy and true, must it be before thou wilt vindicate us and avenge our blood on the inhabitants of the earth?' Each of them was given a white robe; and they were told to rest a little while longer, until the tally should be complete of all their brothers in Christ's service who were to be killed as they had been.[6]

[1] Heb. 12: 3–13.
[2] Perhaps Sadducaic and just conceivably Egyptian Zadokite.
[3] Jas. 5: 10 f.   [4] Jas. 1: 2–4, 12.
[5] *Despotes*; see p. 71.   [6] Rev. 6: 9–11.

Christianity

But Revelation is equally clear in its assurance of the totality and certainty of Christ's victory, and it uses the apocalyptic method in order to convey that assurance imaginatively:

Then one of the elders turned to me and said, 'These men that are robed in white—who are they and from where do they come?' But I answered, 'My lord, you know, not I.' Then he said to me, 'These are the men who have passed through the great ordeal; they have washed their robes and made them white in the blood of the Lamb. That is why they stand before the throne of God and minister to him day and night in his temple; and he who sits on the throne will dwell with them. They shall never again feel hunger or thirst, the sun shall not beat on them nor any scorching heat, because the Lamb who is at the heart of the throne will be their shepherd and will guide them to the springs of the water of life; and God will wipe all tears from their eyes.'[1]

No wonder Revelation is able to speak of suffering and sovereignty in the same breath and in the closest possible juxtaposition:

I, John, your brother, who share with you in the suffering and the sovereignty and the endurance which is ours in Jesus...[2]

And that undoubtedly is the key-note of the response to suffering in the New Testament, that it is not something to be explained away either in theory or in practice. It is to be met realistically in the power of Christ and in the certainty of his victory already won. Not in theory, but in a life actually lived, a new factor has been introduced into the human situation: it does not solve all problems, but it becomes a factor in the way leading to their solution:

It was there from the beginning; we have heard it; we have seen it with our own eyes; we looked upon it, and felt it with our own hands; and it is of this we tell. Our theme is the word of life. This life was made visible; we have seen it and bear our testimony; we here declare to you the eternal life which dwelt with the Father and was made visible to us. What we have seen and heard we declare to you, so that you and we together may share in a common life, that life which we share with the Father and his Son Jesus Christ. And we write this in order that the joy of us all may be complete.[3]

[1] Rev. 7: 13–17; note also the preceding verses, 9–12.
[2] Rev. 1: 9. [3] 1 John 1: 1–4.

80

Development

The Christian understanding of suffering has developed in the two related areas, of explanation and practice, which are already apparent in the New Testament. In the New Testament both activities were held in a necessary relationship because they were both derived from a prior 'knowledge' of the cross and resurrection of Christ. Subsequent developments, both in theory and in practice, have remained derivative in the sense that Christians have regarded as fundamental the events of the life and death and resurrection of Jesus conceived *as* events (though some recent developments have raised questions about the nature and meaning of the resurrection as 'event'). What that has meant in effect is that for Christians those events have become a factor which must be taken into account in any attempt to understand suffering or respond to it. It has meant further that even if particular attempts at explanation have been shown to be inadequate, the 'factor' remains as a constituent part of human experience—it remains a factor to be taken into account.

On the explanatory side, it is obvious that Christians have been particularly exercised by the problem of theodicy[1]—by the difficulty of defending the justice and righteousness of God in face of the existence of evil and suffering. In its classical form, if God is all-loving he would surely not be able to tolerate the appalling suffering that is evident in the created order; and if he is almighty, he would be able to do something about it. God turns out to be impotent or deficient in love, or more simply, so far as men are concerned, non-existent. The problem was raised by Paul for himself, and it has remained central ever since.

The earliest creative lines of explanatory development arose out of a fusion of two lines of thought in the New Testament: the story in Genesis of Adam's 'fall', from a state in which all had been seen to be 'very good'[2] into a state of separation from God; together with the personified and personal activities of the devil and his agents. The two were put together in the simplest possible form, by introducing the devil into the Garden as the agent in the temptation of Eve—that is to say, by identifying him with the serpent, or by at least making the identification more specific. The story of the fallen 'sons of God'[3] was also incorporated

---

[1] The Greek *theos* means 'god', *dike* 'justice'.   [2] Gen. 1: 31.   [3] Gen. 6: 1–4.

to produce a picture of fallen and rebellious angels under the leadership of Satan, who are instrumental in the corruption of men.[1] The picture was more imaginatively than intellectually satisfying. It was not really an explanation, since it merely put back one stage the question of why a creature admittedly created 'free', but also created 'good', should ever have chosen to rebel. But imaginatively it was more effective, since it enabled a graphic account to be given of the manifestly evil state of the created order, while at the same time it provided a framework within which individuals could feel there was something worthwhile to be done. In particular it provided a graphic way of describing the work and victory of Christ.

The redemptive work of Christ in dealing with the situation of evil and suffering was, in broadest terms, seen to correspond to the two lines of thought outlined above—in other words, the relief of the situation was believed to correspond to the ways in which it had come into being. Thus the fact of a state of separation from God (i.e. of sin) required the fact of something to restore relationship; in a sacrificial background the most natural illustration was that of the sacrificial victim, hence Christ the Victim. But at the same time, the strong sense of personal activity on the part of the devil required personal activity against him, hence Christ the Victor. Those two ways of understanding the work of Christ, as Victim and as Victor, are related to two different ways of understanding the nature of human deficiency, of which suffering is a part: it is to be seen as a consequence either of an original capacity for goodness which has not yet been realised; or as an original sin which has had its effect on all subsequent individuals, almost like a disease passed from one to another.

The idea of original sin in its fullest form argues that the fall of Adam had its effect on all subsequent individuals because they were 'seminally present' in his loins.[2] They could not escape the effect of that original act of rebellion and alienation because it radically affected human nature. The development of an idea of original sin was in fact very gradual, and in its earliest forms it was regarded more as an inherited tendency or bias than as an inherited disease, as can be seen in J. N. D. Kelly's summary of

[1] The fusion of these lines of thought had, of course, already begun to take place in Judaism; see p. 52.
[2] See e.g., Augustine, *de Civ. Dei*, xiii. 14.

Development

two representative figures of the African Church in the third century, Tertullian and Cyprian:

> The salient feature of Tertullian's anthropology was the conception, borrowed from Stoicism, of the soul as material. Though simple and more subtle, he regards it as a body intimately united with and occupying the same space as the physical body to which it belongs... Every soul, as Tertullian expresses it, is, as it were, a twig cut from the parent-stem of Adam and planted out as an independent tree.[1]

It is a short step from this psychology to the doctrine of original sin. Tertullian is a firm believer in free-will; he defends its existence against Marcion and Hermogenes,[2] never ceasing to repeat that a man is responsible for his acts. Yet free-will is not the only source of our misdeeds; account must be taken of the bias towards sin in which Adam's transgression has involved mankind. 'We have borne the image of the earthy', he remarks, 'through our participation in transgression, our fellowship in death, our expulsion from Paradise.'[3] As the effect of this primeval sin human nature bears a stain, so that 'every soul is counted as being in Adam until it is re-counted as being in Christ, and remains unclean until it is so re-counted'.[4] The demons, he admits, exert a baneful influence, but apart from that 'the evil that exists in the soul... is antecedent, being derived from the fault of our origin (*ex originis vitio*) and having become in a way natural to us. For, as I have stated, the corruption of nature is second nature (*alia natura*)'.[5] Our whole substance has been transformed from its primitive integrity into rebellion against its Creator, the causal connexion being provided by the quasi-physical identity of all souls with Adam. Deceived by Satan, the first man 'infected the whole race by his seed, making it the channel (*traducem*) of damnation'.[6] For this reason even the children of the faithful must be reckoned impure until they have been reborn by water and the Holy Spirit.[7]

Thus Tertullian takes the view that, while Adam received from God true human nature in its integrity, the nature he passed on to his descendants is vitiated by an inclination to sin; an 'irrational element' has settled in the soul (*irrationale autem... coadoleverit in anima ad instar iam naturalitatis*).[8] He is more explicit and outspoken about this sinful bias than previous theologians, in whose eyes corruption and death seem to have been the principal legacy of the Fall; but, although there has been much difference of opinion on the question, his language about 'our participation in (Adam's) transgression', and about the 'impurity' (cf. *immundi*) of unbaptized infants, can hardly be read as

[1] *de Anima*, 19.   [2] *Contra Marcionem*, ii. 5–7.
[3] *de Resurrectione Carnis*, 49; cf. *Contra Marcionem*, i. 22, *de Carne Christi*, 16.
[4] *de An.* 40.   [5] *Ibid.* 39, 41.   [6] *de Test. An.* 39.   [7] *de An.* 39.   [8] *Ibid.* 16.

83

implying our solidarity with the first man in his culpability (i.e. original guilt) as well as in the consequences of his act.[1] Hints of a doctrine akin to his are to be found in Cyprian, who describes the effects of original sin, in language which was to become classical, as 'wounds' (*vulnera*). The Saviour came, he states, in order to heal the wounds received by Adam and to cure the serpent's poison.[2] Again, he speaks of baptism as 'cleansing us from the stain of the primeval contagion'.[3] Arguing for infant baptism, he states that even a new-born child who has never committed actual sin has been 'born carnally after the pattern of Adam, and by his first nativity has contracted the contagion of the ancient death',[4] although the sins involved here are 'not his own, but someone else's'. That he linked the transmissions of sinfulness with the process of generation is confirmed by his appeal to Ps. 51, 5: 'Behold, I was conceived in iniquities, and in sins did my mother bear me'.[5]

On the foundations briefly outlined in the preceding paragraphs much of the explanatory work of Christianity in relation to suffering was built. Some of the main lines of development in Christianity have been summarised recently by John Hick.[6] He traced two related, but in important respects different, paths of thought, which correspond to the two ways in which human deficiency was understood—either as a capacity for goodness which has not been realised or as an original defect which has vitiated all subsequent life. The former is the 'minority' report which Hick has called 'Irenaean', since the first person of importance to put it forward in reasonably articulate form was Irenaeus (*c.* 130–*c.* 202).[7] The latter is the 'majority' report, which

[1] *de Resurr. Carn.* 49, *de An.* 39.　　[2] *de Op. et Eleem.* 1.
[3] *de Hab. Virg.* 23.　　[4] *Ep.* lxiv. 5.
[5] J. N. D. Kelly, *Early Christian Doctrine* (London, 1958), pp. 175–7.
[6] *Evil and the God of Love* (London, 1966).
[7] The view was certainly expressed elsewhere (see, e.g., Tatian, *Or.* 7, Theophilus, *ad Autol.* ii. 24 f., 27), but not by people with such a 'name' as Irenaeus. In point of fact, the 'Irenaean' view is nothing like such a small minority as it might appear from Dr Hick's book. It is a distinctive and frequently-expressed part of Christian spirituality—indeed, it is hard to see how the distinctive patterns of Christian spiritual life could possibly exist without it. The 'Irenaean' view, therefore, appears as an essential element in many Christian spiritual writers, though not necessarily in isolation from the 'Augustinian'. Scarcely any account is given in Dr Hick's book of the great spiritual writers, perhaps because he would like to draw a distinction between 'doing religion' and 'doing philosophy', though in fact the two have frequently been interwoven until recent times. One suspects that the real distinction is not between 'Augustinian' and 'Irenaean' but that those two postions reflect the distinction between (to use Pauline terminology) justification and sanctification.

Hick has called 'Augustinian', since Augustine's formulation of it became deeply and profoundly influential in subsequent Christian thought. Hick summarised the main differences between them as follows:

There is to be found in Irenaeus the outline of an approach to the problem of evil which stands in important respects in contrast to the Augustinian type of theodicy. Instead of the doctrine that man was created finitely perfect and then incomprehensibly destroyed his own perfection and plunged into sin and misery, Irenaeus suggests that man was created as an imperfect, immature creature who was to undergo moral development and growth and finally be brought to the perfection intended for him by his Maker. Instead of the fall of Adam being presented, as in the Augustinian tradition, as an utterly malignant and catastrophic event, completely disrupting God's plan, Irenaeus pictures it as something that occurred in the childhood of the race, an understandable lapse due to weakness and immaturity rather than an adult crime full of malice and pregnant with perpetual guilt. And instead of the Augustinian view of life's trials as a·divine punishment for Adam's sin, Irenaeus sees our world of mingled good and evil as a divinely appointed environment for man's development towards the perfection that represents the fulfilment of God's good purpose for him.[1]

Since these two views have been so influential in the Christian understanding of suffering, it may be as well to allow them to speak briefly for themselves. Irenaeus' views appear in concentrated form in *Adv. Haer.* xxxviii–xxxix:[2]

But if a man say 'How is this? Could not God render man perfect from the beginning?' let him know, that although unto God, who is always just the same, and Unoriginated, in respect of himself all things are possible; yet the things which were made by him, so far as that, coming afterwards, they have each its own beginning of generation, so far they must also fall short of him who made them; for the things just brought into being could not be unoriginated; and so far as they are not unoriginated, so far also they fall short of perfection. And in respect that they are younger, they are also childish, and in the same respect also unpractised, and unexercised for the perfect training. As then the mother is able indeed to bestow perfect nourishment on her babe, but the babe is as yet incapable of receiving the nourishment which is too old for itself: so God also was indeed able himself to bestow on man perfection from the beginning, but man was incapable of receiving it: for he was a babe.

---

[1] Hick, *op. cit.* pp. 220 f.   [2] Trs. *Lib. of Fathers*, pp. 436–40.

For which cause also our Lord in the last times came to us, having summed up all things in himself; not as he could, but as we were able to receive him. For he indeed could have come to us in his own incorruptible glory, but we as yet had no power to endure the greatness of his glory...And for this cause the Son of God became a babe with man, perfect as he was: not on his own account, but because of man's childishness, being so comprehended, as man was able to comprehend him. Not with God was the weakness and defect, but with the newly formed man, because he was not uncreated...

By this order then, and by measures such as these, and by this kind of training, man being originated and formed comes to be in the image and likeness of the Unoriginate God: The Father approving and commanding, the Son performing and creating, the Spirit giving nourishment and growth, and man for his part silently advancing, and going onward to perfection; i.e. coming near the Unoriginate. For the Unoriginate is perfect; and this is God...For how could men have had a training for good, without knowing what is contrary thereto? For our notion of things actually brought within reach is stronger and more undoubted, than the guess which comes of mere suspicion. For as the tongue by taste receives trial of sweet and bitter, and the eye by sight discerns what is black from the white, and the ear by hearing knows the differences of sounds; so also the mind, by experiment of both, receiving a lesson in good, is made stronger to keep the same by obeying God:—first by penitency rejecting disobedience, as a thing bitter and evil; then learning by reflection what sort of thing it must be which is contrary to goodness and sweetness:—so as never even to make trial of the taste of disobedience to God. But if a man shrink from the knowledge of both kinds, and from the two sorts of impressions arising from that knowledge, without knowing it he destroys his own human being.

In the case of Augustine, the most convenient summary is in his own attempt to write a short handbook of Christian faith, entitled appropriately the *Enchiridion*.[1] Here the main themes of Augustine's understanding of evil and suffering appear: evil is not a separate, self-subsistent principle, eternally opposed to God: it is the absence or privation of good, which God has permitted. It is a consequence of the misuse of freewill, which appears in the rebellion of the angels and in the 'original sin' of Adam. God was aware of the possibility of the misuse of freewill and of the consequent possibility of evil, but he permitted it, because it was

---

[1] The Greek word *encheiridion* means 'something in the hand'. The themes, summarised so briefly in the *Enchiridion*, are given a far more practical and detailed exposition in *de Civitate Dei* (*The City of God*).

still in his control, and because it was better to bring good out of evil than to preclude evil from existing.[1] The control of God is demonstrated in the work of Christ which effectively met and redeemed the situation:

> For a Christian it is sufficient to believe that the cause of created things
> ...is none other than the goodness of that Creator who is the one true God, and that there is no existent entity which is not either he or from him; and that he is a trinity, the Father, the Son begotten of the Father, and the Holy Spirit proceeding from that same Father (and Son), yet one and the same Spirit of the Father and the Son.[2]

> By this Trinity, which is supremely and equally and immutably good, all things were created, and while they are neither supremely nor equally nor immutably good, yet they are good each in itself...

> In this universe, even what has the name of evil, when well ordered and placed in its own position, does the more notably commend the good things, causing them to be more pleasing and more laudable by comparison with things evil. For God Almighty...being supremely good, would on no account permit the existence of any admixture of evil in his works unless he were to such a degree almighty and good as to bring good even out of evil. Moreover, that which has the name of evil is nothing else than privation of good. For as, in the bodies of animate beings, to be affected by diseases and wounds is the same thing as to be deprived of health (...for wound or disease is not a substance in itself, but a defect of fleshly substance,...): so also of minds, whatever defects there are are privations of natural good qualities, and the healing of these defects is not their transference elsewhere, but that the defects which did exist in the mind will have no place to exist, inasmuch as there will be no room for them in that healthiness...

> Consequently, that which we call evil has no existence except where there is goodness...So then every natural existence, even if it is a

---

[1] In other words, dualism is excluded. Augustine in his youth had contacts with the Manichaeans, who produced one of the most sophisticated of all dualistic systems, but he rejected it in favour of Christianity. On this see pp. 285–7.

[2] The Trinity expresses in doctrinal form the belief that the nature of God is relationship in terms of being rather than becoming: 'There are two kinds of life, perfect and imperfect. The perfect life is that which belongs to a being which is self-possessed and finds its exercise in the fullness of a movement which leaves nothing to be achieved. The absolute fullness of such life is to be found in God alone. The divine act, whereby God possesses, knows, and loves himself in the Trinity of the divine Persons, is an infinite act, and this act is the life of God in himself...And what is imperfect life? It is the movement of acquisition whereby a being is developed...The life of this world is growth, the life of heaven is possession, and both are the proper activity of my being.' (*The Interior Life*, ed. J. Tissot, Orchard Books ed. pp. 1 f.) Put the other way round, it is a way of trying to express that the nature of the created order reflects that of its creator.

defective one, is good in so far as it is an existence, and evil in so far as it is defective. . . From good things therefore have evil things originated, and only in good things of some sort do they have their existence. Nor was there any other source from which a natural existence of evil could have taken its origin. . .

We have discussed these matters, with the brevity required by the present work, because we have to know the causes of things good and evil, at least in so far as suffices for the way which should lead us to that kingdom in which there will be life without death, truth without error, felicity without discomposure: and we ought never to doubt that of the good things which are our lot the sole and only cause is the goodness of God, while of the evil things the cause is that the will of that mutable good, the angel first, the man afterwards, falls short of that good which is immutable.

This is the first of the rational creature's evils, that is, his first privation of good. After that, even against men's will, has crept in ignorance of the things that ought to be done, along with concupiscence of things hurtful, in whose train follow their attendants, error and sorrow. . . Man has also his peculiar penalty, being punished by the death of his body besides. God had in fact threatened him with the punishment of death if he were to sin:[1] for he gave him the gift of free choice, and yet, so as to keep him under control by his commandment, put him in fear of destruction. So he put him in the felicity of paradise, as it were in a mirrored image of life, so that from there he might by observing righteousness climb up to better things.

Made an exile from thence after his sin, he bound also his offspring, whom by sinning he had marred in himself as root, in the penalty of death and damnation, . . . infected with original sin. . .

This then was the situation. The whole lump of the human race, being under condemnation, was lying down in evils, nay rather was wallowing in them, and was being hurled headlong into ever deeper evils, and, being attached to the faction of those who had sinned, was paying the well-deserved penalty of its impious revolt; . . . not indeed that the Creator's goodness ceases either to continue to supply life and quickening potency to evil angels (for if the continuance of this supply be withheld, life ceases). . . For he judged it better to bring good out of evil than to preclude evil from existing. . .

Thus the human race was held in righteous condemnation, and they were all children of wrath. . . In fact this wrath accompanies every man's birth: which is why the apostle observes, 'For we also were by nature children of wrath, even as the others.'[2] Since men were in this wrath through original sin, and that the more seriously and destructively

---

[1] Gen. 2: 17.   [2] Eph. 2: 3.

the more they added greater and more frequent sins, there was need for a mediator, that is, a reconciler, who should propitiate this wrath by the offering of that one and only sacrifice of which all the sacrifices of the Law and the Prophets were shadows cast beforehand . . . The fact then that we by a Mediator are being reconciled to God, and do receive the Holy Spirit, so as, instead of enemies, to be made into sons—'for as many as are being led by the Spirit of God, these are sons of God'[1]—this is the grace of God through Jesus Christ our Lord.[2]

It is obvious from those passages that the two responses, of Irenaeus and of Augustine, are far from being so different that they are distinct. They have common ground, not only in the framework within which they operate, but also in the belief that what matters is the quality of having lived rather than the quantity of life or the accidental circumstances of existence. That view appears, significantly, in Augustine when he discusses the death of a much-loved friend in his youth. He and Augustine had played together as children and had grown up together in the closest possible friendship. Then the friend caught a fever and died:

Within a few days he relapsed into his fever and died. And I was not there. My heart was black with grief. Whatever I looked upon had the air of death. My native place was a prison house and my home a strange unhappiness. The things we had done together became sheer torment without him. My eyes were restless looking for him, but he was not there. I hated all places because he was not in them. They could not say 'He will soon come', as they would in his life when he was absent. I became a great enigma to myself and I was forever asking my soul why it was sad and why it disquieted me so sorely.[3]

These are the realities of suffering and grief, which are none the less real for having been given a theoretical explanation—indeed, one might say that they have a reality quite apart from attempts to explain how or why they exist, since they are the primary facts of experience—as Augustine immediately went on to point out:

My soul knew not what to answer me. If I said 'Trust in God' my soul did not obey—naturally, because the man whom she had loved and lost was nobler and more real than the imagined deity in whom I was

---

[1] Rom. 8: 14.
[2] *Enchiridion* iii, iv, viii, x (trs. E. Evans, London, 1953), pp. 7–32.
[3] *Confessions* iv. 4 (trs. F. J. Sheed, London, 1954).

bidding her trust... This is the root of our grief when a friend dies,
and the blackness of our sorrow, and the steeping of the heart in tears
for the joy that has turned to bitterness, and the feeling as though we
were dead because he is dead.[1]

To explain how or why this grief and suffering originated does
not dissolve their reality, and of this Augustine was well aware. He
went on to talk, not of explanations, but of the essentially important quality of having laid hold on life at all: if it is to be made
good, it can only be made good by and in God, for all else belongs
to the same transience of suffering. Even if it were false to believe
that this might be the case, it is still the only possible ground on
which to retain hope:

Blessed is the man that loves thee, O God, and his friend in thee, and
his enemy for thee. For he alone loses no one that is dear to him, if all
are dear in God, who is never lost... Wherever the soul of man turns,
unless towards God, it cleaves to sorrow, even though the things outside itself to which it cleaves may be things of beauty. For these lovely
things would be nothing at all unless they were from him. They rise
and set: in their rising they begin to be, and they grow towards
perfection, and once come to perfection they grow old, and they die:
not all grow old but all die. Therefore when they rise and tend toward
being, the more haste they make toward fulness of being, the more
haste they make towards ceasing to be. That is their law. You have
given them to be parts of a whole: they are all existent at once, but in
their departures and successions constitute the whole of which they are
parts... Things pass that other things may come in their place and
this material universe be established in all its parts. 'But do I depart
anywhere?' says the Word of God. Fix your dwelling in him, commit to
God whatsoever you have: for it is from God. O my soul, wearied at
last with emptiness, commit to Truth's keeping whatever Truth has
given you, and you shall not lose any; and what is decayed in you shall
be made clean, and what is sick shall be made well, and what is transient
shall be reshaped and made new and established in you in firmness;
and they shall not set you down where they themselves go, but shall
stand and abide and you with them, before God who stands and abides
for ever.[2]

That passage is of central importance in understanding Augustine, and it shows to what extent the work of explanation is
coincidental to the life of faith and love—or to put it the other

[1] *Confessions* iv. 4, 9. [2] *Ibid.* 9 f.

way round, the life of faith does not depend on its explanations, although, of course, it has usually tried to give some account of itself as it goes along. The emphasis in that passage from Augustine on the quality of having lived, rather than on the quantity of life or the accidents of its expression, has remained a consistent and essential part of the Christian response to suffering. To take another more recent example, it appears in circumstances almost exactly the reverse of Augustine's, in a letter from a young officer in the First World War, contemplating the virtual certainty of his own death—he was in fact killed almost exactly three months after the letter was written:

We make the division between life and death as if it were one of dates— being born at one date and dying some years after. But just as we sleep half our lives, so when we're awake, too, we know that often we're only half alive. Life, in fact, is a quality rather than a quantity, and there are certain moments of real life whose value seems so great that to measure them by the clock, and find them to have lasted so many hours or minutes, must appear trivial and meaningless. Their power, indeed, is such that we cannot properly tell how long they last, for they can colour all the rest of our lives, and remain a source of strength and joy that you know not to be exhausted, even though you cannot trace exactly how it works.[1]

It is obvious that the passage from Augustine has moved on from the realm of argument to that of assertion. It is not explanatory in the same sense that his analysis of the Creation narratives was intended to be explanatory of the origins of evil. It may, therefore, be asked on what grounds, if any, the assertion is made; or is it a disguised way of admitting that no explanation is possible, and that God can only be rescued by assertion? As A. Flew put it:

It often seems to people who are not religious as if there was no conceivable event or series of events the occurrence of which would be admitted by sophisticated religious people to be a sufficient reason for conceding 'There wasn't a God after all' or 'God does not really love us then'. Someone tells us that God loves us as a father loves his children. We are reassured. But then we see a child dying of inoperable cancer of the throat. His earthly father is driven frantic in his efforts to help, but his Heavenly Father reveals no obvious sign of concern.

[1] Quoted from Lord Birkenhead, *The Five Hundred Best English Letters* (London, 1931), pp. 950 f.

Christianity

Some qualification is made—God's love is 'not a merely human love' or it is 'an inscrutable love', perhaps—and we realize that such sufferings are quite compatible with the truth of the assertion that 'God loves us as a father (but, of course,...)'. We are reassured again. But then perhaps we ask: what is this assurance of God's (appropriately qualified) love worth, what is this apparent guarantee really a guarantee against? Just what would have to happen not merely (morally and wrongly) to tempt but also (logically and rightly) to entitle us to say 'God does not love us' or even 'God does not exist'?[1]

An element in Augustine's response to the same question as it occurred to him was, not surprisingly, to regard the person of Christ as coming close to the necessary assurance:

You seek happiness of life in the land of death, and it is not there. For how shall there be happiness of life where there is no life? But our Life came down to this our earth and took away our death, slew death with the abundance of his own life; and he thundered, calling us to return to him into that secret place from which he came forth to us—coming first into the Virgin's womb, where humanity was wedded to him, our mortal flesh, though not always to be mortal; and thence 'like a bridegroom coming out of his bride chamber, rejoicing as a giant to run his course'. For he did not delay, but rushed on, calling to us by what he said, and what he did, calling to us by his death and life, descent and ascension, to return to him. And he withdrew from our eyes, that we might return to our own heart and find him.[2]

The passage as a whole emphasises how essential in the Christian response to suffering is the acceptance of the life and death and resurrection of Jesus, at least as a factor to be taken into account, and perhaps as transforming the whole situation; and the last sentence emphasises how those 'events' become consequential and indeed causative when they are lived with as true, and when they are appropriated in experience. The causal relationship which was demonstrated between Jesus and the Father becomes operative between Christ and the Christian. Thus the Christian response to suffering has always been as much practical as theoretical, living with the consequences of Christ believed to be risen from the dead:

'What religion do I preach?' The religion of love; the law of kindness brought to light by the gospel. 'What is this good for?' To make all

[1] A. Flew in *New Essays in Philosophical Theology* (London, 1955), pp. 98 f.
[2] *Confessions* iv. 12.

who receive it enjoy God and themselves: to make them like God; lovers of all; contented in their lives; and crying out at their death, in calm assurance, '*O grave where is thy victory!* Thanks be unto God, who giveth *me* the victory, through my Lord Jesus Christ.'[1] Will you object to such a religion as this, that it is not reasonable...? Is it not reasonable then, that as we have opportunity, we should do good unto all men? Not only friends, but enemies, not only to the deserving, but likewise to the evil and unthankful. Is it not right that all our life should be one continued labour of love? If a day passes without doing good, may one not well say, with Titus, *Amici, diem perdidi,* 'My friends, I have lost a day!' And is it enough, to feed the hungry, to clothe the naked, to visit those who are sick or in prison? Should we have no pity for those

> Who sigh beneath guilt's horrid stain,
> The worst confinement and the heaviest chain?

...If we have found a medicine to heal even that sickness, should we not, as we have freely received it, freely give?'[2]

Here, again, theoretical and practical considerations are intertwined. The practical response of Christianity arises directly out of the belief that in the life of Christ God has set his mark on the world in a way which even the worst agonies of suffering cannot eradicate. The life of Christ is not usually claimed to dissolve or even explain the realities of suffering, but it becomes for Christians an essential element in their response, even though it does not eliminate the problem or provide any final solution. This twofold sense of certainty as a consequence of Christ and yet uncertainty because the implications have not yet been worked through or established, is already apparent in the New Testament, as E. L. Mascall has summarised:

Here we are on the journey, *in via*; there we shall be in our fatherland, *in patria*. Now we see in a mirror darkly, then we shall see face to face.[3] Now we know in part, but then we shall know even as we are known. Now we are the children of God, but it is not yet made manifest what we shall be. Throughout the New Testament the contrast is emphasized between our present and our final condition. Yet at the same time it is made equally clear that the powers of the age to come are already working in us. We are on the journey it is true, but even now our citizenship is in heaven;[4] we know only in part, but nevertheless we

[1] 1 Cor. 15: 55 ff.
[2] J. Wesley, *An Earnest Appeal to Men of Reason and Religion,* 8th ed. (1806), pp. 10 f.
[3] 1 Cor. 13: 12.   [4] Phil. 3: 20.

know; we see in a mirror darkly, but nevertheless we see; our future state is not yet manifest, yet we are the children of God. And although we are on the journey and not yet in the fatherland, we are nevertheless no more strangers and sojourners but fellow-citizens with the saints and of the household of God.[1] [2]

The sense of sufficient certainty in reflection on Christ and in relationship with him has meant that suffering can be accepted, as he accepted it, as devastatingly real, but as not the final word. That attitude has had both noble and ignoble consequences. On the bad side—in its effects—it led to the argument that a little suffering here is better than eternal loss elsewhere, even to the extent of imposing suffering on others. To some extent it is the recurrent instrumental view of suffering, although it has received particular applications at different times. In the sixteenth century, for example, there were three benefits which it was thought might justify the imposition of suffering on others: the unity of the state, the purity of the Church, and the hoped-for repentance and salvation of those on whom suffering was inflicted. The first two are combined in Canisius' commentary on Matt. 7: 15, 'Beware of false prophets':

The secular authorities and ruling princes should remember that the Christian order concerns them, too, and warns them to exercise their functions and administration in a Christian fashion. Since they have received the sword from God in order to protect the devout and to punish the wicked, as St Paul says, Christ has commanded them to see to it, together with the spiritual leaders, that the sheep of Christ and his church have nothing to fear from the wolves. That is why the enemies of Christ and the Church should not be borne with and tolerated to the common detriment of the Christian people. Since the true Christian faith is indeed like a mother who protects peace, obedience, unity, discipline, charity and all the good things of the civil as well as the spiritual order, the untrue and anti-Christian faith, on the contrary, is the root from which spring division, disorder, rebellion, insolence and all kinds of excesses. If it is right that the civil authority punishes those that counterfeit money, how can one suffer those that counterfeit the word of God?[3] Whoever insults and violates authority is guilty of

---

[1] Eph. 2: 19.   [2] *Grace and Glory* (London, 1961), pp. 20 f.

[3] The reference is to the *locus classicus* in Aquinas, *Summa Theologica* II, 2, 14, qu. 11 art. 3: 'In regard to heretics two points must be kept in mind. The first with regard to heretics themselves. The second with regard to the Church. From the point of view of heretics themselves there is their sin, by which they have deserved not

lese-majesty and must be punished *am Leib und Leben* (in body and life).[1]

As regards the third, the *locus classicus* might be regarded as Calvin, where it appears with concentrated brevity in *Ordonnances Ecclésiastiques*:

All these measures (for the correction of faults) shall be applied in moderation. There shall not be such a degree of rigour that anyone will be cast down—for all corrections are but medicinal, to bring back sinners to our Lord.[2]

Those who took an extreme line in regarding the imposition of suffering as justified by the issues at stake were always opposed by others who appealed for greater tolerance;[3] nevertheless, the acceptance of suffering as of less importance than the goals to be obtained, whether by society or by the individual, could issue in ruthless effects. On the other hand, exactly the same acceptance of suffering has also issued in quite different effects, not least in Christian asceticism and in the foundations of spiritual life. It has also issued in the many, many examples of Christian martyrdom.

only to be separated from the Church, but to be eliminated from the world by death. For it is a far graver matter to corrupt the faith which is the life of the soul than to falsify money which sustains temporal life. So if it be just that forgers and other malefactors are put to death without mercy by the secular authority, with how much greater reason may heretics be not only excommunicated, but also put to death, when once they are convicted of heresy. On the part of the Church there is merciful hope of the conversion of those in error. For this reason she does not immediately condemn, "but only after a first and second admonition," as the Apostle teaches. Only then, if the heretic remains pertinacious, the Church, despairing of his conversion, makes provision for the safety of others; and separating him, by the sentence of excommunication from the Church, passes him to secular judgement to be exterminated from the world by death. St Jerome says, and we read: "The tainted flesh must be cut away, and the infected sheep cast out from the fold: lest the whole house burn, the mass be corrupted, the body become infected and the flock perish. Arius was but a spark in Alexandria, but for want of being immediately quenched, a conflagration has devastated the whole world."" (trs. J. G. Dawson in A. P. d'Entrèves, *Aquinas: Selected Political Writings*).

[1] *B. Petri Canisii Epistulae et Acta* (ed. Braunsberger), VI, pp. 633 f., quoted in J. Lecler, *Toleration and the Reformation* (London, 1960), I, p. 280.

[2] *Corpus Reformatorum*, XXXVIII, 6. The principle might not appear to have been exercised in the case of Servetus, but it is extremely interesting that Servetus *agreed* with Calvin in his view of punishment and also in the view that 'although one should look for correction by other punishments than death', nevertheless there are some conditions of intransigence for which no other penalty is possible: see Calvin, *Works*, VIII, p. 708.

[3] See J. Lecler, *op. cit.* and for the situation in England, see J. W. Allen, *A History of Political Thought in the 16th Century*.

This might be exemplified from any age, or from almost any generation, of the Church's history, with probably more examples in the twentieth century than in any other. In the early Church, the *Martyrdom of Polycarp* is one of the earliest accounts to be written down outside the New Testament. He was brought into the arena before a large crowd to be questioned by the proconsul:

The proconsul asked him if he were Polycarp. And when he confessed that he was, he tried to persuade him to deny (the faith), saying, 'Have respect to your age'—and other things that customarily follow this, such as, 'Swear by the fortune of Caesar; change your mind; say, "Away with the atheists!"'[1]

But Polycarp looked with earnest face at the whole crowd of lawless heathen in the arena, and motioned to them with his hand. Then, groaning and looking up to heaven, he said, 'Away with the atheists!'

But the proconsul was insistent and said: 'Take the oath and I shall release you. Curse Christ.'

Polycarp said: 'Eighty-six years I have served him, and he never did me any wrong. How can I blaspheme my King who saved me?'[2]

Thus here again the foundation of the Christian response to suffering lies in the events of Jesus' life (which include the resurrection as an 'event', however it is to be explained), and in the experience of living as a consequence of those events—that is to say, living in the Spirit: 'let us at least taste how sweet the Lord is, who hath given unto us as a pledge the Spirit, that in him we may perceive his sweetness.'[3] No experiences of suffering can make it as though that life had not been lived. Therefore in the worst agony there remains something which is not destroyed, and which gives grounds, if not for explanation, at least for assurance and hope. In 1946, Leonard Wilson, then Bishop of Singapore, talked on the radio of his experiences as a Japanese prisoner of war:

I speak to you this morning from personal experience of God's comfort and strength. I was interned by the Japanese; I was imprisoned by their military police for many months; I suffered many weary hours of beatings and torture. Throughout that time I never turned to God in

---

[1] Christians were accused of atheism because they denied traditional gods and the divine representation of the Emperor.

[2] *Martyrdom of Polycarp* ix. 2 f. (trs. M. H. Shepherd in *Early Christian Fathers*, London, 1953), p. 152; Polycarp was eventually burnt to death.

[3] Augustine, *de Agone Christiano*, x. 10.

vain; always he helped and sustained. I wish to speak of these experiences, the keynote of which could be summed up in St Paul's words, 'More than conquerors'. . .

It is not my purpose to relate the tortures they inflicted upon us, but rather to tell you of some of the spiritual experiences of that ordeal. I knew that this was to be a challenge to my courage, my faith, and my love.

I remember Archbishop Temple, in one of his books, writing that if you pray for any particular virtue, whether it be patience, or courage, or love, one of the answers that God gives to us is an opportunity for exercising that virtue. After my first beating I was almost afraid to pray for courage lest I should have another opportunity for exercising it; but my unspoken prayer was there, and without God's help I doubt whether I would have come through. Long hours of ignoble pain were a severe test. In the middle of torture they asked me if I still believed in God. When, by God's help, I said, 'I do,' they asked me why God did not save me. By the help of his Holy Spirit I said, 'God does save me. He does not save me by freeing me from pain or punishment, but he saves me by giving me the Spirit to bear it'; and when they asked me why I did not curse them I told them that it was because I was a follower of Jesus Christ, who taught us that we were all brethren.

I did not like to use the words 'Father forgive them.' It seemed too blasphemous to use our Lord's words; but I *felt* them, and I said, 'Father, I know these men are doing their duty. Help them to see that I am innocent.' When I muttered 'Forgive them,' I wondered how far I was being dramatic, and if I really meant it; because I looked at their faces as they stood round, taking it in turn to flog me, and their faces were hard and cruel, and some of them were evidently enjoying their cruelty. But, by the Grace of God, I saw those men not as they were, but as they had been. Once they were little children with their brothers and sisters—happy in their parents' love, in those far-off days before they had been conditioned by their false nationalist ideals. And it is hard to hate little children.

So I saw them not as they were, but as they were capable of becoming, redeemed by the power of Christ, and I knew that I should say 'Forgive.'

It is true that there were many dreary moments, especially in the early morning, in a crowded, filthy cell with hardly any power to move because of one's wounds; but here again I was helped tremendously by God. There was a tiny window at the back of the cell, and through the bars I could hear the song of the Golden Oriole. I could see the glorious red of the flame of the forest tree; and something of God, something of God's indestructible beauty, was conveyed to my

Christianity

tortured mind. Behind the flame-trees I glimpsed the top of Wesley's church, and was so grateful that the Church had preserved many of Wesley's hymns. One that I said every morning, we sang today: 'Christ whose glory fills the skies.'

Gradually the burden of this world was lifted, and I was carried into the presence of God and received from him the strength and peace which were enough to live by, day by day...

But there were other battles to be fought. I do not know how many of you know what real hunger is, but the temptation to greed is almost overwhelming. Here again we were helped. There was a young Roman Catholic in the cell. He was a privileged prisoner; he was allowed food from the outside. He could have eaten all of it, but never a day passed without his sharing it with some people of the cell. It was a small amount we got, but what an enormous difference it made! It raised the whole tone of our life, and it was made possible for others to follow his noble example—to learn to share with one another.

After eight months I was released, and for the first time got into the sunlight. I have never known such joy. It seemed like a foretaste of the Resurrection. For months afterwards I felt at peace with the universe, although I was still interned and had to learn the lesson or the discipline of joy—how easy it is to forget God and all his benefits! I had known him in a deeper way than I could ever have imagined, but God is to be found in the Resurrection, as well as in the Cross, and it is the Resurrection that has the final word.

God, in all His power and strength and comfort, is available to every one of us today. He was revealed to me not because I was a special person but because I was willing *in faith* to accept what God gave. I know what I say is true, not just because the Bible says so, or because the Church has told us, but because I have experienced it myself; I know that whether you are despondent or in joy, whether you are apathetic or full of enthusiasm, there is available for you, *at this moment*, the whole life of God, with its victory over sin and pain and death.[1]

---

[1] Quoted from *A Treasury of the Kingdom* (ed. E. A. Blackburn, Oxford, 1954), pp. 158–62. The notion of creative suffering is even stronger in Eastern (particularly Russian) Orthodoxy. The original draft of this book included a section on the understanding of suffering in Eastern Orthodoxy, but for reasons of space it had to be omitted. It should, however, be borne in mind (in connection with the chapter on Marxism) that whereas Marx's understanding of suffering is related to the Western religious tradition, the implementation of Marxism in Russia is built on a highly distinctive development of that tradition, namely, that of Russian Orthodoxy. For a brief, but deeply suggestive, discussion of the differences, see Iulia de Beausobre, *Creative suffering*, London, 1940; and see also N. Berdyaev, *Spirit and Reality*, London, 1939, ch. v, 'Evil and Suffering as Problems of Spirit'.

3

ISLAM

THE FOUNDATIONS

These are the verses of the Quran and of a book making clear,
a guide and good news for those who believe,
those who perform the (ordained) prayer,
give the (prescribed) charity,
and who have confidence in the hereafter...
Truly you receive the Quran
from One who is wise, all-knowing.[1]

These words, taken from the Quran, are a typical expression of
the basic and fundamental importance of the Quran in Islam.
The status of the Quran as revelation is such that the Quran
forms the basis of all Islamic life and thought:

The departure point of the Islamic religion, the central article from
which all else flows, may be stated as follows: God (the only God
there is...) has spoken to man in the Quran...The Quran is the
Word of God, for Muslims. While controversies have raged among
them as to the sense in which this is true—whether it is the created or
uncreated Word, whether it is true of every Arabic letter or only of the
message as a whole, that it *is true* has never been questioned by them.[2]

This does not mean that Islamic life and thought is confined to
the Quran, since Islam, like any other religion, has its own
principles of continuity and development as it moves on in time
and confronts new and previously unforeseen situations. But it
does mean that Islam is grounded in the Quran, 'the Book in
which there is no doubt',[3] and that any consideration of the
Islamic understanding of suffering must begin with a study of the
Quran.

Islam as a whole stands within the Western tradition, having
particularly close links with the Judaeo-Christian tradition. There
is nothing 'academic' about that observation—that is to say, it is

---

[1] xxvii. 1–3, 6.   [2] J. A. Williams, *Islam* (New York, 1961), p. 15.
[3] xxxii. 1 (2); references to the Quran are to Fluegel's ed.; the numbers in brackets
are the corresponding verses in the Egyptian text, the translations are my own.

99

not a conclusion reached by observing literary and theoretical connections between the Quran and the Judaeo-Christian tradition, although those connections exist. It is, quite simply, what the Quran claims of itself. The Quran claims repeatedly to be the same revelation which God has already entrusted to such faithful servants as Abraham, Moses and Jesus, to mention only the most prominent. Those earlier figures are not confined to Biblical examples—Ad and Thamud and the Sabaeans have also received their prophets. It is fundamental to the Quran that God is One and that in consequence his revelation is One also; God cannot speak now with one voice, now with another; the message is the same, even though the accidents of its expression in particular ages or places differ. The fact that the holy books of Jews and Christians *do* differ, not simply in the forms of expression but also in the substance of their message, is a proof, so far as the Quran is concerned, that Jews and Christians have corrupted the revelation entrusted through their prophets to them. The Quran, therefore, in its own estimate represents the intended revelation of God in its pure form, but that is not to deny its necessary connections with the preceding religious situation:

He has laid out for you as a path the same religion[1] which he enjoined on Noah, and which he revealed to you, and which he enjoined on Abraham and Moses and Jesus, that they should observe the religion and not make divisions within it.[2]

This does not mean that the Quran is a sort of anthology, repeating, parrot-fashion, elements of pre-existing traditions. On the contrary, the Quran *belongs* to a tradition of thought, but it makes a unique interpretation of it, and it expresses it in a very distinctive way. As each nation has had its own prophet, and his message has been related to the circumstances of his own time, so the Quran is, as it says, the Arabic revelation. It is not a different revelation, but the timeless revelation of God related to the Arab situation as opposed to, for example, the Chinese or British. This has to be remembered in connection with the Islamic response to suffering, since the language and imagery of the Quran are directly related to the circumstances in which Muhammad lived, and yet the Quran is regarded definitively as revelation: the mother of the

___
[1] *Din.*   [2] xlii. 11 (13).

Book is laid up in heaven. Thus the words of the Quran are regarded by Muslims as having absolute and timeless importance, and yet it is recognised that they were related to the circumstances of Muhammad's own time.

Applied to suffering, this means, in effect, that suffering is treated in the Quran as it occurs, in direct and simple terms, not as a theoretical problem. Anyone who lives in or near the desert is bound to be aware how vulnerable life is. It is constantly threatened by drought or famine; its closely-knit kinship groups are frequently threatened by death or by external attack. The treatment of suffering in the Quran is to a great extent conditioned by the actual ways in which suffering most usually occurred. The Quran is related to concrete particulars of life, not to theoretical abstractions, and in this it is certainly in line with the Judaeo-Christian tradition. This is really to point out the obvious, but it needs to be remembered, not least because it helps to explain the very direct and simple language in which the rewards of paradise and the pains of hell are described. The imagery is derived directly from the actual 'fall-out' of suffering in a desert, or desert-related, community.

The Quran, therefore, starts where Judaism and Christianity start, with the actual facts of suffering, not with suffering conceived as a theoretical problem. Suffering is a part of what it means to be alive. Yet there is a clear realisation in the Quran that the facts of suffering do create certain problems. In Judaism of the Biblical period the problem was located primarily in distribution, in Christianity it was located primarily in vindication. Where is suffering located as a problem in the Quran? Or, to put it another way, how does suffering occur as a problem in the Quran?

The answer is that it very nearly does not occur at all. Suffering is given repeated consideration in the Quran, but there is a sense in which it is almost dissolved as a problem. That is so, because the Quran emphasises, as a characteristic of God, omnipotence as much as love. It must be said at once that it is not the one to the exclusion of the other. The Quran reiterates constantly the evidences of God's compassion and love, particularly in creation; and right at the beginning of the Quran there stands the underlying and essential foundation of all belief—'praise be to God,... the merciful, the compassionate.' Yet even there the assertion of

Islam

mercy and compassion is in association with omnipotence; only a part of that opening sentence was quoted. In full it reads:

Praise be to God, the Lord of the universe, the merciful, the compassionate.[1]

Thus whereas in Christianity suffering occurs as a problem principally because it conflicts with the assertion that God is love, in Islam it occurs principally because it conflicts with the belief that God is omnipotent. It would be absurd to try to make the distinction absolute; but there is a certain difference in emphasis in Islam and Christianity, which amounts to a difference in the exact location of the problem. The form of the problem in the Quran is stated very clearly in ii. 210 (214):

Do you reckon that you will enter the garden
without there coming upon you the like of those
who have passed away before you?
Evils and griefs afflicted them, and they trembled so much
that the apostle and those who were with him said,
'When will the help of God come?'
Oh, truly, the help of God is near![2]

The problem is the apparent absence of God's control and power—the same sort of problem that had faced Deutero-Isaiah long before in the Exile: did the Exile mean, *ipso facto*, the impotence of God? Did it mean that God is unable to look after his own?[3] What is at issue is the omnipotence of God, and it is made repeatedly clear in the Quran that suffering can only be understood by being contained within that omnipotence. iii. 159 (165), therefore, asks, in the context of the defeat of the Muslims in battle at Uhud:[4]

What! when a blow strikes you, and you have already struck
with its like,
will you say, 'Why has this happened?'
Say: 'It is from your own selves.'
Truly, God has power over every single thing.[5]

[1] i. 2 (3) ff.
[2] Note that even Muhammad is assailed by doubt; this is as it should be, since no supernatural claims are made on behalf of Muhammad's person. The Quran originates with God, not with Muhammad. Muhammad is simply *rasul Allah*, the apostle of God, the one through whom the revelation of God was conveyed to the world.   [3] See p. 20.   [4] See further pp. 107 f.
[5] *'ala kulli shayin qadir*. This is a frequent and much-repeated refrain in the Quran, as will be seen in the ensuing quotations.

It is in this sense that the 'problem of suffering' is, in the Quran, almost dissolved. In effect, the Quran says, 'Take the concept of omnipotence seriously: if your imagination of God is not too small, then suffering cannot be a problem, because the facts of suffering must necessarily be contained within the omnipotence of God.' Suffering occurs only within creation, which is *God's* creation—and assuming that the universe has not got out of his control, then suffering is not out of his control either. Suffering may thus raise questions about the nature of God, but it cannot occur as a problem, since the omnipotence of God is already established, or at least accepted, on other grounds.

Yet even put like that, suffering reasserts itself as a problem, because it calls in question whether the underlying assumption is in fact correct, that the universe is *not* out of God's control. In other words, suffering could occur here as a problem in traditional terms, because it calls in question a basic assertion about the nature of God, i.e. the assertion that 'God has power over every single thing.' Not surprisingly, therefore, much material in the Quran is devoted to substantiating and exemplifying exactly this assertion, that God *is* in control, and that suffering must in some sense be purposeful—that is to say, it must be a part of the purposes of God.

This theme of the power and the control of God, particularly in creation and in history, is so vital that it might almost be described as the essence of the Quran. Thus to give a typical example, which actually connects up this theme with the occurrence of suffering, s. xxxv begins:

> Praise be to God, the originator of the heavens and the earth,
> who appointed the angels to be messengers,
> with wings, two or three or four;
> he extends creation as he wills.
> Truly, God has power over every single thing.
> Whatever God opens to men in the way of mercy
> none can hold back,
> and whatever he holds back
> none can afterwards set loose;
> and he is the powerful, the wise.[1]

[1] xxxv. 1 f.

Islam

There is nothing, not even in the furthest imaginable extent of the universe, which can possibly lie beyond him:

> To God belong the East and the West.
> No matter where you turn
> there is the face of God.
> Truly God is all-embracing, all-knowing.[1]

Supremely he has control over creation, and thus over life and death itself, and this, again, is one of the commonest themes in the Quran:

> Truly, it is God who splits open the grain and the date-stone;
> he brings forth the living from the dead,
> and he brings forth the dead from the living.
> That, precisely, is God.[2]

At the beginning of s. xxii this assertion of the power of God over life and death is directly related to the vicissitudes of human life and in particular to the pitiable state of senility:[3]

> O men, if you are in doubt about the resurrection,
> surely we created you from dust,
> then from a drop of sperm,
> then from a clot of blood,
> then from flesh formed and unformed,
> that we might give you understanding.
> And we set what we will in the wombs for an appointed time,
> then we bring you forth as infants,
> then that you may come of age—
> and some of you die,
> while others are kept back to an abject state of life
> so that (a man) knows nothing having once known much.
> And you see the earth parched;
> then when we send down rain on it
> it stirs and swells and puts forth growth
> of every lively species.
> That is so, because it is God who is the truth,
> it is he who gives life to the dead
> and it is he who has power over every single thing.[4]

---

[1] ii. 109 (115).　　　　　　　　　　　　　[2] vi. 95.

[3] Cf. also xxx. 53 (54); in xlii. 48 (49) f. the same theme is related to the problem of barrenness.

[4] xxii. 5, 6. For another typical example see xl. 69 (67) f., which ends with the classic phrases: *fa'idha qada 'amran fa'innama yaqulu lahu kun fayakunu*, 'When he decrees something, he simply says to it "Be", and it is.'

This, then, becomes a fundamental part of the attitude of Islam, of right relationship with God, submission. It is the acceptance that God's authority and control extend over everything.

> Say: O God, king of kings,
> you give authority to whom you will
> and you remove authority from whom you will;
> you exalt whom you will
> and you diminish whom you will.
> In your hand is all good,
> truly, you have power over every single thing.[1]

Again it is important to remember the circumstances in which Muhammad lived. The necessity was to argue not so much for the existence of God as for an adequate conception of God. The plea of the Quran is that all men should take their profession of God seriously, and that they should not diminish the overriding sovereignty of God by associating anything with him, or by expressing scepticism or doubt.[2]

The obvious and immediate implication of this is that if God is all-powerful, and if the universe is not out of control, then suffering must in some sense come from God. There can be no dualism. The Quran certainly exploits the Judaeo-Christian myth that at the creation of Adam one of the angels, Iblis, resented Adam's pre-eminent position and distinctive relationship with God, and that he refused to acknowledge Adam or bow down before him. God's immediate response was that Iblis must be destroyed, but he was prevailed upon to give him respite. Iblis, therefore, remains, along with his companion Satans and demons, to tempt men and to provoke them to evil. In this way the Quran gives a pictorial, mythological content to the experience of temptation. But the important point is that the activity of Iblis is still within the control of God—it is God, after all, who gave respite to Iblis in the first place, and thus allowed his activity.[3]

This is a simple but clear example of the way in which the Quran cuts through the problem of suffering by saying that it is within the control of God, and that in a sense, therefore, it comes from him. s. lxiv. 11 puts it briefly:

> There is no kind of blow[4]
> except by the leave of God,...

---

[1] iii. 25 (26).   [2] See, e.g., xxix. 61–3.
[3] See, e.g., vii. 10–18 (11–19).   [4] Or, 'affliction'.

Islam

But this raises serious questions about the character of God: to think of God as having created suffering to be an inherent fact of creation might be impressive in terms of omnipotence, but not of compassion. In conjunction, therefore, with the fundamental assertion of the control of God, there is, almost inevitably, a constant exploration of ways in which suffering can be understood as purposeful. It is this which leads directly into the quest for ways in which suffering can be understood as instrumental, and two main answers emerge—or, perhaps more accurately, two answers are suggested with particular frequency.

The first is that suffering is a punishment for sin. This is clearly stated in iv. 80 (78) f., which is dealing with those who proclaim their faith in God, but only so long as all goes well; as soon as they suffer a reverse, they turn on the Prophet of God, and blame him:

> If some good befalls them, they say, 'This is from God',
> but if evil strikes them, they say, 'This is from you.'
> Say: Everything is from God.
> What has come over this people?
> They scarcely understand a single thing that is told them.
> Whatever in the way of good befalls you, it is from God;
> and whatever in the way of evil befalls you, it is from yourselves.
> We have sent you as an apostle to men,
> and God is sufficient as a witness.

In order to support this argument, that suffering is a punishment for sin, the Quran makes a particular appeal to experience, and to what is known to have happened in the past. For this, the biblical narratives proved an especially rich field, since many of them tell of proud and evil men, who felt themselves to be secure but who were overwhelmed by God, often through the instrumentality of natural disasters. The stories of Noah, of Lot, and of Moses with Pharaoh lent themselves to such an argument. Thus in connection with Pharaoh, s. xliii. 55 f. says specifically:

> So when they provoked us
> we exacted retribution from them
> and drowned them all.
> And we made them extinct
> and an example to later ages.

In vii. 92–4 (94–6) a general conclusion is drawn from a preceding list of particular examples:

We never sent any prophet into a town
without catching hold of its people with misery and affliction
that they might perhaps be humble.
Then we made good take the place of evil until they increased
and said, 'Affliction and prosperity visited our fathers.'
So we took them suddenly while they were not giving it a
thought.
Yet if the people of those towns had believed and been godfearing
we would have opened upon them blessings from the heavens
and the earth,
but they practised deceit,
so we took them according to what they had earned.[1]

The Quranic examples are not confined to Biblical material, fruitful though it was. Narratives of other peoples in the past, particularly Ad and Thamud, appear on the same footing. Appeal is also made to local knowledge and experience, particularly to the evidence of the decline and fall of once great cities or empires. In addition the Quran explores success and failure in the history of Muhammad's own time, and here the two battles of Badr and Uhud provided a crucial case. Badr was a conflict in the second year of the *hijra*[2] between a small Muslim force and a much larger Meccan army which was sent to defend the caravan of abu Sufyan. In ordinary terms the Muslims should have been routed, but in fact they won a notable victory.[3] Inevitably, this was taken

---

[1] The point is made with even greater clarity in xi. 102 (100) ff.; see also the 'parable of the city' in xiv. 113 (112) f.

[2] The *hijra* (sometimes in English *hegira*) is the movement of Muhammad and his followers from Mecca to Yathrib (subsequently known as Medina) in A.D. 622. The majority of Meccans bitterly opposed Muhammad, and under this pressure Muhammad sent most of his small band of supporters to Yathrib. He himself stayed in Mecca until the last moment, but with his life threatened he decided to transfer himself and the centre of his operations to Medina. There he began to build up a theocratic community, and from this point on the Quran is increasingly concerned with social legislation under the guidance of God. The Muslim numbering of years starts with the year of the *hijra*, so that subsequent dates are given A.H.—after the *hijra* (but note that since the Muslims follow a lunar calendar, the length of a year is not the same as it is for those who follow a solar calendar, hence Western and Islamic years do not correspond).

[3] If viii. 7 refers to Badr, it shows that the Muslims turned away from the easier task of destroying and looting the caravan, and that they deliberately met the relieving army from Mecca, confident that they would be helped by God; see also viii. 42–8, where God's control at Badr is analysed in a slightly different way.

Islam

to be a sign of God's approval and of his support for the faithful.

> Already there has been for you a sign
> in the two armies that met.
> One was fighting in the cause of God
> the other was resisting in unbelief.
> These saw with their own eyes twice their own number,
> but God strengthens with his help whom he wills.
> Surely in that is a warning for those who open their eyes.[1]

Badr for the Muslims, like the Exodus for the Jews, vindicated their trust and faith in God. But Uhud seemed to call that faith in question. In the following year, A.H. 3, the Meccans returned to the attack with an even larger army, and they defeated the Muslims at the hill Uhud. The question immediately arose: why had God allowed the faithful to be defeated? The question is raised in iii. 117–24 (121–30), and the answer given is—Islam:

> No part of the matter is yours,
> whether he turns towards them, or whether he punishes them;
> for truly they do dark deeds.
> To God belongs everything in the heavens and in the earth:
> he forgives whom he wills,
> he punishes whom he wills,
> and God is forgiving, compassionate.[2]

This may be a commendable attitude, but it is scarcely an answer to the problem. That suffering is a consequence of evil is undoubtedly true in some instances, but not in all. The defeat at Uhud called that answer in question, because it raised the further problem of innocent or undeserved suffering—or perhaps more particularly it raised the problem of *indiscriminate* suffering. It is, once more, the problem of distribution. It would be hard to suppose that each individual in the Muslim community was so equally culpable that the defeat at Uhud was a just punishment![3]

[1] iii. 11 (13).
[2] iii. 123 (128) f.
[3] The defeat at Uhud was, in fact, analysed as a deserved punishment for over-confidence and for regretting that booty had not fallen easily into their hands; but

Furthermore, the Quran warns the faithful not to make the mistake of Job's friends and to assume that where they see suffering there also they see sin.[1] There should, for example, be no attempt to dissociate from the afflicted as though they were the objects of divine displeasure, nor should those who are unable to go to battle in God's cause be blamed. Still less should those who have died in battle be derided as though the survivors were enjoying the special favour of God. Thus the Quran is well aware that suffering may be a punishment for sin in some cases—and it produces an impressive list of examples—but it cannot be so in all cases.[2] The Quran, therefore, produces a second major explanation, namely, that suffering is a trial or test. This again is a constant and repeated theme of the Quran, and it is frequently stated in explicit terms:

> Surely we will test you with something of fear, and of hunger,
> and of loss of wealth and lives and produce;
> yet give good tidings to the patient,
> who, when calamity afflicts them, say,
> 'We belong to God, and to him are we returning.'[3]

even so not all the Muslims were guilty of that offence: see especially iii. 147 (153) f. This problem of indiscriminate suffering is raised elsewhere in the Quran, as, for example, in connection with the treaty of Hudaibiya: was it right to have made a treaty with the pagan enemies of God, or would it not have been better for the Muslims to have attacked Mecca and thus to have become the instruments of God's justice and punishment?

> 'And if there had not been believing men and believing women,
> whom you did not know that you were trampling down,
> and on whose account you would have incurred guilt unwittingly—
> that God may bring into his mercy whom he wills—
> if they had been separated out,
> then we would certainly have punished those of them
> who resisted God with a heavy punishment.' (xlviii. 25 *b*)

[1] xxiv. 60 (61): 'There is no blemish in the blind, and there is no blemish in the lame, and there is no blemish in the sick...' Cf. also xlviii. 17.

[2] This 'agnostic' attitude was later developed by the Murjiites, who argued that the fate of sinners (with particular reference to Muslim sinners) must be left to God and that men are in no position to judge them. The Murjiites held that Muslim sinners were still Muslims, not least because the door of repentance is a part of Islamic faith; the Khawarij, at the other extreme, thought that Muslim sinners weakened the 'household of faith' and that they should be exterminated (the instrumental theory of suffering!). *Mutatis mutandis*, the same problem arose very early in Christianity (within the New Testament period), whether sin after baptism could be forgiven.

[3] ii. 150 (155) f.

Islam

Or again:

> Every soul tastes of death,
> and we test you with evil and with good[1] as a trial,
> and to us you will return.[2]

This means that human beings are, so to speak, 'out on licence', and that to live is to walk on a precarious razor's edge.

> There are some among men who serve God on an edge:[3]
> if good befalls them they are well-content,
> if a trial befalls them they turn completely round.
> They have lost this world and the next;
> that is an unmistakable loss.[4]

This is not left as a casual or coincidental explanation of suffering. The Quran asserts that sooner or later all will be tested in this way:

> If a wound bruises you,
> a similar wound has bruised people previously.
> Such days we deal out among men in turn
> that God may know those who believe,
> and that he may take from among you witnesses,
> (and God has no love for those who do dark deeds)
> and that God may prove those who believe
> and bruise those who disbelieve.
> Did you reckon that you would enter the garden
> without God knowing those of you who make an effort
> and without knowing those who are patient?[5]

That last question means that so far as the Quran is concerned it belongs to the nature of faith that it must and will be tried.[6] The question appears again, in slightly different form, in ii. 210 (214),

---

[1] This at first sight rather casual phrase is in fact extremely important. It means that prosperity is as much a test as suffering: what is at stake is the way in which men behave in God's creation:

> 'When trouble touches a man he cries out to us,
> then when we bestow a favour on him from ourselves he says:
> "This has been given me because of knowledge."
> Far from it, it is a trial,
> but most of them do not realise.' (xxxix. 50 (49).)

[2] xxi. 36 (35).

[3] *'ala harfin:* for several different applications of this phrase see Lane *ad loc.*

[4] xxii. 11.   [5] iii. 134 (140) f.

[6] Just as the Quran appeals to past history to support the argument that suffering is a punishment, so also it appeals to past history to support the view that suffering is a trial. See, for example, xiv. 6, ii. 46 (49), vi. 42.

and xxix. 1 (2) f. makes it clear that a simple profession of faith is not enough:

Do men reckon that they will be left alone if they say, 'We believe', and that they will not be tested? We certainly tested those who lived before them, and God will unquestionably know those who are consistently sincere, and he will unquestionably know those who are false.

This means that Muslims must expect to be tested, and that as Muslims there will be some particular trials which can only assail *them*. So, for example, they will be exposed to the hostility of those who believe that they themselves possess the revelation of God and that the claims of the Quran are false.[1] Or, to give a more precise example, some of the obligatory requirements and prohibitions of Islam were given to be a test, and obviously those apply only to those who, as Muslims, accept them: thus it is forbidden to kill game while in a state of ritual purity:

You who believe: God tests you in the matter of game which is within range of your hands and spears, that God may know who fears him in secret. After that, whoever transgresses, there will be a heavy punishment for him.[2]

Thus suffering in the Quran is a necessary part of the purposes of God: it helps to create a faithful disposition and it also helps to discriminate the sincere from the insincere.[3] What this means, in effect, is that suffering not only forms character, it also exposes it: it reveals a man's true nature. Under pressure a man will reveal what he is really worth:

If we give a man a taste of mercy from us,
and then remove it from him,
at once he is despairing and rebellious;
and if we give him a taste of favours after misfortune has
    touched him,
he is sure to say, 'Evil has left me.'
Truly he is exultant, boastful—
not so those who are patient and who do good deeds:
those are the ones for whom there is forgiveness
and a great reward.[4]

[1] See, e.g., iii. 183 (186).   [2] v. 95 (94).
[3] Suffering has value not only because it produces an equal disposition but also because pain produces compassion. This is argued in xlvi. 14 (15) in connection with respect for parents.
[4] xi. 12–14 (9–11). This ironic observation of human fickleness is repeated frequently in the Quran—see especially xli. 49–51. For further examples see x. 13 (12),

In these two main ways, suffering as a punishment and suffering as a trial, the Quran attempts to reconcile the fact of suffering with a belief in God's omnipotence and compassion. The Quran opts firmly for the theory of instrumentality—for the belief that suffering is an instrument of the purposes of God. In this way the Quran is able to maintain that, despite some appearances to the contrary, God is in control. A number of subsidiary implications flow out from those two basic ways of understanding suffering. If, for example, suffering is a punishment it follows that suffering endured faithfully helps towards acquittal in the final reckoning of sins by God,[1] and that it leads to life.[2] Or again, exposing oneself voluntarily to suffering in the cause of God can be commended or even enjoined. Then again, the effects of suffering are important: faithfully accepted, suffering helps to produce an equal and balanced character—and conversely fear of suffering is a mark of inadequate trust. Despair is blasphemy.[3] No doubt when the faithful are distressed, the godless will mock them and regard their suffering as an evidence of the absence of God, but that is precisely the moment at which to remember that God *is* in control:[4] they may plot and devise against the faithful, but the devices of God far exceed theirs.[5]

xvi. 55–7 (53–5), xxx. 32 (33) f., xxxix. 11 (8), lxx. 19–21. The observation is particularly common in connection with the hazards of travelling by sea. For an example of this, see x. 22–4 (21–3). In xvii. 68 (66) f., the same example is applied to polytheism.

[1] 'Those who left their homes and were driven out of them, and were harmed in my cause, and fought and were killed, I will certainly cover over their evil deeds, and I will bring them into gardens with rivers flowing beneath as a reward from God; and with God is the best of rewards.' iii. 194 f. (195); cf. also xxii. 57–61 (58–62).

[2] 'Let those who fight in the cause of God sell the life of the present world for that of the next world. And whoever fights in the cause of God, whether he is killed or victorious, soon we will give him a great reward.' iv. 76 (74); cf. also ix. 20, xxii. 57 (58).

[3] This is said of the Jews in v. 69 (64): 'The Jews said: "The hand of God is tied." Tied are their hands, and cursed are they for what they have said. In fact the hand of God is opened wide, and he bestows as he wills.' Cf. also xlii. 34–7.

[4] 'If good befalls you it grieves them, but if misfortune lights upon you, they say, "We took care of our own affairs before", and they turn away rejoicing. Say: nothing will light upon us except what God has written (decreed) for us. He is our protector: on God let the believers rest their trust entirely.' ix. 50 f.

[5] 'If good befalls you it grieves them, but if evil lights upon you they rejoice at it. But if you are patient and god-fearing their guile will not harm you in any way. Truly God encompasses what they do.' iii. 116 (120). From this arises the familiar phrase, 'They made plans and God made plans, but God is the best of planners.' iii. 47 (54); see also viii. 30.

Foundations

The instrumental understanding of suffering is sometimes stated in more specific terms, particularly in the belief that God uses suffering in order to bring men to their senses—though often this does not have the desired effect:

> If we had mercy on them
> and removed whatever is upon them in the way of distress,
> they would surely persist in their error, wandering blindly.
> We have taken them in punishment in the past,
> but they have not humbled themselves to their Lord,
> nor have they abased themselves in supplication—
> until the time when we open against them
> a door leading to hard punishment,
> then they are overwhelmed at it.[1]

Furthermore, God deliberately appoints some men (by their preaching and teaching) to be a test—almost, as it were, a wedge driven into the world to separate the good from the evil:

> We did not send before you any of our messengers
> without their eating food and going about in the market-places,
> and we appointed some of you to be a test:
> will you be patient?
> For your Lord is well-aware.[2]

The instrumental theory of suffering is developed in another direction by the suggestion that men can use suffering as an instrument with which to combat or resist evil:

Fight them (those who planned to expel Muhammad): God will punish them by your hands and humiliate them and help you against them, and he will heal the breasts of a believing people.[3]

The Quran, therefore, expresses in various different ways an instrumental view of suffering. In the light of this understanding of suffering, what, according to the Quran, should the response of men be?

To some extent the answer to this has already begun to appear, and it has revealed the outlines of what may be called 'the hard response': if the emphasis with reference to God is on power and control, the emphasis with reference to men's response must be

---

[1] xxiii. 77–9 (75–7). For a historically-based example, see xliii. 47 (48).
[2] xxv. 22 (20).   [3] ix. 14.

on acceptance. The characteristic word used to describe that response is *sabr*, 'patience', 'endurance', as in the passage quoted above:

> Give good tidings to the patient,
> who, when calamity afflicts them, say:
> 'We belong to God, and to God we are returning.'[1]

The Quran repeatedly advocates the attitude of patient endurance:[2] on man's part it is epitomised in the famous phrase, 'I take refuge in God', and that too is advocated by the Quran:

> If a temptation from Satan entices you,
> seek refuge in God.
> Truly he hears and knows.[3]

The attitude is perfectly expressed in vi. 163 (162):

> Say: truly my prayer, my sacrifice, my living, my dying
> belong to God, the Lord of the universe.
> There are none in association with him,
> and thus I am commanded.
> And I am the first of those who submit.[4]

In itself this response scarcely deserves the adjective 'hard'. It only becomes so when it leads to fatalism or indifference: if the control of God is believed to be absolute or even predestinarian, then concern or anxiety about one's own sufferings or about the sufferings of others becomes totally inappropriate. It is not impossible for patience and endurance to become hardened and thick-skinned, and there are certainly passages in the Quran which, in isolation, might be open to that interpretation:

> No misfortune in the earth or in your lives
> can happen without it having been decreed[5]
> before we create it—
> truly that is easy for God—
> that you may not grieve for what escapes you,
> nor exult over what has come to you...[6]

[1] ii. 150 (155) f.
[2] For typical examples see xi. 117 (115), xvi. 127 (126)*b*, xlvi. 34 (35), l. 38 (39), lii. 48.
[3] vii. 199 (200).
[4] *alMuslimun*.
[5] Lit. 'except it is in a book.'   [6] lvii. 22 f.

In direct application of this the Quran suggests that it is foolish to be preoccupied with the inequalities of life: since all comes from God, there is no point in trying to achieve uniformity:

> God has favoured some of you more than others
> in the matter of sustenance,
> And those who have been favoured should not hand over
> their sustenance to what their right hands possess,
> so that they may be equal in that respect.
> Will they then deny the favours of God?[1]

Similarly, there is no sense in lamenting the fate of those who suffer in the cause of God:

> You who believe: do not be like those who resist God and say of their brethren when they journey in the earth or go forth to fight: 'If they had stayed with us they would not have died or been killed'—that God may make that a grief in their hearts. For God gives life and death, and God is aware of what you do.[2]

In terms of this 'hard response' suffering must be understood as a part of the strict justice of God—'God does not desire injustice for any living being.'[3] A reward based exactly on the balance between good and evil[4] awaits all:

> God does not burden a soul except according to its capacity:
> to it belongs what it has earned,
> and against it stands what it has earned,...[5]

Hence your concern should be for yourself, not for the fate of others:

> He who receives guidance receives it for his own self,
> and he who goes astray in error strays to his own loss.
> No bearer of burdens bears the burden of another.[6]

To the sceptics who say, 'But it doesn't look like that'—i.e. 'why do the wicked prosper?'—the Quran replies emphatically, 'Ultimately they do *not* prosper.' They may, like Iblis, have been given a respite, but it is only a postponement, not a cancellation, for 'truly Gehenna will encompass those who reject God.'[7]

---

[1] xvi. 73 (71).
[2] iii. 150 (156).   [3] iii. 104 (108).
[4] The idea of the exact balance is frequent in the Quran.   [5] ii. 286.
[6] xvii. 16 (15)*a*. This, too, can be expressed in terms of the hard response of dissociation, as, for example, in ii. 135 (141).
[7] See the whole section, xxix. 53 f.

Thus the supernatural solution is invoked: present sufferings, in the sense that they are a warning and a more immediate punishment, are a foretaste of those to come—'disgrace in this world, a heavy punishment in the next.'[1] The final reckoning will take place after death—and the word 'final' is exactly right. There will be no alleviation, nor can the pains of hell be regarded as a limited purgation.[2]

The immediate, practical implication of this is that the acceptance of suffering in an attitude of Islam (patient trust in the overriding control and mercy of God) is worthwhile because of the greater rewards to come. The anomalies and vicissitudes of this life can be accepted because the balance will be restored in the life to come. And this, too, could be interpreted as a contribution to the 'hard response': suffering is put firmly in its place. It is insignificant compared with the great rewards of paradise to come, and since it is, in any case, entirely in the control of God there is no point in being over-concerned about it. 'It is the will of Allah' is a phrase that can easily become fatalistic.

But to interpret the Quran in that way would be to misrepresent it. However much the 'hard response' is supported by certain passages in the Quran it is tempered by other passages and themes of equal significance. It is tempered, for example, by the fact that repentance is a door to forgiveness; by the fact that God has always and with great clarity made the issues entirely clear; by repeated assurances of the compassion of God and of the fact that 'he will not tempt you more than you are able.'[3] But above all a fatalistic and indifferent attitude to the occurrence of suffering is ruled out by the Quran itself. Although the Islamic attitude to suffering has at certain times and in certain individuals become fatalistic, that is a perversion of Islam, not its true expression, and the Quran militates against such an attitude.

This can be seen most directly in the fact that the Quran, far from suggesting that the only attitude to suffering should be passive acceptance, repeatedly demands that suffering should be contested and as far as possible alleviated. This is the foundation of the very detailed and specific requirements in the Quran for a

[1] ii. 108 (114)*b*, *et al.* For an exact statement of this see xli. 15 (16).
[2] For a specific statement of this, see ii. 74 (80) f. Cf. also ii. 80 (86).
[3] So, for example, in the prayer which concludes s. ii: 'O our Lord, do not burden us beyond what we have strength to bear. Forgive us and pardon us—you are our protector, so help us against those who disbelieve.'

Foundations

truly Muslim society, that particular instances of suffering and injustice should be removed. To examine the whole of the social teaching of the Quran would be a vast undertaking: here it is sufficient to underline the extreme importance of its existence. According to the Quran, society should be organised to extend and to implement the justice and compassion of God. Hence specific instances of hardship and suffering which existed in Muhammad's time are contested in the Quran: so, for example, war against evil is necessary but war in general should be defensive only;[1] bloodvengeance is alleviated by compensation; customs governing marriage and divorce are changed for the greater protection of women; the position of slaves is safeguarded; the settlement of debts and of estates after death is made more equitable. In more general terms, the Quran encourages an attack on poverty—and *ʒakat*, alms-giving, is one of the 'five pillars of Islam'.[2] It also warns against the evil consequences of anger, and it therefore urges time for reflection and for ascertaining the facts before action.

This concentration on positive action in society to alleviate suffering and injustice probably arose directly out of Muhammad's early experiences. Certainly s. xciii, which epitomises this attitude, is usually understood as referring to Muhammad:

> By the light of day
> and by the night when it is at rest,
> your Lord has not forsaken you
> nor is he displeased.
> Truly what is to come is better for you than what is now,
> and soon your Lord will bestow gifts on you,
> and you will be pleased.
> Did he not find you an orphan and give you shelter?
> Did he not find you wandering and give you guidance?
> Did he not find you in need and give you riches?
> As for the orphan, then, do him no harm;
> as for the beggar, turn him not away;
> and as for the favour of your lord, proclaim it.[3]

[1] These restrictions theoretically control *jihad*, holy war; for the importance of *jihad*, see n. 2 below.

[2] The *arkan udDin* are the five basic elements of Islam. The others are: 'the witness' ('I bear witness that there is no god but God, and that Muhammad is his messenger'); set prayer; fasting; and pilgrimage. Occasionally a 6th 'pillar' is added, *jihad*, or holy war undertaken in the cause of God.

[3] The compassion of Muhammad is also directly referred to in ix. 129 (128). There are, of course, many examples of Muhammad's compassion in *hadith* (traditions about Muhammad; see p. 123).

Islam

This active response to suffering is not a loose or coincidental attachment to the other, more passive, acceptance of suffering as being within the control of God:[1] they are both intertwined as a part of the definition of true religion:

It is not piety that you turn your faces to the East and West, but piety is belief in God, and in the last day, and in the angels, and in the book, and in the prophets, and to give of your substance, however dear to you, to your family, to orphans, to those in need, to travellers, to beggars, for the ransom of slaves, for establishing prayer, and for the giving of regular charity; and those who fulfil whatever agreements they have undertaken, and are patient in evil and misfortune and peril, those are the ones who are sound, and those are they who are god-fearing.[2]

In addition to advocating positive action against particular instances of suffering, the Quran also regards intercession for its removal as legitimate—though in the case of punishment, particularly of final punishment, this is less so. In s. xxvii there occurs a sequence of examples designed to prove the unity and uniqueness of God, in which the question 'Is there any god with God?' occurs as a refrain. One of these examples is the ability of God to answer prayer and remove distress:

He who answers the distressed when he prays to him
and removes the evil and appoints you to be inheritors of the
    earth.
Is there any god with God?
Little indeed do you remember.[3]

This is all the more impressive when it is remembered how much the Quran restricts the scope and efficacy of intercession in general.[4]

In the Quran, therefore, these two attitudes of acceptance and of action are woven together: acceptance that God is in control, and action within the context of his creation. The Quran is able to hold these two together without tension because it has an adequate doctrine of creation. It is God who creates 'weal and

---

[1] Although sometimes the active response appears in isolation: see, e.g., ii. 211 (215), iv. 40–4 (36–40).   [2] ii. 172 (177).   [3] xxvii. 62 (61).

[4] For details, see my article, 'Intercession in the Quran and the Jewish Tradition', *J.S.S.* xi (1966), pp. 69–82. In xlviii. 11 there is a warning to the desert Arabs not to rely on intercession, but ii. 286 provides an example of prayer that God will hold back too severe a burden. The difference is prayer within the faith and prayer without.

woe, light and darkness',[1] and in both it is possible to find him—
indeed, both are necessary if men are to have an adequate conception of their relationship with him and of their relative status
in the universe:

> Blessed be he in whose hand is dominion:
> he has power over every single thing—
> he who created death and life
> that he might try which of you is best in deed.
> He is the mighty, the forgiving.

There is duality, but no dualism:

> The two seas are not equal:
> the one is pleasant, refreshing, sweet to drink,
> the other salt and bitter,
> yet from each you get food, fresh to eat, and
> ornaments to wear...[2]
> The blind and the seeing are not equal,
> nor are the darkness and the light,
> nor shade and blazing heat.
> The living and the dead are not equal:
> truly God can cause whom he wills to hear,
> but you cannot cause those who are in the grave to hear.[3]

But these inequalities are all a part of God's creation and
cannot escape it. There is no 'opposing principle' which can resist
God or frustrate him. Satan and sundry other demons have much
scope, but not unlimited scope,[4] and in any case the final victory
belongs to God. Moreover, because it is eschatological, the
victory of God is the only one that matters: it is the only one that
puts an end to all further suffering and conflict:

> You who believe seek help with patience and prayer:
> truly God is with the patient.
> And do not say of those who are killed in the cause of God,
> 'They are dead.'
> In fact they are living, but you do not perceive.[5]

---

[1] Isa. 45: 7. The theme of God as the creator of 'weal and woe' is frequently
repeated. Among many examples see especially liii. 44 (43) f. (tears and laughter, life
and death), lvii. 1-6.

[2] I.e. river and sea water are not the same, but they both serve essential purposes
within the whole design of God.

[3] xxxv. 13 (12), 20-1 (21-2). See also xxv. 55 (53).

[4] See p. 105 above of Iblis, and see also xix. 86-9 (83-6).

[5] ii. 148 (153) f. Cf. also ii. 26 (28).

Islam

With such a virile and wide-ranging sense of the victory and omnipotence of God, it is not surprising that there is nothing like the profound analysis of tragedy and defeat in the Quran as there is in Judaism or, even more, in Christianity. Jewish Biblical stories, which are sensitive to the tragic complexities of human nature and of its potentialities for evil, appear quite differently in the Quran. They are used to argue or to illustrate quite different points. Thus the story of Cain and Abel as it appears in the Quran argues important Islamic points, but the emphasis is unmistakably different from that of the version in Genesis:

> Recite to them in truth the story of the two sons of Adam:
> they each offered a sacrifice,
> and it was accepted from the one,
> but not from the other.
> He said, 'I will surely kill you.'
> He replied, 'Truly God accepts an offering only from
>   the god-fearing.
> If you stretch out your hand towards me to kill me,
> it is not for me to stretch out my hand towards you to kill you.
> Truly, I fear God, the Lord of the universe.
> Truly, I desire that you should be laden with my sin and with
>   your sin;
> so you will be among the companions of the fire,
> and that is the reward of those who do dark deeds.'
> Then his soul prompted him to kill his brother,
> so he killed him,
> and he became one of those that are lost.
> Then God sent a raven scratching into the earth
> to show him how he should conceal the shameful body of his
>   brother.
> He said, 'Woe is me! Am I not even able to be like this raven
> and conceal the shameful body of my brother?'
> And he became one of the remorseful.[1]

This passage has powerful and compelling matter for reflection, not least in the *ahimsa*[2] response of Abel, but there is nothing here of the stark question which haunts all men in their behaviour, 'Am I my brother's keeper?'[3] Indeed, in a sense the Quran almost answers, 'I am not': 'Truly I desire that you should be laden with

---

[1] v. 30–4 (27–31). Verse 35 (31) goes on to make a direct application to the laws given to the children of Israel governing murder and legal killing.
[2] See p. 223.　　　　　　　　　　　　　[3] Gen. 4: 9.

my sin and with your sin; so you will be among the companions
of the fire...' Abel retains his innocence and fulfills his obligation in warning his brother of the consequences of his deed. But
then he is quit of him.

Even more disastrously, from the point of view of the Islamic
understanding of Christianity, the crucifixion is almost completely
emptied of significance. Since Jesus was one of God's faithful
servants, and since God always protects his servants and is never
defeated, it follows that those who thought they had put an end to
Jesus on the cross must have been mistaken. Hence arises the
famous passage in iv. 156 (158), which, in a list of ways in which
the Jews have broken faith with God, includes,

> ...their saying, 'Truly, we killed the Messiah, Jesus,
> son of Mary, the apostle of God.
> But they did not kill him and they did not crucify him,
> but its (or 'his') likeness was made to appear to them.
> And truly those who differ (or, 'fall into dispute') about him,
> are in doubt concerning him.
> They have no knowledge of him,
> except the following of conjecture.
> Of a certainty they did not kill him,
> but rather, God raised him to himself,
> and God is mighty, wise.

The passage has been much discussed. It is certainly open to
the interpretation that the intention of the Jews to crucify Jesus
seemed to have been carried out, but in fact the appearance of
death was an illusion since God raised Jesus to himself. In that
case it would be a graphic way of describing the power of God in
the resurrection. But the more usual Muslim interpretation has
been to take the phrase *shubbiha lahum* ('his likeness was made to
appear to them') literally, and to understand that his likeness was
given to another who was crucified in his place. In any case, what
undoubtedly remains true is that there is nowhere in the Quran
anything like the profound analysis of the crucifixion that there is,
for example, in St John's Gospel. There cannot be, since although
the Quran is equally well aware that light is made manifest in
darkness and that victory is often contained in what appears to be
defeat, nevertheless the emphasis is always on the victory. The
Quran indeed tells of prophets killed for their faith, but the case

Islam

of Jesus is different because of the claims made by Christians about him. The Christian understanding of the crucifixion certainly cannot be allowed. As Kenneth Cragg has put it:

A recent Muslim writer on Jesus in the Gospels remarks when he comes to the Garden of Gethsemane 'Here the role of history ends and the role of credal faith begins.' He means that what happens after the arrest, history does not tell: faith, perhaps credulity, take over the story. But history is plain enough. If the Muslim does not follow it, it is because his prejudgement has intervened arbitrarily to break its course and to disallow there what it wills to reject.[1]

This means that although Christianity and Islam belong to the same tradition, they represent a completely different ethos within it. As has often been remarked it is epitomised in the different attitudes of Jesus and Muhammad when facing the possibility of their own defeat and death: Jesus in Gethsemane opted for the way to the cross, Muhammad at the *hijra*[2] opted for the way of success, for the way of co-operating with the power of God, and of becoming God's agent in the elimination of evil and injustice. It is not surprising that contacts between Islam and Christianity have usually been (to borrow a phrase) like 'brontosaurus calling to brontosaurus in the ice-age, with no one to interpret between them.' Despite the efforts of an increasing number of Muslims and Christians to break down this intransigent situation, there is no immediate prospect of any considerable change. The Quran predefines the nature of the relationship between them, and Islamic history has, to a great extent, meant the implementation of the Quran:

> What thing is history, O Self-unaware?
> A fable? Or a legendary tale?
> Nay, 'tis the thing that maketh thee aware
> Of thy true self...
> The bond of Turk and Arab is not ours,
> The link that binds us is no fetter's chain
> Of ancient lineage; our hearts are bound
> To the beloved Prophet of Hejaz,
> And to each other are we joined through him.
> Our common thread is simple loyalty
> To him alone.[3]

[1] *The Call of the Minaret*, p. 295.   [2] See p. 107.
[3] M. Iqbal, *The Mysteries of Selflessness*.

Development

In its attitudes to suffering the Quran represents the Western tradition in a positive and confident form. The facts of suffering are clearly recognised, but in general they are regarded as instrumental in the purposes of God. The two elements of the power of God and the responsibility of men lie side by side, but they are also held together in a sufficient doctrine of creation. How then has this understanding of suffering been expressed in Islamic history?

Theologically, a problem came to the forefront almost at once —almost, one might say, with the rise of theology itself; one of the earliest and most persistent theoretical problems in Islam was the need to reconcile more exactly those two elements of omnipotence and freewill. In that discussion, the question of human responsibility inevitably arose, and with it the question of whether suffering was or was not deserved.

The most immediate response was to stress the control of God in a determinist, even predeterminist, sense. Thus the *hadith*, the traditions of Muhammad's life and teaching, represent an almost entirely determinist position. A. J. Wensinck's judgement, 'Tradition has not preserved a single *hadith* in which *liberum arbitrium* is advocated',[1] has been modified by Montgomery Watt on the grounds that it is far too sweeping, but he accepted that it was 'true in the main.'[2] Applied to suffering, there is a much greater stress in *hadith* on God determining its occurrence and knowing of it in advance:

Truly, each of you is formed in his mother's womb for forty days, then he becomes a clot for the same length of time, then he becomes formed flesh for the same length of time. An angel is sent to him with four

---

[1] 'To all appearance, the main attitude of Islam was in favour of predestination. Tradition has not preserved a single *hadith* in which *liberum arbitrium* is advocated. If this should be due to the extirpation of such traditions at a time when the doctrine of free will had received the stamp of heresy, we may adduce evidence from the works of John of Damascus, who flourished in the middle of the eighth century A.D. and who was well acquainted with Islam. According to him (*Migne*, XCIV, cols. 1589 ff.) the difference regarding predestination and free will is one of the chief points of divergence between Christianity and Islam.' A. J. Wensinck, *The Muslim Creed* (Cambridge, 1932), p. 51.

[2] W. Montgomery Watt, *Free Will and Predestination in Early Islam* (London, 1948), p. 27. In contrast he refers to three Traditions from alBukhari's section of Traditions on *Qadar* (Divine Disposition, see below, p. 124), viii, iv. 2 and 15.

commands, for his sustenance, the length of his life, whether he is to
be wretched or happy, (and his work).[1]

Or again:

From Ubada b. alSamit:...I heard the Apostle of God, peace etc., say:
'God first created the Pen. He said, Write. It asked, What shall I write?
He said, Write the destinies of all things until the coming of the hour.'[2]

But it was not long before a reaction set in against this over-em-
phasis on the omnipotence of God, which in effect was in danger of
reducing men to puppets. The implications of the early determinist
point of view have been effectively summarised by M. S. Seale:

When the Quran says: 'God created you and your works,'[3] it is using
the language of religion to declare God to be the only Lord and
Creator. The statement is innocuous, and could be spiritually helpful if
taken to mean no more than that God was and is a beneficent maker
and provider. But this is in fact a key verse used by determinists to
declare God to be the *only* Creator and only initiator, asserting that he
alone is the one who acts at any time. Man is reduced to the status of a
puppet who is moved about willy-nilly on the stage of human existence.
Their interpretation of this and similar verses borders on perversity
when they go on to assert that even wrong-doing and unbelief are not
in man's hands: God must have willed them or they would not have
occurred. They cast scorn on the idea that God could be disobeyed
against his will.[4]

The reaction against this strong determinism crystallised in the
school of thought known as the Qadariyya,[5] who maintained that

[1] alBukhari, *Qadar* i. 1; see also Muslim, *Qadar* iii. The tradition appears in different
forms, and usually includes the sex of the child as the fourth decree instead of its
work.　　　　　[2] abuDawud, *Sunna* xvi.　　　[3] xxxvii. 94 (96).
[4] M. S. Seale, *Muslim Theology* (London, 1964), p. 16.
[5] The word *qadar* means in the Quran 'command' or 'plan'. M. S. Seale has argued
that neither *qadar* nor *qada'* have a deterministic sense in the Quran, but that they
were subsequently and almost immediately *given* a determinist sense by those who
on other grounds wanted to maintain a determinist position: 'Muslim com-
mentators and modern translators of the Quran, under the influence of the Syriac
pusqono and *helqo*, gave these Quranic terms a connotation which they only came to
have in post-Quranic times. The translators thus introduced destiny where there is
no mention of it in the original text.' (Seale, *op. cit.* p. 38; for the whole discussion
see pp. 38–42.) The Qadariyya maintained that the 'plan' of God included
sufficient scope for the exercise of free will. Not a great deal is known in coherent
form about the Qadariyya, and it may be that 'school of thought' is too formal a
phrase, and that the name refers more loosely to any who defended free will.
Nevertheless, there does appear to have been some organisation (see, e.g.,
Montgomery Watt, *Free Will and Predestination*..., p. 51).

Development

men initiate their own actions and thus determine their destiny. God remains in control, but he delegates actions and thus responsibility to men:

A group of Qadariyya is called Mufawwida.[1] They maintain that they are entrusted to themselves in such a way they have power for everything good through such delegation, without the help or guidance of God.[2]

The Qadariyya were in turn opposed, and indeed bitterly reviled, because it seemed that their emphasis gave men far too great an independence from God. They were called Parsis, or dualists—Persia being the home of Zoroastrianism with its reputed acceptance of a dualistic conflict between good and evil.[3]

In medieval *kalam*[4] the tension between the two attitudes was, to a great extent, resolved through the concept of *kasb* or *iktisab*, 'acquisition'—in contrast to *tafwid* 'delegation'. God created the potentialities, men acquire them and make them their own. The founders of the two great schools of orthodox theology, alAshari and alMaturidi, both formulated a doctrine of acquisition, though with a difference in emphasis:

Acquisition. The disciples of alAshari gave this explanation: God creates in a man the resolve to do something and the deed. The man has no effective but only an acquisitive part in the deed. Acquisition is the connection of human power with the deed, but without causation. There is a proverb, 'More subtle than the acquisition of alAshari.'

AlMaturidi; external acts and inclination, motive, and will are all the work of God; the direction of man's power to one of two possible acts is acquisition and it is not the work of God. When this resolve has come into being God creates the act.[5]

AlAshari had originally been a Mutazilite,[6] but was converted from their views and became one of the greatest orthodox

---

[1] From *tafwid*, 'delegate'.   [2] alMalati, *Tanbih*, p. 133.
[3] On Zoroastrianism and dualism, see pp. 270–4.   [4] Formal theology.
[5] Quoted from A. S. Tritton, *Muslim Theology* (London, 1947), p. 175.
[6] The Mutazilites were a major group in early Islamic theology. They were recognised by five principles: the absolute unity of God, the righteousness of God, that God rewards good and punishes evil, that sinful Muslims are corrupt, and that men must maintain good and resist evil. The Mutazilites held that reason was essential in faith, and they therefore discussed far wider questions in relation to the problem of suffering: they asked, for example, what was the purpose of animal suffering and whether it will receive compensation in the next life (alAshari, *Maqalat alIslamiyin*, i. 240 f.). They also asked how the sufferings of children could be reconciled with the compassionate control of God—and, significantly, the majority response applied the instrumental theory of suffering: they said that the

125

Islam

theologians. In view of the fact that he holds such a revered position, it is significant that he tended to revert to an emphasis on the absolute control of God. AshShahrastani, for example, quoted him as saying:

God is Lord of his creation. He does what he wishes and effects what he desires. If he sent all beings to paradise there would be no injustice, or if he sent them all to Gehenna there would be no wrong. Wrongdoing means disposing of things not one's own, or putting them in the wrong place. But since God is the owner of all things without exception, it is impossible to think of wrong-doing in connection with him, and it is impossible to attribute injustice to him.[1]

However, alAshari modified this apparently extreme position by pointing out that it is possible to allow evil without being its immediate or direct cause. This comes out clearly in his exegesis of the passage in the Quran on Cain and Abel.[2] He pointed out that Abel willed a course of action which resulted in sin—murder—because he refused the alternative, self-defence. He thus willed his own murder which is sinful, and if he had not willed it, it could not have occurred as it did. He made the act possible, but it would be absurd to describe him as the agent of the act of murder.

In these theological debates the problem of suffering was never far from the surface, though it was usually contained within the wider and more general questions of omnipotence and freewill. Thus it played an indirect part in alAshari's 'conversion' from the Mutazilites. In asSubki's version of the story, he entered into debate with his teacher, alJubbai, and asked him:

'What do you say of a believer, an unbeliever and a child?' He said: 'The believer is in heaven, the unbeliever is in Gehenna, and the child is in a place of safety.' He asked, 'What if the child asks God why he did not allow him to grow up so that he might earn a larger reward?' He said, 'God would say that he knew he would be a sinner if he grew up.' AlAshari commented, 'The unbeliever would then ask God why he had not killed him earlier to prevent his sin.'[3]

suffings of children were intended to be an example to older people, and to break down hardness of heart. Such sufferings would certainly receive compensation in the next life, since otherwise the justice of God would be destroyed (*Maqalat*, i. 242).
[1] *Kitab alMilal walNihal* (ed. Cureton, 1846), i, p. 73.   [2] Quoted on p. 120.
[3] *Tabaqat ashShafiiya*, ii. 250. The story appears frequently: see, e.g., W. C. Klein, trs. *Ibana* (New Haven, 1940), pp. 25 ff., W. Spitta, *Zur Geschichte abulHasan alAshari* (Leipzig, 1876), p. 42.

126

Reason, in the shape of the Mutazilites, could give no answer, and alAshari turned away from them and put his reliance on revelation—on what God in his mercy had willed to reveal and make known to his creatures. He became, to use the terms of another religion, a 'Barthian'. Thus the orthodox answer reestablished the supremacy of the Quran, as indeed it was bound to, seeing that the Quran was regarded as the word of God. To some extent the two elements of omnipotence and responsibility were reconciled, but in the final analysis, the attempt to fathom the character of God was bound to end up with the phrase, *bila kaif*— the following is believed about God 'without knowing how.'

Kalam was by no means the totality of Islamic life and thought. For many Muslims suffering did not occur as an academic problem but as a fact of life. But in general no new solutions emerged. The Islamic response to suffering throughout the ages has most usually been 'the Quran writ large in life'. This is not to say that the discussion was not considerably extended: it was, particularly as new instances of suffering occurred which had not been mentioned or discussed in the Quran. Thus it has already been pointed out that *hadith* is largely deterministic, but at the same time it also extended the discussion. For example, the question of animal-suffering occurs, and it is made clear that every effort should be made to alleviate it; or again, brief statements in the Quran are amplified, as in the extension of the Quranic commendation of those who are killed in the cause of God: the question was asked whether that applies only to those who die in battle:

From abu Huraira: the Messenger of God, peace etc., said: 'Whom do you reckon to be a martyr[1] among yourselves?' They said, 'Messenger of God, whoever is killed in the cause of God, he is a martyr.' He said: 'In that case the martyrs of my community would be few: he who is killed in the cause of God is a martyr, he who dies in the cause of God is a martyr, he who dies of the plague is a martyr, he who dies of cholera is a martyr.'[2]

Or to take another example, it has been seen already that the Quran encourages men to accept suffering as a trial and as a chastisement for sins already committed. Several traditions

[1] Lit. 'witness' (*ashShahid*).
[2] Muslim, *Mishkat*, 18. All things faithfully and patiently done bear witness to God.

Islam

developed this further by suggesting that it is often the best men who suffer most, because this shows how close and how dear they are to God. Furthermore, there is repeated emphasis that suffering, especially sickness, patiently endured remits sins.[1]

But although much of the Islamic attitude to suffering has in practice been the implementation of the Quran, it has often produced very distinct expressions of Islam in different areas and different ages. That, in part, is a result of the ability of Islam to adapt itself to the cultures it overruns. Islam remains the controlling factor, but it accommodates and absorbs a great deal of what those cultures hold as valuable. As Hampeté Ba has put it:

Islam, in Africa, has no more colour than water; that is what explains its success. The colours of the earth and stones where it flows, become its colours also.[2]

In the case of suffering, that certainly happened in the rise of Sufism. Sufism is the name given to the great mystical movements in Islam, beginning in about the eighth century A.D.[3] It was often frowned upon and even persecuted by orthodox theology, the most famous martyr being alHallaj, who was executed in 922.[4] Sufism was a diverse phenomenon, but in its early days it was influenced by ascetic and monastic practices outside Islam. That at once introduced the note, which so often belongs to mysticism, of voluntary privation or suffering.[5] The Quran, as has been seen, commends voluntary suffering undertaken in the cause of God, but the asceticism of monks was regarded as being blasphemous. It seemed to imply that creation is evil, and that it must be discarded. It thus came close to dualism, a position which seemed to orthodox Muslims absolutely irreconcilable with the Quranic

[1] See, e.g., alBukhari, *Sahih*, lxxv. 1 and 3.
[2] Quoted C. F. Molla, 'The Rising Tide', *Frontier* (1966/7), p. 261.
[3] Of course, mystics and ascetics existed in Islam from a much earlier period, perhaps from the time of its origin, particularly in the imitation of the simple life of the Prophet. For summaries of the early ascetics, see A. S. Tritton, *Muslim Theology*, pp. 11 ff., and A. J. Arberry, *Sufism* (London, 1950), pp. 31 ff.
[4] Sufis were opposed, because in their quest for direct and immediate relationship with God, they often seemed far from the Quran—though in fact they appealed to the Quran for support, particularly those verses, such as l. 15 (16) or ii. 182 (186), which emphasise the closeness of God to men. On the Quranic connections of Sufism, see M. Valiuddin, *The Quranic Sufism* (Delhi, 1959).
[5] Various etymologies have been suggested for the name 'Sufi'. The most convincing still remains that it was a nickname applied to those who for ascetic reasons wore a wool garment, *suf*. See further p. 129.

128

Development

emphasis on the unity of God. Yet in Sufism asceticism very similar to that of Christian monasticism played a prominent part. AlKalabadhi, summarising some of the meanings of the name Sufi current in his own time (d. *c.* 385/995), wrote:

Some say: 'The Sufis were only named Sufis because of the purity (*safa*) of their hearts and the cleanliness of their acts.'...[1] Others have said: 'They were only called Sufis because their qualities resembled those of the people of the Bench (*suffah*), who lived in the time of God's Prophet (God's blessing and peace be upon him!)' Others have said: 'They were only named Sufis because of their habit of wearing wool (*suf*).'

Those who relate them to the Bench and to wool express the outward aspect of their conditions: for they were people who had left this world, departed from their homes, fled from their companions. They wandered about the land, mortifying the carnal desires, and making naked the body: they took of this world's goods only so much as is indispensable for covering the nakedness and allaying hunger. For departing from their homes they were called 'strangers';...One of them was asked: 'Who is a Sufi?' He replied: 'He who neither possesses nor is possessed.' By this he meant that he is not the slave of desire. Another said: '(The Sufi is) he who possesses nothing, or, if he possesses anything, spends it.' Because of their clothes and manner of dressing they were called Sufis: for they did not put on raiment soft to touch or beautiful to behold, to give delight to the soul; they only clothed themselves in order to hide their nakedness, contenting themselves with rough haircloth and coarse wool... Wool is also the dress of the Prophets[2] and the garb of the Saints.[3]

[1] Various other explanations are then given.

[2] The view that the prophets before Muhammad had been ascetics appeared very early on. alHasan alBasri (d. 110/728), sometimes claimed by later Sufis as the first of their line, wrote: 'Be wary of this world with its cunning traps. It is like a snake which is smooth to handle but deadly in its poison...The world was offered to our Prophet, with all its opportunities and treasures...but he refused it...He tied a stone to his stomach when he was hungry. And as for Moses...it is said in the stories that God revealed to him, "Moses, when you see poverty coming close, say, 'Welcome to the mark of those who are righteous.' But when you see riches coming near, say, 'Behold, a sin whose punishment has been laid up long before.'"' If you wish, you could name as a third example the Lord of the Spirit and the Word, Jesus, for in the things to do with him there is a clear sign. He said, "My daily bread is hunger, the mark set upon me is fear, my clothing is wool, my feet are my transport, the moon by night is my lamp, the sun by day is my fire, my food and sustenance are whatever the earth brings forth for the cattle and beasts of the earth. When night falls I possess nothing, yet there is no one richer than I.'" (*Hilya*, II, pp. 134 ff.)

[3] *Kitab atTaarruf liMadhhab ahl atTasawwuf*, §1 (trs. A. J. Arberry, *The Doctrine of the Sufis*, Cambridge, 1935).

129

Islam

It is not surprising that the mystics frequently appealed to an instrumental view of suffering—not simply because it is implicit in the Quran, but also because it reinforces the practice of asceticism. Thus one of the greatest of the Muslim mystics, JalaludDin Rumi,[1] wrote:

> ...our sense of guilt is evidence of Free-will,
> If we are not free, why this shame? Why this sorrow, and guilty
> confusion and abashment?
> Why do masters chide their pupils? Why do minds change and
> form new resolutions?
> You may argue that the asserter of Free-will ignores God's
> Compulsion, which is hidden like the moon on a cloud;
> But there is a good answer to that; hearken, renounce
> unbelief and cleave to the Faith!
> When you fall ill and suffer pain, your conscience is awakened,
> you are stricken with remorse and pray God to forgive your
> trespasses.
> The foulness of your sin is shown to you, you resolve to come
> back to the right way;
> You promise and vow that henceforth your chosen course of
> action will be obedience.
> Note, then, this principle, O seeker: pain and suffering make
> one aware of God.[2]

Sufism thus represents a major development of Islamic understandings of suffering. Equally spectacular developments in connection with suffering took place in the first major schism of Islam into what came to be known as Sunni and Shia Islam. The causes of this division, which continues to the present day, are extremely complex. Ostensibly, the dispute was over the succession to Muhammad, but although that was certainly a central issue, there were many other causes and motives at work. As regards the succession, the issue, so far as the Shiites were concerned, was simple. In their view, only members of Muhammad's family should be considered as successors. In fact, the first three caliphs ('successors') were not of his immediate family; but the fourth, Ali, was a cousin, who married Muhammad's daughter, Fatima. Thus from the Shiite point of view Ali was the first legitimate caliph, the other three being usurpers. In fact Ali's position was insecure, since the governor of Syria, Muawiyya, sought power

[1] 1207–73.
[2] *Mathnawi* i. 616 (trs. R. A. Nicholson, *Rumi*, London, 1950, pp. 155 f.).

Development

for himself. Ali was driven into increasing obscurity, and was assassinated by a dissatisfied member of a break-away group (the Kharijites),[1] ibn Muljam. Ali's elder son, alHasan, succeeded him, but publicly renounced his claims to be caliph, in favour of Muawiyya and in return for a large pension. He died at Medina of consumption. His brother, alHusain, was a stronger character, and he was urged by supporters of the family of Muhammad to assert his right to be caliph—particularly since Muawiyya had by this time been succeeded by his own, less forceful, son, Yazid. On his way to join his supporters in Iraq, alHusain was intercepted by a patrol, and his small party was surrounded at Karbala. For ten days no attempt was made to capture alHusain, and it seems evident that Yazid hoped for his voluntary surrender. But on 10 Muharram (the first month of the Muslim year) 61 A.H. (10 October, 680), the troops surrounding alHusain and his small party made a move to capture him. His supporters resisted, and the 'police-action' turned into a slaughter. alHusain was killed without offering any resistance. A report to Yazid stated laconically: 'It did not last long; just time to slay a camel or take a nap.'

The implications for the Shiite understanding of suffering are obvious: the three deaths, of Ali, Hasan and Husain, became martyrdoms. The Kharijite connections of ibn Muljam were quietly forgotten, and it was made out that he was a Sunni; the death of Hasan was ascribed to Muawiyya's agency; and the death of Husain spoke for itself. These three martyrdoms released among the Shiites a whole complex of ideas and emotions about suffering and the effect of the death of the innocent. This can be seen in the reverence paid to the martyrs at the places of their martyrdom, but above all it is concentrated in the *ta'ziya*, the re-enactment of the martyrdoms in dramatic form. The passion plays of the Shiites exist in many different forms, but essentially their purpose is to enable the participants, both actors and spectators, to enter into the events as they are re-created, and thus to realise the saving benefits of innocent suffering. In the version, for example, transcribed by Lewis Pelly, Husain approaches the moment of his death with the following reflections:

Husain. Trials, afflictions, and pains, the thicker they fall on man, the better, dear sister, do they prepare him for his journey heavenward.

[1] See n. 2, p. 109.

131

Islam

We rejoice in tribulations, seeing they are but temporary, and yet they work out an eternal and blissful end. Though it is predestined that I should suffer martyrdom in this shameful manner, yet the treasury of everlasting happiness shall be at my disposal as a consequent reward. Thou must think of that, and be no longer sorry...The soil of Karbala is the sure remedy of my inward pains...

Shimar [addressing Husain]. Stretch forth thy feet toward the holy *qibla*, the sacred temple of Makkah.[1] See how my dagger waves over thee! It is time to cut thy throat.

Husain. O Lord, for the merit of me, the dear child of thy Prophet; O Lord, for the sad groaning of my miserable sister; O Lord, for the sake of young Abbas rolling in his blood, even that young brother of mine that was equal to my soul, I pray thee, in the Day of Judgement, forgive, O merciful Lord, the sins of my grandfather's people, and grant me, bountifully, the key of the treasure of intercession. [*Dies.*][2]

At the very end of the play, Jibril (the archangel Gabriel) gives him, through the agency of Muhammad, the key that he had longed for:

Gabriel. Peace be unto thee, O Muhammad the elect, God hath sent thee a message, saying, 'None has suffered the pain and afflictions which Husain has undergone. None has, like him, been obedient in my service. As he has taken no steps save in sincerity in all that he has done, thou must put the key of Paradise in his hand. The privilege of making intercession for sinners is exclusively his. Husain is, by my peculiar grace, the mediator for all.'

Muhammad. Good tidings, O Husain! act thou according to thy will. Behold the fulfilment of God's promise. Permission has proceeded from the Judge, the gracious Creator, that I should give to thy hand this key of intercession. Go thou and deliver from the flames every one who has in his lifetime shed but a single tear for thee, every one who has in any way helped thee, every one who has performed a pilgrimage to thy shrine, or mourned for thee, and every one who has written tragic verses for thee. Bear each and all with thee to Paradise.

Husain. O my friends, be ye relieved from grief, and come along with me to the mansions of the blest. Sorrow has passed away, it is now time for joy and rest; trouble has gone by, it is the hour to be at ease and tranquillity.

The Sinners [entering Paradise]. God be praised! by Husain's grace we are

[1] Mecca.
[2] *The Miracle Play of Hasan and Husain* (London, 1879), II, pp. 86, 102 f.

132

Development

made happy, and by his favour we are delivered from destruction. By Husain's loving-kindness is our path decked with roses and flowers. We were thorns and thistles, but are now made cedars owing to his merciful intercession.[1]

This emphasis on the saving effects of martyrdom (and of the three martyrs in particular) introduced an entirely new note into Islam, and one which has remained to a great extent alien to Sunni Islam.[2] Yet still, in both expressions of Islam, the far more general response to suffering has been to reiterate the Quran and apply it to whatever new circumstances of suffering arise, and that has remained true down to the present day. It is, of course, exactly what would be expected, since in Islam there has been nothing like the re-evaluation of the concepts of inspiration and revelation, or of their connection with history and time, as there has been in Christianity. It is not surprising, therefore, that the same Quranic attitudes reappear as much in the present as in the past. Of this, a particularly good example is M. F. Jamali's *Letters on Islam*,[3] written while he was in prison. A former Prime Minister of Iraq, he was arrested in the 1958 revolution and condemned to death. After eighteen months awaiting execution his sentence was commuted to life imprisonment, and he was released at the end of three years in prison. While he was in prison he wrote a series of letters to his son explaining the importance of Islam; in the Introduction to the published edition of these he wrote:

It was the will of Allah the Sublime that I should remain alive and not be hanged...Having escaped death I now feel as if I had travelled to another world and returned anew to the world of the living. That is why I consider it my duty to inform my brethren (all living human beings) about what I felt while close to the gallows for a year and a half.

There is no doubt that the awe of death dominates every living man when he is exposed to peril, for man, like any living organism, strives by nature to survive. But, in my case, besides the feeling of awe for death, I had another feeling, that of comfort and inner peace resulting from the following factors:

(1) A deep faith (which became deeper after the Revolution of 1958) in Allah the Sublime, and confidence that His Will will prevail over everything.

[1] *Op. cit.* II, pp. 347 f.
[2] Cf. the restraint placed by Muhammad on intercession, for which see my article already referred to, 'Intercession in the Quran...'.   [3] Oxford, 1965.

Islam

No man or group of men can change what Allah has destined. If my time had come to die, then death would have been inevitable. While under sentence of death I felt that the blessing of faith and the spiritual peace which goes with it is the most precious treasure in this life. Poor is the individual who is devoid of faith, for he is no more than a bankrupt man devoid of the greatest blessing which ennobles humanity; for faith gives man the assurance of spiritual survival so that he will not fear death or worry about trivial matters in life.

(2) Peace of conscience which, after faith, is a second blessing in this life...I do not claim that my judgement has always been sound, for perfection belongs to Allah alone, but, whatever I did was motivated by my conscientious convictions. Clear conscience, then, emanating from both the love and fear of Allah, is the second treasure which every man should seek if he desires to have peace and happiness in this life and the next.

(3) Friends.

The sympathy and kindness which was conveyed to me from friends and acquaintances made me feel that the judgment of Mahdawi was no more than a sweeping revolutionary judgment not based on right or sound logic...The truth is that the sympathy of brothers and friends in Iraq and the Arab world and the world at large was the greatest human consolation for me in the dark moments through which I passed. The possession of friends, then, is the third blessing which was mine.

Faith in Allah, clear conscience, and loyal friends, are three blessings which give life meaning and value and provide one with peace and comfort in time of tragedies and calamities. These three blessings make up the message which I carry from the vicinity of the gallows to those who seek a free and happy life, a life which does not terminate with physical death but is renewed hereafter.[1]

Here, indeed, is the Quran 'writ large'—as is the whole exposition of Islam in the *Letters*. It is instructive to compare it with the *Letters and Papers from Prison*, written by Bonhoeffer in a similarly exposed position, knowing the probability of his eventual execution by the Nazis. There are many passages of great similarity, although they were expressed out of a completely different background:

I can still hear the hymns we sang in the morning and evening, with all the voices and instruments. 'Praise to the Lord, the Almighty, the King of creation... Shelter thee under his wings, yea, and gently

[1] *Letters on Islam*, pp. viii f.

Development

sustaineth.' How true it is, and may it ever remain so![1] ...I can't help thinking of that lovely song of Hugo Wolf which we sang a number of times recently:

> Over night come joy and sorrow.
> Both are gone before tomorrow,
> Back to God to let him know
> How you've borne them here below.

It all turns upon that 'how' far more than anything that happens to you from the outside. It allays all the anxieties about the future which so often torment us[2] ...What a blessing it is in such times as this to belong to a large and closely-knit family where each trusts the other and stands by him. I often used to think when pastors were sent to prison that it was easier for those who were unmarried. But I had no idea then what the love of wife and family could mean in the coldness of prison life, and how in just such times of separation the feelings of belonging together through thick and thin is actually intensified.[3]

Faith, clear conscience, and loyal friends; the same three characteristics reappear in those three passages. But at the same time there are even more essential differences:

The key to anything is the 'in him'. All that we rightly expect from God and pray for is to be found in Jesus Christ. The God of Jesus Christ has nothing to do with all that we, in our human way, think he can and ought to do. We must persevere in quiet meditation on the life, sayings, deeds, sufferings and death of Jesus in order to learn what God promises and what he fulfils. One thing is certain: we must always live close to the presence of God, for that is newness of life; and then nothing is impossible for all things are possible with God; no earthly power can touch us without his will, and danger can only drive us closer to him. We can claim nothing for ourselves, and yet we may pray for everything. Our joy is hidden in suffering, our life in death. But all through we are sustained in a wondrous fellowship. To all this God in Jesus has given his Yea and his Amen,[4] and that is the firm ground on which we stand.[5]

In that last sentence lies the essential difference; where Jamali looked for factors giving comfort and inner peace, and found them in God, Bonhoeffer looked for God after the pattern of Christ in the worst extremes of discomfort and distress, and found him in the pangs of a new birth.[6]

[1] *Letters and Papers from Prison* (London, 1963, paperback ed.), pp. 13 f.
[2] *Ibid.* p. 16.   [3] *Ibid.* p. 21.
[4] 2 Cor. 1: 20.   [5] *Letters and Papers*..., p. 130.
[6] See especially *ibid.* p. 130.

135

Islam

But it remains worthy of note that many of their utterances, particularly in devotion and prayer, are indistinguishable, and it is hard to know, when confronted with them out of context, which of the two men might have given expression to them:

Lord God, great misery has come to me, my weight of cares is crushing me, I know not what to do. O God, be merciful and help, give strength to bear what you have sent...Relying on your grace, I place my life completely in your hands: do with me according to your will, and as is good for me. In life or death I am with you, and you with me, my God. Lord, I wait for your salvation, and for your kingdom...The struggle within the self, then, between the forces of good and the forces of evil continues, and blessed is he in whose soul the mercy of God and his guidance dominate.[1]

[1] *Letters and Papers* ..., pp. 170 f.; *Letters on Islam*, p. 73.

4

MARXISM

THE FOUNDATIONS

Marx's connections with the Western religious tradition are evident and self-confessed. Although in many respects he reacted strongly against that tradition and reserved some of his severest criticism for the ways in which it had been expressed, he nevertheless remained firmly attached to it, not least in the fact that many of his early insights arose out of reading and accepting Feuerbach's criticisms of Hegel.[1] Certainly, he pushed on much further than Feuerbach in attempting to eliminate vague idealism from human thought and motivation, but he had no doubt at all about the liberating effect of Feuerbach in the first place. In 1843 Feuerbach published his *Preliminary Theses on the Reform of Philosophy*. Marx commented:

I advise you speculative theologians and philosophers to rid yourselves of the notions and preconceptions of the old speculative philosophy if you want to get to things as they are in reality, i.e. to the truth. And there is no other road to truth and freedom for you than the road through 'the brook of fire' (Feuer-bach). Feuerbach is the *purgatory* of our time.[2]

Thus although Marx reacted strongly against the ways in which the Western religious tradition had come to be expressed, he remained in a dialectical relationship with it, and he by no means escaped its categories of thought. In connection with suffering, this can be seen immediately in the fact that Marx concentrated, not on suffering as a theoretical problem, but on the actual facts and occurrences of suffering as he observed them. Suffering lies at the foundation of Marx's thought because he was first stirred to his vehement and passionate appeals for revolutionary action by his observations of the appalling conditions in which working people lived and died. Uncontrolled industrial development had

[1] See, e.g., R. Tucker, *Philosophy and Myth in Karl Marx*, Cambridge, 1961.
[2] MEGA, 1/1, p. 175 (Tucker, pp. 80 f.).

Marxism

produced conditions of horrifying severity, and throughout *Das Kapital* Marx coldly—but angrily—set down the facts of human suffering. He protested, for example, against the employment of women and children on terms which involved virtual bondage:

Previously, the workman sold his own labour power, which he disposed of nominally as a free agent. Now he sells his wife and child. He has become a slave dealer. The demand for children's labour often resembles in form the inquiries for negro slaves, such as were formerly to be read among the advertisements in American journals. 'My attention', says an English factory inspector, 'was drawn to an advertisement in the local paper of one of the most important manufacturing towns of my district, of which the following is a copy: "Wanted, 12 to 20 young persons, not younger than what can pass for 13 years. Wages, 4 shillings a week. Apply, etc."'[1] The phrase 'what can pass for 13 years' has reference to the fact that, by the Factory Act, children under 13 years may work only 6 hours. A surgeon officially appointed must certify their age. The manufacturer, therefore, asks for children who look as if they were already 13 years old. The decrease, often by leaps and bounds, in the number of children under 13 years employed in factories, a decrease that is shown in an astonishing manner by the English statistics of the last 20 years, was for the most part, according to the evidence of the factory inspectors themselves, the work of the certifying surgeons, who overstated the age of the children agreeably to the capitalist's greed for exploitation and the sordid traffick needs of the parents.[2]

Marx returned frequently to the theme of slavery as, for example, in connection with the Nottingham lace trade, on which he quoted the remarks of Mr Broughton Charlton, in 1860. He stated that,

there was an amount of privation and suffering among that portion of the population connected with the lace trade, unknown in other parts of the kingdom, indeed in the civilised world... Children of nine or ten years are dragged from their squalid beds at two, three or four o'clock in the morning, and compelled to work for a bare subsistence until ten, eleven, or twelve at night, their limbs wearing away, their frames dwindling, their faces whitening, and their humanity absolutely sinking into a stone-like torpor, utterly horrible to contemplate... The system, as the Rev. Montagu Valpy describes it, is one of unmitigated slavery... We declaim against the Virginian and Carolinian cotton-

[1] A. Redgrave, *Reports of Inspectors of Factories* (31 October 1858), pp. 40 f.
[2] *Das Kapital*, iv. 15.3 (Chicago, p. 193).

planters. Is their black market, their lash, and their barter of human flesh more detestable than this slow sacrifice of humanity which takes place in order that veils and collars may be fabricated for the benefit of capitalists?[1]

In *Das Kapital* Marx made much use of available reports and statistics, and to that extent, at least, the claim is justified that he represents the beginning of social science; but there is certainly nothing dispassionate in his use of the figures. Lane Lancaster has commented: 'We misconceive the nature of the communist appeal unless we understand that the moral impetus of that appeal came from the bitter indignation that Marx felt when he contemplated the injustice implied in these figures.'[2]

Marx was not alone in this passionate fury about the conditions of human suffering in nineteenth-century industrial society. Engels shared his anger, and in 1845 he produced a long work entitled *The Condition of the Working Class in England*, which includes his famous description of London:

A town, such as London, where a man may wander for hours together without reaching the beginning of the end, without meeting the slightest hint which could lead to the inference that there is open country within reach, is a strange thing... The hundreds of thousands of all classes and ranks crowding past each other, are they not all human beings with the same qualities and powers, and with the same interest in being happy? And have they not, in the end, to seek happiness in the same way, by the same means? And still they crowd by one another as though they had nothing in common, nothing to do with one another, and their only agreement is the tacit one, that each keep to his own side of the pavement, so as not to delay the opposing streams of the crowd, while it occurs to no man to honour another with so much as a glance. The brutal indifference, the unfeeling isolation of each in his private interest becomes the more repellent and offensive, the more these individuals are crowded together, within a limited space. And, however much one may be aware that this isolation of the individual, this narrow self-seeking is the fundamental principle of our society everywhere, it is nowhere so shamelessly barefaced, so self-conscious as just here in the crowding of the great city. The dissolution of mankind into monads, of which each one has a separate principle and

[1] *Daily Telegraph* (17 January 1860), *Kapital*, iii. 10.3, pp. 117 f. On the lace trade see also iv. 15.8, pp. 229 f.
[2] *Masters of Political Thought, Hegel to Dewey* (London, 1959), p. 165; for a perceptive assessment of the effects of this on Marx's thought, see R. G. Collingwood, *An Autobiography* (Penguin ed., 1944), pp. 102 f.

a separate purpose, the world of atoms, is here carried out to its utmost extreme... What is true of London, is true of Manchester, Birmingham, Leeds, is true of all great towns. Everywhere barbarous indifference, hard egotism on one hand, and nameless misery on the other...[1]

In these passages from Marx and Engels it is possible to feel the old prophetic anger of Israel stirring again.[2] Lenin commented on this work of Engels on England:

Engels was the *first* to say that *not only* was the proletariat a suffering class, but that, in fact, the disgraceful economic condition of the proletariat was driving it irresistibly forward and compelling it to fight for its ultimate emancipation.[3]

The inevitability of class-struggle arises directly out of the conditions which have imposed suffering on the mass of the population. Those conditions can be summarised in a single word—a word that is the key to the Marxist understanding of suffering—'alienation'. The passages just quoted exemplify that word time after time—

'greed for exploitation'; 'slow sacrifice of humanity'; 'the unfeeling isolation of each in his private interest'; 'the dissolution of mankind into monads, of which each one has a separate principle and a separate purpose.'

Marx and Engels observed the realities of life around them in nineteenth-century Europe. They saw that much human suffering —not all, but much human suffering—was caused by the conditions in which people were compelled by society to live: what caused the slums of Manchester and Nottingham and Bradford? What caused the terrible fate of children who worked such hours that they scarcely saw daylight at all? Some might say that it was the uncontrollable pace at which the Industrial Revolution developed; ideals were overtaken by events. But what caused the Industrial Revolution to develop in that uncontrolled way, so that even when the pace slackened, the slums survived and went on increasing? The answer seemed to Marx and Engels quite apparent: the cause lay in the relentless pursuit of profit. In capitalist societies everything is subordinated to the plain necessity of running a profitable business. In their view the root

---

[1] Marx and Engels, *On Britain*, 2nd ed. (Moscow, 1962), pp. 56 f.
[2] See p. 8.
[3] *Marx, Engels, Marxism* (Moscow, 1951), p. 60; 'Frederick Engels', *Collected Works* II, pp. 22 f.

Foundations

cause of much human suffering lies in the conditions necessary
for the perpetuation of capitalist societies—those societies, that is,
in which the overriding motive and condition for survival is
competitiveness. It is essential to a capitalist society that its
members must be in competition with one another.

In such societies, therefore, all the classic conditions for
alienation are present, men alienated from each other in conflicting classes, and alienated in themselves because the conditions
of a free and integrated life are not possible in a capitalist system.
If profit is the condition for success—or indeed for survival itself
—ruthless competition and exploitation will never be eliminated.
Marx sometimes talked of the original sin of capital, but it is
really the original sin of greed:

> The less you eat, drink and buy books; the less you go to the theatre,
> the dance hall, the public house; the less you think, love, theorize, sing,
> paint, fence, etc., the more you *save*—the *greater* becomes your treasure
> which neither moths nor dust will devour—your *capital*. The less you
> *are*, the less you express your own life, the greater is your *alienated* life,
> the more you *have*, the greater is the store of your estranged being...All
> passions and all activity must therefore be submerged in *greed*. The
> worker may only have enough for him to want to live, and may only
> want to live in order to have that.[1]

The pursuit of profit and the passion of greed seemed to Marx
to dominate human activity in capitalist societies. Human liberty
and capacity to take enjoyment from life seemed to be subordinated to that 'inhuman power'.[2] Men have been controlled by it in
building up the societies in which they live; by giving free rein to
it as an overriding motive they have allowed it to reduce their
own lives to bondage. Men cannot develop what Marx called
'free and spiritual energies'; instead they mortify the body and
destroy the spirit in pursuit of profit. And in doing so they trample
not only on themselves but also on each other—hence the evil
and suffering involved in alienation.

Marx, in his analysis of alienation, was not so absurd as to
believe that he had explained the reason for *all* human suffering.
Obviously, much suffering is caused by the accidental potentialities
of the human organism; or, to put it more simply, all men die.

[1] *Economic and Political Manuscripts*, ed. D. J. Struik (trs. M. Milligan, New York, 1964), p. 150.
[2] *Unmenschliche Macht, Econ. MSS.* p. 156 (trs. Milligan).

But what he did believe was that he had penetrated the reason why *much* human suffering does in fact occur; the conditions necessary for the survival of capitalist societies make it inevitable that there will be conflict, strife and ruthless competition.

Political economy starts with the fact of private property, but it does not explain it to us. It expresses in general, abstract formulas the *material* process through which private property actually passes, and these formulas it then takes for *laws*. It does not *comprehend* these laws, i.e. it does not demonstrate how they arise from the very nature of private property. Political economy does not disclose the source of the division between labour and capital, and between capital and land. When, for example, it defines the relationship of wages to profit, it takes the interest of the capitalists to be the ultimate cause, i.e. it takes for granted what it is supposed to explain. Similarly, competition comes in everywhere. It is explained from external circumstances. As to how far these external and apparently accidental circumstances are but the expression of a necessary course of development, political economy teaches us nothing. We have seen how exchange itself appears to it as an accidental fact. The only wheels which political economy sets in motion are *greed* and the war *amongst the greedy—competition*...

Do not let us go back to a fictitious primordial condition as the political economist does, when he tries to explain. Such a primordial condition explains nothing; it merely pushes the question away into a gray nebulous distance. It assumes in the form of a fact, of an event, what the economist is supposed to deduce—namely, the necessary relationship between two things—between, for example, division of labour and exchange. Theology in the same way explains the origin of evil by the fall of man; that is, it assumes as a fact, in historical form, what has to be explained.

We proceed from an economic fact *of the present*.

The worker becomes all the poorer the more wealth he produces, the more his production increases in power and size. The worker becomes an ever cheaper commodity the more commodities he creates. With the *increasing value* of the world of things proceeds in direct proportion the *devaluation* of the world of men. Labour produces not only commodities; it produces itself and the worker as a *commodity*—and this in the same general proportion in which it produces commodities.[1]

The absurdity of this situation is that in an industrial, capitalist society the worker can never own the product of all his energy and labour. It belongs to someone else, who makes a profit out of

---

[1] *Econ. MSS*. pp. 106 f. (trs. Milligan).

it, not for the worker's benefit, but for himself. Thus the worker is alienated from his work, and in most cases he cannot find any satisfaction or fulfilment in it. He is part of a process that does not belong to himself and is not in his control.[1]

The inhuman ways in which men live in association with each other—or rather in veiled and potentially hostile association with each other—are the direct consequence of a situation in which it is necessary to exploit one's fellow-men in order to survive. Again it must be emphasised that Marx did not spin this out of his head as an abstract theory: he observed the facts of suffering in capitalist, industrial societies, and on the basis of his empirical observations he then tried to analyse the causes. It is true that the passages just quoted have the appearance of abstract theorising, but that is largely because they were taken from Marx's earliest writings, when he was trying to give some coherent form to his first insights and observations. What he then went on to do was to translate those tentative thoughts into *economic* theory. This has considerable bearing on the Marxist understanding of suffering, because it means that Marxism is one of the few places in the western tradition (or in the eastern, if it comes to that) where human suffering is reduced to an equation. Putting it as simply as possible, Marx regarded an article's value as being controlled by what he called 'the socially necessary amount of labour'. An article is worth exactly what it costs to produce, and in that cost there are two factors: first, whatever you need of previously produced goods for the article in question, plus the costs of whatever materials are used; this combination Marx called *constant capital*, which may be represented by C; secondly, whatever has to be paid in wages for the production of the article in question, not above the labourer's subsistence, and this he called *variable capital* or V:

The surplus of the total value of the product over the sum of the values of its constituent factors is the surplus of the expanded capital over the capital originally advanced. The means of production on the one hand, labour-power on the other, are merely the different modes of existence which the value of the original capital assumed when from being money it was transformed into the various factors of the labour-process. That part of capital then which is represented by the means of production, by the raw material, auxiliary material and the instruments of labour,

[1] See especially the important passage, *Econ. MSS.* pp. 110 f. (trs. Milligan).

143

does not in the process of production undergo any quantitative alteration of value. I therefore call it the constant part of capital, or more shortly, *constant capital*. On the other hand, that part of capital represented by labour-power does, in the process of production, undergo an alteration of value. It both reproduces the equivalent of its own value, and also produces an excess, a surplus-value, which may itself vary, may be more or less according to circumstances. This part of capital is continually being transformed from a constant into a variable magnitude. I therefore call it the variable part of capital, or shortly, *variable capital*.[1]

In a straightforward society, according to Marx, the value of an article is $C + V$, though in combination they may produce a value over and above the strict costs of production, a surplus-value S. In capitalist societies the factor which distorts value is the disposition of S, since it is the income produced by an act of production which goes to those who have no direct share in the act of production—that is to say, it is the income of the capitalists, which becomes an additional item in the cost of an article:

If we now compare the two processes of producing value and of creating surplus-value, we see that the latter is nothing but the continuation of the former beyond a definite point.[2]

So the equation becomes $C + V + S = $ Value, and it is the addition of S which makes this the equation of alienation—that is to say, the equation of much human suffering. The surplus value has to be found from somewhere. Surplus value is *not* the same as profit; an article must be sold profitably, if only for the purpose of reinvestment for the production of the next article.[3] Surplus value is an additional cost, and it is found, in capitalist society, by reducing labour to a commodity. So, for example, if a man works a 7-hour day, he covers the cost of his own employment in 2 hours, and he covers the cost of the raw materials in 1 hour— $C + V$. For the remaining 4 hours he is producing S, surplus-value, the capitalist income. It is this in-built exploitation which deprives the worker of more than half of his product, and which

---

[1] *Marx on Economics*, ed. R. Freedman (Penguin, 1961), p. 69. (*Kapital* i. 8.)
[2] *Kapital* i. 7.2.
[3] Marxist economists have, in recent years, been making varied attempts to reassess the place of profit as an incentive. For summaries of this, see Prof. E. Liberman, quoted in *The Economist* (26 February 1966), pp. 782, 786. See further, 'Marxist Economic Theory Today', *The World Today* (December 1967), pp. 493–505.

alienates him from the product of his own energy and labour. It simply is not his. It is in this way that much human suffering can be reduced to an equation. The form of the equation was described by Marx in *Kapital* i. 9.1:

> Since on the one hand the value of the variable capital and of the labour-power purchased by that capital are equal, and the value of this labour-power determines the necessary portion of the working day; and since on the other hand the surplus-value is determined by the surplus portion of the working day, it follows that surplus-value bears the same ratio to variable capital as surplus labour does to necessary labour, or in other words, the rate of surplus-value $\frac{s}{v} = \frac{\text{surplus-labour}}{\text{necessary labour}}$.
>
> Both ratios, $\frac{s}{v}$ and $\frac{\text{surplus-labour}}{\text{necessary labour}}$ express the same thing in different ways; in the one case by reference to materialized, incorporated labour, in the other by reference to living, fluent labour.
>
> The rate of surplus-value is therefore an exact expression of the degree of exploitation of labour-power by capital, or of the labourer by the capitalist.[1]

It may perhaps seem tendentious to have written of suffering being reduced to an equation, but it has been done deliberately: that potentially depersonalised way of understanding the causes of human suffering has had its effect on the way in which many Marxists have actually responded to suffering.[2] In what way, then, according to Marx, *should* men respond to the facts and occurrences of suffering?

[1] *Marx on Economics*, p. 83; *Kapital* i. 9.1.

[2] It should perhaps be pointed out that Marx himself did not hold a depersonalised view, because at the foundation of his economic theory he put the belief that the value of a product depends on the human labour embodied in it: 'A commodity is in the first place an object outside us, a thing that by its properties satisfies human wants of some sort or another. The nature of such wants—whether, for instance, they spring from the stomach or from fancy—makes no difference. Neither are we here concerned to know how the object satisfies these wants, whether directly as means of subsistence or indirectly as means of production...Let us now consider the residue of each of these products; it consists of the same unsubstantial reality in each, a mere congelation of homogeneous human labour, of labour-power expended without regard to the mode of its expenditure. All that these things now tell us is, that human labour-power has been expended in their production, that human labour is embodied in them...A use-value or useful article, therefore, has value only because human labour in the abstract has been embodied or materialized in it. How then is the magnitude of this value to be measured? Plainly, by the quantity of the value-creating substance, the labour, contained in the article. The quantity of labour, however, is measured by its duration, and labour-time in its turn finds its standard in weeks, days, and hours.' (*Kapital*, i. 1.1.)

It is in his answer to this question that Marx made his greatest contribution to the world as it now is. Marx knew perfectly well that there were many philanthropists, many devoted clergymen in Victorian England, who were as well-aware as he was that the living and working conditions of the great mass of the population were intolerable; and Marx also knew perfectly well that there were many who were doing a great deal to relieve the sufferings of the poor. But Marx believed that those efforts were completely misguided: certainly they gave relief to people's distress, but only within the conditions which gave rise to that distress in the first place. The conditions remained unchanged. Marx, in contrast, said, 'Change the conditions, and you will then remove the causes of that particular distress.'

Marx made no claim that he could remove *all* distress, or that he could produce a Utopia. For that reason, although he was greatly influenced by them, he reacted strongly against the so-called Utopian socialists in France—those who thought that a perfect or near-perfect world might be produced without struggle. So far as Marx was concerned they were talking, like the idealist philosophers, in abstractions and generalities. No doubt such talk was appropriate in its time, but the unfolding developments of history had left it far behind.[1]

What Marx demanded, in contrast, was that the true socialist should face up to actual facts of suffering, should try scientifically to analyse the causes of that distress, and should then take *action* to remove those causes.

The philosophers have only *interpreted* the world, in various ways; the point, however, is to change it.[2]

What is required is action not words. Marx's response to suffering is to take action to remove the conditions which give rise to it, wherever they can be ascertained. He himself concentrated on social conditions, but he was well-aware that other areas of

---

[1] For Marx's scornful attack on Utopian socialists, see especially *Manifesto*, iii. 3. For Engels' estimate of the Utopian socialists, see particularly 'Socialism: Utopian and Scientific', in *Marx and Engels, Selected Works*, ii (Moscow, 1962), pp. 117-27; *Anti-Dühring*, pp. 364 f. See also Marx, 'Der politische Indifferentismus' in *Marx/Engels Werke*, xviii, §301, and 'Erster Entwurf zum "Bürgerkrieg in Frankreich"', in *Marx/Engels Werke*, xvii, §557: 'The misery of the workers was there, but not yet the conditions for their own movement.'

[2] *Theses on Feuerbach* xi.

research—medical, for example, or technological—were of great importance as well. The people against whom he militated fiercely were those who *thought* about suffering, and who, by producing metaphysical theories about its origin, felt that they had done something about it. Equally misguided, in his view, were those who gave relief within the conditions without changing the conditions themselves, and above all, those who reinforced the *status quo* by consoling sufferers with the spurious suggestion that the inequalities of this life will all be put right in another. This is one of the main reasons why Marx was so angrily suspicious of religion; in practice it obscures the realities of suffering and evil, by giving them a metaphysical explanation (which in fact explains nothing), and by transferring the removal of distress to another world.[1]

The strength of this feeling, that in the face of suffering words are no substitute for action, came out very clearly in an interview with Sartre, republished in *Encounter* in 1964.[2] The interviewer asked Sartre whether he was still as pessimistic as he appeared to be in his early book *La Nausée*:

'The first Sartrean universe was scarcely rose-coloured. Have you stopped seeing the world in that light?'
'No. The universe remains dark. We are animals struck by catastrophe...But I discovered suddenly that alienation, exploitation of man by man, under-nourishment, relegated to the background metaphysical evil which is a luxury. Hunger is an evil full-stop.'

Here exactly is the plea for realism which the theoretical world evades:

'What I lacked was a sense of reality. I have changed since. I have slowly learned to experience reality. I have seen children dying of hunger. Over against a dying child *La Nausée* cannot act as a counter-weight.'

Or as Engels put it with equal brevity:

Communism is not a doctrine, but a movement; it is based not on principles, but on the facts.[3]

---

[1] See, e.g., the opening of the Introduction to *The Critique of Hegel's Philosophy of Right*.
[2] *Encounter* (June 1964), pp. 61 f.
[3] 'Die Kommunisten und Karl Heinzen', in *Marx/Engels Werke*, IV, §321.

Marxism

Exactly the same point was also made in forthright language by Marx:

The criticism of religion ends with the teaching that man is the highest essence for man, hence with the categorical imperative to overthrow all relations in which man is a debased, enslaved, abandoned, despicable essence, relations which cannot be better described than by the cry of a Frenchman when it was planned to introduce a tax on dogs: Poor dogs. They want to treat you as human beings.[1]

Thus the basic principle of the Marxist attitude to suffering is to face the realities of suffering and to change the conditions which give rise to them. But that frequently demands a complete revolution, which may, in itself, involve suffering. It may well, for a start, involve self-sacrifice in order to change conditions which have given rise to injustice or alienation, and that applies as much to those who are bearing the burden of existing suffering (that is, in social terms, the workers, the proletariat) as it does to those who are better off. In fact, of course, it often applies *more* to the workers, because in the nature of the case the initiative in revolution is unlikely to be taken by those who possess private property or who make a profit out of the labours of others. It must, therefore, be left to the workers to make this supreme effort to regain the conditions of their freedom. But that in turn can only be achieved if the proletariat is prepared to annihilate in itself its own petty self-interests: in other words, the individuals who take part in the revolution must be prepared to give up the small stake that most of them have in the capitalist world. Crucial, therefore, in the Marxist expectation of revolution is self-change, not as a prelude to revolution but as the actual process of revolution. As the worker abandons his own subservience to self-interest, his own stake in private property, however small it may be, so the total reappropriation of *all* private property becomes inevitable. When it is complete, alienation, at least in the old sense, will be impossible, because the conditions which give rise to it will have been removed. It is the act of reappropriation which is Marx's definition of the proletarian revolution. It is what he calls 'communist action'. The revolution at once implies not only self-change but self-sacrifice and suffering:

[1] *Critique of Hegel*, Introduction, quoted from *Marx and Engels on Religion* (Moscow, n.d.), p. 50.

Both for the production on a mass scale of this communist consciousness and for the success of the cause itself, the alteration of men on a
mass scale is necessary, an alteration which can only take place in a
practical movement, a *revolution*; this revolution is necessary, therefore,
not only because the *ruling* class cannot be overthrown in any other
way, but also because the class *overthrowing* it can only in a revolution
succeed in ridding itself of all the muck of ages and become fitted to
found society anew.[1]

The question at once arises whether it is realistic to expect that
the worker, already in poverty, will impoverish himself still
further by giving up his stake in the capitalist world. Marx
thought it was: if only the workers could have their eyes opened
to their exploited condition, and to the causes of their condition,
and also to the fact that it is in their power to change their
condition, then they will immediately 'lose their life in order to
find it'. After all, they have nothing to lose but their chains.[2]
Hence Marx came increasingly to stress the importance of opening
men's eyes to the true facts of their condition: in the very process
of waking up and looking around them the revolution has already
begun. So the third Thesis on Feuerbach reads:

The materialist doctrine concerning the changing of circumstances and
education forgets that circumstances are changed by men and that the
educator must himself be educated... The coincidence of the changing
of circumstances and of human activity or self-changing can only be
grasped and rationally understood as revolutionary *practice*.

Again the emphasis is on action not words, and Marx certainly
realised that revolutionary action may involve, not simply the
acceptance of suffering in a good cause, but also the infliction of
suffering. The revolution is achieved, not simply by self-change,
but by actual struggle which is a consequence of that self-change:

The antagonism between the proletariat and the bourgeoisie is a class
struggle, whose most complete expression is a total revolution. Is it
astonishing, moreover, that a society founded on the *opposition* of
classes should end in a brutal *contradiction*, in a hand-to-hand struggle as
its last act? Let us not say that the social movement excludes a political
movement. There is no political movement which is not at the same
time social. It is only in an order of things where there are no longer

[1] Marx and Engels, *The German Ideology* (Moscow, 1962), p. 86.
[2] *Communist Manifesto*, end.

Marxism

classes and class antagonism that *social evolution* will cease to involve *political revolution*. Until then, the last word of social science, on the eve of every general reconstruction of society, will always be:

> 'Le combat ou la mort; la lutte sanguinaire ou le néant.
> C'est ainsi que la question est invinciblement posée.'[1]

Suffering may, therefore, be necessary in order to create the conditions in which some people—not necessarily oneself but perhaps one's successors—can attain true happiness and individuality. It is important to remember that this was the goal of Marx's endeavour, the full and free liberation of human energies in a society that does not rule out that liberation for a large number of people because of the accidents of their birth.[2] Nevertheless, that goal cannot be reached overnight. There is an inevitable *interim* period of struggle and self-sacrifice before the revolution can be finally achieved and the authoritarian control of the State can fade away:

> The question then arises: What changes will the State undergo in communist society? In other words, what social functions will remain there which are analogous to the present functions of the State? The question can only be answered scientifically, and one does not get a flea-hop nearer to the problem by any number of juxtapositions of the word 'people' with the word 'State'. Between capitalist and communist society lies the period of the revolutionary transformation of the one into the other. There corresponds to this also a political transition period in which the State can be nothing but the *revolutionary dictatorship of the proletariat*.[3]

This means that although Marx was not Utopian, and although he recognised that the revolution would produce its own new problems, he was, all the same, working towards an objective in the future, the full implementation of communist action. It was obviously necessary that the revolution should be protected against reaction and hesitation in the *interim* period. There was, therefore, always the possibility that Marxism might be given a ruthless interpretation, and that it would be understood to support the principle that 'the end justifies the means'. And that

---

[1] *Poverty of Philosophy* (MEGA 1/6, pp. 227 f., trs. Bottomore); *Karl Marx: Selected Writings in Sociology*...(Penguin, 1963). The quotation is from George Sand.
[2] Apart from the passages already quoted, see also *Econ. MSS.* p. 135.
[3] *Critique of the Gotha Programme* (trs. Bottomore), p. 261.

principle, as has been apparent in recent history, belongs also to the Marxist understanding of suffering:

> There were many dreamers, some of them geniuses, who thought that it was only necessary to convince the rulers and the governing classes of the injustice of the contemporary social order, and it would then be easy to establish peace and general well-being on earth. They dreamt of a socialism without a struggle. . . The services rendered by Marx and Engels to the working class may be expressed in a few words thus: they taught the working class to know itself and be conscious of itself, and they substituted science for dreams.[1]

Thus did Lenin estimate the achievement of Marx and Engels; and it was to Lenin that the task fell of making the first major development of Marxism, its implementation in practice.

THE DEVELOPMENT

The revolution in Russia in 1917 was, to put it mildly, a precarious business. Not only was the country physically and economically exhausted as a result of the war with Germany, but the revolutionaries themselves were much divided. Trotsky, describing the situation in 1918, wrote:

> One unconsciously asked the question whether the life forces of the exhausted, shattered, despairing land would last until the new regime was in the saddle. Provisions were not at hand. There was no army. The state apparatus was being put together. Conspiracies were festering everywhere.[2]

At the end of 1918 there were at least eighteen separate 'governments' in Russia (or what had been Russia) alongside the Bolshevik government which had moved to Moscow.[3] Those who had been fostering revolutionary feelings were more accustomed to query orders than obey them. The establishing of authority was imperative, if the revolution was to survive, and Lenin quietly and with increasing confidence began to assert

---

[1] V. I. Lenin, 'Frederick Engels', in *Collected Works*, II, p. 20; see also 'Our Programme', in *Collected Works*, IV, pp. 210 f.

[2] Trotsky, *Lenin*, p. 152.

[3] Some of the rival governments took over states which had previously been a part of the Russian empire, such as Finland or Georgia. Generally speaking, Lenin was prepared to let them go, at least for the time being. The problems of establishing central authority were too great to allow concern about the edges of empire.

authority and set up the structures through which it could be implemented. Perhaps most significant was the almost immediate formation of the Special Commission to Resist Counter-revolution and Sabotage, known from its initials as *Cheka*. One of the most hated institutions of the Empire had been the Okhrana, the secret police, yet within two months[1] of the October revolution the Okhrana had been replaced by the Cheka. It is hard to see how the revolution could have survived without the exercise of the strong authority epitomised in the Cheka, even though its full implications did not emerge until the time of Stalin.

It is quite probable that Lenin meant what he said when he replied to criticisms that the Bolshevik regime was too oppressive:

> They reproach us that we use terror, but such terror as practised by the French revolutionaries who guillotined unarmed people we have not resorted to, and I hope we shall not use.[2]

It is certainly true that Lenin, surrounded by intrigue and criticism, made great efforts to carry people with him by persuasion or argument. But the plain fact remained that the enemies of the revolution—and the enemies *within* the revolution—were not paper-enemies:

> The historical truth is that in every profound revolution, the *prolonged, stubborn and desperate* resistance of the exploiters...is the *rule*. Never—except in the sentimental fantasies of the sentimental fool Kautsky—will the exploiters submit to the decision of the exploited majority without trying to make use of their advantages in a last desperate battle or series of battles.[3]

In Russia the uprisings were entirely real, and there was no pretence, either, in the threats and attempts at assassination. On 30 August 1918, a woman attempted to shoot Lenin as he left a factory after making a speech,[4] and although there was no evidence to connect her with any widespread plot, the occasion was made an opportunity to 'sift out' and eliminate a large number of those who *might* have been involved. What Lenin sought to create was 'a party of iron...tempered in the struggle'.[5]

---

[1] The Cheka came into being on 7 December 1917.
[2] Lenin, *Collected Works*, XXVI, p. 261.
[3] Lenin, 'The Proletarian Revolution...', *Collected Works*, XXVIII, pp. 253 f.
[4] He was in fact hit by two bullets, but not seriously wounded.
[5] Lenin, 'Left-Wing Communism—an Infantile Disorder', *Collected Works*, XXXI, p. 44.

Development

The fatal, but inevitable, steps were already being taken. There was no other way in which the revolution could be defended and made secure, and the end would therefore have to justify the means. Lenin had an extremely strong sense of the historical inevitability of revolution—and for that reason he preferred to wait for the natural collapse of capitalism rather than to try to cut the corners or hasten the process by waging wars against capitalist countries—but at the same time he knew that a part of the process of revolution would be *counter-revolution*.[1] It is possible that Lenin was not so directly involved as Trotsky in the physical assertion of authority,[2] but he had no doubts about the necessity for suffering in the cause of revolution. Replying, for example, to the view that workers should have no need to suffer in a workers' state, he said:

'Revolution', he says, 'should be undertaken only if it does not injure too much the situation of the workers.' I ask, is it allowable in the Communist Party to speak in such a way? That is a counter-revolutionary way of speaking...When we established the dictatorship the workers became more hungry, and their standard of living went down. The victory of the workers is impossible without sacrifices, without a temporary worsening of their situation.[3]

The need for a period of strong authority was exactly what Marx had come to articulate in his *Critique of the Gotha Programme* when he talked of the revolutionary dictatorship of the proletariat.[4] Lenin spelt out what that meant:

Every state is a machine for the suppression of one class by another... The most *democratic* bourgeois republic is a machine for the oppression of the proletariat by the bourgeoisie. The dictatorship of the proletariat, the proletarian state, which is a machine for the suppression of *the bourgeoisie by the proletariat*, is not a 'form of government', but a

[1] See particularly 'War and Revolution' in *Collected Works*, XXIV, p. 417, 'The Impending Catastrophe and how to Combat it', *C.W.* xxv, p. 359.
[2] It was usually Trotsky who appeared—literally appeared—on the scene of disturbances to restore order. As a result, in the Kronstadt mutiny of 1921 it was Trotsky, 'the bloody field marshal', who was the object of hatred, not Lenin.
[3] *Collected Works*, XXXI, p. 233. Cf. 'Materials Relating to the Revision of the Party Programme', in *Collected Works*, XIV, p. 470. For the central importance of the acceptance of suffering in Lenin's estimate of revolution, see the passage quoted on p. 154.
[4] See p. 150 above.

Marxism

state of a different type. Suppression is necessary because the bourgeoisie will always furiously resist being expropriated.[1]

The argument that the end justifies the means was carried many stages further by Lenin's successor, Stalin. It is, perhaps, unnecessary to examine his policies in detail. The attitudes underlying them came out very clearly in an interview between Stalin and H. G. Wells, the record of which was published in the *New Statesman*, 27 October 1934. H. G. Wells, who was visiting Moscow at the time, suggested that Communist appeals for revolution and violence were old-fashioned:

Wells: 'I watch Communist propaganda in the West, and it seems to me that in modern conditions this propaganda sounds very old-fashioned, because it is insurrectionary propaganda. Propaganda in favour of the violent overthrow of the social system was all very well when it was directed against tyranny. But under modern conditions, when the system is collapsing anyhow, stress should be laid on efficiency, on competence, on productiveness, and not on insurrection. It seems to me that the insurrectionary note is obsolete. The Communist propaganda in the West is a nuisance to constructive-minded people.'

Stalin: 'Of course the old system is breaking down, decaying. That is true. But it is also true that new efforts are being made by other methods, by every means, to protect, to save this dying system. You draw a wrong conclusion from a correct postulate. You rightly state that the old world is breaking down. But you are wrong in thinking that it is breaking down of its own accord. No: the substitution of one social system for another is a complicated and long revolutionary process. It is not simply a spontaneous process, but a struggle; it is a process connected with the clash of classes. Capitalism is decaying, but it must not be compared simply with a tree which has decayed to such an extent that it must fall to the ground of its own accord. No; revolution, the substitution of one social system for another, has always been a struggle, a painful and a cruel struggle, a life-and-death struggle...

Yes, you are right when you say that the old social system is breaking down; but it is not breaking down of its own accord. Take Fascism for example. Fascism is a reactionary force which is trying to preserve the

[1] 'The Proletarian Revolution...', *Collected Works*, XXVIII, pp. 107 f. Lenin repeatedly underlined the point. It appears in its most familiar form in the brief definition: 'The dictatorship of the proletariat implies a recognition of the necessity to suppress the resistance of the exploiters by force, and the readiness, ability and determination to do it.' *Collected Works*, XXX, p. 340.

old world by means of violence. What will you do with the Fascists?
Argue with them? Try to convince them? But this will have no effect
upon them at all. Communists do not in the least idealize methods of
violence. But they, the Communists, do not want to be taken by
surprise; they cannot count on the old world voluntarily departing from
the stage; they see that the old system is violently defending itself, and
that is why the Communists say to the working class: Answer violence
with violence; do all you can to prevent the old dying order from
crushing you; do not permit it to put manacles on your hands, on the
hands with which you will overthrow the old system. As you see, the
Communists regard the substitution of one social system for another,
not simply as a spontaneous and peaceful process, but as a complicated,
long, and violent process. Communists cannot ignore facts.'[1]

Much of Stalin's interpretation has been disowned as a heretical
or aberrant interpretation of Marx. Isaac Deutscher, for example,
has said that it seems to him 'as incongruous to blame Marx for
Stalin as it would be to blame the Bible and Aristotle for the
dogmas of the medieval Church and the Inquisition'.[2] Yet the fact
remains that Marx was peculiarly open to that particular interpretation, however much he might have disowned it himself. It is
not difficult to give the principles of 'self-change' and 'self-
sacrifice' a ruthless application by saying that the individual is
dispensable, and that it is better for a few to suffer, even inno-
cently to suffer, than for the process of revolution to be deflected.
This is always a real possibility in the Marxist understanding of
suffering. For however far Stalin carried it to excess, he was
supported by many of his associates and theoreticians, taking the
line that the actions, however regrettable they may have been,
were necessary in defence of the revolution. The point is
extremely well exemplified in the case of Karl Radek.

Radek was a journalist of incisive style, who wrote with a
passionate intensity. A volume of his articles was published in
this country in 1935, and in a Preface to that book, A. J. Cummings described Radek as follows:

There is no doubt at all of Radek's passionate devotion to the well-
being of the Soviet Union and the whole Soviet philosophy. His
uncompromising faith in the Revolution; his ruthless contempt for
bourgeois and social-democratic weaklings; his refusal to show mercy

[1] Quoted from *Newstatesmanship*, ed. E. Hyams (London, 1963), pp. 115 f.
[2] *Listener* (3 August 1967), p. 140.

to men and institutions outside the Soviet ideal; and his cheerfully confessed acceptance of the familiar view so convenient to the authors of revolutionary violence, that the end justifies the means—all these are characteristics not difficult to discover in this extraordinarily interesting collection of his writings.[1]

Radek certainly wrote with a savage and merciless intensity. Of the trial of A. A. Fedotov he wrote:

On the stage in the Hall of Columns stood an old man. He was half blind and the bright lights seemed to him like the fiery eyes of millions who wanted to penetrate his secrets. Suddenly he felt that he was naked...He tried to explain something in a whisper, but the loud-speakers bellowed out even the rattle and the shaking in his breast.

An old man, and his speech was incoherent, and in spite of the detestable ulcers of his soul he excited pity. Even the State prosecutor on whose shoulders the republic and the proletariat had placed the heavy duty of knowing no mercy, seemed reluctant to hold the probe with which he had to investigate those old wounds. But he was obliged, like a doctor, to be firm. He was obliged to probe deeply into the living body. He forced his voice to be calm and strong and questioned unmercifully...[2]

Commenting on Bertrand Russell's visit to Russia, Radek underlined the inescapable necessity for strife and suffering in the way of revolution:

Mr. Russell declares that he is an opponent of communism for the same reason that he is a pacifist. Civil war like any war brings appalling distress, and its utility is very problematic. In the struggle, he says, civilisation is destroyed...

In order to conquer it is necessary to establish a powerful authority, and any powerful authority leads to abuses. Mr. Russell has before him two attempts to establish a powerful authority. He has before him the British government and the other allied capitalist states which plunged the world into unprecedented international butchery and now that it is over are continuing the ruin. Mr. Russell has little liking for Lloyd George and still less for Winston Churchill. He has also before him the authority of Soviet Russia making intense efforts to lead the masses out of the distress created by capitalism, an authority making heroic efforts to establish new foundations for human life. But for struggle against the whole capitalist world this authority could never limit

---

[1] K. Radek, *Portraits and Pamphlets* (London, 1935), pp. xviii f.
[2] *Op. cit.* p. 230.

Development

itself to guerrilla warfare. It had to form the Red Army, to create a huge provisioning apparatus, to centralize all its economic life...

But what is Mr. Russell to do as between these two evil governments strengthening their respective authorities? When he gets back from his sentimental journey, now what does he do? After taking a bath he flings himself into an armchair by the fireside—how delightful English open fire-places are! And though he's not a commissar, he does not have to suffer from lack of coal, even if the poor in the East End of London are freezing. And Mr. Russell, having put on his slippers and donned his dressing-gown, reads in the papers about the agony of Europe which has gone on even in his absence...

It is not a very good look-out for the capitalist world facing the stupendous catastrophe of a whole epoch of history, if it cannot produce a better philosophy than that of Mr. Russell, who reminds us of Aesop's fable about an exceeding unphilosophic character—namely, the ass—which, placed midway between a trough of hay and a trough of oats, died of starvation philosophizing which was the better. We offer Mr. Russell our apologies for comparing him with such an unphilosophical creature, and we also present our apologies to that grey-coated toiler for comparing it with such a parasitic creature as a middle-class 'philosopher'.[1]

It is not surprising that Radek had a great admiration for Stalin, whom he described appropriately as 'a sword forged in the fire of revolution'.[2] The qualities which Radek most admired in Stalin were those of consistency in developing Marxist–Leninist theory,[3] and of ruthless determination in putting theory into practice. One of the articles in the book is a panegyric on Stalin. In it Radek wrote of the lessons that Stalin learned in early life:

From that time one of the basic features of Stalin as a leader has been his great rigour in attacking fundamental problems. Once he has felt his way to a real solution of a problem, whatever the difficulties he fights for that solution with the greatest possible persistence...The second fruit...was his great vigilance in regard to opportunism. No matter how well disguised, no matter in what wonderfully coloured robes it hid its miserable body, Stalin was always able to see through to the opportunist reality underneath and fight ruthlessly against it.[4]

---

[1] *Op. cit.* pp. 214–16. It is of interest to note that Mao Tse-tung also criticised Russell for his views that Communist objectives can be attained without violence or bloodshed. See Li Jui, *Mao Tse-tung...* (Peking, 1957), p. 135.

[2] Radek, *op. cit.* p. 12.

[3] Radek particularly emphasised Stalin's development of Lenin's teaching that the unequal development of capitalism formed a proper basis for the building of socialism in a single country. See *op. cit.* pp. 6–12.   [4] *Op. cit.* p. 13.

Nothing could exemplify this more clearly than Radek's support for Stalin's policy of exterminating the Kulaks—a policy which some of the Party resisted:[1]

The Rights croaked that the fight against the kulaks would inevitably lead to a break with the rural population. They held that it was necessary to slow down the pace of industrialization, and give freedom of development to kulak farming and trust that it would 'grow into socialism'...By shaking the iron Leninist discipline of the Party it would have opened wide the gates for kulak counter-revolution...A concession to the pressure of the Rights on this question would have had the same effect as if Lenin in the October days had permitted vacillation on the question of the uprising. And just as Lenin needed to be firmly convinced of the correctness of Marxism in order to have no wavering in adopting the decision for the uprising, Stalin's determination to carry through the Five-Year Plan and to liquidate the kulaks as a class was an expression of his firm conviction that Lenin's theory of the possibility of building socialism in the U.S.S.R. was correct.[2]

Radek produced this panegyric on Stalin in January 1934, but he projected it into the future and wrote it as though it were a speech delivered on the fiftieth anniversary of the October Revolution—as though it were one of the many speeches which were in fact made in 1967. He heads it:

The ninth of a series of lectures...delivered in 1967 at the School of Interplanetary Communications on the fiftieth Anniversary of the October Revolution.[3]

It is, inevitably, a document full of ironies. Radek concluded, for example, by describing the May Day parades of 1932 and 1933 presided over by Stalin and his immediate colleagues, and in his last paragraph he wrote:

And towards that compact, calm, rocky figure of our leader Stalin, rolled the vast waves of love and confidence of the masses marching by, firm in knowledge that there, on Lenin's tomb, stood the General Staff of the coming victorious world revolution.[4]

[1] From the very earliest days the Bolsheviks had been bothered by the problem of the Kulaks and the whole rural peasant population. They seemed to represent an almost monumental resistance to the collectivisation of farms and agriculture.
[2] *Op. cit.* pp. 24 f. Cf. also his treatment of internal Party struggles, pp. 20 f.
[3] *Op. cit.* p. 3.   [4] *Op. cit.* p. 34.

Development

Of all the things that were said about Stalin in the year of the fiftieth Anniversary, 'Love' has not been prominent among them. But the irony of Radek's 'speech' goes even deeper: that same ruthless determination which he so admired in Stalin, and which led to the liquidation of the kulaks and to the ironing out of internal Party dissent, led also to his own extermination. Radek was himself executed after the Trial of the Seventeen in January 1937. Again with unconscious irony A. J. Cummings wrote in the Preface to Radek's book:

Radek is fifty years of age...Radek is still going strong; apparently there is no reason why he should not live to a ripe old age.[1]

There was indeed no reason except for the iron logic of necessity. It was, in Stalin's interpretation of Marxism–Leninism, necessary for the implementation of the Revolution that Radek— and many others—should go. Radek's writings, together with his fate, pierce to the very heart of the Marxist understanding of suffering. For if by some miracle he were allowed one last column in *Pravda*, written from the other side of the grave, it is not in the least inconceivable that he would argue that his death was in fact necessary and justified. Marxism is not, and cannot be, a static, objectifiable dogma; it is an empirical process of revolution, of changing the world, and in that process, at particular stages of its unfolding development, the individual must be subservient. This is not to say—although it often is said—that Marxism must necessarily suppress the individual in the mass. On the contrary, Marx's basic concern was to rescue individuals from the sub-human conditions to which capitalism had subjected them *en masse*. Nevertheless, in the process of that emancipation individual rights and claims may have to be given up—voluntarily, if possible, but by compulsion if not. Yet the aim remains the recovery of true individuality in a free and open society. The question, obviously, raised against Marxism is whether it can achieve that open society, and whether, therefore, it can in practice achieve what it asserts in theory, the true realisation of individuality without coercion or restraint (beyond what is necessary for good order and the preservation of society itself).

In view of all this, one of the most significant developments in contemporary Marxism is the attempt to recover (at least in

[1] *Op. cit.* p. x.

theoretical terms) the worthwhileness of the individual. Far from contradicting Marx, this is a reassertion of his theory—though events in Czechoslovakia show how wide the gap remains between Marxist theory and actual practice. Nevertheless, the *theoretical* interest in the place of the individual exists, as can be seen, for example, in the work of the Polish philosopher, Leopold Kolakowski. His particular concern has been with the moral issues of Marxist philosophy, and with the tendency of historical determinism to undermine the worthwhileness of moral choice. It can lead, all too easily, into moral inertia:

All that is needed to have a belief in the inevitability of progress is to have a parallel belief in the progressive nature of everything that is inevitable.[1]

Just as the sovereignty of God in Islam has sometimes received a fatalistic interpretation—or misinterpretation—so, obviously, historical determinism is open to the interpretation—or misinterpretation—that moral choice is itself determined and therefore of no real effect in the historical process. Despite Plekhanov's early rejection of that view,[2] Kolakowski has still had to defend freewill and moral responsibility, as when he asserts, 'Practical choice is a choice of value, that is to say a moral act for which everybody individually takes personal responsibility...Individual action remains in the sovereign control of the individual.' In an article entitled 'The Narcotic of the Great Demiurge' (a bizarre title, since it alters Marx's dictum on religion, and makes *Marxism* the opiate of the people!) Kolakowski wrote:

No one is released from the moral responsibility of condemning a crime because of his theoretical conviction about the inevitability of the crime. No one is released from the moral duty of struggling against a system, doctrine or social condition which he considers as wretched and inhuman because he regards them as historically inevitable. We protest against such form of moral relativism which assumes that criteria for moral evaluation of human behaviour can be deduced from the knowledge of the secrets of the *Weltgeist*.[3]

Kolakowski has also asked whether Marxism has taken sufficient account of the variations, including the corruptibility, of

---

[1] *Der Mensch ohne Alternative* (1960), p. 119.   [2] See, e.g., *Selected Works*, I, pp. 738–43.
[3] Pt. II of an article entitled 'Responsibility and History' ('Odpowiedzialnść i historia'), *Nowa Kultura* (1957), quoted from H. Skolimowski, 'Creative Developments in Polish Marxism', *Cambridge Review* (4 March 1967), p. 257.

human nature. In 1963 he published what might be described as a Screwtape Letter, an essay entitled 'A Shorthand Report of a Metaphysical Press Conference given by the Devil in Warsaw on December 20th, 1963'.[1]

> The Devil is falling into oblivion. So be it. Sometimes I visit churches to hear the sermons. I listen attentively with perfect composure, trying not to smile. It is becoming more and more unusual for any preacher—even a poor village priest—to mention me: in the pulpit, in the confessional, anywhere. The man is ashamed to do it, simply ashamed. Why, people might say, 'Dear me, a fossil. He still believes in fairy-tales.'

Kolakowski then asks whether it might not be the case that the devil describes something real, the reality of evil, not as a metaphysical concept but as the only appropriate description of certain events or behaviour. He is asking, in other words, whether it is not somewhat naïve to suppose that all you need to do to remove certain instances of suffering is to remove the conditions that give rise to them: it underestimates the human factor.

> You say that evil can be constantly controlled, with no holds barred. That is why you speak of it with such explosive pathos, revealing your apprehension, your desires, your day-dreams, and the confidence you have in the future. All quite wrong gentlemen. There is not a particle of pathos in the word 'evil'. It is neither a horrific word nor a high-flown one: it is absolutely matter-of-fact. It indicates precisely what is at stake, it is as straightforward as the word 'stone' or 'cloud'; it says exactly what it means, unfailingly finds the heart of its reality, goes straight to the mark. Evil *is*.
>
> No, you will have none of this. With manic obstinacy you go on saying: 'It simply happened, that is all. But it might have happened otherwise. Evil is an accident; it happens purely by chance, now here, now there, and it fails to happen if one meets it with enough energy'. . . . You witness cruelty that is of no use to anyone, a pointless, joyless passion to destroy, and it does not occur to you that it might be the Devil at work. All the explanations are available to you, all the names you need to solve the problem in any form it can assume. You have your Freud, who helps you talk about aggression and the death-instinct; your Jaspers, to tell you about the passions of the night in which man tries to wrest the secrets of the deity from it. You have your

---

[1] In *Traktat über die Sterblichkeit der Vernunft, Philosophische Essays* (Stuttgart, 1967), trs. in part in *Herder Corr.* (April 1967), 126 ff.

Nietzsche and the rest of your psychologists, all adept at hiding me. They contrive to say nothing about a matter on the pretext that they are about to unveil it.

But can you really leave things this way, with a veil drawn over them?...Do a little digging and find yourselves.[1] For a moment give words back their original meaning...Dwell on the long lost literal sense of words...A stone is a stone; the Devil is the Devil.

The emphasis on the meaning of words in that passage betrays how much Kolakowski has been influenced by the very strong school of linguistic philosophy which flourished in Poland before the War. This has made it all the easier for the official party line to denounce Kolakowski and to disown him as a Marxist, though he himself continues to claim to be one.[2] As an outsider his direct influence on Marxism has been slight, but his indirect influence has been quite considerable. It can be seen, for example, in the work of Adam Schaff, a Professor of Philosophy at Warsaw University, who is by no means in agreement with Kolakowski, but who also recognises the central importance of the quest for the status of the individual. In recent years he has taken up the question raised by Sartre about the human concern of Marxism. In *Critique de la Raison Dialectique* Sartre suggested that existentialism, by emphasising *human* existence as the truly important fact for the individual, filled a gap in classical Marxism, but that when Marxist theory filled in this gap, then existentialism, in a true Marxist fashion, would wither away:

When Marxist enquiries accept the human dimension (that is the existential plan) as the basis for anthropological knowledge, existentialism will lose its *raison d'être*.[3]

Schaff's response has been to appeal to Marxism to recover the emphasis in Marx's works, particularly in his early works, on exactly this point: the whole purpose of revolution is the emancipation of men at present in bondage.

The division of labour offers us the first example of how, as long as man remains in natural society, that is, as long as a cleavage exists between

---

[1] Cf. Eckhart, *Fragments*, 37: 'To get at the core of God at his greatest, one must first get into the core of himself at his least, for no one can know God who has not first known himself. Go to the depths of the soul...for all that God can do is focused there.' Trs. R. B. Blakney, *Meister Eckhart* (New York, 1941), p. 246.

[2] He was expelled from the United Polish Labour Party in 1966.

[3] See Skolimowski, *op. cit.* p. 258.

the particular and the common interest, as long, therefore, as activity is not voluntarily, but naturally, divided, man's own deed becomes an alien power opposed to him, which enslaves him instead of being controlled by him. For as soon as the distribution of labour comes into being, each man has a particular, exclusive sphere of activity, which is forced upon him and from which he cannot escape. He is a hunter, a fisherman, a shepherd, or a critical critic, and must remain so if he does not want to lose his means of livelihood; while in communist society, where nobody has one exclusive sphere of activity but each can become accomplished in any branch he wishes, society regulates the general production and thus makes it possible for me to do one thing today and another tomorrow, to hunt in the morning, fish in the afternoon, rear cattle in the evening, criticise after dinner, just as I have a mind, without ever becoming hunter, fisherman, shepherd or critic...[1]

In a way, according to Schaff, the early insights which Marx had about relationships and alienation are more important than his extensive writings, which work out the implications in economic theory:

Economics for Marx, although he devoted his entire life to it, is not the end in itself. Marx was and remained the philosopher and sociologist for whom man is the central concern...His researches in economics are not the end in itself...but only a means of achieving the main goal which is the *liberation of man*.[2]

Or as Marx put it himself in a brief but crucial quotation:

The development of the capacities of the *human* species, although at first it takes place at the cost of the majority of human individuals and even classes, in the end breaks through this antagonism and coincides with the development of the individual.[3]

Schaff began a recent essay on 'Marxism and the Philosophy of Man' with the words:

There is nothing new in the statement that the central problem of socialism—of *any* socialism, and Marx's socialism in particular—is the problem of man, with its most essential aspect of creating conditions for man's happiness and full development. For *any* socialism, whether

---

[1] Marx, *The German Ideology* (Moscow, 1962), pp. 44 f.
[2] Skolimowski, *op. cit.* p. 260.
[3] 'Theories of Surplus-Value' in Marx and Engels, *Collected Works*, XXVI, 2 (Russian ed. p. 123).

Marxism

ancient or modern, utopian or scientific, has its roots in rebellion against social evils, poverty and exploitation, slavery and oppression, and all other sources of human suffering. *Any* socialism, even if incapable of saying *what human happiness is*, is always ready to say what its obstacles are, and to imply in its programme ways and means of eliminating the sources of man's misery.[1]

It remains true that there is no individuality apart from society: the 'Robinson Crusoe' option simply does not exist. The insights of Marx into the nature of society thus remain decisively important for Schaff—though here again the connections with the Western religious tradition are particularly obvious:

> For if the individual is always *social*—that is, if he is a product of society which he creates—then he is in a sense dialectically involved in society; and if the problem of his happiness and development is to be interpreted as liberation from unhappiness and barriers to development, then the problem of the individual, and of his happiness and full development, presents itself to us as a *social* problem. What will be of decisive importance is not moral self-improvement, the will of the hero as an arbitrary creator of history or prayers to some supernatural force, but the ability to set in motion those *social* forces which alone are capable of removing the *social* barriers to individual happiness. Thus, although we begin with the *individual*, we are not only aware of his *social* aspects, but we also perceive the *social* way to the implementation of *individual* aims.[2]

The recovery of that emphasis in Marxism indicates the extent to which it is rediscovering its roots in the Western tradition, though it will necessarily remain an expression of the Western tradition greatly developed and transformed. It may, perhaps, seem inevitable that Marxism should remain closely connected with the Western tradition, since Marx himself was so closely involved with it, but in fact some other expressions of Marxism

---

[1] In *Socialist Humanism*, ed. E. Fromm (London, 1967), p. 129. This volume of collected essays by various writers appeared after this book was written, otherwise greater use might have been made of it to illustrate the changing emphasis in contemporary Marxism. In fact, it provides a good example *in English* of the tendencies in Marxism described in this chapter, although the (perhaps inevitable) absence of Chinese contributions makes the volume unbalanced. Any discussion of Marxist developments should, of course, include an account of Marxism in the 'third world'. This is of particular importance in relation to suffering because of the development of the notion of 'the gentle revolution'; but this is not adequately documented, and it is not, therefore, open to the same treatment in this book.

[2] *Op. cit.* pp. 132 f.

Development

are developing *away* from the Western tradition, by attaching Marxist insights to completely different cultures and traditions. Of that, a particularly good example is the expression of Marxism in China, and a survey of Chinese Marxism will thus provide a convenient 'bridge' from the Western to the Eastern tradition.

CHINESE MARXISM

The problems of studying Marxism in any country are great (because of the difficulty of access to sources), but in the case of China they are particularly acute—not least because of the added difficulty of language. The latest official version of the works of Mao Tse-tung has been carefully edited, so that a comparison between the earlier and the later versions sometimes reveals considerable differences.[1] That in itself can be important, because it helps to indicate the directions in which Chinese Marxism has developed, but it demands extremely careful handling and comparison of whatever sources are available. Nevertheless, despite the difficulties of the sources, certain general tendencies have emerged which indicate quite clearly that there have been serious attempts to develop Marxism in China in an independent way. Those attempts can be summarised in the familiar phrase, 'the sinification of Marxism', giving to Marxism a content directly related to the Chinese situation and needs. It is that which may eventually give to Chinese Marxism a greater dynamic in the world, not because of its ideas, which at the moment seem fairly barren, but because of the methods and reasons by which it has reached its distinctive understanding of how Marxism should function in the different cultures and civilisations of the world. This means, in effect, that it is possible in the Chinese estimate for an individual to be consistently Marxist without denying whatever pride he may have in his own native culture and civilisation. Peking, in other words, does not have to be an outpost of Moscow. Separate development is not always congenial to Moscow, but it is close to what Marx and Engels had foreseen:

Chinese socialism may stand in the same relation to the European variety as Chinese philosophy stands to the Hegelian...But when in their imminent flight across Asia our European reactionaries will

---

[1] But note the estimate of J. Ch'en, minimising the importance of the differences, in *Mao and the Chinese Revolution* (Oxford, 1965), p. 14.

ultimately arrive at the Wall of China, at the gates that lead to the stronghold of arch-reaction and arch-conservatism, who knows if they will not find there the inscription:

'République Chinoise:
Liberté, Égalité, Fraternité?'[1]

It remains true, of course, that the application of Marxism in Russia is equally a 'naturalisation' of Marxism, and that the sinification of Marxism is no more surprising than its 'russianisation'. There is no such thing as 'pure' Marxism apart from its practice, since Marxism is action rather than theory.[2] It cannot be detached from the context in which it is, or is to be, expressed, however much it may modify or control that context. Thus the diversification of Marxism is implicitly to be expected, and the sinification of Marxism is a particularly good example of how it happens. In connection with suffering, this means that the Maoist understanding of the place of suffering is likely to be predominantly Marxist, but that it will have received very distinctive interpretations from the process of sinification. In order to isolate those distinctive notes, it is necessary to look briefly at the background and process of sinification, even though some of the material may not, at first sight, seem directly relevant to the estimate of suffering. In fact, it *is* relevant, in so far as it helps to explain the distinctive features of the Chinese interpretation.

The sinification of Marxism appears now, in the official versions of published works, as having been a consistent and intentional policy almost from the start—that is, from the early 1920s when Communism was beginning to become coherent and organised in China. In fact what appears to have happened is that in the early years the sinification process was largely accidental and non-theoretical. Only later and gradually, for various empirical reasons, did it become a self-conscious policy. What it has produced in effect is an amalgamation of indigenous ideas and Marxist ideas, rather than a preconceived or creative fusion of them. This is not to say that no theoretical attempts have been made to hold the two together. In 1937, for example, when the Chinese Communists were in fact already negotiating for an

---

[1] Marx and Engels, 'First International Review', in *On Colonialism* (Moscow, 1962), p. 14.   [2] See pp. 146–8 above.

alliance with the 'bourgeois reactionaries', the Kuomintang, because of the increasing Japanese threat, Mao Tse-tung said in an interview:

> The Communists absolutely do not tie their viewpoint to the interests of a single class at a single time, but are most passionately concerned with the fate of the Chinese nation, and moreover with its fate throughout all eternity... The Chinese Communists are internationalists; they are in favour of the world Communist movement. But at the same time they are patriots who defend their native land... This patriotism and internationalism are by no means in conflict, for only China's independence and liberation will make it possible to participate in the world Communist movement.[1]

The increasingly separate development of Chinese Marxism has laid it open to the charge of being 'revisionist'. The charge has been rejected with scorn and has been applied instead by the Chinese to such people as 'the rural peasant', Khrushchev. Yet the Chinese have been sufficiently aware of the changes made for great stress to be laid on Mao Tse-tung's role as a Marxist theoretician, as though sinification was a logical next step in theoretical development. That may well be so, but in true Marxist fashion the practical factors, which made the process of sinification virtually inevitable, came first. Six main factors stand out as having been of particular importance in this process, and together they have a considerable bearing on the estimate of suffering in Chinese Marxism.

The first, and perhaps most obvious, is the immense pride that most Chinese have in their history and civilisation. To give just one example, taken from the reformer Liang Ch'i Ch'ao:

> The greatest country in the greatest of the five continents of the world, —which is it? My country, the Middle State, the Flowery Land! The people who number one-third of the human race,—who are they? My countrymen of the Middle State, the Flowery Land! Annals which extend back without a break for over four thousand years,—of what country are these? Of my country, the Middle State, the Flowery Land! My country contains four hundred million inhabitants, who all speak what is fundamentally the same language, and use the same

[1] Mao Tse-tung's interview with Agnes Smedley, quoted in S. Schram, *Mao Tse-tung* (London, 1966). It remains, of course, important to note the order of priorities; compare also Stalin's attitude to those who advised compromise with the Kulaks in order that the collectivisation of the rural areas could more peacefully be put into effect.

167

script: of no other country can this be said. Her ancient books hand down events which have occurred during more than thirty centuries past: of no other country can this be said... My country, the Middle State, the Flowery Land, stands proudly alone, having survived, in one unbroken line, ever increasing in size and brilliancy, down to the present day. And in the future it will spread into a myriad branches, to be fused together in one furnace. Ah, beautiful is my country! Ah, great are my countrymen! Now, ere inditing a rough outline of their story, I must purify myself thrice with perfume and the bath; then, looking up to heaven, with many prostrations, thank God that I was born in this lovely land, as one of the sons of this great people.[1]

This was the atmosphere in which Mao grew up, and Mao undoubtedly shared this pride in China's long and ancient civilisation.[2] It comes out particularly in his poetry, where he draws constantly on the history and mythology of China in order to illustrate and explain the present. For example, the reference made above[3] to Khrushchev as a 'rural peasant' comes from an allusion in a poem written by Mao in July 1959. At that time Khrushchev was applying forms of pressure to bring China into line and to retain the central authority of Moscow. Mao, with his background of pride in China's far more ancient civilisation, had no intention of giving way gracefully—and indeed from this point on he increasingly articulated his view that China had justifiably succeeded Russia as the centre of the world revolution. He wrote this poem to indicate his independence:

> Beside the Great River the Mountain rises majestically.
> I ascend four hundred spirals to reach its verdant peaks.
> Coldly I scan the world towards the sea;
> Warmly the wind carries rain to this riverside.
> Clouds hang above the nine tributaries flowing by the tower
>   of the Yellow Crane,
> Waves race down to the ancient state of Wu, giving off white
>   mist.
> Who knows where Magistrate T'ao has gone?
> Could he be farming in the Land of Peach Blossoms?[4]

[1] 'My Country', quoted from H. A. Giles, *Gems of Chinese Literature (Prose)* (London, 1923), pp. 277 f. Liang Ch'i Ch'ao was born in 1872, and was an ardent republican reformer.
[2] For the nationalistic pride of his ethics teacher, Yang Ch'ang-chi, see S. Schram, *op. cit.* pp. 39 f. [3] See p. 167.
[4] Trs. J. Ch'en, *Mao and the Chinese Revolution*, p. 351. Cf. the translation of S. Schram in *Problems of Communism* (1964), p. 40 (reprd. in *Mao Tse-tung*, p. 299).

Chinese Marxism

Like much of Mao's poetry, it reads at first glance like a series of clues from *The Times*' crossword, but in fact it is fairly easy to unravel: Magistrate T'ao is the poet T'ao Ch'ien, who died in A.D. 427. At one point he became a magistrate, though his period of office only lasted eighty days, since a more senior official came to visit him expecting to be received with all due honour and obsequiousness on the part of T'ao. T'ao, however, refused, with the words, 'How can I bow down before an insignificant rural peasant for five handfuls of rice?' The reference to the Peach-blossom Spring is in fact to a work of that name by T'ao, in which T'ao described his idea of Utopia. Mao, who was, at the time of writing this poem, urging what he called 'the Great Leap Forward', was obviously asking whether perhaps, in People's China, they were about to put into practice what for T'ao had been only a dream. Like a true Marxist, Mao is concerned with realities, not with idealistic dreams.

Sometimes Mao's pride in China's past has been expressed in more direct ways. For example, amongst the most valued of Mao's writings are his directives on the conduct of guerrilla warfare, to which in practice Mao has had to devote a great deal of his life, first against the Government of Chiang Kai-shek, then in co-operation with the Kuomintang against the Japanese, and then finally (after the War) against the Kuomintang once more, in order to establish the People's Republic. In those directives Mao is often extremely close to classical writers who wrote in great detail about the conduct of war.[1] There is a clear dependence on the tactics proposed by the ancient writers. Or again, Mao has sometimes expressed pride in the past in more romantic ways, as, when a boy, he read 'blood-and-thunder' stories of moments in China's history—stories which had a very considerable effect on him, perhaps akin to being brought up on the *Boys' Own Paper* of the same period.

National pride, therefore, represents a basic factor in the sinification of Marxism. The second factor arises directly out of the first, namely, the fact that the China in which Mao and his contemporaries grew up directly *contradicted* their instinctive pride. At the beginning of the twentieth century, the condition of China was desperate. It was internally divided and restless, its forms of government were antiquated and autocratic. Confucian

[1] See, e.g., the translation by S. B. Griffith of *Sun Wu: The Art of War* (Oxford, 1963).

ethics did much to reinforce the *status quo*, not least because they took an autocratic system of government for granted and did not discuss what ought to be done if any figures in the hierarchy—ruler, father, instructor or husband—abused their position. The situation was made worse in China by the fact that until the end of the nineteenth century the European powers wanted the benefits of free trading without the responsibilities of actual imperial power. They therefore sought to maintain peaceful conditions, not by direct control, but by pressure applied to the Manchu dynasty. Lord Curzon described Britain's policy in China as 'a riddle unsoluble by man',[1] but in fact the clue to its solution was simple: the policy of Britain and of other trading nations was to take whatever steps seemed necessary or desirable to maintain conditions in which trade and expansion would be possible. But such a policy of informal imperialism was certainly 'unsoluble' and unfathomable to the Chinese, and the Manchu dynasty found itself making repeated concessions to foreigners from whom it received virtually no assistance in maintaining order or in coping with increasing discontents in society.[2]

This meant that China was in a thoroughly confused state. It was also in a thoroughly revolutionary state, although on the whole the discontent was not co-ordinated. There were, for example, many secret societies, but no universal agreement between them on intentions or method. Thus Huang Hsing announced in December 1903, at the founding of his Society for the Revival of China—in itself a very typical name:

Speaking of the province of Hunan, there has been a rapid growth of revolutionary ideas among the army and the students...Furthermore, members of the secret societies who also harbour anti-Manchu ideas have long spread and consolidated their influence, but they dare not start first; they are like a bomb full of gunpowder ready to blow up, waiting for us to light the fuse.[3]

The reference to the province of Hunan is of interest, because Hunan is Mao's home province. According to several writers, the

[1] J. D. Hargreaves, 'Lord Salisbury, British Isolation and the Yangtze Valley, June–September, 1900', *B.I.H.R.* xxx (1957), p. 70.
[2] The celebrated 'gunboat' was an important factor in dispersing riots in China, particularly in the 1890s, but the gunboat was more often used as a pressure on the Manchu dynasty to take action itself: it would be used if the Manchu dynasty did not itself restore order and suppress the riots.
[3] Quoted from S. Schram, *Mao Tse-tung*, p. 30.

Chinese Marxism

Hunanese are traditionally famous for two things, eating red peppers and being extremely vigorous in everything they do. There is a proverb to the effect that 'China will only be conquered when all the Hunanese are dead.'[1] The proverbial vigour of the Hunanese was by no means always directed into revolutionary channels. It was the Hunanese, for example, who had supported the Manchu dynasty and been instrumental in breaking the Taiping rebellion. Perhaps the real truth is that Hunan was one of the main centres of intense Chinese patriotism, and that their energies were given to any cause which seemed to serve that purpose. Thus the Hunanese were prominent in the anti-missionary riots of the 1890s, since missionaries seemed to be the first incursion of foreigners and of Western domination. It was in Hunan that an anti-Christian agreement was drawn up in 1891 threatening any who uttered 'the Jesus pig squeak', and promising support for the Emperor if he ran into trouble with any Western powers as a result of pursuing that policy. The Hunanese, therefore, at the end of the nineteenth century appear as supporters of the traditional order. But when confidence was lost in the ability of that order to revive China, it is not surprising that their energies became revolutionary. It is thus appropriate that it was a man from Hunan who eventually lit the fuse of which Huang Hsing had spoken.

If those two factors are put together—intense pride in China, plus extreme dissatisfaction with the weak and chaotic state of China at the beginning of the twentieth century—the third factor which has produced the distinctive form of Chinese Marxism becomes at once apparent: a multiplicity of experiments going on in this century to revive China's greatness and destiny. It is this factor which is perhaps the real key to Mao's character.

At the beginning of this century there was an almost feverish search going on for ways in which China could once again be made great and independent. One obvious way was the way of revolution, but the many occasions on which revolution flared up were uncoordinated and the anger was dissipated. Mao identified himself with a revolutionary movement in 1911, but what positive action there was had all taken place before he could join in. No doubt Mao learnt from those early experiences the truth of Chateaubriand's observation, that he who only half-makes a revolution digs his own grave.

[1] *Op. cit.* p. 29.

Marxism

Another way for the revival of China was that of reformation. The movement for reformation was in fact quite strong in China, and it was eventually taken up by the young emperor, Tsai-t'ien, who instituted a wide programme of reform in 1898. It was largely a response to the way in which the Sino-Japanese war had exposed the frightening weakness of China, and the reforms were essentially Chinese in form and origin—that is to say, they arose directly out of Confucianism. Yet even so the forces of reaction moved swiftly and effectively. The Emperor was imprisoned, and his advisers were either imprisoned with him or executed. The way of reformation by co-operation was closed.

Another related possibility was reformation involving a complete break with the traditional past. This particularly proposed that China should learn and absorb from the West. In 1911, for example, there first appeared a review which was to have a tremendous influence in the building up of the early Communist Party. It was called *Youth, Ch'ing-nien*, but it was soon renamed *New Youth, Hsin Ch'ing-nien*. One of the founders of this journal was Ch'en Tu-hsiu, who was later to become the first general secretary of the Chinese Communist Party. He thought that what he called 'Mr Democracy' and 'Mr Science' would be the salvation of China: what he advocated was the establishment of a secular state on Western lines which would remove the dead hand of Chinese traditionalism. Understandably, he was attacked by guardians of the traditional order, on the grounds that he was disintegrating the old values, and in 1919 he replied to those charges in *New Youth*:

We, of course, admit that we are guilty of all the charges. But if we go to the root of the matter, we are not really guilty. We committed the alleged crimes entirely for the sake of supporting two gentlemen: Mr Democracy and Mr Science. In order to support Mr Democracy, we must oppose Confucianism, the code of rituals, chastity, traditional ethics, and politics; in order to support Mr Science, we must oppose traditional arts and crafts and traditional religion; in order to support Mr Democracy and Mr Science, we cannot but oppose the so-called national heritage and old-style literature.[1]

Ch'en's analysis of the situation has been effectively summarised by Benjamin Schwartz:

[1] *New Youth* vi. 1 (1919), p. 10 (trs. Kwok).

Buddhism and Taoism by their radically antiworldly bias had paralyzed the energies of China for centuries. Confucianism on its side had suffocated the individual in a network of family and social obligations. The final result had been passivity, stagnation, and impotence in the face of the challenge from the West. The answer to this challenge could be found only in the West itself... What did the West have that the East lacks? The answer in China's view was quite clear—democracy and science...

Ch'en's conception of the role of science reminds one above all of the Russian nihilists. Like them, he saw in science a weapon, a corrosive to be used in dissolving traditional society... By stridently proclaiming on the authority of science that the material atom was the only ultimate reality, he was quickly able to dispose of the whole basis of the 'religion of rites', as well as of the mysticism of Buddhism and Taoism.[1]

There were many others who shared the same view, that the only hope for China lay in taking over from the West those things that had made the West prosperous and powerful. Wu Chih-hui, for example, also believed in Mr Science and Mr Democracy, and he hoped that to the family would be added another member, Miss Morality. The sixth article of his materialist creed reads:

I believe that morality is a product of culture; there is no such thing as low morals in a high culture. The early religions of the major civilizations were all illusory talk; they bred a philosophy of death. China has already received Mr Science (dealing with knowledge), and Mr Democracy (dealing with public morality). What we now lack is a private morality, which we shall call Miss Morality.[2]

Wu Chih-hui had earlier stated his belief that education would eventually 'bring men to their senses' and remove the need for autocratic authority:

The name 'anarchy' is the most auspicious in the world... The state without government uses seventy or eighty per cent of its total effort to educate people in scientific knowledge, and twenty or thirty per cent to teach the ethics of nongovernment. Anarchy, the result, is inevitable and will have ethics but not laws. One will have 'from each

[1] B. I. Schwartz, *Chinese Communism and the Rise of Mao* (Harvard, 1951), pp. 9 f. See also, 'Biographical Sketch, Ch'en Tu-hsiu, Pre-Communist Phase', *Papers on China*, II (Harvard, 1948).

[2] D. W. Y. Kwok, *Scientism in Chinese Thought, 1900–1950* (Yale, 1965), p. 57, summarising *A New Belief* from *Wu Chih-hui hsien-sheng wen ts'un* (Shanghai, 1925).

according to his ability', but cannot call that 'duty'; one will have 'to each according to his need', but cannot call that 'right'. When everyone voluntarily places himself in the realm of truth and equity, and when the state of the ruler and the ruled exists no longer, then we will have true anarchy.[1]

In that passage the Marxist influence is obvious, since the quotation is direct,[2] but neither Ch'en Tu-hsiu nor Wu Chih-hui began as specific, overt Marxists. Ch'en Tu-hsiu eventually became a member of the Communist Party in China, but it was as a result of a diverse quest for emancipation. The same could be said of Mao Tse-tung. He grew up in the midst of the many conflicting proposals about what might be done in China, and in a sense his early life, as a student and as a worker, can be summarised as a search for the method of national recovery. A book that influenced him greatly in early days was F. Paulsen's *A System of Ethics*. Mao's copy is annotated copiously in his own hand, and one of the notes (written at some time about the beginning of the 1914–18 War) reads:

In the past I worried over the coming destruction of our country, but now I know that fear was unnecessary. I have no doubt that the political system, the characteristics of our people, and the society will change; what I am not yet clear on are the ways in which the changes can be successfully brought about. I incline to believe that a (complete) reconstruction is needed. Let destruction play the role of a mother in giving birth to a new country.[3]

This means that Mao Tse-tung did not begin as a doctrinaire socialist, nor was he a socialist because someone had brought him up to be one. He came to Marxism as a result of an exploratory process, trying almost everything before he found in Marxism the most effective method of recovery. There is, of course, a tendency in official works to read his Marxism back into the earliest possible period, but the truth is that he really cast around. He fluctuated between being a student and a worker, he joined the police, signed on in a soap-factory, decided to become a classical lawyer, but before he could begin he had enrolled in a commercial school. After a month of that he decided he would be

[1] 'T'an we-cheng-fu chih hsien-t'ien' (*Collected Works*, VIII, pp. 49, 51), trs. Kwok.
[2] The direct quotations are from the end of the *Communist Manifesto*.
[3] Trs. Ts'ai Yuan-p'ei, quoted from Ch'en, *Mao and the Chinese Revolution*, p. 44.

better at educating himself, and he read a large number of translations of Western liberal writers, such as Rousseau, Mill, Spencer and Darwin. Then he went back to school. This diffuse background is extremely important, because it means that by the time Mao became Marxist he knew fairly clearly why he disliked the alternatives, and it also means that he became a Marxist, not on rigid, doctrinaire, grounds, but on an experimental basis. Mao has described the process himself, which has an obvious relevance to his understanding of the place of suffering:

In his book *'Left-Wing' Communism: an Infantile Disorder* written in 1920, Lenin described the quest of the Russians for revolutionary theory.[1] Only after several decades of hardship and suffering did the Russians find Marxism. Many things in China were the same as, or similar to, those in Russia before the October Revolution. There was the same feudal oppression. There was similar economic and cultural backwardness. Both countries were backward, China even more so. In both countries alike, for the sake of national regeneration progressives braved hard and bitter struggles in their quest for revolutionary truth...

Imperialist aggression shattered the fond dreams of the Chinese about learning from the West. It was very odd—why were the teachers always committing aggression against their pupil?... Doubts arose, increased and deepened. World War I shook the whole globe. The Russians made the October Revolution and created the world's first socialist state. Under the leadership of Lenin and Stalin, the revolutionary energy of the great proletariat and labouring people of Russia, hitherto latent and unseen by foreigners, suddenly erupted like a volcano, and the Chinese and all mankind began to see the Russians in a new light. Then, and only then, did the Chinese enter an entirely new era in their thinking and their life. They found Marxism-Leninism, the universally applicable truth, and the face of China began to change.[2]

[1] The Peking ed. adds as a footnote the following quotation from Lenin: 'For nearly half a century—approximately from the forties to the nineties—advanced thinkers in Russia, under the oppression of an unparalleled, savage and reactionary tsardom, eagerly sought for the correct revolutionary theory and followed each and every 'last word' in Europe and America in this sphere with astonishing diligence and thoroughness. Russia achieved Marxism, the only correct revolutionary theory, veritably through *suffering* (italics in text), by half a century of unprecedented torment and sacrifice, of unprecedented revolutionary heroism, incredible energy, devoted searching, study, testing in practice, disappointment, verification and comparison with European experience.'
[2] *Selected Works of Mao Tse-tung* (Peking, 1961), IV, pp. 412 f.

Marxism

It is not surprising, in view of his experimental quest for a method of national recovery, that Mao's Marxism has remained experimental and empirical, and that it has not been dominated by Russian theory. Mao has remained attracted by the possibility of containing genuine disagreement and argument within the overriding progress of the Revolution. It issued in the famous 'Hundred Flowers Campaign' in 1956, which was based on the view that, since the central truths of Marxism must prevail, limited argument and discussion can be allowed, particularly in the arts and sciences.[1] In fact, criticisms were soon being addressed, not to the details, but to the underlying principles of Marxism, and the Campaign was closed down in the spring of 1957. Yet the fact remains that Mao's Marxism has always had something of 'the hundred flowers' about it.[2] It has been empirical rather than doctrinaire.

His Marxism first began to crystallise in 1919, particularly in the 'May the Fourth' movement, which was a violent demonstration against the pro-Japanese policies of Chang Ching-yao and the Peking Government. It was out of that highly nationalistic background that Mao wrote some articles for a student review, of which he was the editor, *The Hsiang River Review*. The first article appeared on 21 July, and it was entitled, 'The Great Union of the Popular Masses'. In the articles there is nothing very distinctively Marxist: he welcomed the victory of the Russian revolution, and he encouraged the progress of the army of the red flag throughout the world. But what he was really saluting was the courage of anyone prepared to stand up and fight. Yet although there is little in the article that is specifically Marxist, one factor of extreme importance does emerge: the stress on the people as a revolutionary force.

Mao's teacher, Li Ta-chao, had developed ideas about the moral superiority of the peasants living their simple and uncomplicated lives, but Mao was not interested in sentimentalising. What he suddenly grasped was the potentiality of the people as a whole to

[1] See, 'On the Correct Handling of Contradictions among the People', *Quotations from Chairman Mao Tse-tung* (Peking, 1966), pp. 302 f. (the 'Little Red Book').
[2] See especially Lu Ting-yi, 'Let a Hundred Flowers Bloom, Let a Hundred Schools of Thought Contend' (26 May 1956), text in *Communist China (1955-9)*; *Policy Documents with Analysis* (Harvard, 1962), pp. 151–63; Mao Tse-tung, 'On the Correct Handling of Contradictions among the People' (27 February 1957), text in *Communist China...*, pp. 273–94 (ed. R. R. Bowie and J. K. Fairbank).

become an irresistible force—provided that they were organised and directed to a common end. It was this grasp of the irresistible potentiality of the people as a revolutionary force which made Mao's development into Marxism inevitable. Furthermore, it has dominated his thought down to the present time. It was the reason, for example, why he called the atom-bomb 'a paper tiger'. Compared with the force of a united people, who know what they want and are determined to get it, the atom-bomb is nothing.[1] Hence arose his famous statement, published in the *Peking Review*:[2]

I debated this question [i.e. atomic warfare] with a foreign statesman [Nehru]. He believed that if an atomic war was fought, the whole of mankind would be annihilated. I said that if the worst came to the worst and half of mankind died, the other half would remain while imperialism would be razed to the ground and the whole world would become socialist; in a number of years there would be 2,700 million people again and in fact more. We Chinese have not yet completed our construction and we desire peace. However, if imperialism insists on fighting a war, we will have no alternative but to make up our minds and fight to the finish before going ahead with our construction. If every day you are afraid of war and war eventually comes, what will you do then?[3]

Such attitudes are, of course, directly relevant to Mao's estimate of the place and necessity for suffering. In the West those statements were usually interpreted as a sign of aggressive and almost insane belligerence. But really they are nothing of the kind. They arise out of a genuine belief—a belief which has been verified time after time in Mao's experience—that the people constitute such a powerful force that any obstacle, however great, can be swept aside, even the atom-bomb. It might justifiably be said that Mao is the one man in the world who has learnt to stop worrying and live with the bomb.

The stress on the revolutionary force of the people has been a consistent note of Mao's thought and writing throughout his life. To give just one example, at the beginning of 1927 Mao set out on a close tour of inspection of rural areas in central China. He

---

[1] See *Selected Works*, IV, pp. 21 f.
[2] 6 September 1963, p. 10.
[3] Quoted from S. Schram, *Mao Tse-tung*, p. 291.

wrote up his observations with an intense fervour in a report that has become a classic of Chinese Marxism:

> In a very short time, in China's central, southern and northern provinces, several hundred million peasants will rise like a mighty storm, like a hurricane, a force so swift and violent that no power, however great, will be able to hold it back. They will smash all the trammels that bind them and rush forward along the road to liberation. They will sweep all the imperialists, warlords, corrupt officials, local tyrants and evil gentry into their graves...A revolution is not a dinner party, or writing an essay, or painting a picture, or doing embroidery; it cannot be so refined, so leisurely and gentle, so temperate, kind, courteous, restrained and magnanimous. A revolution is an insurrection, an act of violence by which one class overthrows another.[1]

This is the central and formative fact in Mao's expression of Marxism; it might even be called the overriding fact. Mao, looking back on the 4 May movement on its twentieth anniversary in 1939, wrote that it was more important to realise and to implement this conception of the power of the people than to give an intellectual assent to Marxist theory:

> In the Chinese democratic revolutionary movement, it was the intellectuals who were the first to awaken...But the intellectuals will accomplish nothing if they fail to integrate themselves with the workers and peasants. In the final analysis, the dividing line between revolutionary intellectuals and non-revolutionary or counter-revolutionary intellectuals is whether or not they are willing to integrate themselves with the workers and peasants and actually do so. Ultimately it is this alone, and not professions of faith in the Three People's Principles or in Marxism, that distinguishes one from the other. A true revolutionary must be one who is willing to integrate himself with the workers and peasants and actually does so.[2]

The genuine innovation in that passage, and one of the distinctive contributions that Mao has made to Marxism, is that he stressed the revolutionary force not just of the people but of the *rural* people in particular.[3] Classical Marxism had originated in the

---

[1] 'Report on an Investigation of the Peasant Movement in Hunan' (March 1927), *Selected Works*, I, pp. 23–4, 28.
[2] *Selected Works*, II, p. 238.
[3] See particularly 'Analysis of the Classes in Chinese Society' (1926), *Selected Works*, I, pp. 13–19.

conditions produced by capitalism in the huge industrial cities of Europe. Lenin wrote:

The very conditions of their lives make the workers capable of struggle and impel them to struggle. Capital collects the workers in great masses in big cities, uniting them, teaching them to act in unison. At every step the workers come face to face with their main enemy—the capitalist class. In combat with this enemy the worker becomes a *socialist*, comes to realise the necessity of a complete reconstruction of the whole of society, the complete abolition of all poverty and all oppression. Becoming socialists, the workers fight with self-abnegating courage against everything that stands in their path, first and foremost the tsarist regime and the feudal landlords.[1]

But Mao very rapidly learned that the Chinese situation was entirely different. To attempt to initiate the revolution in the large cities, like Shanghai, made it all too easy for opponents to isolate the revolutionaries and eliminate them—as happened in Chiang Kai-shek's ruthless suppression of the Shanghai workers in April 1927. The real 'suffering class' was that of the peasants. Marxist theory, therefore, had to be applied in China to a different set of circumstances. The theory held, but it had to be applied experimentally.

Thus the third factor which has given Chinese Marxism its distinctive form is the fact that Mao and his associates came into Marxism in an exploratory way. As a result, the Chinese expression of Marxism has continued to be experimental and empirical. That at once leads on to the fourth factor: the situation of China as a nation in this century has meant that Mao's Marxism was *compelled* to be empirical rather than doctrinaire. For most of this century the survival of China itself has been at issue, particularly under pressure and eventually invasion from Japan. The Communists, therefore, have repeatedly had to collaborate with their natural enemies, in particular with the Kuomintang, the government of Chiang Kai-shek. Always the Revolution remained

[1] 'The Lessons of the Revolution', *Collected Works*, XVI, pp. 301 f. It should perhaps be pointed out that the experimental development of Marxism in other times and other countries is exactly what Lenin had predicted: 'Absolutely hostile to all abstract formulas and to all doctrinaire recipes...under no circumstances does Marxism confine itself to the forms of struggle possible and in existence at the given moment only, recognising as it does that new forms of struggle...inevitably arise as the given social situation changes.' 'Guerilla Warfare', *C.W.* XI, p. 213; see also 'Report...22 October 1918', *C.W.* XXVIII, p. 123; 'Eighth Congress of the R.C.P. (B).', *C.W.* XXIX, p. 174; 'The Third International and its Place in History', *C.W.* XXIX, p. 308.

Marxism

the objective, and the actual terms of collaboration kept in mind the eventual revolutionary situation, yet still the sheer facts of existence demanded that external threats should be removed first, before the internal revolution could take place. This means that Mao has always been prepared to take things as they come, not as the Party line from Moscow might have dictated. There was even a brief period at the end of the war when he regarded America as a potential ally, an attitude not unlike that of David joining the Philistines![1]

A fifth and more precise factor that has led to China's individual position has been the ambivalence, and indeed the ambiguity, of China's relation with Russia. Quite naturally, after the Revolution, Russia regarded herself as the centre and supreme authority in all Communist matters. This meant that the Russian leaders, particularly Stalin, expected to be consulted on all questions of policy and decision, either directly or through local experts. In theory there is much to be said for giving the World Revolution some central authority and control, but in practice the Chinese rapidly discovered that Russian advice was solely for the benefit of the Russians, and for the extension and protection of Russian interests. The Russians scarcely seemed able to take the Chinese Communists seriously. For quite a long period Stalin thought it would be most effective to work through Chiang Kai-shek and the Kuomintang, since both he and Trotsky thought that the Kuomintang was the genuinely peasant party— though Trotsky in fact urged a far more revolutionary policy. In 1926 and 1927 Stalin instructed the Communists to call off the peasant revolution and to join the Kuomintang, in order to push it further to the left.[2] Even as late as 1949, the year of the

[1] 1 Sam. chs. 27–9.

[2] The policy collapsed in ruins when, in 1927, Chiang Kai-shek felt strong enough to dispense with the support of the Communists, and turned his army against them. See C. Brandt, *Stalin's Failure in China, 1924–1927* (Harvard, 1958), chs. 4 and 5. Stalin's uncertain policy was a direct continuation of Lenin's. Lenin had regarded Sun Yat-sen as the most hopeful Chinese leader, and in 1920, in a famous debate with the Indian Communist M. N. Roy, he maintained against Roy that the proletariat in such countries as China was too weak and too ill-organised to carry out an effective revolution. He therefore argued that it was better to work through reformers, such as Sun Yat-sen, until the time came when Communism could take over. Stalin's attempt to apply this point of view to Chiang Kai-shek was even more spectacularly unsuccessful. See especially J. P. Haithcox, 'The Roy–Lenin Debate on Colonial Policy: a New Interpretation', *Journal of Asian Studies*, XXIII (1963), pp. 93–101.

Chinese Marxism

Communist victory in China, the Soviet Ambassador was the only foreign diplomat to go with the Nationalist Government to Canton when it surrendered Nanking to the Communists. Always Russian interests predominated: in the Friendship Treaty of 1950, Russia retained its hold on Port Arthur and Dairen until 1952—and even then did not return them. Furthermore Mao was compelled to recognise the independence of the Mongolian People's Republic and its inclusion in the Russian sphere of influence.

The incoherence and the self-centredness of Russian advice was quite apparent to the Chinese, and although for a long time no formal break was made, the Chinese inevitably viewed the Russians with a somewhat detached disillusionment. That disillusionment formed a vital factor in the sinification of Marxism.

A sixth factor of almost equal importance is the fact that much of the traditional Chinese background lends itself to a Marxist expression. It must be emphasised (in view of the extravagant claims sometimes made) that this is more in general than specific terms. It is not that Mao has made a profound analysis of Chinese philosophy, which he has then applied to Marxism. It is, rather, a part of the general atmosphere in which his ideas and his search for a method of national recovery have taken shape. Of particular importance in this respect is the well-known 'secularity' of much Chinese thought. Generally speaking, Confucianism, for example, is not so much a religion as a way of life. It is an educational system which enables those who devote themselves to it to order and regulate their lives in society. It is quite possible for a man to be a Confucian in the world, and in his religious or spiritual life to be a Taoist or a Buddhist—rather like, as A. C. Graham has put it, 'being a Christian and a gentleman'.[1] Again, that must not be exaggerated. Confucianism has often been developed into varied and fervently held forms of religious expression. But the fact remains that Confucianism has a sufficiently 'this-wordly' concern for Confucian writers repeatedly, throughout the centuries, to have made specific attacks on religion: to give just one example, Hu Yin in the twelfth century wrote:

Man is a living thing; the Buddhists speak not of life but of death. Human affairs are all visible; the Buddhists speak not of the manifest

---

[1] *The Concise Encyclopaedia of Living Faiths*, p. 365.

but of the hidden. . . What man cannot avoid is the conduct of ordinary life; the Buddhists speak not of the ordinary but of the marvellous. What determines how we should behave in ordinary life is moral principle; the Buddhists speak not of moral principle but of the illusoriness of sense-perception. It is to what follows birth and precedes death that we should devote our minds; the Buddhists speak not of this life but of past and future lives. Seeing and hearing, thought and discussion, are real evidence; the Buddhists do not treat them as real, but speak of what the ear and eye cannot attain, thought and discussion cannot reach.[1]

Obviously this kind of attitude is very congenial to the rise of Marxism, but Mao's Marxism did not arise directly out of it, nor does it depend upon it. Indeed, from a Marxist point of view Confucian society, however 'secular' it may theoretically be, is exactly the sort of society which demands revolution.

Thus the so-called 'secular tradition' in China had a general rather than a particular effect on the development of Marxism. In particular points of application and in the ways in which it was actually given expression in society it was severely criticised, and it was not directly related to Marxist theory. Nevertheless, parts of that tradition have supplied useful material with which to reinforce Marxism. It has already been pointed out that many Chinese at the turn of the century combined pride in China's heritage with shame at what China had become. The same is true of Mao Tse-tung: he often quotes from Chinese classics, but pours scorn on the sort of society which grew out of them. Sometimes, of course, his dependence on the classical tradition is direct, as in his use of the ancient manuals of guerrilla warfare,[2] but in general he quotes classical writers, not analytically, but in order to illustrate or to reinforce. What becomes creative in Mao's Marxism is not the analysis of one particular writer or another; it is rather the conjunction of a Chinese secular tendency with a Western tradition that has developed in a similar direction. The Chinese 'secular tradition' is not systematic or organised. It has received many different forms of expression in the long centuries of Chinese history. As a result, Mao has never been bound to any particular elements within it. It is important, for the understanding of Chinese Marxism, to bear this in mind, because Chinese thought has often been oversimplified in the West, even to the

---

[1] Quoted *op. cit.* pp. 365f.   [2] See p. 169.

extent of being virtually identified with Confucianism. Confucius was simply one teacher among many—although it is true that he was quite rapidly recognised as one of the greatest, and his Analects are one of the Four Books, the four basic classics of Chinese education and philosophy before the revolution. But Confucius is by no means the totality of Chinese thought—and in fact Mao has more in common with one of the earliest *opponents* of Confucius, Mo Tzu, than he does with Confucius himself, as can be seen from Mo Tzu's criticisms of Confucianism: Mo Tzu concentrated his attack on Confucianism under four headings,[1] which in his view were sufficient to bring the world to ruin:

Mo Tzu said to Ch'eng Tzu:[2] In the teaching of the Confucianists there are four principles sufficient to ruin the empire: The Confucianists hold heaven is unintelligent and the ghosts are inanimate. Heaven and spirits are displeased. This is sufficient to ruin the world. Again they (practise) elaborate funerals and extended mourning. They use several inner and outer coffins, and many pieces of shrouds. The funeral procession looks like house moving. Crying and weeping last three years...This is sufficient to ruin the world. And they play the string instruments and dance and sing and practise songs and music. This is sufficient to ruin the empire. And, finally, they suppose there is fate and that poverty or wealth, old age or untimely death, order or chaos, security or danger, are all predetermined and cannot be altered. Applying this belief, those in authority, of course, will not attend to government and those below will not attend to work. Again this is sufficient to ruin the world.[3]

Mao, one imagines, would not have much sympathy with the first of those criticisms, either way. But the last three certainly represent his attitudes. Furthermore, Mo Tzu held that the state, if it is to produce the greatest good for the greatest number, must be totalitarian and the authority of its ruler absolute:

Mo Tzu said: As we look back to the time when there was yet no ruler, it seems the custom was 'everybody in the world according to his own standard'. Accordingly each man had his own standard, ten men had ten different standards, a hundred men had a hundred different standards—the more people the more standards...Knowing the cause of the confusion to be in the absence of a ruler who could unify the standards in the world, (Heaven) chose the virtuous, sagacious and wise in the world and crowned him emperor, charging him with the

[1] His whole attack on Confucianism was more detailed and will be found in *Mo Tzu* 39.   [2] A Confucianist.   [3] *Mo Tzu* 48 (trs. Mei).

Marxism

duty of unifying the wills in the empire... It was really to procure benefits and eliminate adversities for the people, and to enrich the poor and increase the few, and to bring safety where there is danger and to restore order where there is confusion—it was for this that the political leaders were appointed.[1]

If one takes out of that paragraph the assertion that such a State is established by the will of God and the spirits, and substitutes for it the belief that it is established by the will and conscious action of a united people, it becomes an almost perfect summary of what Mao has tried to achieve.[2] Yet it is not so much that Mao has derived direct inspiration from Mo Tzu, as that their views on some points coincide. According to *Huai-nan-tzu* 20, 'the disciples of Mo Tzu were 180 in number, all of whom he could order to enter fire or tread on sword blades, and whom even death would not cause to turn on their heels'. Again, one can easily imagine the zest with which Mao would accept that as an appropriate description of himself and his followers, particularly in the pre-war period and at the time of the Long March.[3] But it is not the case that Mao has made an exegetical study of Mo Tzu in order to derive ideas from him. It is rather that Mo Tzu is one of many who represent this tradition of thought in China, concentrating on the ways in which society can best be established in an orderly manner. It is the whole tradition, rather than particular elements within it, which has been so profoundly influential.

The six factors outlined above have been instrumental in bringing about the sinification of Marxism. Yet however much that process may have been compelled on the Chinese as a result of the situation in which they found themselves, it is in itself a profound and deeply-held concept. Certainly Mao Tse-tung has no doubt about its validity and necessity.[4] It explains why, if it

[1] *Mo Tzu* 12 (trs. Mei).
[2] Even Mo Tzu's most distinctive contribution, universal love, represents in broadest outline something like the communist vision: see especially *Mo Tzu*, 'Universal Love', iii. 16, trs. B. Watson, *Mo Tzu: Basic Writings* (Columbia, 1963), pp. 39 f. The difference between the two 'visions' lies, of course, in the methods thought to be necessary to realise them: see *Mo Tzu: Basic Writings*, p. 44.
[3] See p. 187.
[4] See especially *Selected Works*, II, pp. 196, 209 f. The original form of the speech (before revision for *Selected Works*) will be found in B. Compton, *Mao's China, Party Reform Documents, 1942–1944* (Seattle, 1952), pp. 61–3. In its original form Mao was even more scathing about those who dabble in *Das Kapital* without knowing anything of their own country. See also the reference back to that speech in *Selected Works*, II, p. 65.

continues on its present course, the eventual appeal of Chinese Marxism in the world is likely to be functional rather than dogmatic. It suggests a method whereby pride in nationality can be combined with *effective* national recovery. Marxism can be brought into a positive relation with indigenous cultures—it does not depend on having a Hegel in the family. Yet there is no doubt that Marxism is the stronger partner, and that traditional institutions may be put under severe pressure if they conflict with the revolutionary process.[1] The dominance of Marxism can be seen quite clearly in Mao Tse-tung's understanding of the place of suffering, even though the sinified form of Marxism introduces its own distinctive notes.

Like Marx, Mao began with actual occurrences of suffering. In general terms this is exactly what led him into Marxism, as has been seen: the condition of China initiated his search for a method of national recovery. It was not simply that the country was run down, but that the existing order was appallingly harsh in its treatment of particular individuals. Thus although Mao was intensely proud of China's history and traditions, he was also acutely aware of its defects, and of the way in which the traditional order caused intolerable suffering for certain individuals. To take a particular example, in 1919 a young girl committed suicide in Changsha because her parents had forced her to marry against her will. Mao wrote and published nine articles in thirteen days in the local daily newspaper, attacking the restraints placed on individual freedom by the old traditional society.

The same concern has remained constant throughout Mao's life. In 1931 he wrote: 'Under feudal domination the oppression and suffering borne by women is far greater than that of man.' In the 1950 Marriage Law he implemented his dislike of that injustice. The preamble to it begins:

Abolish the feudal system of marriage characterized by the use of constraint, respect for men but contempt for women, and indifference to the interests of sons and daughters. Put into practice a system of marriage characterized by freedom to marry for men and women, one

---

[1] All the same, it must be remembered that much of the ambivalence of China's domestic policies is a result of the attempt to hold the two sides together. It is even more true of China's foreign policies, where the endeavour not to get involved is at least in part a consequence of a genuine wish to allow the revolutionary movements in different countries to find their own level—though, naturally, pragmatic motives are not unimportant.

Marxism

wife to one husband, equal rights for men and women, and the protection of the legal rights of wives, sons, and daughters.[1]

In more general terms, Mao early on analysed the causes which gave rise to domination and suffering in traditional China:

A man in China is usually subjected to the domination of three systems of authority: (1) the state system (political authority)...; (2) the class system (clan authority), ranging from the central ancestral temple and its branch temples down to the head of the household; and (3) the supernatural system (religious authority), ranging from the King of Hell down to the town and village gods belonging to the nether world, and from the Emperor of Heaven down to all the various gods and spirits belonging to the celestial world. As for women, in addition to being dominated by these three systems of authority, they are also dominated by the men (the authority of the husband). These four authorities—political, clan, religious and masculine—are the embodiment of the whole feudal-patriarchal system and ideology, and are the four thick ropes binding the Chinese people, particularly the peasants ... Our present task is to lead the peasants to put their greatest efforts into the political struggle, so that the landlords' authority is entirely overthrown. The economic struggle should follow immediately, so that the land problem and the other economic problems of the poor peasants may be fundamentally solved. As for the clan system, superstition, and inequality between men and women, their abolition will follow as a natural consequence of victory in the political and economic struggles.[2]

The attitude of positive response to conditions which have given rise to suffering characterises many of Mao's political actions, particularly in Agrarian Reform. The effect, not unnaturally, has been to rock the boat. Land and family lie close to the inmost heart of any society, and to try to transform them in a generation is likely to prove traumatic. But in true Marxist fashion that *is* where Mao begins, tackling the actual facts and occurrences of suffering, with a determination to change the conditions which give rise to them. And Mao is equally true to the Marxist position in being prepared to accept the possible necessity for violence and suffering in the process of change or revolution. One example has already been seen in his acceptance of an atomic war as being

[1] Quoted from S. Schram, *Mao Tse-tung*, p. 260.
[2] *Hunan Report, Selected Works*, I, pp. 44, 46.

a way of clearing the stage for socialism.[1] There are many other examples in Mao's own life. He and his followers have been prepared to accept quite extraordinary degrees of privation and suffering in the cause of revolution—above all, in the Long March, one of the truly great epics of human endurance. It took place at the end of 1934 and beginning of 1935, and it refers to the escape of the encircled remnants of the Communist First Front Army from central China to the north. Jerome Ch'en has effectively summarised the character of the Long March:

One may compare the Long March with Hannibal's journey across the Alps and say smugly that the Chinese did better, or with Napoleon's retreat from Moscow and say coldly that the Chinese did worse. But it must be admitted that man has never seen the equal of it before or since. It was a flight in panic; yet it was also an epic of human endurance. In 370 days, from 16 October 1934 to 20 October 1935 the First Front Army under Mao Tse-tung walked on and on, to cover a distance of 6,000 miles.[2]

In what must be one of the greatest understatements of modern history, Mao, when asked in 1946 what his intentions had been at the start of the Long March, replied, 'If you mean, did we have any *exact plans*, the answer is that we had none.'

But exactly that same willingness to accept personal suffering has also meant a willingness to accept that *others* may have to suffer. And that, too, is essentially Marxist. There is no doubt at all of Mao's clear determination to establish and implement the revolution, and it may certainly involve ruthlessness in destroying counter-revolutionaries. One of the earliest examples is the so-called Futien Incident in 1930, when the leaders of the Twentieth Red Army tried to displace Mao Tse-tung and change his agrarian policies. Mao's response was to eliminate, in one way or another, something like 3,000 officers and men of the Red Army.

The same determination can be seen even earlier, in the *Hunan Report*:

When the local tyrants and evil gentry were at the height of their power, they literally slaughtered peasants without batting an eyelid... Such was the cruelty of the local tyrants and evil gentry in former days, such was the White terror they created in the countryside, and now that the peasants have risen and shot a few and created just a little reign

[1] See p. 177.   [2] *Mao and the Chinese Revolution*, p. 185.

187

of terror in suppressing the counter-revolutionaries, is there any reason for saying they should not do so?[1]

Exactly the same pragmatic, but implicitly Marxist, acceptance of suffering as necessary to implement and safeguard the revolution can be seen repeatedly in Chinese actions and policies. In the case of Tibet, for example, the suppression of the 1959 rebellion was justified in the People's Congress on the grounds that the elimination of reactionaries resisting the reincorporation of Tibet into China was necessary, and that in any case the previous sufferings of the people of Tibet were far greater. The removal of that crushing burden was a sufficient justification in itself:

The existing social system in Tibet is an extremely backward system of serfdom. The degree of cruelty which characterized the exploitation, oppression and persecution of the labouring people by the serf-owners can hardly be paralleled in any other part of the world...With the putting down of the rebellion started by the reactionary elements of the former Tibet Local Government who are opposed to reform, conditions have been provided for the smooth realization of the desire for reform of the broad mass of the Tibetan people. The Preparatory Committee for the Tibetan Autonomous Region should, in accordance with the Constitution, the aspirations of the broad mass of the Tibetan people and the social, economic and cultural characteristics of Tibet, carry out democratic reforms in Tibet step by step so as to free the Tibetan people from suffering and lay the foundations for the building of a prosperous, socialist new Tibet.[2]

It is exactly the point from which Marx began: only convulsive and violent action can overthrow the vested interests of traditional societies. The end is so self-evidently desirable that the means scarcely need to be justified. The way in which Stalin developed that view has already been seen. In the case of Mao, it must be said that an attempt has been made to keep this instrumental view of suffering within limits: it is limited by what is strictly

---

[1] *Selected Works*, 1, pp. 38 f. It is worth noting that the original version of the Report had 'one or two' instead of 'a few'. Either Mao became less mild or else the Report was brought into line with the extent of what actually happened; but even then 'a few' is a considerable understatement.

[2] *Peking Review* (29 April 1959), pp. 6 f., quoted in *Documents on China's Relations with South and South-East Asia, 1949–1962* (Bombay, 1964), p. 444. Chinese actions were, of course, further justified in the Chinese view on the grounds that Tibet was originally a part of China, and that it should be referred to as 'the Tibet region of China'.

necessary for the defence of the revolution. Commenting on the Futien Incident, Stuart Schram has written:

It is undoubtedly excessive to claim, as have some extremely hostile critics, that the whole affair was simply a plot by Mao to kill off his rivals. But the affair does provide the first large-scale example of his ruthlessness. It also brought into action the very efficient secret police which he had created. There is no evidence whatever that Mao Tse-tung, like so many who have wielded absolute power (Stalin in particular), takes pleasure in killing or torturing the enemies of the revolution or of his own power. But he has never hesitated to employ violence whenever he believed it necessary. One must immediately add that he would never have survived otherwise.[1]

Perhaps that may sound like special pleading, but in fact there is much to support it. One example has already been mentioned briefly, the Hundred Flowers Campaign. Even though it was short-lived, the present convulsions in China are *in part* a consequence of the genuine convictions underlying that policy. It is not hard to find other examples. In his notes on *Problems of Strategy in China's Revolutionary War*, written in 1936 in order to draw lessons from the second phase of the Civil War, Mao set almost at the head a section entitled, 'The aim of War is to Eliminate War':

War, this monster of mutual slaughter among men, will be finally eliminated by the progress of human society, and in the not too distant future too. But there is only one way to eliminate it and that is to oppose war with war, to oppose counter-revolutionary war with revolutionary war, to oppose national counter-revolutionary war with national revolutionary war, and to oppose counter-revolutionary class war with revolutionary class war. History knows only two kinds of war, just and unjust. We support just wars and oppose unjust wars. All counter-revolutionary wars are unjust, all revolutionary wars are just...When human society advances to the point where classes and states are eliminated, there will be no more wars, counter-revolutionary or revolutionary, unjust or just; that will be the era of perpetual peace for mankind. Our study of the laws of revolutionary war springs from the desire to eliminate all wars; herein lies the distinction between us Communists and all the exploiting classes.[2]

Like many other manifestos, the naïve simplicity of that passage almost turns into a parody of itself. Yet although words are often

---

[1] S. Schram, *Mao Tse-tung*, pp. 152 f.   [2] *Selected Works*, i, pp. 182 f.

Marxism

divorced from deeds, there is at least no doubt that Mao has repeatedly attempted to place a limit on crude violence.[1]

Perhaps the basic reason why Mao regards the infliction of pain and suffering as being of limited value (even though he has used them, sometimes on a wide scale) is that he has such a fundamental conviction about the power of a united people—the overwhelming power of concerted conscious action.[2] It is far better, therefore, to penetrate the springs of action, and to possess the minds of men, than to try to influence them by external pressures or threats. Rather than try to plug gaps in the dykes as they occur, it is better to persuade the waters to fall back of their own accord. Inevitably this conviction, that mind has the power to influence matter, has resulted in somewhat unrealistic statements, and this again has been effectively summarised by Stuart Schram. He quotes from a study of Mao's thought:

Many living examples show that there is only unproductive thought, there are no unproductive regions. There are only poor methods for cultivating the land, there is no such thing as poor land. Provided only that people manifest in full measure their subjective capacities for action, it is possible to modify natural conditions.

Schram comments: 'Stalin, too, had entertained extravagantly ambitious ideas on the possibility of transforming deserts into gardens, but he had never suggested that deserts did not exist.'[3]

Marx called for 'self-change' as the actual process of the revolution itself;[4] Mao implements that by thought-reform, by so possessing the minds of men that the full power of conscious action can be directed in revolutionary channels:

Apart from their other characteristics, China's 600 million people have two peculiarities; they are, first of all, poor, and secondly, blank. That may seem like a bad thing, but it is really a good thing. Poor people want change, want to do things, want revolution. A clean sheet of paper has no blotches, and so the newest and most beautiful words can be written on it, the newest and most beautiful pictures can be painted on it.[5]

[1] See, for example, the directive in *Selected Works*, IV, pp. 201 f.
[2] See pp. 176–8.
[3] S. Schram, *Mao Tse-tung*, p. 295.
[4] See p. 149.
[5] Quoted from S. Schram, *Mao Tse-tung*, p. 292.

That attitude leads on potentially into areas of suffering, whose dimensions have scarcely yet begun to be comprehended. In a way, the control of other minds is an almost irresistible step for a Marxist to take, since it offers supremely an effective chance to change the conditions rather than the actual details of life. It acquires a particular force in China as a result of the strange conjunction in Chinese Marxism of Western and Eastern traditions—the instrumental view of suffering, which becomes implicitly so strong in classical Marxism when it says that the price to be paid for the revolution is worth it; and combined with that, the rather flat, dispassionate and frequently heroic way in which traditional China has often estimated the place of suffering and of death. The conjunction of the two were graphically expressed by Mao in a poem written in 1959, when he visited his native village of Shaoshan for the first time since 1927:

> I curse the time that has flowed past
> Since the dimly-remembered dream of my departure
> From home, thirty-two years ago.
> With red pennons, the peasants lifted their lances;
> In their black hands, the rulers held up their whips.
> Lofty emotions were expressed in self-sacrifice:
> So the sun and moon were asked to give a new face to heaven.
> In delight I watch a thousand waves of growing rice and beans,
> And heroes everywhere going home in the smoky sunset.[1]

Such a view depends on the credibility of the belief that the sacrifice and consequent suffering are worthwhile; and in Mao's repeated assertions that they *are* worthwhile the conjunction of East and West is most apparent:

All men must die, but death can vary in its significance. The ancient Chinese writer Szuma Chien said, 'Though death befalls all men alike, it may be heavier than Mt Tai or lighter than a feather.' To die for the people is of more weight than Mt Tai, but to work for the fascists and die for the exploiters and oppressors is lighter than a feather.[2]

---

[1] Trs. Ch'en, p. 350. Schram's translation of ll. 6 and 7 is perhaps more graphic: 'Only because so many sacrificed themselves did our wills become strong, So that we dared command the sun and moon to bring a new day.' Mao made the same point prosaically in *Basic Tactics*: 'All we are afraid of is getting killed by the enemy. But when we have been oppressed by the enemy to such a point as this, how can we still fear death? And if we do not fear death, what is there to fear about the enemy? So when we see the enemy, whether he be strong or weak, we must act as though he is bread which can satisfy our hunger, and at once devour him.'   [2] *Selected Works*, III, p. 227.

Marxism

In China a particular expression of the Western tradition has joined hands with a particular expression of the Eastern tradition, the Chinese—one that in many ways lent itself to that amalgamation. Would other forms of the Eastern tradition be open to the same process, or did China's self-conscious and aggressive independence make it a special case? What *are* the other expressions of the Eastern tradition—or what, to return to the theme, is the understanding of suffering in the great religions of the East?

5

HINDUISM

INTRODUCTION

To summarise the thought of any religion is difficult, but in the case of Hinduism it is impossible. It is the essence of Hinduism that there are many different ways of looking at a single object, none of which will give the whole view, but each of which is entirely valid in its own right. A statue may be viewed from many angles. Each aspect helps to convey what the statue is like, but no single aspect is able to comprehend the statue as a whole, still less does the act of viewing it from one particular angle or another constitute 'the statue itself'. Again the statue may be described in quite different terms, each of which is entirely appropriate in its own way, but none of which is exhaustive. It may be described physically in terms of its mass displacement, or geologically in terms of the stone from which it is carved, or aesthetically in terms of the impression conveyed to the viewer. Each of these descriptions has something entirely valid and informative to say about the nature of the object described, but none of them is identical with the statue itself. Similarly the universe can be viewed and described in an almost infinite variety of ways, each of which may be entirely appropriate and valid from the point of view of the particular observer concerned, but none of which is necessarily exhaustive. It follows that a particular individual is unlikely to reach final and exclusive certainties in his quest for knowledge and understanding. If he makes the necessary effort and applies the necessary disciplines he will make progress in establishing what is true for himself, and in many fields this 'truth' will be shared by many others, even to the extent of it being virtually universal. But no matter how great the consensus of opinion, he cannot be absolutely sure that the discoveries of other individuals, even if they are in a minority and in apparent conflict with his own, are not equally valid so far as those other individuals are concerned.[1]

---

[1] Cf. the idea of 'many-sidedness' in Jainism, discussed on p. 283.

Hinduism

Applied to religion, this means that, so far as the Hindu is concerned, claims on the part of any religion to exclusive religious truth cannot be allowed. There are many paths to the summit, different in themselves, but gradually converging and leading to the same place. This is expressed in the classic statement of Radhakrishnan:

The truth, which is the kernel of every religion, is one and the same; doctrines, however, differ considerably since they are the applications of the truth to the human situation...Rites, ceremonies, systems and dogmas lead beyond themselves to a region of utter clarity and so have only relative truth...Every word, every concept is a pointer which points beyond itself. The sign should not be mistaken for the thing signified. The sign-post is not the destination.[1]

The goal, or summit, may also be described in different ways, but again the reality is more than its partial description.[2] This attitude of tolerance is applied as much *within* Hinduism as it is to other religions. Thus K. M. Sen writes in typical fashion:

Different religious leaders have belonged to different schools, and most Hindus are rather proud of the fact that there have not been any violent conflicts or persecution, thanks to mutual tolerance. This is a field where no one theory can claim to explain all the mysteries, and tolerance may well be the path to wisdom rather than that to confusion.[3]

The acceptance of diversity in religion as having positive value and importance explains why it is impossible to give a systematic account or summary of Hinduism: to attempt to do so would contradict its very nature. What is essential in Hinduism is that each individual should act with integrity, seeking to appropriate what is true for himself on whatever level that may be. Thus the act of a villager in putting a wreath of flowers on a tree as an act of recognition of the deity is as valid as the most sublime utterance of a mystic or the most detached philosophical analysis of the nature of reality. The point was put very clearly by Vivekananda, in a passage arguing that the caste system is natural and good, even though it produces suffering for some people,

[1] S. Radhakrishnan, *East and West, the End of their Separation* (New York, 1954).
[2] See particularly S. Radhakrishnan, *The Principal Upanishads* (London, 1953), pp. 143 f.
[3] K. M. Sen, *Hinduism* (London, 1963), pp. 84 f.

Introduction

since there must be different levels of attainment and ability in society:

Caste is a natural order. I can perform one duty in social life, and you another; you can govern a country, and I can mend a pair of old shoes, but there is no reason why you are greater than I, for can you mend my shoes? Can I govern the country? I am clever in mending shoes, you are clever in reading Vedas, but there is no reason why you should trample on my head...Caste is good. That is the only natural way of solving life. Men must form themselves into groups, and you cannot get rid of that. Wherever you go there will be caste. But that does not mean that there should be these privileges. They should be knocked on the head. If you teach Vedanta to the fisherman, he will say, I am as good a man as you, I am a fisherman, you are a philosopher, but I have the same God in me as you have in you. And that is what we want, no privileges for any one, equal chances for all; let every one be taught that the Divine is within, and every one will work out his own salvation...[1]

The acceptance of diversity, even when crystallised in the caste system, is made viable in Hinduism by the belief in *karma*, the exact accumulation of an individual's actions (sometimes referred to as the exercise of the moral law in the universe), and by the related belief in *samsara*, the round of rebirth into other forms of existence whose level depends, by the working of *karma*, on the quality of the individual's previous existence:

Until we negate the ego and get fixed in the Divine Ground we are bound to the endless procession of events called *samsara*. The principle which governs this world of becoming is called *karma*. There are moral and spiritual laws as well as physical laws. If we neglect the laws of health, we injure our health; if we neglect the laws of morality, we wreck our higher life...The law of *karma* is not external to the individual. The judge is not without but within. The law by which virtue brings its triumph and ill-doing its retribution is the unfolding of the law of our being.[2]

It is thus possible to rise or fall in subsequent existences according to the integrity with which one has lived previously: 'As a man puts on new clothes in this world, throwing away those which he formerly wore, even so the soul of man puts on new bodies which are in accordance with its acts in a former life.'[3]

[1] *The Complete Works of the Swami Vivekananda* (Almora, 1924–32), III, pp. 245 f., 460.
[2] S. Radhakrishnan, *The Principal Upanishads* (1953), pp. 113 f.
[3] *Vishnu Smriti* xx. 50.

Hinduism

It follows that a man of a low caste may hope to appear subsequently in a higher caste, provided that he has lived with integrity according to the duties and obligations of the caste in which he has found himself in his present existence. Very roughly, the idea of living according to the pattern of life appropriate to one's own level of attainment and position in society is what is meant by *dharma*, and a vast amount of Hindu literature is devoted to spelling out in detail what the various 'patterns of life' should be.[1]

In such circumstances, the aim of the individual should be to escape from inappropriate action (*adharma*) and from his involvement in the transient, impermanent world to which he is bound by *samsara*. Instead, he should aim at detachment, leading ultimately to total release (*moksha*), and this he can achieve by becoming aware of the true nature of his own self. His living body (*jiva*) may come and go, and the elements of which it is composed may return to the earth from which they came, but the essential Self (*atman*), Being-itself manifested in human shape, does not perish or dissolve:

Just as a person casts off worn-out garments and puts on others that are new, even so does the embodied soul cast off worn-out bodies and takes on others that are new. Weapons do not cleave this self, fire does not burn him; waters do not make him wet; nor does the wind make him dry. He is uncleavable. He cannot be burnt. He can be neither wetted nor dried. He is eternal, all-pervading, unchanging and immovable. He is the same for ever.[2]

In Hinduism the individual Self, *atman*, came to be understood as a manifestation of *Brahman*, Being-itself. *Brahman* is being or existence as such, which manifests itself in the almost infinite variety of forms which can be perceived in the universe. *Moksha*, release, is achieved when the individual realises that he *is Brahman*, that his *atman* is an aspect or manifestation of *Brahman*. The way in which *atman* is related to *Brahman* is understood differently in Hinduism, depending on whether *Brahman* is understood in a theistic or non-theistic way.[3] But in any case, *moksha* is still understood as having been achieved when the individual realises (not simply as an intellectual proposition but with a total and

[1] For a brief summary of the high importance of *dharma*, see *Taittiriya Aranyaka* x. 79.　　　[2] *Bhagavadgita* ii. 22–4 (trs. Radhakrishnan).
[3] I.e. (to put it roughly) it depends on whether Brahman is understood as being God or 'energy/matter'. The three main ways in which the relation of *atman* and *Brahman* have been understood are those of Shankara, Ramanuja and Madhva. See further pp. 227–8.

Introduction

complete commitment) that his apparently differentiated self, together with the apparently different entities of the universe, are not really distinct at all, but are in fact aspects or manifestations of the underlying reality, *Brahman* or Being-itself.

The fact remains that the objects which men perceive *do* appear to be distinct and separate. But that is only the superficial appearance. It is not the reality of the thing in itself. What appears real and substantial, this chair or this table, is in fact a part of the ceaseless ebb and flow of *Brahman* manifesting itself now in one form, now in another. The 'solid ground' is *Brahman*, not the object as perceived, since perception is fraught with deception, and it is in any case relative to the perceiver. The most usual example of this is that of the snake and the rope: what appears at a distance to be a snake coiled on the path turns out on closer examination to be a length of rope. The universe is filled with 'appearance' of that sort. The relativity of perception and the insubstantial transitoriness of superficial appearance are known as *maya*—sometimes translated as 'illusion', although, as will be seen, it is really a word of far greater subtlety.[1]

The brief summary given above of some of the basic concepts of Hinduism is not intended in any way to be a 'summary of Hindu doctrine'. It is an attempt to introduce some of the words and ideas which will occur repeatedly in the following pages and which have a bearing on ways in which Hindus have understood suffering. Broadly speaking, one might say that suffering belongs to the world of *maya* and *samsara*, and that by seeing the relativity of suffering an individual is able to progress on the way of *moksha*—there is, therefore, a considerable emphasis on asceticism as a practical way of getting suffering in its right perspective. But those broad generalisations have been very differently applied in practice, and even the simple definitions given above of some of the most basic words would not be accepted by all Hindus. There was even one group, for example, the Carvakas, who remained attached to Hinduism and yet who rejected the concept of *samsara*.[2] Furthermore, in the earliest stages of religion in India, even in the *Vedas*,[3] some of those apparently essential and

---

[1] See p. 229.
[2] See, e.g. Madhva Acarya, *Sarvadarsanasamgraha* (trs. E. B. Cowell and A. E. Gough, London, 1904), p. 2.
[3] The *Vedas* are very early religious texts—mostly hymns and chants. They are discussed further on pp. 198 ff.

basic concepts do not appear. That is principally because Indian beliefs were greatly affected by the Aryan invasion during the second millennium B.C. The Aryans were a war-like people who invaded from the north-west and rapidly overran the old Indus civilisation. Details of pre-Aryan religious beliefs are difficult to recover, but certainly they reasserted themselves in the midst of Aryan beliefs during and after the Vedic period. The *Vedas* are largely a consequence of the Aryan invasion, and although they reveal a fusion of the two elements, Aryan and non-Aryan, some of the beliefs which were later to be of the greatest importance do not appear in the *Vedas* in articulate form. It is quite probable, for example, that *samsara* is a pre-Aryan belief which only gradually reasserted itself after the Aryan invasion. Certainly, as will be seen, it does not appear very clearly in the *Vedas*, although traces of it are there.

It follows that the study of Hindu estimates of suffering is a study of the ways in which these and other basic concepts emerged, and of the many various ways in which they have been applied in different areas of Hinduism. It may, therefore, seem misleading to divide the material into 'foundations' and 'development', particularly since the whole spectrum of thought and practice, from the most primitive to the most profound, is expressed in every generation and is accepted as potentially appropriate for the individuals concerned. But there *are* foundations in Hinduism in the sense that certain writings are accepted as authoritative, and are frequently referred to as Scripture. The exact status of those writings is, as might be expected, disputed, but still, those particular writings have a distinct importance, and it is worth briefly examining them to see how they deal with the apparent facts of suffering.

THE FOUNDATIONS

The most important Scriptures of Hinduism are known as *sruti*, 'what is heard', or perhaps 'revelation'. They consist of the four *Vedas*, the extensions of the *Vedas* known as the *Brahmanas* and the *Aranyakas*, and the further extension of those in the *Upanishads*. The word *Veda*, from *vid*, 'to know', means knowledge. Another word commonly applied to the *Vedas* is *agama*, which emphasises the unbroken tradition of this knowledge and which points to the fact that the *Vedas* are not a single or unified composition, but the end-result of a long process of formation in the second and first millennia B.C. There are four *Vedas*, of which the most sacred is the *Rig-Veda*. It is primarily a collection of hymns addressed to a variety of gods who for the most part represent dominant aspects of nature and the universe. The *Sama-Veda* is largely a collection of verses from the *Rig-Veda* rearranged for chanting at various ceremonies and sacrifices. The *Yajur-Veda* is also related to ritual observances, and it contains instructions and formulae for the performance of sacrifices. These three *Vedas* are sometimes referred to together as *Trayi*, or *Trayi-Vidya*, the threefold *Vedas*. The fourth *Veda*, *Atharva-Veda*, is generally reckoned to be later in its date of composition, and it is made up chiefly of spells and chants designed to ward off evil and ensure prosperity in life.

From that brief description it will be clear that the *Vedas* belong to an extremely early stage of religious consciousness. The hymns of the *Rig-Veda* depict men trying to come to terms with themselves and with the universe by personifying in the form of gods the most notable aspects and strongest forces. It was not a simple or naïve polytheism, and there seem always to have been strong tendencies to understand individual gods as aspects of one supreme God or of 'divinity-itself'. Nevertheless, an elaborate network of relationships with the gods grew up in sacrificial and ritual terms, hence the importance of the *Sama* and *Yajur-Vedas*. These relationships with particular deities have changed in detail through the centuries, but in general they remain a dominant and obvious part of popular Hinduism. It is not surprising that the *Brahmanas*, the earliest extension of the *Vedas*, deal principally with sacrificial matters, providing greater elaboration and discussion of ritual details. Yet for some the attempt to integrate and explain the universe in sacrificial, theistic terms was not satisfying because it failed to answer basic questions about the nature of the universe—and, indeed, about the nature of the gods themselves. The *Vedas* and the *Brahmanas* themselves recorded such questions:

> Striving for strength bring forth a land for Indra, a truthful
>   hymn if he in truth existeth.
> One and another say, There is no Indra. Who hath beheld him?
>   Whom shall we honour?[1]

---

[1] *Rig-Veda* viii. 89.3 (trs. R. T. H. Griffith, *The Hymns of the Rigveda*, 2 vols., Benares, 1920–6).

Hinduism

For this reason the *Vedas* were developed in another related direction in the *Aranyakas*. Strictly speaking the *Aranyakas* are a part of the *Brahmanas*, but the material contained in them is for the most part different. The *Aranyakas* are largely speculative and philosophical, and those speculations reached their consummation in the *Upanishads*.

The *Upanishads* are treatises which are different in form and content, but alike in raising and attempting to answer fundamental questions about the nature of existence. They are known as *Vedanta*, which means 'the end of the *Vedas*'; and, in the case of the *Upanishads*, *Vedanta* means 'end' in both senses: they are the final part of accepted Scripture, but they are also the consummation of Vedic teaching. Yet this would be misleading if it gave the impression of an orderly and progressive development. All parts of Hindu Scripture overlap and merge with each other, and it is almost impossible to isolate the date at which any particular item was written. Furthermore, *Upanishads* continued to be produced until there were more than 200, and the accepted number varied.[1] Shankara, one of the greatest of all Indian philosophers, commented on eleven, but he mentioned another four in his commentary on the *Brahma-Sutra*. Hume translated thirteen,[2] Radhakrishnan eighteen.[3] This ambiguity on the edges of the 'canon' is typical of Hindu unwillingness to draw dogmatic lines where none are strictly necessary.

The Vedas

The *Vedas* have a direct and straightforward understanding of suffering. The personification of forces and aspects of nature as gods meant that suffering could be understood as a consequence of personal activity in the universe on the part of the gods. Potentially, therefore, suffering could be understood and dealt with by an appropriate relationship with particular deities, which was frequently expressed in ritual forms. In a sense, suffering is the essence of the universe, since the universe is a chain of killing and being killed, of devouring and of being devoured: 'The whole (world) is just food and the eater of food.'[4] Sacrifice was a form of

---

[1] *Muktika Up.* put the total at 108.
[2] R. E. Hume, *The Thirteen Principal Upanishads* (Oxford, 1921).
[3] S. Radhakrishnan, *The Principal Upanishads* (London, 1953).
[4] *Brihad-aranyaka Up.* i. 4.6 (trs. Radhakrishnan).

identification with the process, and a way of trying to bring it into some sort of control.[1]

The universe thus has a triple aspect, the devourer, the devoured, and the relationship between them, devouring or sacrifice. Sacrifice is an identification with the inherent process of creation, and it enables an individual to have hope that the 'process' will work on his behalf. Many of the Vedic prayers, therefore, express a desire for harmony and well-being in simple terms, as in this example:

O Rudra of dark and red form who makest the evil-doers suffer, O Lord of food, himself bereft of any possessions, of all these men and animals (already named), do not frighten any one; let not anyone of them perish; let none of them fall ill. O Rudra! that benign aspect of yours which acts like a daily tonic, a benign remedy for terrible suffering, make us happy with that aspect[2] of yours so that we may live. To Rudra, the almighty God of matted locks who crushes his opponents, we foster this worshipful thought of ours, so that there may be peace to our men and cattle, the world may be well-nourished, and this (our) village will be free from diseases...Strike not, O Rudra! at our little son, at our life or cattle and horses; slay not in anger our men; we worship you with offering and obeisance.[3]

It should not be thought from this that all suffering was held to be the consequence of arbitrary action on the part of the gods, which men could only hope to manipulate or influence by sacrificial bribes. On the contrary, the concept of *karma*, as the exact moral balance of the universe, was already apparent, though in the earliest days it tended to be personified as the god Varuna. Varuna in the earliest texts was the ruler of the unseen world, exercising control over the relations between men and gods. It was Varuna who was ultimately responsible for all that happened, 'for he is the one who possesses *maya*'.[4] This means that occurrences which at first sight seemed unaccountable, whether they were good or evil, were in fact to be explained as the consequence of Varuna's greater knowledge: 'The Lord who punishes is

---

[1] See, e.g. *Bhagavad Gita* iii. 10–14.
[2] On the two aspects of a single God, see further p. 205–7.
[3] *Satarudriya* §10 (trs. Raghavan). The *Satarudriya* is a collection of hymns and prayers in eleven sections assembled from various parts of the *Veda*.
[4] *Rig-Veda* vi. 48.14, x. 99.10. *Maya* here means 'the power to bring the apparent forms of existence into being'; see p. 229.

Hinduism

Varuna. He is the king whose duty it is to punish.'[1] He is the foundation and guarantee of natural and moral law, and he is able to implement it because he is omniscient:

Even as erring people, we, O God Varuna, every day violate ceaselessly the observance of your ordinance. Do not make us the victims of death, you who kill those that disregard you; do not make us the objects of your fatal wrath...He knows the track of the birds in the sky. Sovereign of the seas, he knows the path of ships...He knows the gods who live in heaven. The wise, law-abiding Varuna is enthroned as a king, governing all and beholding all things that have been or shall be.[2]

It is reasonably clear that this is a personified form of *karma*, and it perhaps explains why, in later mythology, Varuna became far less significant. When *karma* emerged more clearly as a separate principle Varuna fell away in importance and ended up as the god of death. But in early times it was Varuna who raised sacrifice above the level of manipulative bribery by personifying the assertion of an entirely just cause-and-effect in the universe. This is not to deny that sacrifice could itself be an important 'cause' of benefit and prosperity. But Varuna meant that the gods could not be made an excuse for irresponsible behaviour or for the occurrence of suffering. Furthermore, the existence of suffering was not seen as being brought to bear on men entirely from the outside; it was recognised that much evil and suffering is a result of internal desire and anger, or in other words, of men who have lost control of themselves—though even here the loss of control is sometimes described in terms of possession.[3]

Thus the *Vedas* are by no means concerned simply with the details of sacrifice and ritual, but also with the assertion of moral order in the universe:

O Varuna! whatever offence we mortals may have committed against the divine beings, whatever moral orders of yours we have, in our ignorance, violated, punish us not, O God, on account of that sin... O shining Varuna! sharpen our thought and capacity, whereby we disciplining this mind (of ours) may embark on the boat that conveys us safely over all evil.[4]

[1] *Manu Smriti* ix. 24.5. The *Lawbooks of Manu* are a basic source in the second category of Hindu scripture, discussed below on pp. 219 ff.
[2] *Rig-Veda* i. 25.7–9 (trs. Daniélou).   [3] See especially *Yajur-Veda* x. 61.
[4] *Rig-Veda* vii. 89.5, viii. 42.3 (trs. Raghavan).

Foundations

Suffering was therefore seen as a result of a conflict inherent in creation. Duality, but not dualism, is apparent in almost all the particulars of creation, as S. Radhakrishnan has described it: 'Cosmic process is one of universal and unceasing change and is patterned on a duality which is perpetually in conflict, the perfect order of heaven and the chaos of the dark waters. Life creates opposites, as it creates sexes, in order to reconcile them.'[1]

In the *Vedas*, that duality received personified form in gods (*sura*) and anti-gods (*asura*). Mythologically the anti-gods represent those forces and inclinations which bind men in bondage to their senses and thus prevent their spiritual progress and growth:

In contrast to the gods, the antigods are the inclinations of the senses which, by their nature, belong to the obscuring tendency, and which delight in life, that is, in the activities of the life energies in all the fields of sensation.[2]

That general idea was made more particular by the identification of certain gods with the evil and destructive aspects of existence. Thus death was personified as the god Yama, a name which means 'the binder' or 'restrainer'. Although he is moved by pity, he remains frightening and terrible, and there is every need to propitiate him with offerings:

> Him who has passed along the mighty ridges,
> And has spied out the path for many travellers,
> Vivasvant's son, the gatherer of people,
> Yama, the king, do thou present with offering...
> Broad-nosed and brown are the messengers of Yama,
> Greedy of lives they rove among the people.
> May they give back to us a life propitious
> Here and today, that we may see the sunlight.[3]

The personification of misery and suffering is found in the goddess Nirriti: 'She is the embodiment of all sins...the one who has dominion over gambling, women, sleep, poverty, disease

---

[1] S. Radhakrishnan, *The Principal Upanishads*, p. 59. On duality and dualism, see further ch. 7.

[2] Shankara, *Commentary on Chandogya Up.* i. 2.1 (trs. Daniélou). In later mythology it was thought that the *asuras* were originally good, but that when they multiplied they grew jealous and self-assertive. As a result they became envious of any who were happy, and they tried to provoke as much misery as they could: 'In due course, as a result of their change of heart, I saw that divine Law had vanished from their midst and that they were inspired by anger and rage' (*Mahabharata* xiii. 8360). [3] *Rig-Veda* x. 14.1–2, 12 (trs. Macdonnell).

and all other kinds of trouble. She is the wife of lawlessness (*adharma*), the son of Varuna. Her sons are death, fear and terror.'[1]

In her ceremonies the officiants are dressed in black, and her images and symbols are picked out in red.

> Those who habitually destroy the simple and harm with their
> evil minds the righteous,
> Hand them over to the embrace of Nirriti.[2]

But the gods who most obviously represent evil and destructive tendencies in the universe are the related group Siva, Rudra, Kali. The cult of Siva, known in general as Shaivism, goes back to an early period, but in the *Vedas* the destructive god is Rudra.[3] The nature of Siva has changed greatly during the course of time, but consistent tendencies can be discerned. Siva is the Lord of Sleep, and he represents the tendency of all things to move towards dissolution and destruction. In his most destructive guise he appears as Bhairava, the terrible destroyer. He is the one who wields the thunderbolt, he is armed with innumerable arrows, and he drives in his chariot like a destroying wind razing the earth as he goes.[4] It is obvious that Siva-Rudra must be propitiated, and, on the basis of the threefold relationship of devourer, devoured and devouring, the propitiation of the devourer sometimes took on frightening and awe-inspiring forms. In post-Vedic Hinduism Siva reappears in a multiplicity of forms and images, but frequently he is depicted wearing a garland of skulls and carrying a noose with which to bind offenders.[5] The goddess Kali, the power of Time, is an aspect of Siva, the Destroyer, and in many ways she is even more terrible:

Most fearful, her laughter shows her dreadful teeth. She stands upon a corpse. She has four arms. Her hands hold a sword and a head and show the gestures of removing fears and granting boons. She is the auspicious divinity of sleep, the consort of Siva. Naked, clad only in space, the goddess is resplendent. Her tongue hangs out. She wears a garland of heads. Such is the form worthy of meditation of the Power of Time, Kali, who dwells near the funeral pyres.[6]

---

[1] *Mahabharata* i. 67.52.   [2] *Rig-Veda* vii. 104.9.
[3] Rudra is the Destroyer and lord of Tears.
[4] See, for example, *Rig-Veda* ii. 33.3, 10; v. 42.11; x. 126.6.
[5] Saivism developed a vast literature; for a brief summary, see C. Sharma, *A Critical Survey of Indian Philosophy* (London, 1960), pp. 386 ff.
[6] *Kali Tantra* (trs. Daniélou, p. 271).

The personification of evil in the forms cf gods and goddesses represents, graphically and dramatically, the way in which suffering was believed to arise out of a fundamental conflict and tension in the universe. If death and suffering are a consequence of personal activity on the part of various gods, it means that their occurrence can potentially be regulated by the ways in which an individual relates himself to the gods concerned. The many images and rites devoted to the destructive gods indicate how powerful was their effect in popular imagination. The value of polytheistic representation is that it enables individuals to come to terms with an otherwise faceless and impenetrable universe. It gives life and vitality to an otherwise abstract process, and it enables an individual to participate imaginatively in that process. Suffering is the relationship between devourer and devoured; it is the process of being devoured, and as such it is the relationship between the two conflicting principles of the universe, the urge to life and the urge to death.[1]

This understanding of suffering might seem to imply a basic dualism, a conflict between two eternally opposed principles. In fact, nothing could be further from the truth. There is certainly conflict and duality, but no dualism; the conflict takes place within the same frame, and what appear to be two principles are in reality aspects of a single entity seen from different sides. The clearest illustration of that lies in the fact that all the gods who represent evil and destructive tendencies *also* represent the opposite qualities. It depends how you look at them. Thus Yama, the Lord of Death, is frightening in appearance, but he is also handsome—in other words, death may be abhorrent or it may be welcome: it depends how you look at it. To the upright man Yama appears gracious:

His sacred string is of gold. His face is charming, smiling. He wears a crown, earrings, and a garland of wild flowers.[2]

But to the man who has given way to evil,

his limbs appear three hundred leagues long. His eyes are deep wells. His lips are thin, the colour of smoke, fierce. He roars like the ocean of destruction. His hairs are gigantic reeds, his crown a burning flame.

[1] For this, see particularly the chant recorded in *Taittiriya Up.* iii. 10.5.
[2] *Padma Purana* (trs. Daniélou, p. 133).

The breath from his wide nostrils blows off the forest fires. He has long teeth. His nails are like winnowing baskets. Stick in hand, clad in skins, he has a frowning brow.[1]

Exactly the same is true of the other gods who personify evil and suffering.[2] Siva is not only fearful but also auspicious. Since he is the Lord of Death he can also be the destroyer of death. He destroys, but also he wanders through the world filled with the urge to create life. In later Shaivism the harsh elements of Siva often disappeared, and the coming of suffering or death was set in a moral context:

> In love the Lord (Siva) punishes,
> to the end that a sinner may correct his ways
> and pursue what is right.
> All that he does flows out of his love.[3]

Rudra, too, is the Lord of Tears, but he is also the most beneficent of gods.[4]

Shvetashtavara Up. iii 5 f. combines the two aspects by playing on the name Siva—*ya te rudra siva tanur aghorapapakashini*...:

Rudra, your body which is auspicious, unterrifying, showing no evil— with that most benign body, O dweller in the mountains, look upon (manifest yourself to) us. O Dweller among the mountains, make auspicious the arrow which thou holdest in thy hand to throw. O Protector of the mountain, injure not man or beast.

Even Nirriti has her good side, since she is the protector of those who, by being born into evil families, are handicapped, and yet who, despite that, remain virtuous. Kali, as well, has a dual aspect: the Power of Time is initially destructive, but when all has been destroyed, Kali is the state of ensuing peace and stillness, and in that capacity she is known as 'transcendent night'. Kali is only to be feared from the point of view of attachment to transient pleasures, since she breaks that attachment remorselessly. But

---

[1] *Padma Purana* (trs. Daniélou, p. 133). See also the hymn to Yama (parts of which have already been quoted on p. 203), *Rig-Veda* x. 14.

[2] It is true also of many other gods who have not been specifically described or mentioned here, particularly of Agni (Fire) and Indra (in the Vedic period one of the greatest of the gods, but subsequently 'relegated' to become simply an aspect of Siva). See, e.g., *Rig-Veda* i. 143, i. 32.

[3] *Shivananasiddhiyar* ii. 15.23.

[4] See the prayer from the *Satarudriya*, quoted already on p. 201. Rudra is 'both kind and terrible, a destroyer and a protector; he has a dark and clear countenance, he has matted locks and no hair' (*Satarudriya* §5).

from the point of view of the progress of the soul she is to be approached with joyful expectation.

The *Vedas* thus have a far more complex understanding of suffering than at first sight might have seemed to be the case. In personified form, the gods represent the view that occurrences of apparent suffering cannot be defined as evil or afflictive in advance. It depends how they are viewed and assimilated. Of course there are many unpleasant occurrences which men, understandably, have no desire to experience, and for that reason the *Vedas* contain many prayers to the gods that they may appear in their beneficent, rather than their destructive, capacity.[1] But basically suffering is an experience, a part of the universe of being, which needs to be seen in perspective. It may in fact be extremely beneficial, particularly if it is the foundation of better things, or if it is the knife which cuts humans off from their attachment to unworthy objects: it may, in other words, initiate dissatisfaction and the quest for *moksha*. That at once explains why asceticism, privation voluntarily accepted, is so important in Hinduism. It is a part of the process of 'getting suffering in perspective'.

In the *Vedas* suffering is seen as a part of the universal order expressed imaginatively, in personified form, in the various aspects of the gods. There is a clear sense that at least a part of the right attitude to suffering is to see it in relation to the whole. The elements of *maya*, of 'the way things appear', are already present. So too are the elements of *karma* and *samsara*, although *samsara* only appears in rudimentary form. It was certainly envisaged that the soul would pass from its present abode in the body and take up its dwelling in other forms of existence, as can be seen, for example, in the prayers recited over a dead person as his body is about to be cremated:

Let your eye go to the Sun; your life to the Wind; by the meritorious act that you have done, go to heaven, and then (for rebirth) to the earth again, or resort to the Waters if you feel at home there; remain in the herbs with the bodies you propose to take.[2]

[1] The nature of the gods in the *Vedas* is even more revealing of later Hinduism in the way that the gods, who at first sight seem straightforwardly polytheistic, are in fact a foreshadowing of the full elaboration of monism (the undifferentiated understanding of the Universe). The gods not only represent different sides of the same thing, such as death or time; they also represent aspects of 'divinity-itself'. This does not appear in the *Vedas* as a clear, articulated theory, but it is expressed. See, e.g., *Rig-Veda* i. 164.4 ff.; x. 121.1 ff. (the 'Hymn to the Unknown God').
[2] *Rig-Veda* x. 16.3 (trs. Raghavan).

Hinduism

The later *Vedas* also advocate the quest for *moksha* in the sense of achieving identification with the Supreme Being, the one who pervades all existence.

You are the man and woman, boy and girl; you are the old man tottering about with a staff, and you are the child new-born. You are of all forms...He who knows the long-thread on which these beings are woven, he knows indeed the thread of threads, he shall know the great Brahman...Free from desire, delighting in knowledge, immortal, self-born, satisfied with its own bliss, deficient in no way; knowing that firm, unaging, (ever) young Self, the Wise one fears not from death.[1]

None of this was worked out in the *Vedas* in any kind of detail, elaborate or otherwise. But the elements were there, and they were rapidly developed and explored. Much of the material produced went into the *Aranyakas*, but supremely it issued in the *Upanishads*.

The *Upanishads*

The *Upanishads* have already been briefly described.[2] They contain a great variety of material, some of it similar to that found in the *Vedas*. There are prayers addressed to various gods,[3] primitive chants,[4] and also formulae designed to produce success or well-being in life.[5] Furthermore, the *Vedas* were recognised as being an important foundation of life.[6]

Nevertheless, although the *Upanishads* are undoubtedly Vedanta, the end and consummation of the *Vedas*, they emerged at least in

---

[1] *Atharva-Veda* x. 8.27, 37, 44. Cf. *Shvetashvetara Up.* iv. 1 ff. (trs. Radh.): 'He who is one, without any colour, by the manifold exercise of his power distributes many colours in his hidden purpose and into whom in the beginning and at the end the universe is gathered, may he endow us with a clear understanding. That indeed is Agni, that is Aditya, that is Vayu and that is the moon. That, indeed, is the pure. That is Brahma. That is the waters. That is Praja-pati (the Lord of creation). You are woman, you are man. You are the youth and the maiden too. You, as an old man, totter along with a staff. Being born you become facing in every direction. You are the dark-blue bird, you are the green (parrot) with red eyes. You are (the cloud) with the lightning in its womb. You are the seasons and the seas. Having no beginning you abide through omnipresence. (You) from whom all worlds are born.' [2] See p. 200.

[3] See, for example, the prayer addressed to Indra in *Taittiriya Up.* i. 4.1–3.

[4] One of these has already been quoted. *Chandogya Up.* i and ii, and *Taittiriya Up.* i deal with chants at some length.

[5] *Brihadaranyaka Up.* vi. 4.14 ff., for example, suggests what diet should precede the attempt to beget a particular sort of child. Thus if a son of fair complexion is desired, the parents-to-be should have rice cooked with milk, and they should eat it with a little clarified butter.   [6] See, e.g. *Maitri Up.* vii. 10.

Foundations

part as a protest *against* certain tendencies in Vedic religion. The increasing elaboration of sacrifices in the *Brahmanas*, together with the resulting emphasis on the importance of the priestly class, meant that Vedic religion had become 'top-heavy'. It is probable that both Buddhism and Jainism emerged as a part of a widespread dissatisfaction with an increasingly formal and ritualistic ordering of religious and spiritual life. Certainly the *Upanishads* contain strong protests against sacrifices performed for their own sake without any understanding.[1]

It is not that sacrifices or rituals are evil, but that they have only a limited value.[2] Similarly, study of the *Vedas* is a means to an end, not the end in itself. So Krishna tells Arjuna in the Uttaragita: 'Just as a donkey bearing the weight of sandal-wood knows its weight but not its fragrance, so also is a Brahmana who knows the text of the *Vedas* and scriptures but not their significance.'[3] Generally speaking, therefore, the *Upanishads* are a consequence of the efforts of many individuals to discover, in more detached and intellectual terms, the significance of the pictorial myths and rituals of the *Vedas*. It is by no means the case that myths were discarded in the *Upanishads*, but they appear usually as vehicles for developed ideas. Thus the material in the *Upanishads* has often moved a long way beyond the *Vedas*, but it is not completely detached or independent. This can be seen most clearly in the way in which the same idea may be expressed in one place in mythological terms, and in another place in completely abstract discourse.

Applied to suffering, this means that much of the old Vedic way of understanding suffering reappears, but that it tends to subserve more profound ideas. The most obvious illustration of this is the way in which suffering is understood as a result of a basic conflict and tension in the universe. In several passages this is portrayed through the ancient myths of the creation of the

---

[1] See, e.g. *Mundaka Up.* i. 2.7–10.

[2] The continuing, parallel, importance of sacrifice can be seen in the way that sacrificial imagery and ideas are applied to life, either in general (*Chandogya Up.* iii. 16.1 ff.), or to specific details, such as eating *Maitri Up.* vi. 9), or being a student (*Chandogya Up.* viii. 5.1 ff.), or sexual intercourse (*Brihadaranyaka Up.* vi. 4.1 ff., *Chandogya Up.* v. 9.1 f.). It can also be seen in the fact that the *Upanishads* include instructions for the right-performance of various ceremonials; see, e.g., *Chandogya Up.* iv. 16.1–5, which ends: 'When the sacrifice is well supported the sacrificer is well supported. By having sacrificed he becomes better off.'

[3] Trs. Radhakrishnan, *Upanishads*, p. 196; cf. *Muktika Up.* ii. 65.

Hinduism

world. Both *Brihadaranyaka Up.*[1] and *Chandogya Up.*[2] explain the possibilities of good and evil as being a result of conflict between the gods and demons. The version in *Chandogya Up.* begins:

When the gods and the demons, both descendants of Prajapati (the lord of creation), contended with each other, the gods took hold of the *udgitha*,[3] thinking, with this, we shall overcome them. Then they meditated on the *udgitha* as the breath in the rose. The demons afflicted that with evil. Therefore, with it one smells both the sweet smelling and the foul smelling, for it is afflicted with evil.

Then they meditated on the *udgitha* as speech. The demons afflicted that with evil. Therefore with it one speaks both the true and the false, for it is afflicted with evil.

Chandogya Up. goes on to consider, in the same way, the eye, the ear, the mind, and the breath. The version in *Brihadaranyaka Up.* is even more elaborate. The opening chapter of that *Upanishad* is an account of the creation of the world, based on the great horse-sacrifice. In i. 3.1 it reaches the point where the gods and the demons come into conflict:

There were two classes of the descendants of Prajapati, the gods and the demons. Of these, the gods were the younger and the demons the elder ones. They were struggling with each other for (the mastery of) these worlds. The gods said, come, let us overcome the demons at the sacrifice through the *udgitha*. They said to speech, chant (the *udgitha*) for us; 'So be it', said speech, and chanted for them. Whatever enjoyment there is in speech, it secured for the gods by chanting; that it spoke well was for itself. The demons knew, verily, by this chanter, they will overcome us. They rushed upon it and pierced it with evil. The evil which consists in speaking what is improper, that is that evil.

The *Upanishad* then goes on to apply the same formula to the life-breath, the eye, the ear, the mind and the vital-breath in the mouth. The form of words is more precise than that in the other version, and it illustrates how the *Upanishads* move beyond an interest in the myth for its own sake, and use it as a way of exploring reality. In this case, it is an effective way of illustrating the belief that there is duality, but no dualism: evil and suffering are a consequence of the ways in which neutral objects are used—or misused. Originally and basically the universe was undifferentiated;

---

[1] i. 3.1 ff.   [2] i. 2.1 ff.
[3] The *udgitha* is the sacred syllable AUM which is a symbol of the Supreme, unutterable, Reality.

the various forms in which creation has taken shape give the appearance of diversity, but Being-itself, *Brahman*, remains a unity. That can only be realised if the different forms of the universe are penetrated and seen as aspects of the whole:

At that time this (universe) was undifferentiated. It became differentiated by name and form (so that it is said) he has such a name, such a shape. Therefore even today this (universe) is differentiated by name and shape (so that it is said) he has such a name, such a shape. He (the self) entered in here even to the tips of the nails, as a razor is (hidden) in the razor-case, or as fire in the fire-source. Him they see not for (as seen) he is incomplete, when breathing he is called the vital force, when speaking voice, when seeing the eye, when hearing the ear, when thinking the mind. These are merely the names of his acts. He who meditates on one or another of them (aspects) he does not know for he is incomplete, with one or another of these (characteristics). The self is to be meditated upon for in it all these become one. This self is the foot-trace of all this, for by it one knows all this, just as one can find again by foot-prints (what was lost).[1]

This brings us at once to the very heart of the *Upanishads*, and to their central affirmation about suffering: to create duality is to create suffering. Suffering is a result of introducing duality into a non-dualistic situation. Existence is a unity. All that is, is an aspect or manifestation of Being-itself, *Brahman*. To break down that unity is to introduce tension and conflict and strife:

For where there is duality as it were, there one sees the other, one smells the other, one tastes the other, one speaks to the other, one hears the other, one thinks of the other, one touches the other, one knows the other. But where everything has become just one's own self, by what and whom should one see, by what and whom should one smell, by what and whom should one taste, by what and to whom should one speak, by what and whom should one hear, by what and of whom should one think, by what and whom should one touch, by what and whom should one know? By what should one know him by whom all this is known? That self (is to be described as) not this, not this.[2] He is incomprehensible for he cannot be comprehended. He is

---

[1] *Brihadaranyaka Up.* i. 4.7 (trs. Radh.).

[2] This is the famous clause, *neti neti* (here in full: *sa esha neti nety atma*). Being-itself cannot be described by the name of one of its manifestations, nor can it be approached objectively in the form of another person as distinct from oneself. All that is is an expression of Being-itself. It is, therefore, impossible to touch an object as though it were different from oneself, since both toucher and touched are expressions of Being-itself.

indestructible for he cannot be destroyed. He is unattached for he does not attach himself. He is unfettered, he does not suffer, he is not injured. Indeed, by what would one know the knower?[1]

To regard the apparently different forms of the universe as being always and irreconcilably differentiated is to have only the most primitive and inadequate conception. True perception is to see the unity behind the manifest forms.[2] It follows that suffering cannot be, so to speak, an ultimate reality. The experience of suffering is real enough, but it must be seen in relation to the whole. The individual who has an adequate grasp of *Brahman* will find that suffering falls away in significance. Since everything that happens is a manifestation of *Brahman*, it follows that true understanding only arises when the accidents of time and space are penetrated and are seen to reveal *Brahman*. *Brahman* pervades all things without being exhausted in any one of them; which means that suffering or sorrow cannot be the final truth about existence:

As fire which is one, entering this world becomes varied in shape according to the object (it burns), so also the one Self within all beings becomes varied according to whatever (it enters) and also exists outside (them all). As air which is one, entering this world becomes varied in shape according to the object (it enters), so also the one Self within all beings becomes varied according to whatever (it enters) and also exists outside (them all). Just as the sun, the eye of the whole world, is not defiled by the external faults seen by the eye, even so, the One within all beings is not tainted by the sorrow of the world, as he is outside (the world).[3]

It follows that suffering, however agonising or distressing it may be, is still only relative. The realisation of *Brahman* means that suffering immediately falls into place: 'As water does not cling to the lotus leaf, so evil deed does not cling to one who knows it.' Suffering is a result of becoming attached to transient objects as though they were the final reality. To do that at once introduces the tensions of duality and rivalry where none ought to obtain, since it places one object above another. The *Upanishads* repeatedly state that an individual becomes what he has aimed at.

[1] *Brihadaranyaka Up.* iv. 5.15 (trs. Radh.). The same occurs in slightly shorter form in *ibid.* ii. 5.1. Cf. also *ibid.* iii. 9.26, iv. 2.4, iv. 4.22.
[2] See, e.g. *Brihadaranyaka Up.* iv. 4.18 f.
[3] *Katha Up.* ii. 2.9–11 (trs. Radh.).

Foundations

Verily, this whole world is *Brahman*: from which he comes forth, without which he will be dissolved and in which he breathes. Tranquil, one should meditate on it. Now verily, a person consists of purpose. According to the purpose one has in this world, so does he become on departing hence. So let him frame himself for a purpose.[1]

Thus if the individual self aims at *Brahman* in the right way, he comes to realise that he *is Brahman*, an aspect of Being-itself. But if he aims for any lesser objective, he cannot hope to get any higher than that lesser objective. If he places his full reliance on what he perceives through his senses, he remains sensual. He cannot expect to see the distant horizon if he is not prepared to look further than the end of his nose. Thus the seven organs of perception, the eyes, ears, nostrils, and mouth are referred to as 'the seven hostile kinsmen',[2] intimate friends who yet mislead if too great reliance is placed upon them. Love of this life and attachment to its pleasures lead inevitably to distorted action and inadequate understanding, because such attitudes are myopic: they prevent an individual from seeing the whole picture.[3]

This means that attachment to the objects of this world, as though they have an eternal validity, is in fact the most terrible bondage. The individual self remains bound to the world and reappears in future existences still attached to those objects: 'Some souls enter into a womb for embodiment; others enter stationary objects according to their deeds and according to their thoughts.'[4] The merit of good works and of sacrifices postpones the moment of rebirth, but it does not obliterate it,[5] and the process of rebirth is governed by the inexorably just working-out of *karma*:

Like the waves in large rivers there is no turning back of that which has been done previously; like the tide of the ocean, the approach of one's death is hard to keep back. Like a lame man, bound by the fetters made of the fruits of good and evil, like the condition of a man in prison, lacking independence, like the condition of one in the realm of death,

---

[1] *Chandogya Up.* iii. 14.1 (trs. Radh.). Cf. also *Maitri Up.* iv. 6, where the same is expressed in theistic terms. For a more detailed statement, see *Brihadaranyaka Up.* i. 4.16, iv. 4.5, and cf. also *Chandogya Up.* iii. 2.3.

[2] *Brihadaranyaka Up.* ii. 2.1.

[3] See, e.g., *Brihadaranyaka Up.* iv. 7.3.

[4] *Katha Up.* ii. 2.7 (trs. Radh.).

[5] See, e.g., *Chandogya Up.* v. 10.5–7. For a shorter version see *Brihadaranyaka Up.* vi. 2.15 f.

beset by many fears, like one intoxicated with liquor, intoxicated with the liquor of delusion, rushing about like one possessed by an evil spirit, like one bitten by a great serpent, bitten by the objects of sense, like gross darkness, the darkness of passion, like jugglery, consisting of illusion, like a dream, false appearances, like the inside of the banana tree, unsubstantial, like an actor changing dress every moment, like a painted scene, falsely delighting the mind; and therefore it has been said, 'Objects of sound, touch and the like are worthless objects for a man.' The elemental self, through attachment to them, does not remember the highest state.[1]

The world thus appears to consist of conflicting opposites, of evil and good, of pain and pleasure, of suffering and healing. Anyone who isolates one part of this duality as though it were the whole transcendent truth is led into one-sided and unbalanced action. Release is only possible when the parts are *seen* to be parts, and *Brahman* is realised as the sole truth; and that realisation may take a long time and many existences to attain:

Through the ripening of the fruits of his past actions he does not attain any rest, like a worm caught within a whirlpool. The desire for liberation arises in human beings at the end of many births through the ripening of their past virtuous conduct.[2]

Suffering, therefore, is only a problem so long as it appears to be a final and inescapable truth. But when it is realised that the self is not bound for ever to the transient world of suffering, but rather that it *is Brahman*, then suffering can no longer occur. Suffering may be a way in which *Brahman* becomes manifest, but it is not *Brahman* itself:

As a man when in the embrace of his beloved wife knows nothing without or within, so the person when in the embrace of his intelligent self knows nothing without or within. That, verily, is his form in which his desire is fulfilled, in which the self is his desire, in which he is without desire, free from any sorrow. There (in that state) a father is not a father, a mother is not a mother, the worlds are not the worlds, the gods are not the gods, the *Vedas* are not the *Vedas*...He is not followed (affected) by good, he is not followed by evil for then he has passed beyond all the sorrows of the heart.[3]

The realisation of *Brahman* isolates the individual from suffering, because it involves detachment as opposed to attachment, and

---

[1] *Maitri Up.* iv. 2 (trs. Radh.).   [2] *Paingala Up.* ii. 11 (trs. Radh.).
[3] *Brihadaranyaka Up.* iv. 3.21 f. (trs. Radh.).

Foundations

suffering arises only when an individual attaches himself to limited or transient objects as though they are permanent.[1]

So far, therefore, it has been seen that instances of suffering are a direct result of the working out of *karma*, and that an individual self acquires the fruits of its own deeds and thoughts, in future existences if not in this. This means that morality is connected with suffering in Hinduism as much as it is in Judaism, but it is a *different* connection. The problem of Job cannot arise, because it may always be the case that occurrences of suffering are a consequence of activities, not simply in this existence, but in previous ones as well. Suffering occurs as a problem only when duality in the universe, the contrast between pain and pleasure, is seen as an abiding truth about existence: then, inevitably, the individual self spends itself in trying to find a solid and secure home in objects that prove ephemeral and transitory. Suffering ceases to be a problem when it is realised that the individual self can transcend occurrences of suffering by finding its identity in *Brahman*.

Thus the goal of life, and the only possible way of dealing with suffering, is to realise the famous equation of the *Upanishads*, *atman* is *Brahman*—this apparently differentiated self, which is subjected to the hazards and vicissitudes of life, is not independent or isolated, nor is it inextricably bound up with its experiences. Like all other forms of existence, it is an aspect or manifestation of *Brahman*: *tat satyam, sa atma, tat tvam asi*...'That is the true. That is the self. That art thou.' All previous distinctions will disappear. When Aruni tried to help his son, Shvetaketu, to understand this, he said:

'Just as, my dear, the bees prepare honey by collecting the essences of different trees and reducing them into one essence, and as these (juices) possess no discrimination (so that they might say) "I am the essence of this tree, I am the essence of that tree," even so, indeed, my dear, all these creatures though they reach Being do not know that they have reached the Being. Whatever they are in this world, tiger or lion or wolf or boar or worm or fly or gnat or mosquito, that they become. That which is the subtle essence, this whole world has for its self. That is the true. That is the self. That art thou, Shvetaketu.'
'Please, Venerable Sir, instruct me still further.'[2]

[1] See, e.g. *Brihadaranyaka Up.* iv. 4.23 (trs. Radh.).
[2] *Chandogya Up.* vi. 9 (trs. Radh.).

The instruction continues with many other examples (including the famous one of salt in water),[1] but the heart of it is contained in the repeated words, *tat tvam asi*. In those words, also, is contained the essence of the Hindu understanding of suffering. It must be seen in relation to the whole, as being a part of the illusory world. It seems real, as the objects of the world seem real, but they are in fact manifestations of *Brahman*, and they have no reality in themselves.

The *Upanishads* do not try to assert that suffering is an illusion in the sense that it is not an actual experience. The long narrative in *Chandogya Up.* viii. 7–15, which tells of Indra's progress in spiritual understanding, takes up exactly that point. Indra comes to understand that the body may suffer but that the Self which pervades it is not affected. But he then reflects:

'He is not slain (when the body is slain). He is not lame (when the body) is lame, yet it is *as if* they kill him, *as if* they unclothe him. He comes to experience as it were what is unpleasant, he even weeps as it were. I see no good in this.'

Prajapati, who is instructing Indra, explains that true realisation of the Self is like being in a dreamless sleep. But that is not to deny the possibility of many 'as it were' experiences before that state is reached. In fact, the *Upanishads* realise that to be born is to come into contact with evil and suffering. The material body is full of corruption and potential conflict—a potentiality which is realised if the self gives way to its desires and passions:

'O Revered One,[2] in this foul-smelling, unsubstantial body, a conglomerate of bone, skin, muscle, marrow, flesh, semen, blood, mucus, tears, rheum, faeces, urine, wind, bile and phlegm, what is the good of the enjoyment of desires? In this body which is afflicted with desire, anger, covetousness, delusion, fear, despondency, envy, separation from what is desired, union with the undesired, hunger, thirst, old age, death, disease, sorrow and the like, what is the good of the enjoyment of desires? And we see that all this is perishing, as these gnats, mosquitoes and the like, the grass and the trees that grow and decay...In such a world as this, what is the good of enjoyment of desires? For he who has fed on them is seen to return (to this world) repeatedly. Be

[1] For the analogy of salt in water applied to *Brahman*, see also *Brihadaranyaka Up.* ii. 4.13, iv. 5.13.
[2] The ascetic Shakayanya, from whom Brihadratha is seeking wisdom.

Foundations

pleased, therefore, to deliver me. In this world I am like a frog in a waterless well.'[1]

But how is the frog to leap from the depths of his barren well? Only by realising that the body is the support of *atman*; it forms the platform from which *atman* can 'leap' into *Brahman*:

Just as a caterpillar when it has come to the end of a blade of grass, after having made another approach (to another blade) draws itself together towards it, so does this self, after having thrown away this body, and dispelled ignorance, after having another approach (to another body) draw itself together (for making the transition to another body)...But the man who does not desire, he who is without desire, who is freed from desire, whose desire is satisfied, whose desire is the self; his breaths do not depart. Being *Brahman* he goes to *Brahman*.[2]

Such an understanding of suffering might seem escapist, a selfish attempt to escape from the miseries and perplexities of the present world. But that is not the case. *Brahman* cannot be realised simply as an intellectual proposition. The realisation that *atman* is *Brahman* cannot be attained by pretending that the world does not exist, but only by seeing the world for what it is, in the right perspective, and by acting appropriately in the world. Appropriate action is a vital element in Hinduism. It means acting according to the pattern of life that belongs to one's present circumstances, concerned with the action only, and not with the fruits or rewards that might accrue from it. In other words, the way an individual acts demonstrates the extent to which he has realised *Brahman*; detachment from the world is necessary, but not as a way of escape from living appropriately. There can be no short-cut: 'This is, indeed, the antidote for the elemental self, acquirement of the knowledge of the Veda and the due performance of one's own duty. Pursuit of the duties of the stage of life to which each one belongs, this is the rule for one's own duty...'[3]

Thus there cannot be attainment or realisation of *Brahman* unless it is founded on appropriate action, *dharma*. *Mahanirvana Tantra* even described the abandoning of parents or family in order to become a recluse as a great sin.[4] Thus the *Upanishads*

---

[1] *Maitri Up.* i. 3 f. (trs. Radh.).   [2] *Brihadaranyaka Up.* iv. 4.3, 6 (trs. Radh.).
[3] *Maitri Up.* iv. 3 (trs. Radh.); there are four basic stages, but many different sub-divisions. For a brief description of the four stages, see *Jabala Up.* 4.
[4] viii. 18. Cf. vii. 7.

Hinduism

regard suffering as a part of the way the world has come to be, but not as the final truth or reality. Suffering is only a problem for those who cannot see it in the perspective of *Brahman*. *Brahman* is the underlying reality, the One without a second, where there can be no duality and hence no conflict, no becoming but only being, and hence no strife. The proper response to suffering is detachment from the objects and desires which give rise to suffering, and in that detachment to realise the truth that *atman* is *Brahman*.[1]

He sorrows not, because he is not connected with the sources of sorrow.[2]

But *Brahman* cannot be realised unless the individual performs his duties and obligations in the world—for their own sake, and not because they are an end in themselves, or because they will bring honour and reward. The *Upanishads* tend to assert this as a principle rather than in detail. It was left to the development of Hinduism to spell out in detail what *dharma* means in practice,[3] not least as a way of engaging the griefs and sufferings of life.

THE DEVELOPMENT

Hinduism has sometimes been criticised on the grounds that its emphasis on individual salvation, understood as *moksha* or release from the bondage of this world, has made it indifferent to the world as it is. It has been suggested that the Hindu, if he is true to his faith, will not be concerned about the sufferings of his fellow-creatures, nor will he feel any compulsion to take any action to relieve the distresses of the world. A. A. Macdonell, for example, expressed a common criticism of India when he wrote:

A result of the combined doctrine of transmigration and *karma* is, it is true, to reconcile men to their fate as the just retribution for deeds

---

[1] *Moksha* is frequently described in the *Upanishads* as attainment of *Brahman*, although the actual portrayal varies. It is sometimes pictorial, sometimes theistic, sometimes monistic. See, e.g., *Brihadaranyaka Up.* v. 10.1, *Shvetashvatara Up.* iv. 14, *Mundaka Up.* iii. 2.5–9.
[2] Shankara on *Brihadaranyaka* i. 5.19.
[3] That is a comparative judgement. The later sources deal specifically and in detail with the organisation of life. The *Upanishads* certainly deal with *dharma*, but not in such detail. See, e.g., *Chandogya Up.* ii. 23.1.

Development

done in a previous life, but on the other hand, it paralyzes action, drives to asceticism, and makes action self-regarding, since it becomes the aim of every man to win salvation for himself individually, by acquiring the right knowledge. There is consequently little scope for the development of other-regarding virtues, as each individual is intent on gaining his own salvation.

But such an attitude, however much it may, for the sake of argument, have been expressed in practice, is a travesty of Hinduism, not its true expression.[1] Hinduism came to see the development of men as taking place in four general 'areas', *Dharma*, *Artha*, *Kama* and *Moksha*. Broadly speaking, *dharma* refers to the moral and idealistic needs of men, though it is frequently used more particularly to refer to two comprehensive ideals, the organisation of society into clearly defined classes, and the organisation of individual lives within those classes into precise stages. *Artha* refers to material needs, and has a particular reference to the exercise of authority, and *kama* refers to the needs of the senses. None of these is escapist, nor can one be pursued to the exclusion of the others if a well-balanced life is to be achieved.[2] It may be true that *moksha* is the final goal, but *moksha* cannot be attained or even hoped for without realising the three other ends of life first. As P. H. Prabhu has put it, 'In modern terminology, these are the three principal motivating forces or urges or drives around which the whole life and conduct of man could be comprehended. And therefore, the management and conduct of his social and individual life is conceived and formulated in terms of these three, with reference to the ultimate end of life viz., *Moksha*.'[3]

A vast literature grew up in Hinduism devoted to the practical issues of life, and this entirely practical concern with the circumstances of life is in itself an important part of the Hindu understanding of suffering. Much of the literature has continuing authority in Hinduism because it forms a second category of

---

[1] Hence the claims of the Maharishi to be representing the forgotten truth of Hinduism, that meditation is not world-renouncing, but world-affirming.

[2] The correct balance of all three is emphasised in *Manu Smriti* ii. 224: 'Some say that *dharma* and *artha* are good, others say that *kama* and *artha* are good, and others that *dharma* alone or *kama* alone is good, but the correct position is that the three should exist together without encroaching on each other.' Cf. also *Manu Smriti* xii. 95.

[3] P. H. Prabhu, *Hindu Social Organization* (Bombay, 1963), p. 12.

Hinduism

scripture, known as *smriti*, 'what is remembered'.[1] The *smritis* are technically derivative, because they are held to be based on tradition which goes back to the *Vedas*, and the *smritis* are regarded as spelling out in detail what in practice was done in the true expression of Vedic religion. Certainly it is true that the *smriti* texts cannot be regarded as a development in Hinduism in the sense that they form a part of a strict sequence. On the contrary, they often contain very ancient material. What they represent, in general, is the attempt to set down, in accessible form, guidance and instruction for life, gathered from many different sources.

It is completely impossible to summarise the ways in which the *smriti* and other related texts deal with suffering, since they consider almost every conceivable situation which might give rise to suffering and suggest appropriate action. What is essential is that this element in Hinduism should be recognised and appreciated as being in itself an essential part of the Hindu response to suffering. There is no *moksha* that is not built on *dharma*. If it is true that *moksha* is impossible while an individual is bound by *karma* to the endless round of *samsara*, then it follows that *moksha* cannot be achieved unless it is founded on *dharma*; that is to say, if release from the bondage of this world is impossible while the weight of evil works and desires keeps an individual attached to this world in the process of rebirth, then it follows that there can be no release unless it is based on good works and renunciation which redress the balance.

[1] The main works in this category are known collectively as *Dharma Sastras*. The *Dharma Sastras* fall into four groups: *Sutras*, *Smritis* or *Sastras*, Commentaries, and *Nibandhas*. Two particularly influential works are the *Manu Smriti* (sometimes referred to as *The Lawbook of Manu*) and the later and more developed *Yajnavalkya Smriti* (Yajnavalkya being the famous wise man who appears frequently in the *Upanishads*). In addition, there are also many works which took up the old legends and traditions of India and used them as a vehicle for illustrating the ideals of life. Of particular importance are the *Puranas* and the *Epics* (*itihasa*). It is impossible to describe these briefly, because in effect they are encyclopaedias of Hindu beliefs, manners and customs. The best known and most frequently quoted are the *Vishnu* and *Bhagavata Puranas*, and the *Ramayana* and *Mahabharata Epics*. The *Mahabharata* contains the most revered and deeply loved of all the scriptures, the *Bhagavadgita*. The *Gita* and the *Upanishads*, together with an elliptical commentary on the *Upanishads* attempting to reconcile apparent contradictions, known as the *Brahma Sutra*, form the three most influential parts of authoritative scripture. They are sometimes referred to as 'the threefold canon' (*prasthana-traya*). The *Gita*, in order to indicate its relationship to the *Upanishads*, is sometimes referred to as *Bhagavadgita Upanishad*. 'The whole *Veda* is the basis of *Dharma*, as also the *Smritis* and the conduct of those that know the *Vedas*, the conduct of the good and the conscience of the disciplined.' *Manu Smriti* ii. 6 (trs. Raghavan).

Development

It follows that *karma* and *samsara* remain the key to the explanation of suffering, whether it occurs in individual circumstances or as a result of the condition in life in which an individual finds himself:

The acts done in former births never leave any creature. In determining the working out of *karma* the Lord of Creation saw them all. Man, since he is under the control of *karma*, must always have in mind how he can restore the balance and rescue himself from evil consequences.[1]

Such an attitude might seem to be fatalistic, but in fact it is the opposite: if one's present state is a consequence of what has gone before, the urgency of responsible and appropriate action becomes greater, not less, and the *smriti* texts repeatedly emphasise it. Thus in the dialogue in the *Mahabharata* between Dharmavyadha, the dutiful hunter, and Brahmana, Dharmavyadha accepts that his lowly position, which involves violence and killing, is a result of his former misdeeds. It is impossible to escape the consequences of what has gone before, but for that reason it is all the more essential to fulfil the obligations of being a hunter as conscientiously as possible—even though it means the infliction of pain and suffering. Brahmana assures him, 'Since those evil actions belong to the duties of your profession, the penalty of evil *karma* will not attach to you.'[2]

Here is the essence of *dharma*, doing whatever is appropriate in the circumstances in which one finds oneself. During a lifetime there can be progress between stages; and between existences there can be progress among the castes, but progress depends—greatly though not entirely—on fulfilling the duties appropriate to a particular stage or caste:

Man, who could normally live up to a hundred years, must apportion his time and take to *dharma*, *artha* and *kama* in such a way that these are mutually integrated and do not harm each other. As a boy he must attend to accomplishments like learning; in youth he should enjoy himself; in later life he should pursue the ideals of virtue and spiritual liberation.[3]

Dharma is not the gratification of desires. It is rather, action without attachment to the consequences. Thus when Yudhishtira in the *Mahabharata* called *dharma* 'the only boat that can carry

[1] *Mahabharata Vanaparva* 207.19 f. [2] *Mahabharata Vanaparva* 215.11 f.
[3] *Kama Sutra* i. 2.1 (trs. Raghavan).

Hinduism

men to salvation', [1] he also said that he pursued *dharma*, not because it was immediately rewarding, nor even because it led to salvation, but because he felt a strong, natural tendency to pursue that course. 'Fire consents to be extinguished, but submits not to be cold.' [2] Of course, it is just possible that that might be given a ruthless interpretation—the pursuit of one's own obligation and duty at the expense of others. *Dharma*, far from obliging men to relieve suffering, might compel them to *inflict* suffering. Such seemed to be implied in Dharmavyadha's attitude to hunting, referred to above. Later he goes on to say:

Men kill countless creatures that live on the ground when they trample them underfoot. The wisest and best-instructed men kill many creatures in various ways, even when sleeping or resting. Both earth and sky are full of living organisms which are killed by men quite unconsciously in their ignorance. [3]

The infliction of suffering may be necessary as a part of appropriate action, and, as will be seen, the problem of the *Gita* arises out of exactly that consideration. [4] But generally speaking, the opposite is the case. The *Manu Smriti*, particularly, emphasises to such an extent the central importance of causing no harm or pain to anyone, that it appears as a part of the summary of law for the four castes:

Abstention from injuring (creatures), veracity, abstention from unlawfully appropriating (the goods of others), purity and control of the organs, Manu has declared to be the summary of the law for the four castes. [5]

It is not that certain acts can be predefined as necessarily evil, but that abstention from them *can* be predefined as conducive to detachment and self-awareness:

Without doing injury to non-living beings, flesh can be had nowhere; and the killing of living beings is not conducive to heaven; hence

---

[1] *Mahabharata Vanaparva* 207; see also *ibid. Santi.* 174.45 ff.
[2] Cf. also *Apastamba Dharma Sutra* xx. 1–3: 'One must not observe the ordained duties with a worldly end in view. For in the end they bear no fruit. Just as when a mango is planted to bear fruit, shade and fragrance also result concomitantly, even so the ordained duty that is performed is attended by material gains' (trs. Raghavan).
[3] *Mahabharata Vanaparva* 207.30 ff. Cf. the Jain reaction to the same observation, pp. 281–2.
[4] See p. 225.   [5] *Manu Smriti* x. 63 (trs. Bühler). See also *ibid.* iv. 238.

Development

eating of flesh must be avoided...There may be no harm in eating flesh, in drinking or in sexual indulgence; creatures are by nature prone, but refraining therefrom holds great fruits.[1]

In the repeated claim that *dharma* involves compassion rather than ruthlessness the seeds of *ahimsa*, non-violence, are sown. *Ahimsa* does not appear as a clearly articulated concept, even in the *Upanishads*,[2] but as advice it is frequently repeated. It appears, for example, in the famous response of the bear to the tiger, quoted by Sita in the *Ramayana*:

You should not retaliate when another does you injury. Good conduct is the adornment of those who are good. Even if those who do wrong deserve to be killed, the noble ones should be compassionate, since there is no one who does not transgress.[3]

In these texts, therefore, there is a serious recognition of the reality of suffering and of the need to take action against it—not because it is the ultimate reality, but, more prosaically, simply because it is there. Suffering is not necessarily evil as such: it can be undertaken voluntarily as a way of progressing towards renunciation and detachment. But the underlying sense of tension and conflict in the universe remains as strong as it was in the *Vedas*; and in the *Epics*, particularly in the *Ramayana*'s long accounts of the conflict against the demon king Ravana, it re-appears in mythological form. There is every need to take sides and to make a stand. Furthermore, much suffering is a direct result of *karma*, and the downward slide must be checked. This applies not only to oneself, but also to others, and there is an obligation to try and make *dharma* widely known and accepted;[4] it is a part of the purpose of the *smriti* texts to do exactly that: to

[1] *Manu Smriti* v. 48, 56 (trs. Raghavan).
[2] *Ahimsa* is far stronger in Buddhism and Jainism, and was probably reasserted in Hinduism in reaction to those two 'break-away' movements; see further pp. 266, 281.
[3] Quoted by Sita to Hanuman after the death of the demon King of Ceylon, Ravana. Hanuman (the monkey god and devoted helper of Rama in his fight against the evil king) had begged Sita to be allowed to destroy the demon guards. Sita replied: 'No. They were under the King's control and simply carried out his orders. Who can be angry with the servants? Now that Ravana is dead, they will pursue me no more.' For the whole passage see *Ramayana Yuddha Kanda*.
[4] *Manu Smriti* ii. 159 points out that this cannot be compelled on anyone—i.e. suffering ought not to be used as an instrument to encourage others to combat suffering: 'The teaching to fellow beings of what is beneficial must be done in a non-violent manner; he who desires *Dharma* should employ his words sweetly and finely' (trs. Raghavan).

bring people to an awareness of the causes of suffering, and to show in what ways suffering can be alleviated or avoided.[1]

Thus the purpose of texts dealing with *dharma* is to give guidance on appropriate action in as many of the foreseeable situations of life as is possible. Obviously, the possible variations are enormous, and the texts themselves recognise that they cannot catch the whole of life in their net. Again, Brihaspati pointed out that decisions taken by looking up a *smriti* text and trying to apply the letter of the *sastra* literally are the very contradiction of *dharma*. What is required is a rational consideration of the circumstances in which can then be applied the collective wisdom and experience of the *sastras*. The *Mahabharata* makes the same point when it says that, in deciding what is *dharma* or *adharma*, the wise person will rely on an intelligent understanding (*buddhi*) of the situation.[2]

Thus the texts dealing with *dharma* do not attempt to dictate rigid and invariable patterns of life; they aim to provide authoritative guidance in order to assist individuals to act in such a way that they will attain self-fulfilment and release from the recurring bondage of pain and suffering. What *dharma* recommends is an even disposition in the face of either happiness or sorrow—in other words, perfect detachment:

In this respect it is said that they (who) are possessed of wisdom, beholding that the world of life is overwhelmed with sorrow both bodily and mental, and with happiness that is sure to end in misery, never suffer themselves to be stupefied...Happiness and misery, prosperity and adversity, gain and loss, death and life, in their turn, wait upon all creatures. For this reason the wise man of tranquil self would neither be elated with joy nor be depressed with sorrow.[3]

There is an inescapable duality in human experience, and the *Mahabharata*, like the *Upanishads*, holds that the only way to reconcile that duality is not to pursue one or other side of it as being the *summum bonum*, but to rise above it and see the experiences of duality as passing and transitory moments: 'Happiness always ends in sorrow, and sometimes proceeds from sorrow itself. He, therefore, that desires external happiness must abandon both.'[4] The purpose of *dharma* is to show how the even disposition

---

[1] For an example of this, see Kautilya, *Arthasastra* viii.
[2] *Mahabharata Santiparva* 141.102.
[3] *Ibid.* 190.6; 25.31 (trs. Ray).
[4] *Ibid.* 25.24 (trs. Ray).

can be attained and exercised in the face of both happiness and sorrow. *Dharma* does not point to a single rigid solution, but, rather, it underlines the diversity of human activity which is so characteristic an emphasis of Hinduism. There are many different levels to be worked through before an individual attains *moksha*, and any attempt to find a single path is likely to prove quite irrelevant to the majority of human beings. Yet there is, in fact, one work which does try to gather some of the many threads of Hindu belief into a unity, and that is the *Bhagavadgita* (the *Gita*).[1]

The *Gita* is particularly relevant to the subject of suffering, because it begins with the fact of human suffering—or more particularly, it begins with the problem raised earlier, that the following of *dharma* may necessitate the infliction of suffering on others. The *Gita* is a part of the *Mahabharata* (though it has a quite independent status and existence in Hinduism, which is the reason for its separate consideration here), and it occurs at a moment in the narrative when the Kauravas and the Pandavas, two tribes descended from the same ancestor, are about to engage in strife for the vacant throne of the Kurus. Yudhishthira, of the Pandavas, is the heir by choice of the deceased king, but he has been usurped by his cousin, Duryodhana. One of the great heroes of the Pandavas is Arjuna, and just as the battle is about to commence Arjuna realises that the opposing army is made up of his own family and friends. He feels, therefore, that he ought not to fight, and he turns to his charioteer, Krishna (who is the god Vishnu in human form, and has taken the side of the Pandavas), and tells him that he cannot go into battle. His arguments display a strong sense of the tragedy of suffering:

There saw Arjuna standing fathers and grandfathers, teachers, uncles, brothers, sons and grandsons, as also companions; and also fathers-in-law and friends in both the armies. When the son of Kunti (Arjuna) saw all these kinsmen thus standing arrayed, he was overcome with great compassion and uttered this in sadness:
'When I see my own people arrayed and eager for fight, O Krishna, my limbs quail, my mouth goes dry, my body shakes and my hair stands on end...It is not right that we slay our kinsmen, the sons of Dhritarashtra. Indeed, how can we be happy, O Madhava (Krishna), if we kill our own people? Even if these whose minds are overpowered

---

[1] The high status of the *Gita* has already been briefly described on p. 220. It is that very high status which makes a study of the *Gita* essential in any consideration of Hindu thought or beliefs.

Hinduism

by greed see no wrong in the destruction of the family and no crime in treachery to friends, why should we not have the wisdom to turn away from this sin, O Janardana (Krishna), we who see the wrong in the destruction of the family? In the ruin of a family, its ancient laws are destroyed: and when the laws perish, the whole family yields to lawlessness...Alas, what a great sin have we resolved to commit in striving to slay our own people through our greed for the pleasures of the kingdom! Far better would it be for me if the sons of Dhritarashtra, with weapons in hand, should slay me in the battle, while I remain unresisting and unarmed.'

Having spoken thus on the field of battle, Arjuna sank down on the seat of his chariot, casting away his bow and arrow, his spirit overwhelmed by sorrow.[1]

The immediate response of Krishna, in *Gita* ii. 11–38, advances two lines of argument to encourage Arjuna to take up arms, even though it will result in pain and suffering. The first is that he should consider the nature of the real self and the way in which it is related to the body which appears to suffer. In fact, if the self, *atman*, is realised to be an aspect of *Brahman*, the true 'self' cannot suffer. Part of this passage has already been quoted,[2] and its application to suffering scarcely needs elaborating. The second line of argument is an appeal to *dharma*. This is significant, because Arjuna had appealed to a form of *dharma* as a reason for not taking up arms: the pillars of the world would be shaken if families fell into internecine strife. But Krishna points out that the overriding duty is to fulfil one's own *dharma*, particularly since the injuries it causes are only superficially serious—the real self cannot be affected by external accidents:

Further, having regard for thine own duty, thou shouldst not falter; there exists no greater good for a *kshatriya* (warrior) than war enjoined by duty. Happy are the warriors, O Partha (Arjuna), for whom such a war comes of its own accord as an open door to heaven. But if thou doest not this lawful battle, then thou wilt fail thy duty and glory and will incur sin...Either slain thou shalt go to heaven; or victorious thou shalt enjoy the earth; therefore arise, O Son of Kunti (Arjuna), resolve on battle. Treating alike pleasure and pain, gain and loss, victory and defeat, then get ready for battle. Thus thou shalt not incur sin.[3]

[1] *Gita* i. 26–30, 37–40, 43, 45–7 (trs. Radh.).
[2] See p. 196.
[3] *Gita* ii. 31–3, 37–8 (trs. Radh.).

Development

It might seem that there is a contradiction between those two lines of argument: the first advocated detachment from 'the changes and chances of this fleeting life', and the second advocated commitment to life in order to fulfil one's *dharma*. How can detachment and involvement be combined? The *Gita* immediately meets the point by stating that it is possible to act without becoming attached or 'bound up' in the action itself:

To action alone hast thou a right and never at all to its fruit; let not the fruits of action be thy motive; neither let there be in thee any attachment to inaction. Fixed in *yoga*, do thy work, O winner of wealth (Arjuna), abandoning attachment, with an even mind in success and failure, for evenness of mind is called *yoga*.[1]

This is the essence of the Hindu response to suffering. Not unnaturally, Arjuna asks Krishna how such a disposition of mind can be attained. The main part of the *Gita* is an exposition of the ways in which such detachment and discovery of *Brahman* can be attained. Three broad avenues are described and explained, the way of work (devotion to duty),[2] the way of knowledge or of perceptive understanding,[3] and the way of devotion, or *bhakti*. *Bhakti*, devotion to God, is an important part of the *Gita*, as it is of Hinduism generally. It implies conceiving of *Brahman*, Being-itself, in personal and theistic terms. In the *Upanishads* several passages tend towards an understanding of *Brahman* in absolute terms, beyond personality, and therefore beyond relationships of worship or love or praise. That non-dualistic interpretation was developed with great skill by Shankara, with whose name the *advaita* school of Hinduism is particularly linked. *Advaita*[4] can easily accommodate theism, by saying that gods are as much an aspect or manifestation of *Brahman* as anything else, and that *bhakti* is an important stage in spiritual progress. The *Upanishads* sometimes make that accommodation.[5] But others regarded a theistic interpretation as being the truth about *Brahman*, not as a

[1] *Yoga* is defined in the *Gita* as 'skill in action' (*yogah karmasu kaushalan*). *Yoga* is the means of acquiring evenness in disposition and also the exercise of it. The conclusion of the *Gita* (see especially xviii. 1, 2, 5, 6, 8–11, 50–4) makes the same point in greater detail—'the abandonment of the fruit of all works...is relinquishment.'
[2] *Karmayoga*. [3] *Jnyanayoga*.
[4] Non-dualism, frequently referred to as monism.
[5] As, for example, in *Mundaka Up.* ii. 1.1 ff. For a particularly famous passage, in which the many gods are reduced to one and the one is identified with Brahman, see *Brihadaranyaka Up.* iii. 9.1–9.

Hinduism

stage to be discarded and left behind. That line of thought was developed particularly by Ramanuja, who regarded devotion as belonging to the highest bliss. The self, in attaining *Brahman*, is not absorbed in *Brahman* to such an extent that it loses its individuality. In a sense, it continues to stand over against God in adoration and worship and love. Thus selves remain many, not one; yet at the same time the self is not distinct: the self and the whole universe can be thought of as the body of God, who is their soul and who animates them. They are, therefore, characteristic of God and cannot exist without him, but the self retains a measure of independence which makes it what it is.[1] The self cannot escape from God, but at the same time it is not lost in God:

Giving up all other ordained observances, abandoning all my desires inclusive of salvation, O Lord! I took refuge under your feet that measured the whole universe. You alone are my mother, my father, my kinsmen, my teacher, my learning, my wealth; O God of gods! You are my everything.[2]

Bhakti has important applications to the understanding of suffering, because it implies that God is knowable and accessible in this life. In reverse, it also means that God may perhaps participate in this life to assist and support those in distress. The incarnate forms of God are known as *avatars*, or *avataras*. Exactly that view of God appears in the *Gita*, as it does also in many other expressions of Hinduism. Thus in the *Gita* Krishna (himself a manifestation in human form of the supreme God Vishnu) assures Arjuna:

'Though I am unborn, and My self is imperishable, though I am the lord of all creatures, yet, establishing Myself in My own nature, I come into (empiric) being through My power.[3] Whenever there is a decline of righteousness and rise of unrighteousness, O Bharata (Arjuna), then I send forth Myself. For the protection of the good, for the destruction of the wicked, and for the establishment of righteousness, I come into being from age to age. He who knows thus in its true nature My divine birth and works is not born again, when he leaves his body, but comes to Me, O Arjuna. Delivered from passion, fear, and anger, absorbed in Me, taking refuge in Me, many purified by the austerity of wisdom have attained to My state of being.'[4]

[1] Hence the system is known as *vishishtadvaita*, or 'qualified non-dualism'.
[2] Ramanuja, *Sharanagatigadya* (trs. Raghavan).
[3] *Maya*, the ability to make things appear in manifest form.
[4] *Gita* iv. 6–10 (trs. Radh.).

Development

Thus it can be hoped that God will make himself manifest in incarnate form to relieve the distresses of the world and to take action against evil and corruption: 'Whenever righteousness declines and unrighteousness increases, the Almighty Lord, Hari, creates himself.'[1] Hari is in fact Vishnu in his role of removing sorrows and bringing comfort.

The idea of incarnation again underlines the fact that Hinduism does not underestimate the harsh realities of suffering. Furthermore, stories of the incarnations of God to relieve suffering remain exemplary and inspiring for Hindus to do likewise. Nevertheless, suffering is a part of *maya*, the way things have been brought to pass and happen to be in manifest, apparent form.[2] To that extent suffering is coincidental. It may be felt as an utterly real experience, but it is not the final truth about reality or about the self which has begun to realise its oneness with the totality of Being-itself. The proper response, therefore, to suffering must be detachment, thereby seeing suffering in its relative perspective. Such an attitude might seem escapist, but it is not, since there cannot be any adequate detachment that is not tested by the way in which it is sustained in the very fullest involvement. That, in the *Gita*, was the difference between the passionate and the dispassionate involvement. However, the fact remains that there is a constant temptation in Hinduism to allow detachment to slide imperceptibly into indifference. The view, based on *karma*, that an individual's present position and suffering are a consequence of his previous actions, is all too readily open to that fatal transformation, and it can produce a rigidity and acceptance of the *status quo* which is almost paralysing. It hardly needs to be reiterated that such a transformation is a corruption of Hinduism,

---

[1] *Bhagavata* iv. 24, 56. The *Bhagavata*, like the *Epics*, tells many stories of God becoming incarnate in the world.

[2] The word *maya* has had many different meanings in the course of time, but centrally it means 'the ability or power to express oneself in different forms', as in *Rig-Veda* vi. 47.18, *anekarupagrahanasamarthyam*. In that verse, Indra, in his battle with the demons, takes many forms through his power of *maya* (*mayabhih*); cf. x. 54.2. *Maya* is thus the power of *Brahman* to bring itself into manifest forms of existence or appearance: see *Katha Up*. ii. 2.9. *Maya* can be viewed from at least three points of view: first, the actual 'bringing into being'; second, the apparent nature of what has been brought to be (i.e. illusion); third, the acceptance of those apparent forms as 'real' (i.e. delusion); 'Deluded by my *maya*, the ignorant look for me who am hidden' (*Guruda Purana*). Thus Sayana on *Rig-Veda* iii. 27.7 observed that the most common meanings of *maya* in the *Rig-Veda* are *prajna* (intelligence) and *kapata* (deceit). To translate *maya* as 'illusion' is very much to oversimplify the word.

not its true expression. But the temptation is there, and it is one of which Indians themselves are entirely aware—to point it out is not to criticise externally and unsympathetically, but to repeat what many Hindus have themselves expressed. As a result, much of the Hindu discussion of suffering in modern times has been an exploration of the ways in which detachment can be safeguarded from turning into indifference.

The problem was raised, precisely and specifically, by Sri Aurobindo, one of the greatest interpreters of Hinduism in recent times, in *The Life Divine*. The passage is worth quoting at length, because it shows how central the question is, and how, also, it is met in intellectual terms:

Individual salvation can have no real sense if existence in the cosmos is itself an illusion. In the monistic view the individual soul is one with the Supreme, its sense of separateness an ignorance, escape from the sense of separateness and identity with the Supreme its salvation. But who then profits by this escape? Not the supreme Self, for it is supposed to be always and inalienably free, still, silent, pure. Not the world, for that remains constantly in the bondage and is not freed by the escape of any individual soul from the universal illusion. It is the individual soul itself which effects its supreme good by escaping from the sorrow and the division into the peace and the bliss. There would seem then to be some kind of reality of the individual soul as distinct from the world and from the Supreme even in the event of freedom and illumination. But for the illusionist the individual soul is an illusion and non-existent except in the inexplicable mystery of *maya*. Therefore we arrive at the escape of an illusory non-existent soul from an illusory non-existent bondage in an illusory non-existent world as the supreme good which that non-existent soul has to pursue! For this is the last word of the knowledge, 'There is none bound, none freed, none seeking to be free'...

These things, it is said, cannot be explained; they are the initial and insoluble miracle. They are for us a practical fact and have to be accepted. We have to escape by a confusion out of a confusion. The individual soul can only cut the knot of ego by a supreme act of egoism, an exclusive attachment to its own individual salvation which amounts to an absolute assertion of its separate existence in *maya*. We are led to regard other souls as if they were figments of our mind and their salvation unimportant, our soul alone as if it were entirely real and its salvation the one thing that matters. I come to regard my personal escape from bondage as real while other souls who are equally myself remain behind in the bondage!

Development

It is only when we put aside all irreconcilable antinomy between Self and the world that things fall into their place by a less paradoxical logic. We must accept the many-sidedness of the manifestation even while we assert the unity of the Manifested. And is not this after all the truth that pursues us wherever we cast our eyes, unless seeing we choose not to see? Is not this after all the perfectly natural and simple mystery of Conscious Being that It is bound neither by its unity nor by its multiplicity? It is 'absolute' in the sense of being entirely free to include and arrange in its own way all possible terms of its self-expression. There is none bound, none freed, none seeking to be free,—for always That is a perfect freedom. It is so free that it is not even bound by its liberty. It can play at being bound without incurring a real bondage. Its chain is a self-imposed convention, its limitation in the ego a transitional device that it uses in order to repeat its transcendence and universality in the scheme of the individual *Brahman*...

The liberation of the individual soul is therefore the keynote of the definite divine action; it is the primary divine necessity and the pivot on which all else turns. It is the point of light at which the intended complete self-manifestation in the many begins to emerge. But the liberated soul extends its perception of unity horizontally as well as vertically. Its unity with the transcendent one is incomplete without its unity with the cosmic many. And that lateral unity translates itself by multiplication, a reproduction of its own liberated state at other points in the multiplicity. The divine soul reproduces itself in similar liberated souls as the animal reproduces itself in similar bodies. Therefore, whenever even a single soul is liberated, there is a tendency to an extension and even to an outburst of the same divine self-consciousness in other individual souls of our terrestrial humanity and,—who knows?—perhaps even beyond the terrestrial consciousness. Where shall we fix the limit of that extension? Is it altogether a legend which says of the Buddha that as he stood on the threshold of *nirvana*, of the non-being, his soul turned back and took the vow never to make the irrevocable crossing so long as there was a single being upon earth undelivered from the knot of the suffering, from the bondage of the ego?[1]...[2]

For most people, however, the problem occurs in practical rather than theoretical terms. It occurs in the actual circumstances of life, and it occurs, therefore, acutely in political decisions.

[1] The allusion is to the Buddhist idea of the *boddhisattva*, the enlightened one who suspends the moment of his own final release and attainment in order to assist those who are weighed down in bondage. For a discussion of the idea, see pp. 259 ff.
[2] Sri Aurobindo, *The Life Divine*, quoted from *A Source Book in Indian Philosophy*, ed. S. Radhakrishnan and C. A. Moore (Princeton, 1957), pp. 586–8.

Hinduism

Nehru, for example, saw that much of the distress of India was due to detachment of the wrong sort, detachment in the sense of indifference and acceptance of the *status quo*. It was this rigidity which had slowly come to paralyse India and to produce the squalor and suffering of many of its inhabitants:

The search for the sources of India's strength and for her deterioration and decay is long and intricate. Yet the recent causes of that decay are obvious enough. She fell behind in the march of technique, and Europe, which had long been backward in many matters, took the lead in technical progress...

Why this should have happened so is more difficult to unravel, for India was not lacking in mental alertness and technical skill in earlier times. One senses a progressive deterioration during centuries...A rational spirit of inquiry, so evident in earlier times, which might well have led to the further growth of science, is replaced by irrationalism and a blind idolatry of the past. Indian life becomes a sluggish stream, living in the past, moving slowly through the accumulations of dead centuries. The heavy burden of the past crushes it and a kind of coma seizes it. It is not surprising that in this condition of mental stupor and physical weariness India should have deteriorated and remained rigid and immobile, while other parts of the world marched ahead.[1]

It is not that Nehru undervalued or despised the traditional foundations. On the contrary, he had a deep sense of India's history. He saw clearly, for example, the values in a well-ordered society towards which the caste-system contributed.[2] Yet despite the values represented by the caste-system, Nehru was equally aware that the abuse and over-rigidity of the system had led to unjustifiable suffering. The attempt to make the system more flexible became a major part of his policy. In this he was following the inspiration and example of Gandhi. In connection with the attempt to achieve Indian independence he wrote:

What could we do? How could we pull India out of this quagmire of poverty and defeatism which sucked her in? Not for a few years of excitement and agony and suspense, but for long generations our people had offered their 'blood and toil, tears and sweat'. And this process had eaten its way deep into the body and soul of India, poisoning every aspect of our corporate life, like that fell disease which consumes the tissues of the lungs and kills slowly but inevitably. Sometimes we thought that some swifter and more obvious process

[1] J. L. Nehru, *The Discovery of India* (London, 1946), pp. 33 f.
[2] See especially *ibid.* p. 61.

resembling cholera or the bubonic plague, would have been better; but that was a passing thought, for adventurism leads nowhere, and the quack treatment of deep-seated diseases does not yield results. And then Gandhi came. He was like a powerful current of fresh air that made us stretch ourselves and take deep breaths; like a beam of light that pierced the darkness and removed the scales from our eyes; like a whirlwind that upset many things, but most of all the working of people's minds. He did not descend from the top; he seemed to emerge from the millions of India, speaking their language and incessantly drawing attention to them and their appalling condition. Get off the backs of these peasants and workers, he told us, all you who live by their exploitation; get rid of the system that produces poverty and misery.[1]

Gandhi's life was devoted to that end. In connection with suffering, his most memorable contribution was the practical assertion of *ahimsa*, or non-violence. The word *ahimsa* scarcely appears in the principal *Upanishads*, although the attitude implied in the word is advocated. The word *ahimsa* appears in *Chandogya Up*. iii. 17.4 in a list of virtues:

Austerity, almsgiving, uprightness, non-violence, trustfulness, these are the gifts for the priests.

Otherwise, *ahimsa* only seems to have become prominent after the emergence of Buddhism. By the time of Patanjali's *Yoga Sutra* (2nd century B.C.), *ahimsa* appears first in the list of 'restraints', *yama*.

Restraint, observance, posture, regulation of breath, abstraction (of the senses), concentration, meditation and trance are the eight accessories of *yoga*. Of these, the restraints are: *ahimsa*, veracity, abstinence from theft, continence, and abstinence from avariciousness. They are the great vow, universal, and not-limited by life-state, space, time, and circumstance.[2]

However, a later commentary on those verses in the *Yoga-bhasya* of Vyasa, confined *ahimsa* to particular circumstances. Some injuries are unavoidable in the perfectly proper and obligatory pursuit of *dharma*—as Krishna and Dharmavyadha also argued:[3]

Ahimsa is limited to life-state, as for example, the injury inflicted by a fisherman is limited to fish alone, and to none else. The same is limited

---

[1] *Ibid.* p. 303.
[2] *Yoga Sutra* ii. 29–31 (trs. Prasada). Cf. also *Mahabharata Santiparva* 21. 11, 37. 10, 114. 65.   [3] See pp. 221–2, 226.

Hinduism

to space, as, for example, in the case of a man who says to himself, 'I shall not injure at a sacred place.' The same is limited to time, as, for example, in the case of a man who says to himself, 'I shall not cause injury on the sacred day of the *caturdashi* (the fourteenth) of the lunar fortnight.' The same...is limited by circumstance, as, for example, when a man says to himself, 'I shall cause injury only for the sake of gods and *brahmins* and not in any other way.' Or as, for example, injury is caused by soldiers in battle alone and nowhere else... Universal is that which pervades all conditions of life, everywhere, always, and is nowhere out of place. They are called the great vow.[1]

It is clear that Gandhi attempted to assert *ahimsa* as the great vow, so far as that was possible, though even he realised that there were occasions when violence was the only creditable course of action—as, for example, when the choice lies between cowardice and violence.[2]

But in general he saw *ahimsa* as the supreme moral strength:

I...justify entire non-violence, and consider it possible in relation between man and man and nations and nations; but it is not 'a resignation from all real fighting against wickedness'. On the contrary, the non-violence of my conception is a more active and more real fighting against wickedness than retaliation whose very nature is to increase wickedness. I contemplate a mental, and therefore a moral, opposition to immoralities. I seek entirely to blunt the edge of the tyrant's sword, not by putting up against it a sharper-edged weapon, but by disappointing his expectation that I would be offering physical resistance. The resistance of the soul that I should offer instead would elude him. It would at first dazzle him, and at last compel recognition from him, which recognition would not humiliate him but would uplift him.[3]

Gandhi was sometimes accused by his fellow-Indians of distorting Hinduism and of getting the various elements of Hinduism out of balance.[4] In the case of *ahimsa* he claimed to be implementing the ancient traditions of India:

I am not a visionary. I claim to be a practical idealist. The religion of non-violence is not meant merely for the *rishis* and saints. It is meant for

[1] Vyasa, *Yoga-Bhyasa* on *Yoga Sutra* ii. 31.
[2] See M. Gandhi, *Non-violence in Peace and War*, 1, pp. 1 f.
[3] *Ibid.* p. 44.
[4] In the famous dispute between Gandhi and Tagore, Tagore accused him of being too socially active, and of being over-concerned with the material needs of the poor, without giving sufficient consideration to the spiritual emancipation that must accompany the material. 'Mind is no less valuable than cotton thread.' Despite their differences the two remained very close.

Development

the common people as well. Non-violence is the law of our species as violence is the law of the brute. The spirit lies dormant in the brute, and he knows no law but that of physical might. The dignity of man requires obedience to a higher law—to the strength of the spirit.

I have therefore ventured to place before India the ancient law of self-sacrifice. For *satyagraha*[1] and its offshoots, non-cooperation and civil resistance, are nothing but new names for the law of suffering. The *rishis*, who discovered the law of non-violence in the midst of violence, were greater geniuses than Newton. They were themselves greater warriors than Wellington. Having themselves known the use of arms, they realised their uselessness, and taught a weary world that its salvation lay not through violence but through non-violence.

Non-violence in its dynamic condition means conscious suffering. It does not mean meek submission to the will of the evil-doer, but it means the pitting of one's whole soul against the will of the tyrant. Working under this law of our being, it is possible for a single individual to defy the whole might of an unjust empire to save his honour, his religion, his soul and lay the foundation for that empire's fall or its regeneration.[2]

But there were other Hindus who saw the implementation of *ahimsa* as a betrayal of Hinduism, not as its true expression. By one of the greatest of all tragic ironies Gandhi, the prophet of *ahimsa*, died a violent death. It is entirely possible that the nationalist who committed the assassination saw in that action the fulfilment of his own *dharma*. For the real problem of suffering in Hinduism is that there *may* not be a problem. It depends from which point you start. Yet still, in many ways, *ahimsa* is the true culmination of the many strands of thought and practice which make up the Hindu understanding of suffering. And Tagore, who differed from Gandhi in particulars, nevertheless admired Gandhi for the way in which he embodied the principle of *ahimsa* and brought it back to life in the world. In the context of the struggle for independence, he wrote to C. F. Andrews:

The West has its unshakable faith in material strength and prosperity; and therefore, however loud grows the cry for peace and disarmament, its ferocity growls louder, gnashing its teeth and lashing its tail in impatience. It is like a fish, hurt by the pressure of the flood, planning to fly in the air. Certainly the idea is brilliant, but it is not possible for a

[1] 'The term *satyagraha* was coined by me in South Africa to express the force that the Indians there used for full eight years.' Gandhi, *Young India*.
[2] M. Gandhi, *Non-violence in Peace and War*, p. 2.

235

fish to realize. We, in India, have to show the world what is that truth which not only makes disarmament possible but turns it into strength.

The truth that moral force is a higher power than brute force will be proved by the people who are unarmed. Life, in its higher development, has thrown off its tremendous burden of armour and a prodigious quantity of flesh, till man has become the conqueror of the brute world. The day is sure to come when the frail man of spirit, completely unhampered by airfleets and dreadnoughts, will prove that the meek are to inherit the earth.

It is in the fitness of things that Mahatma Gandhi, frail in body and devoid of all material resources, should call up the immense power of the meek that has been waiting in the heart of the destitute and insulted humanity of India. The destiny of India has chosen for its ally the power of soul, and not that of muscle. And she is to raise the history of man from the muddy level of physical conflict to the higher moral altitude...

We, the famished ragged ragamuffins of the East, are to win freedom for all humanity. We have no word for 'Nation' in our language. When we borrow this word from other people, it never fits us. For we are to make our league with *Narayan*,[1] and our triumph will not give us anything but victory itself; victory for God's world. I have seen the West; I covet not the unholy feast in which she revels every moment, growing more and more bloated and red and dangerously delirious. Not for us is this mad orgy of midnight, with lighted torches, but awakement in the serene light of the morning.[2]

[1] The divine spark or essence in men.
[2] ed. C. F. Andrews, *Letters to a Friend*, pp. 127 f.

6

BUDDHISM

THE FOUNDATIONS

To outside observers Buddhism has frequently seemed a pessimistic religion. Despite the serene countenance with which the Buddha is almost invariably portrayed, Buddhism has seemed to be preoccupied with suffering and grief: 'Take the Book of Ecclesiastes, remove from it every reference to God, and you have a fair representation of the philosophy which forms the basis of Buddhism. "All is vanity."'[1] But in fact to describe Buddhism as pessimistic is mistaken, although it is easy to see how that impression arises. Awareness of suffering, without any pretence or deception about it, lies at the very root and foundation of Buddhism. The Buddha's insight, in its most concentrated form, is found in the Four Noble Truths. In general terms they are usually expressed as: the existence of suffering, the causes of suffering, the cessation of suffering, and the path that leads to the cessation of suffering. There is thus no doubt at all that awareness of suffering is a deeply essential part of Buddhism, as Lama Govinda has emphasised:

Descartes, the famous French philosopher, started his philosophy with the formula: 'Cogito, ergo sum,' 'I think, therefore I am.' The Buddha went one step further in starting with an even more universally established principle, based on an experience that is common to all sentient beings: the fact of suffering.[2]

Of all religions, Buddhism is the one which concentrates most immediately and directly on suffering. But of course to be *aware* of suffering is by no means the same thing as to be necessarily pessimistic. It would in fact be more appropriate to describe Buddhism not as 'pessimistic' but as 'realistic', since it begins, quite simply, with the common facts of experience:

Suffering in Buddhism is not the expression of pessimism or of the world-tiredness of an aged civilization: it is the fundamental thesis of

---

[1] H. Moore, *The Christian Faith in Japan* (S.P.G. 1904), p. 27.
[2] Lama Anagarika Govinda, *The Psychological Attitude of Early Buddhist Philosophy* (London, 1961), pp. 47 f.

a world-embracing thought, because there exists no experience which is equally universal. Not all sentient beings are thinking beings, and not all thinking beings reach the stage in which this faculty conceives its own nature and importance; but all sentient beings endure suffering; because all are subject to old age, decay and death...It was this experience of common suffering that caused the Bodhisattva[1] to leave his home, his family, his wealth, and to sacrifice his royal position; and consequently he took it later on as the starting point of his ethical and philosophical system. Without fully understanding this axiomatic truth of suffering one cannot really understand the other parts of his teaching.[2]

That quotation illustrates the central importance of suffering in Buddhist thought. Awareness of suffering is not symptomatic of gloom or despondency; it is, rather, the realistic observation of the way things happen to be. But the Buddha's teaching[3] went far beyond simple observation of the facts: by penetrating the causes of suffering—the underlying reasons why suffering occurs—he showed the way in which suffering can be transcended and brought to cease. The way leading to the cessation of suffering is summarised in the Noble Eightfold Path. These basic insights occur in their most concentrated form in the First Sermon of the Buddha at Benares:[4]

Thus have I heard. The Blessed One was once living in the Deer Park at Isipatana near Baranasi.[5] There he addressed the group of five bhikkhus:[6]

'Bhikkhus, these two extremes ought not to be practised by one who has gone forth from the household of life. What are the two? There is devotion to the indulgence of sense-pleasures, which is low, common, the way of ordinary people, unworthy and unprofitable; and there is devotion to self-mortification, which is painful, unworthy and unprofitable.

'Avoiding both these extremes, the Tathagata (Perfected One)[7] has realized the Middle Path: it gives vision, it gives knowledge, and it

---

[1] The Buddha in his capacity of the Enlightened One who wishes to share enlightenment with others.

[2] Govinda, *op. cit.* p. 48.   [3] The Buddha lived *c.* 6th cent. B.C., see pp. 260 ff.

[4] The *Dhammacakkappavattana-sutta*, the setting in motion of the wheel of truth: *Samyutta-nikaya* lvi. 11 (trs. Rahula).   [5] Benares.

[6] The word *bhikkhu* means 'one who begs for food', and is the word used to describe Buddhist monks.

[7] 'He who has thus come' or 'thus attained', a title of the Buddha as the Perfected One.

Foundations

leads to calm, to insight, to enlightenment, to Nibbana.[1] And what is that Middle Path...? It is simply the Noble Eightfold Path, namely, right view, right thought, right speech, right action, right livelihood, right effort, right mindfulness, right concentration. This is the Middle Path realized by the Tathagata, which gives vision, which gives knowledge, and which leads to calm, to insight, to enlightenment, to Nibbana.

'The Noble Truth of suffering is this: Birth is suffering; ageing is suffering; sickness is suffering; death is suffering; sorrow and lamentation, pain, grief and despair are suffering; association with the unpleasant is suffering; dissociation from the pleasant is suffering; not to get what one wants is suffering—in brief, the five aggregates of attachment are suffering.

'The Noble Truth of the origin of suffering is this: It is this thirst (craving) which produces re-existence and re-becoming, bound up with passionate greed. It finds fresh delight now here and now there, namely, thirst for sense-pleasures; thirst for existence and becoming; and thirst for non-existence (self-annihilation).

'The Noble Truth of the Cessation of suffering is this: It is the complete cessation of that very thirst, giving it up, renouncing it, emancipating oneself from it, detaching oneself from it.

[1] *Nibbana* is the Pali form of the Sanskrit *nirvana*; on *nirvana* see below, p. 252. Most Buddhist terms have a Pali and Sanskrit equivalent because classic Buddhist texts have been preserved in both languages—as also a large number have been preserved in Tibetan or Chinese translations. The Buddhist scriptures are thus vast in extent. That is partly because the Buddha made no attempt to hand over an organised body of systematic doctrine. For a time his teaching was passed on in oral form, and around it gathered the interpretations and elaborations of later monks and disciples. Eventually the teaching was brought together in two basic collections, or 'baskets', *pitaka*, the *Vinaya-Pitaka* dealing with monastic life (*vinaya*), and the *Sutta-Pitaka*, containing five collections of discourses. A third *pitaka* was added, the *Abhidhamma-Pitaka* (Sanskrit *Abhidharma*). These three together form the *Tipitaka* (Sanskrit *Tripitaka*), the Three Baskets, which constitute the Pali Canon. It is not usually thought that the Pali Canon contains the words of the Buddha alone—though traditionally the formation of the Baskets is put within a few weeks of the Buddha's passing from the world. According to tradition, it took place at the First Council of *arhants* (enlightened ones), when Kassapa questioned Upali and Ananda, and their record of the Buddha's teaching formed the first two Baskets. But in fact there is nothing self-contradictory about the view that the Pali Canon—as also the other Canons—contains teaching in addition to that of the Buddha. On the contrary, it emphasises an essential element in Buddhism, that the Buddha pointed to the necessity for individual effort. No one, not even the Buddha, can make that effort on behalf of someone else: 'You yourself must strive. The Blessed Ones (Buddhas) are (only) preachers. Those who enter the path and practise meditation are released from the bondage of Mara (Death, sin)' (*Dhammapada* xx. 4 (276)). The purpose of the Buddha was not to dominate others by his teaching, but to inspire and help them to follow the path and attain release from bondage. It is entirely appropriate, therefore, that comments and interpretations of that teaching should be included in the Canons if they served the same purpose.

Buddhism

'The Noble Truth of the Path leading to the Cessation of suffering is this: It is simply the Noble Eightfold Path, namely right view; right thought; right speech; right action; right livelihood; right effort; right mindfulness; right concentration.'

The word for 'suffering' in that passage is *dukkha* (Sanskrit *duḥka*). It is a word of far greater depth and complexity than is implied by the rather bald translation 'suffering'. It is true that it has an ordinary reference to pain, or grief, or misery, and in that sense it is the opposite of *sukha*, meaning 'happiness' or 'contentment'; but it also refers to impermanence, emptiness, lack of wholeness or perfection. Thus *dukkha* refers more to the general nature of the universe than to particular instances of suffering: change and impermanence are characteristic of the universe. That understanding of *dukkha* makes it possible to express the Four Truths in a more general way, without actually introducing the word 'suffering' at all: a thing exists or an event occurs; that occurrence or that event depends on the existence of a particular cause or condition; if that cause or that condition ceases to exist; then what is caused by it cannot exist either. But although the Four Truths *can* be expressed in detached terms, in point of fact they are usually expressed with reference to suffering—that there *is* suffering, that suffering is caused (it is not imposed arbitrarily by an outside will), that removing the causes of suffering leads to the cessation of suffering, that the way to transcend and remove the causes of suffering is both known and attainable.

Dukkha can be understood—and experienced—on three levels: in the first place, there is the fact of suffering inherent in the life-process—in birth, old age, sickness, death, and all the other accidents to which life is subject—in other words, the plain facts of suffering, *dukkha-dukkha*. Secondly, there is the suffering of sentient, conscious creatures who know the gap between what they desire and what they obtain, and who are aware of the transitory nature of all things—in other words, happiness does not last for ever, and there is suffering involved in change, *viparinama-dukkha*. Thirdly, there is suffering which arises out of the actual nature and constitution of human beings—in other words, suffering that is inherent in what human nature is, and this is known as suffering arising from the aggregates[1] of

---

[1] On the five aggregates, see pp. 242–5.

existence, *samkhara-dukkha*. Clearly, those levels of suffering are neither sequential nor exclusive: what is certain is that everyone eventually comes to realise the reality of suffering on *all* those levels as a plain matter of experience. The first two levels are particularly obvious and inescapable: 'Change and decay in all around I see.' It is the context in which every individual lives out his life. But then, according to the Buddha, he becomes aware that he is not distinct from his context, that he himself is a part of that same 'change and decay', and that his own self is not exempt from the process of change.

This leads on at once to distinctively Buddhist ground, because it raises the difficult but vital question: who or what is the 'self' that becomes aware of the reality of *dukkha* and of its own participation in the process of change? There is in fact, according to the Buddhist, *no* self. What is felt to be the 'I', the self residing in the body, is nothing of the kind. There is no soul or self which exists as a separate essence or entity, or which experiences physical and mental happenings. There is only the human complexity, made up of the elements and energy which have flowed together in a particular human form, and which are in a constant state of change. The sense of being a 'self', or of being an individual, is a result of the way in which physical entities and energies have been combined in human form. That is why, instead of talking about a soul or self, which might be supposed to exist (and survive) independently of the body, it is far more realistic to talk of 'not-self', or, in the Buddhist terminology, *anatta*.

To arrive at the conclusion *anatta*, no-self, is to understand the importance of the third level of suffering described briefly above, *samkhara-dukkha*. It is, in a sense, the realisation that the aggregates which constitute a human being are no more permanent than those which constitute a tree or a blade of grass: 'All flesh is grass, and all the goodliness thereof is as the flower of the field.'[1] But whereas the prophet of Israel felt himself to be contained within a knowledge and experience of God which he could not abandon and which made him go on immediately to assert that the word of God endures for ever, the Buddha insisted that it was the greatest folly and delusion to try and rescue something from the wreck. There is no self. There is nothing which

---

[1] Isa. 40: 6.

Buddhism

can, so to speak, be disentangled from the body and be isolated from the inexorable process of the body's decay and death. The Buddha was well-aware that this is a terrifying realisation. For a time, after he had come to realise it for himself, he hesitated whether he should try to teach it to anyone else.[1] When he *did* teach it, it certainly provoked a cold fear among many who contemplated for the first time the possibility of their own 'self'-annihilation. On one occasion a disciple came and asked, 'Sir, is there a case where one is tormented when something permanent in oneself is not found?' The Buddha replied:

Yes, bhikkhu, there is. A man has the following view: 'The universe is that *Atman*,[2] I shall be that after death, permanent, abiding, everlasting, unchanging, and I shall exist as such for eternity.' He hears that Tathagata, or a disciple of his, preaching the doctrine aiming at the complete destruction of all speculative views... aiming at the extinction of 'thirst', aiming at detachment, cessation, *Nirvana*. Then that man thinks: 'I will be annihilated, I will be destroyed, I will be no more.' So he mourns, worries himself, laments, weeps, beating his breast, and becomes bewildered.[3]

There is, therefore, nothing that can be called the self, if by that is meant an unchanging, abiding substance. There are only the aggregates of existence, the flowing together of energy and matter into particular shapes or forms. In the famous and much-repeated illustration of the Chariot, Nagasena makes the point to Milinda:[4]

Then King Menander went up to the Venerable Nagasena, greeted him respectfully, and sat down. Nagasena replied to the greeting, and the King was pleased at heart. Then King Menander asked: 'How is your reverence known, and what is your name?'

'I'm known as Nagasena, your Majesty, that's what my fellow monks call me. But though my parents may have given me such a

---

[1] He eventually persuaded himself that it was right to share his insight with others by taking a lotus pool as an analogy: some lotuses are sunk beneath the water, some are floating on the surface of the water, but some have risen above the water; so there are different levels of understanding, and at least some would be able to understand what the Buddha said. (*Mahavagga*, ed. Saddhatissa, p. 4).

[2] See p. 196 for the Hindu understanding of *atman*.

[3] *Majjhima-nikaya* i, P.T.S. pp. 136 f. (trs. Rahula).

[4] The Greek king Milinda, or Menander, ruled in north-west India in about the second century B.C. The *Milindapanha*, or *Questions of King Milinda*, is one of the most important early texts.

name...it's only a generally understood term, a practical designation. There is no question of a permanent individual implied in the use of the word.'

'Listen, you five hundred Greeks and eighty thousand monks!' said King Menander. 'This Nagasena has just declared that there's no permanent individuality implied in his name!' Then, turning to Nagasena, 'If, Reverend Nagasena, there is no permanent individuality, who gives you monks your robes and food, lodging and medicines? And who makes use of them? Who lives a life of righteousness, meditates, and reaches Nirvana? Who destroys living beings, steals, fornicates, tells lies, or drinks spirits?...If what you say is true there's neither merit nor demerit, and no fruit or result of good or evil deeds. If someone were to kill you there would be no question of murder. And there would be no masters or teachers in the (Buddhist) Order and no ordinations. If your fellow monks call you Nagasena, what then is Nagasena? Would you say that your hair is Nagasena?' 'No, your Majesty.'

'Or your nails, teeth, skin, or other parts of your body, or the outward form, or sensation, or perception, or the psychic constructions, or consciousness? Are any of these Nagasena?' 'No, your Majesty.'

'Then are all these taken together Nagasena?' 'No, your Majesty.'

'Or anything other than they?' 'No, your Majesty.'

'Then for all my asking I find no Nagasena. Nagasena is a mere sound! Surely what your Reverence has said is false!'

Then the Venerable Nagasena addressed the King.

'Your Majesty, how did you come here—on foot, or in a vehicle?' 'In a chariot.'

'Then tell me what is the chariot? Is the pole the chariot?' 'No, your Reverence.'

'Or the axle, wheels, frame, reins, yoke, spokes or goad?' 'None of these things is the chariot.'

'Then all these separate parts taken together are the chariot?' 'No, your Reverence.'

'Then is the chariot something other than the separate parts?' 'No, your Reverence.'

'Then for all my asking, your Majesty, I can find no chariot. The chariot is a mere sound. What then is the chariot? Surely what your Majesty has said is false! There is no chariot!...'

When he had spoken the five hundred Greeks cried 'Well done!' and said to the King, 'Now, your Majesty, get out of that dilemma if you can!'

'What I said was not false,' replied the King. 'It's on account of all these various components, the pole, axle, wheels, and so on, that the vehicle is called a chariot. It's just a generally understood term, a practical designation.'

Buddhism

'Well said, your Majesty! You know what the word 'chariot' means! And it's just the same with me. It's on account of the various components of my being that I'm known by the generally understood term, the practical designation Nagasena'.[1]

Thus the aggregates of existence form a recognisable and perceivable object, but they do not produce or sustain an abiding substance. In the case of human beings it is reckoned that there are five 'aggregates of existence', known as *khandhas* (Sanskrit *skandhas*). They are *rupakkhandha* (the aggregate of matter; though note that the term 'matter' should not be taken to suggest substantiality: it is the coincidence of solidity, fluidity, heat, motion and their derivatives in corporeal form); *vedanakkhandha* (the aggregate of sensations); *sannakkhandha* (the aggregate of perceptions); *samkharakhandha* (the aggregate of mental directions or formations; the meaning of that will be discussed below); *vinnanakkhandha* (the aggregate of consciousness).

It is true that the *khandhas* in association produce a perceptible form, but to call it a 'being', or Nagasena, or John Smith, is a convenience. It does not imply an eternal, indestructible Being or self;[2] as it is put in the famous verse of Buddhaghosa: 'Suffering as such exists, but no sufferer is found; The deeds are, but no doer is found.' To try to extract something substantial or indestructible from the five *khandhas* is the greatest possible delusion, for the *khandhas* themselves are insubstantial: they are a part of the ceaseless change and flow of all things. Not for a single second do they remain the same. They pursue their course of birth, decay and death, and they carry the individual with them in that process because they *are* the individual. Thus an individual's existence is not a solid rock which has somehow been cast into the stream of life and death, and around which swirl and eddy the various experiences of life. It is an indistinguishable part of that stream: it *is* the swirl and eddy of a rapidly moving stream, and it can no more halt the process of change than can a river halt its progress to the sea. Existence, properly understood, is not 'solid': it is a rapidly changing sequence, which moves from one moment to the next. Like the frames of a film being projected on to a screen, there is the appearance of continuity; each frame is in fact a separate photograph, but the sequence of each

---

[1] *Milindapanha* (Trenckner ed. pp. 25 f., trs. A. L. Basham, *Sources of Indian Tradition*, (ed. Bary), pp. 106 ff.).   [2] See, e.g., *Samyutta-nikaya*, i. 135.

photograph is so close that it gives the appearance of continuous movement. Similarly, human life is made up of a series of individual moments. The sequence is so close that it gives the appearance of continuity, because each 'moment' is the cause of the next. Yet in fact from one moment to another the aggregates of existence are changing and shifting, and their association with each other subtly alters. To try to cling to the *khandhas* and halt the process of rapidly fleeting change is simply to be blind to the facts—'here we have no abiding city'.[1] Perhaps one might wish it otherwise, but it cannot be: *dukkha* is the truth of existence, and the *khandhas* are not immune from it: that is the third level of *dukkha*.[2]

Existence is thus a chain of causation, of unceasing cause and effect.[3] Yet the fact remains that the human individual is aware that this is so; furthermore, he is aware of continuity produced by the rapidly moving sequence of cause and effect which is the product of the five *khandhas* of his existence. This means that the particular way in which the *khandhas* are combined in human form produce the experience of self-awareness. It is not that the *khandhas* are substantially different from the other aggregates or constituent elements of the universe: it is, rather, that in the particular way in which they are associated in human beings they produce certain effects. In this connection, the fourth *khanda*, *samkharakkhanda*, is of particular importance. What it means, roughly, is that human beings have the ability, on a limited scale, to organise and direct the stream of being. In the first place, they can become aware of the rapidly moving phenomena around them, and they can organise their awareness into pictures of reality. In the second place, they can to some extent direct and modify the process of change; they cannot halt it, but they can alter the course it takes. In other words, instead of struggling against the stream, they can go with it; instead of being carried headlong on the flood, they can ride upon it with confidence because they are aware of what is happening.

The ability to ride the flood with understanding and thereby to achieve some direction and control, is related to the concept of dependent origination. It is impossible for an individual to avoid being the consequence of what has gone before—that is to say, it is

---

[1] For a good expression of this, see *Visuddhi-magga* xviii (trs. Warren).
[2] See p. 240.
[3] The 'chain of causation' in human life is examined in greater detail on p. 246.

Buddhism

impossible to stand apart from the chain of cause and effect, since that chain of causation is precisely what it means to exist. On the other hand, it is possible to work within that process and give it one direction rather than another. The purpose of the Buddha's teaching was to point out the direction which would lead to release from the otherwise unbreakable chain. But it is a path that can only be taken *within* the chain of cause and effect, by setting the chain going in that particular direction. This basic insight is summarised in one of the most fundamental concepts of Buddhism, *paticca-samuppada*—'origination by way of cause', 'conditioned co-production', 'conditioned genesis'. *Paticca-samuppada* breaks down the unending circle of birth, death and again-becoming[1] into twelve stages, each of which is conditioned and conditioning. The sequence runs: (1) as a result of ignorance, volitions; (2) as a result of volitions, consciousness; (3) as a result of consciousness, mental and physical phenomena; (4) as a result of those phenomena, the six faculties (the five senses plus mind); (5) as a result of the six faculties, contact (or engagement with the world); (6) as a result of contact, feeling; (7) as a result of feeling, craving; (8) as a result of craving, clinging; (9) as a result of clinging, the process of becoming; (10) as a result of becoming, again-becoming; (11) as a result of again-becoming, arise; (12) decay, death, grief, lamentation, suffering. *Paticca-samuppada* is the process by which life arises, exists and continues. Since each of the factors is conditioned and at the same time conditioning, there is no 'starting-place': the process is an endless circle.[2]

It goes almost without saying that the aggregate of volition or mental directions can be used for good or ill. Most people use it in an attempt to go *against* the stream, or, to transfer the metaphor back to the unending circle of *paticca-samuppada*, they use volition to try to break out of the circle. They try by mental effort and will-power to rescue something substantial from the flow of change. But there is nothing to be rescued. On the other hand, there is the sense and experience of continuity, which is produced by the rapidly passing sequence of one momentary state being the cause of the next. Those who abstract that continuity and cling to it as though it were evidence of a substantial 'self' do exactly that: they cling to that continuity and bind themselves to it. They become bound to the continuation of that process in 'again-

[1] See p. 247.   [2] The twelve links are listed in *Samyutta-nikaya* xxii. 90.

246

becoming', *punabbhava* (*ponobhavika*), or, as it is more popularly
known, rebirth.

Punabbhava in Buddhism does *not* mean that suddenly, miracu-
lously, a 'self' turns up after all, which passes from one life to
another. On the contrary, the Buddha rejected the two opposite
extremes of total annihilation and eternal *atman*,[1] and discovered
the Middle Way between the two. If life is a sequence of moments
linked in a chain of causation, the moment beyond death is the
next link in the chain. As there has been a sense of continuity and
yet no continuous 'self', there is nothing surprising in that sense
of continuity extending beyond the moment of death. Life is a
series of 'events' or 'happenings', and death takes its place in the
series of events, giving rise to the next 'event'. Thus there is no
'self' that is reborn; there is an on-going continuity of again-
becoming. Life itself is a constant sequence of moments, which
come into being and almost instantaneously die as each moment
gives rise to the next. In each moment the individual is born and
dies, but he continues. The same happens in and through the
moment of death. Thus Nagasena explained the meaning of
continuity and change to Milinda:

'It is as if, sire, some person might light a lamp. Would it burn all
night long?'

'Yes, revered sir, it might burn all night long.'

'Is the flame of the first watch the same as the flame of the middle
watch?'

'No, revered sir.'

'Is the flame of the middle watch the same as the flame of the third
watch?'

'No, revered sir.'

'Is it then, sire, that the lamp in the first watch was one thing, the lamp
in the second watch another, and the lamp in the last watch still another?'

'O no, revered sir, it was burning all through the night in dependence
on itself.'

'Even so, sire, a continuity of *dhammas*[2] runs on; one uprises,

---

[1] See p. 242.

[2] *Dharma* (Pali *Dhamma*) is another word of immense complexity. Here it means
approximately 'that state of life produced by previous causes'. The general
meanings of *dharma* have been effectively summarised (so far as they can be) by
Bh. Sangharakshita: 'Dharma (Pali *dhamma*) is the key-word of Buddhism. So
great is the frequency with which it appears in the texts, and so numerous the
vitally important ideas connoted by its various shades of meaning, that it would
scarcely be an exaggeration to claim that an understanding of this protean word is

another ceases; it runs on as though there were no before, no after; consequently neither the one (*dhamma*), nor another is reckoned as the last consciousness.'[1]

The analogy of the lamp occurs again in the *Milindapanha* with a slightly different application:

The King said: 'Revered Nagasena, does that which does not pass over reconnect?'

'Yes, sire, that which does not pass over reconnects.'

'How, revered Nagasena...? Make a simile.'

'Suppose, sire, some man were to light a lamp from (another) lamp; would that lamp, sire, pass over from that (other) lamp?'[2]

It follows that the actual form which the event of *punabbhava* ('again-becoming') produces depends on what has gone before— not only the immediately preceding moment (the immediate cause), but also the whole chain of causation lying behind it. In that sense, the chain of causation, the exact effect produced by previous 'happenings', is *karma* (Pali *kamma*). *Karma* is the exact working-out of cause and effect:

Even a flight in the air cannot free you from suffering,
After the deed which is evil has once been committed.
Not in the sky nor in the ocean's middle,
Nor if you were to hide in cracks in mountains,
Can there be found on this wide earth a corner
Where karma does not catch up with the culprit...
Whatever deeds a man may do, be they delightful, be they bad,
They make a heritage for him; deeds do not vanish without
    trace...
The iron itself creates the rust,
Which slowly is bound to consume it.
The evil-doer by his own deeds
Is led to a life full of suffering.[3]

synonymous with an understanding of Buddhism. For all its laconic diction and telegraphic abbreviations, the Pali Text Society's *Pali–English Dictionary* has found it impossible to dispose of all the meanings, applications and combinations of this term in an article of less than 6,000 words...Buddhaghosa...groups the various meanings of the term under four main heads: (1) *pariyatti*, or doctrine as formulated; (2) *hetu*, or condition, causal antecedent; (3) *guna*, or moral quality or action, and (4) *nissatta-nijivata*, or the "phenomenal" as opposed to the "noumenal", "animistic entity".' (*A Survey of Buddhism*, p. 92.)

[1] *Milindapanha* 40 (trs. Horner).   [2] *Milindapanha* 71 (trs. Horner).

[3] The Sanskrit *Dharmapada*, *Karmavarga* vi. 4–5, 8, 19 (trs. Conze). The Sanskrit *Dharmapada* differs from the Pali *Dhammapada*. The Pali *Dhammapada* is one of the most basic and important Buddhist writings.

It follows that particular instances of suffering are a direct consequence of a sufficient preceding cause. The Buddha explained in that way the violent death of the saintly Moggallana: it was a consequence of his having beaten his parents at a previous moment in the chain of his existence. Thus particular instances and occurrences of suffering are contained within the general understanding of *dukkha*, *samsara* and *karma*:

The King said: 'Revered Nagasena, what is the reason that men are not all the same, some being short-lived, some long-lived, some weakly, others healthy, some ugly, others comely, some of few wishes, others of many wishes, some poor, others rich, some belonging to low families, others to high families, and some being weak in wisdom, others having wisdom?'
The Elder said: 'But why sire, are trees not all the same, some being acid, some salt, some bitter, some sharp, some astringent, others sweet?'
'I think, revered sir, that it is because of a difference in seeds.'
'Even so, sire, it is because of a difference in *kammas* that men are not all the same... And this, Sire, was also said by the Lord: 'Young men, beings have their own *kamma*, they are heirs to *kamma*, *kamma* is the matrix, *kamma* the kin, *kamma* the arbiter, *kamma* divides beings, that is to say into low and lofty.'[1]

Karma is particularly bound up with *samkharakhandha*, mental directions or volition. What the individual sets out to obtain, what he desires, what he clings to as being most precious to him, becomes a particularly important cause in the process of change, and it produces its inevitable effect.[2] The greatest folly, therefore, is to cling to the *khandhas* as though they can provide an abiding refuge in the storm. To cling to the *khandhas* and regard them as all-important is to *make* them all-important, even though they are not. It sets the chain of causation going in a false direction, one which makes the moment of 'again-becoming' an inevitable consequence since it produces a continuation of clinging and bondage. That is why *dukkha*, impermanence or change, can rightly be called 'suffering': the chain of continuity is unbroken and there seems to be no way of escape.

With that brief background in mind, it is now possible to look more closely at the meaning of the Four Truths and the Eightfold Path in relation to suffering. It has already been seen that the

[1] *Milindapanha* 65 (trs. Horner).
[2] Hence in *Anguttara-nikaya* iii. 415 *karma* is described *as* volition.

Buddhism

First Truth is a simple observation that suffering exists. Elaborations of the First Truth generally take the form of exemplifying instances of suffering as they occur in ordinary human experience.[1] It is perhaps this concentration on detailed examples of suffering which gives rise to the view that Buddhism is pessimistic.[2] Yet in fact, although the Buddha concentrated on the experiences of suffering, he did not in any way deny that there are equally experiences of happiness. In fact, in the *Anguttara-nikaya* there is a list of various kinds of happiness (*sukhani*) comparable to the list of the most common experiences of suffering.[3] Thus it is recognised that there are great joys in family life, in pleasures of the senses, in mental well-being, and in many other ordinary human experiences. In the *Dhammapada* there is a section on 'Happiness', which includes the appeal,

Let us live happily then, we who possess nothing. Let us dwell feeding on happiness like the shining gods...Health is the greatest of gifts, contentment is the greatest wealth; trust is the best of relationships. *Nirvana*[4] is the highest happiness.[5]

And yet the very fact that men are aware of being happy and at the same time are aware that happiness does not last for ever is in itself a source of grief. The transitory nature of happiness points directly to the overriding truth of *dukkha*. Once again, it is not a question of being pessimistic. It is, rather, a question of being realistic about the facts of existence as they are: *dukkha* is simply a fact, and that is the First Truth.

The Second Truth is 'the arising (*samudaya*) of *dukkha*': *dukkha* manifestly exists, but what gives rise to it—what causes it? The answer is 'thirst' or 'craving', *tanha*. The meaning of *tanha* has already been briefly outlined. Broadly speaking, it means trying to cling to something in the stream of change and decay as though that 'thing' were substantial. *Tanha* is briefly described in a passage that occurs in several texts:

It is *tanha* which produces continuing existence and again-becoming. It goes hand in hand with insatiable greed, it is adept at finding new

---

[1] See, e.g., Sariputta's exposition of *dukkha* in *Majjhima-nikaya* iii. 248–52; Sariputta (Sariputra) is traditionally regarded as having developed the Buddha's teaching in a more analytical way.   [2] See p. 237.   [3] Colombo ed. p. 49.
[4] On the meaning of *nirvana*, see p. 252—here it can be taken to mean roughly 'release from the chain of causation and again-becoming'.
[5] *Dhammapada* xv. 3, 8 (200, 204), trs. Radhakrishnan.

pleasures, now in one thing, now in another, particularly in thirst for pleasures of the senses, thirst for existence and becoming, thirst for total annihilation.[1,2]

It should not be thought that *tanha* is a kind of 'first cause' of *dukkha*; on the contrary, *tanha* itself is caused; it is itself a part of *dukkha*. Nevertheless, *tanha* is a particularly frequent cause *within dukkha*, and gives rise to *dukkha*. The reason for this is that human beings long to cling to something, or to find something substantial in the relentless flow of change. But it is like building a house on sand: there is nothing substantial there. The grains fall apart and dissolve, and the house crumbles into dust. *Tanha* epitomises the greatest human delusion, 'going against the stream', trying to live as though death were not an inescapable part of the sequence of change. *Tanha* clings to life, and forgets that life is a moving pattern.[3] The nature of *tanha* in this respect has been put very clearly by Lama Govinda:

Change either appears as birth and growth or as decay and death, though both these aspects are inseparably connected with each other like the two sides of the same coin. Just as the same door may be called entrance or exit according to the standpoint of the observer, so is the same process which we call birth or death according to our limited perception, our one-sided point of view. By not seeing the unity of these two sides we fail to realize that we cannot desire the one without inviting the other. Clinging to life means clinging to death. The very essence of life is change, while the essence of clinging is to retain, to stabilize, to prevent change. This is why change appears to us as suffering. If we did not regard objects or states of existence from the standpoint of possession or selfish enjoyment, we should not feel in the least troubled by their change or even by their disappearance; on the contrary, we enjoy change in many cases, either because disagreeable states or objects are removed or because it provides us with new experiences or reveals to us a deeper insight into the nature of things and greater possibilities of emancipation...It is therefore not the 'world' or its transitoriness which is the cause of suffering but our attitude towards it, our clinging to it, our thirst, our ignorance.[4,5]

---

[1] *Kama-tanha, bhava-tanha, vibbhava-tanha.*

[2] See, e.g., *Samyutta-nikaya* v, P.T.S. p. 421.

[3] *Tanha* appears as stage 7 > 8 in the chain of conditioned genesis; see p. 246.

[4] 'Ignorance' is in fact a technical term, *avijja*, which might perhaps be better translated as 'self-delusion'. It refers to the way in which men refuse to face the realities of existence, and pretend that something or some 'self', can be rescued from the flow of change. *Avijja* thus goes hand in hand with *tanha*.

[5] Govinda, *The Psychological Attitude...*, pp. 54 f.

Buddhism

Is the situation, then, hopeless? Are men forever bound by their ignorance and craving to the chain of causation? The Buddha believed—and discovered—not. Thus the Third Truth is 'the cessation (*nirodha*) of *dukkha*', the plain truth that *dukkha* can be brought to cease. The experience of the cessation of *dukkha* is as real as the experience of *dukkha*, and in its complete and unassailable realisation it is known as *nirvana (nibbana)*. Nirvana, the cessation of change and of the chain of causation, lies completely beyond description: it can only be realised, not described. In briefest terms it can be defined as the cessation of clinging or thirst (*tanha*), and *nirvana* is sometimes referred to as exactly that, *tanhakkhaya*, 'extinction of *tanha*'. Nirvana is certainly not 'heaven' —that is, it is not the relationship of an eternal soul with its creator. It is even inaccurate to talk of 'entering' *nirvana* after death, as though *nirvana* were a literal or metaphorical place. The word used to describe those who have realised *nirvana* is *parinibbuto*, which means 'completely extinct' or 'totally blown out', in the sense that there is no further 'again-becoming'—'the steadfast go out (*nibbanti*) like this lamp'.[1]

From that it will be clear that it is easier to talk of *nirvana* in negative terms than to give it a positive description:

A wanderer who ate rose-apples spoke thus to the venerable Sariputta:
'Reverend Sariputta, it is said: 'Nirvana, Nirvana.' Now, what, your reverence, is Nirvana?'
'Whatever, your reverence, is the extinction of passion, of aversion, of confusion, this is called Nirvana.'
'Is there a way, your reverence, is there a course for the realisation of this Nirvana?'
'There is.'[2]

Sariputta's reply, explaining the way to the realisation of *nirvana*, belongs to the Fourth Truth, 'the way to cessation of *dukkha*', which will be considered shortly. In connection with the Third Truth, it underlines the extent to which the Buddha and his disciples were unwilling to describe *nirvana*, but preferred to talk about the way leading to it. If it has to be described, it is best done in terms of cessation:

The King said: 'Revered Nagasena, is stopping *nibbana*?'
'Yes, sire, stopping is *nibbana*.'

---
[1] *Suttanipata* 235; cf. also *Majjhima-nikaya* i, P.T.S. p. 487; iii, P.T.S. p. 245.
[2] *Samyutta-nikaya* iv. 251 (trs. Horner).

Foundations

'How, revered sir, is stopping *nibbana*?'

'All those foolish average men, sire, who rejoice in the inner and outer sense-fields, approve of them and cleave to them—they are carried away by that stream, they are not utterly free from birth, old age and dying, from grief, sorrow, suffering, lamentation and despair, they are not, I say, utterly free from anguish. But, sire, the instructed disciple of the ariyans does not rejoice in the inner and outer sense-fields, does not approve of them or cleave to them. For him, not rejoicing in them, not approving of them or cleaving to them craving is stopped; from the stopping of craving is the stopping of grasping; from the stopping of grasping is the stopping of (karmic) becoming; from the stopping of (karmic) becoming is the stopping of birth; from the stopping of birth, old age and dying, grief, sorrow, suffering, lamentation and despair are stopped. Thus is the stopping of this whole mass of anguish. In this way, sire, stopping is *nibbana*.'[1]

But although it is easier to talk of *nirvana* in terms of what it is *not*, it by no means follows that *nirvana* is annihilation. On the contrary, the Buddha rejected the two extremes of annihilation and eternal *atman*, and realised *nirvana* as a middle term between the two:

A monk whose mind is thus released cannot be followed and tracked out even by the gods including Indra, Brahma, and Prajapati, so that they could say, 'There rests the consciousness of a released person.' And why? Even in this actual life, monks, I say that a released person is not to be thoroughly known. Though I thus say and thus preach, some ascetics and brahmins accuse me wrongly, baselessly, falsely and groundlessly, saying that the ascetic Gotama is a nihilist, and preaches the annihilation, destruction and non-existence of an existent being. That is what I am and do not affirm. Both previously and now I preach pain and the cessation of pain.[2]

Pain and the cessation of pain are *both* realisable experiences. *Nirvana* is not even a 'future' state. It can be realised here and now. Precisely because it is cessation of suffering it is easier to describe it in negative terms—in terms of what it has left behind—but the state of cessation is itself so blissful that it does receive positive descriptions as well. Thus Bh. Sangharakshita has summarised some of the most important negative terms: uninterrupted, uncreate, infinite, inextinguishable, cessation of suffering, freedom from longing, uncompounded, farther shore, the beyond,

---

[1] *Milindapanha*, 68 f. (trs. Horner).   [2] *Majjhima-nikaya* i. 140 (trs. Thomas).

253

deliverance, extinction, indiscernible, unoppressed, the absolute, unendangered, unattached, deathless, release, liberation, final deliverance, dispassionate, stillness, purity, allayment.[1] But equally Rhys Davids collected some of the most important positive descriptions: the harbour of refuge, the cool cave, the island amidst the floods, the place of bliss, emancipation, liberation, safety, the supreme, the transcendental, the uncreated, the tranquil, the home of ease, the calm, the end of suffering, the medicine for all evil, the unshaken, the ambrosia, the immaterial, the imperishable, the abiding, the further shore, the unending, the bliss of effort, the supreme joy, the ineffable, the detachment, the holy city.[2]

But it is immediately apparent that some of the terms in the two lists coincide, and that they can be either negative or positive depending on the standpoint of the observer. The truth is that *nirvana* lies beyond 'negative' and 'positive': it lies beyond description. It simply *is*, the state in which *dukkha* has ceased.[3]

The question inevitably arises whether or not this is wishful thinking. The experience of *dukkha* is common, the experience of *nirvana* is not: what guarantee is there that *nirvana* is in fact realisable? For the Buddhist, the basic answer is found in the life of the Buddha himself: because he attained *nirvana* he knew what he was talking about. The fact that others have also realised *nirvana* is important confirmation, but essentially the 'pledge' of *nirvana* lies in the fact that the Buddha attained it. The experience of the cessation of suffering was, to him, as real as the experience of suffering, and that gave to his teaching a glowing eloquence:

As long as my vision of true knowledge was not fully clear... regarding the Four Noble Truths, I did not claim to have realized the perfect Enlightenment that is supreme in the world with its gods, with its Maras and Brahmas, in this world with its recluses and brahmanas, with its princes and men. But when my vision of true knowledge was fully clear... regarding the Four Noble Truths, then I claimed to have realized the perfect Enlightenment that is supreme in the world... And a vision of true knowledge arose in me thus: My heart's deliverance is unassailable. This is the last birth. Now there is no more again-becoming.[4]

---

[1] *A Survey of Buddhism*, p. 62.
[2] *Early Buddhism*, p. 172. For a discussion of the positive aspects of *nirvana* see *Milindapanha* 268–71.
[3] For a good attempt at description, see *Udana* 80 f. (viii. 1 f.).
[4] Conclusion of the First Sermon at Benares, *Samyutta-nikaya* lvi. 11 (trs. Rahula).

Foundations

In coming to realise the possibility of *nirvana*, there is no alternative but to rely on the testimony of those who have experience of it, and of them all the Buddha is supreme.[1] It is this which forms the basis and constitutes the assurance of the Buddha's teaching. Not only did he observe the fact of *dukkha* with a realistic eye, but by penetrating the causes of *dukkha* he discovered that it could be made to cease; and not only did he discover that it could be made to cease, he showed the way that leads to its cessation. The way leading to the cessation of *dukkha* is the Fourth Noble Truth. It is known as the Middle Path (*majjhima patipada*), because it avoids the extremes of sensual indulgence and rigorous self-mortification. The Buddha tried both, and found them equally unsatisfactory.[2] He pointed instead to a middle way made up of the Noble Eightfold Path (*ariya-atthangika-magga*).

The Eightfold Path has already been given in outline in the First Sermon (quoted on p. 239). It is right view (understanding), right thought, right speech, right action, right livelihood, right effort, right mindfulness, right concentration. Together those eight factors form the three foundations of Buddhist life: wisdom (*panna*), ethical conduct (*sila*), and mental discipline (*samadhi*).[3] Right view and right thought constitute wisdom; right speech, right action and right livelihood constitute ethical conduct; right effort, right mindfulness and right concentration constitute mental discipline. It would be far beyond the scope of this book to examine in detail the meaning and implications of the Eightfold Path, since it would amount to a survey of virtually the whole of Buddhism. However, it may be helpful at least to quote Sariputta's analysis, in the continuation of the passage referred to on p. 250.[4] In that passage Sariputta had analysed the First Noble Truth. He continued by explaining the remaining three Truths:

What now is the Noble Truth of the origin of suffering? It is any craving that makes for re-birth and is tied up with passion's delights and culls satisfaction now here now there—such as the craving for sensual pleasure, the craving for continual existence, and the craving for annihilation.

[1] For a clear discussion of this, see *Milindapanha* 69, 70.
[2] See the First Sermon, quoted on p. 238.
[3] For texts illustrating the three foundations, see E. Conze, *Buddhist Scriptures* (Penguin, 1959), pp. 70–180. The material is arranged under the three headings.
[4] *Majjhima-nikaya* iii. 248–52 (trs. Chalmers).

Next, what is the Noble Truth of the cessation of suffering?—It is the utter and passionless cessation of this same craving,—the abandonment and rejection of craving, deliverance from craving, and aversion from craving.

Lastly, what is the Noble Truth of the Path that leads to the cessation of suffering?—It is just the Noble Eightfold Path, consisting of right outlook, right resolves, right speech, right acts, right livelihood, right endeavour, right mindfulness and right rapture of concentration.

Right outlook is to know suffering, the origin of suffering, the cessation of suffering, and the path that leads to the cessation of suffering.

Right resolves are the resolve to renounce the world and to do no hurt or harm.

Right speech is to abstain from lies and slander, from reviling, and from tattle.

Right acts are to abstain from taking life, from stealing, and from lechery.

Right livelihood is that by which the disciple of the Noble One supports himself, to the exclusion of wrong modes of livelihood.

Right endeavour is when an almsman brings his will to bear, puts forth endeavour and energy, struggles and strives with all his heart, to stop bad and wrong qualities which have not yet arisen from ever arising, to renounce those which have already arisen, to foster good qualities which have not yet arisen, and, finally, to establish, clarify, multiply, enlarge, develop, and perfect those good qualities which are there already.

Right mindfulness is when realizing what the body is—what feelings are—what the heart is—and what the mental states are—an almsman dwells ardent, alert, and mindful, in freedom from the wants and discontents attendant on any of these things.

Right rapture of concentration is when, divested of lusts and divested of wrong dispositions, an almsman develops, and dwells in, the first ecstasy with all its zest and satisfaction, a state bred of aloofness and not divorced from observation and reflection. By laying to rest observation and reflection, he develops and dwells in inward serenity, in (the) focussing of heart, in the zest and satisfaction of the second ecstasy, which is divorced from observation and reflection and is bred of concentration—passing thence to the third and fourth ecstasies.

This, sirs, constitutes the Noble Truth of the Path that leads to the cessation of suffering...

The effect of the Eightfold Path is to reverse the twelve links of conditioned genesis: through the cessation of ignorance, volitions cease; through the cessation of volitions, consciousness ceases; as a result of the cessation of consciousness, mental and physical phenomena cease...; as a result of the cessation of again-becoming, decay, death, suffering cease. The Eightfold Path is the gradual relinquishment of one's hold on the chain of causation.[1] For this reason there is a sense in which the whole of the Buddha's teaching can be concentrated in two deeply-revered and sacred verses:

Let the past be what it has been, let the future be what it will be, I will teach you *dharma*: if this is, that becomes; from the arising of this, that arises; if this is not, that does not come to be; from the ceasing of this, that ceases.[2]

The second verse is Assaji's[3] summary of the Buddha's teaching. When Sariputta heard it he is said to have attained the first level of sanctity:

The Tathagata has explained the origin of things proceeding from a cause. He has also explained their cessation. That is the teaching of the great Shramanah.

Although the Buddha knew the reality of *nirvana*, he did not point to himself as important—in fact, exactly the reverse: he pointed *away* from himself and emphasised the necessity for each disciple to undertake the discipline for himself. There is no other way in which *nirvana* can be realised and attained, except by under-taking for oneself the path that leads towards it. It is never suggested that the path is easy, but it is always maintained that the path is possible: '"Unwearied digging..."—This lesson the Blessed One taught while living at Savatthi. About what? About a monk who gave up effort.'[4]

It is precisely in that noble and austere teaching of self-reliance and self-responsibility that the seeds of one of the major Buddhist developments in connection with suffering lie; for if it were really true that each individual should pursue his own salvation without reference to anyone else, it would expose Buddhism to the charge of being escapist or selfish. It was the realisation of this that led to

[1] See p. 246.
[2] *Majjhima-nikaya* ii. 32 *et al.*
[3] Assaji was one of the Buddha's first five disciples.
[4] *Vannupatha-jataka.* The emphasis on individual responsibility appears with supreme clarity in the Farewell Sermon of the Buddha, the *Mahaparinibbana Sutta.*

Buddhism

a more profound analysis of the motives of the Buddha in his teaching, and that in turn led to the elaboration of the Bodhisattva ideal. It was a truly momentous development.

THE DEVELOPMENT

In the last Sermon of the Buddha it was stated that 'with the Tathagata there is no such thing as the closed fist of the teacher'.[1] What that has meant in effect is that although the essentials of the Buddha's teaching have been generally agreed and accepted by all Buddhists, there has been great variety of interpretation and application, and Buddhism thus exists on different levels and in different forms. Divisions in Buddhism arose quite early on. More than twenty varying schools of interpretation are mentioned as having emerged within about 200 years of the parting of the Buddha from his disciples.[2] The exact details of many of those groups are uncertain, although three appear to have been particularly important, the Theravadins (Sanskrit Staviravadins), Sarvastivadins, and Mahasanghikas. The Theravadins have remained an important group, and it is Theravada Buddhism which predominates in S. Asia, particularly in Ceylon, Burma and Siam. The other groups have virtually disappeared, but out of them coalesced the major development in Buddhism, Mahayana. The word *mahayana* means 'great vehicle', as opposed to the name given by the Mahayana to the Theravadins, 'Hinayana' or 'Lesser Vehicle'.

The reasons for the development of Mahayana Buddhism in distinction from Theravada are many.[3] Generally speaking, Theravadins tended to be conservative and cautious, sticking closely to the text of the basic scriptures in the Pali Canon. In other words, there was a tendency to 'close the fist of the teacher'. Some of the points at issue between them were relatively small,

[1] The technical connotations of 'the closed fist' are discussed in *Milandapanha* 144.
[2] Most lists give eighteen or occasionally twenty schools of interpretation, but the actual schools mentioned vary from list to list. For the Buddha's date, see p. 260.
[3] For a brief summary of the way in which Mahayana emerged out of the early schools, see Bh. Sangharakshita, *A Survey of Buddhism*, pp. 191 ff. Mahayana itself is not a monolithic unity. It exists in many different groups and forms of expression, and it continues to change: 'Mahayana Buddhism belongs to the progressive school and is ever ready for change or metamorphosis and for adapting and accepting the cultural and social conditions of every land and every time' (Thich Nhat Hanh, *Vietnam! The Lotus in the Sea of Fire* (London, 1967), p. 13).

but one of the most vital and important differences arose out of the question raised at the end of the preceding section. Some of the Buddha's teaching, taken at face-value and without very deep reflection, might give the impression of extreme self-centredness—of a concentration on one's own attainment of *nirvana*, without much reference to the fate of anybody else. Thus the *Dhammapada* says:

> By oneself, indeed, is evil done; by oneself is one injured. By oneself is evil left undone; by oneself is one purified. Purity and impurity belong to oneself. No one purifies another.
> Let no one neglect his own task for the sake of another's, however great; let him, after he has discerned his own task, devote himself to his task.[1]

But a 'selfish' interpretation is in fact contradicted by the life of the Buddha, who far from pursuing enlightenment on his own, shared it with others in his teaching. It is true that he shunned any temptation to 'dominate' others by his teaching, and that he insisted that its truth could only be ascertained by experiment—a starving man faced by a banquet cannot satisfy his hunger by sending another to eat on his behalf. But the Buddha clearly felt great concern and compassion for his fellow-men caught in the chain and bondage of *dukkha*, and he tried to share with them his own insight into the way of release. It was out of contemplation of the life and of the motives of the Buddha in going out of his way to help others that Mahayana Buddhism came to articulate a major development in connection with suffering, the Bodhisattva ideal.

The word *bodhisattva* is made up of two parts, *bodhi*, meaning 'enlightenment', and *sattva*, meaning 'being' or 'essence'. The term *bodhisattva* refers to a person who directs his essential being towards the attainment of enlightenment. Much Mahayana literature describes the details of the ten stages which lead to the attainment of full Buddhahood.[2] The first six refer to the acquiring of the six perfections, or *paramitas*. In Mahayana Buddhism the *Paramitas*, 'means of reaching the beyond', are so fundamental that it is sometimes referred to as 'The Vehicle of the *Paramitas*'. The six perfections are generosity, morality (to the extent of

---

[1] *Dhammapada* xii. 9 f. (165 f.), trs. Radhakrishnan.
[2] For the most concentrated expression, see the *Sutra of the Ten Stages*.

Buddhism

dying rather than stealing, killing or lying), even-disposition, constant endurance, concentration (or meditation) and wisdom. To master the six perfections[1] may take many aeons and many occasions of again-becoming, but when the *bodhisattva* (the disciple seeking enlightenment) has mastered them, he is then on the edge of *nirvana*. It is at that point, and as the next 'stage', that the *bodhisattva* voluntarily turns away from his *own* realisation of *nirvana*, and returns to help others in the world.[2] Aware of the bondage and suffering of others, and full of compassion for them, he postpones his own final attainment in order to stand beside his fellow beings:

> Compassion speaks and saith:
> 'Can there be bliss when all that lives must suffer?
> Shalt thou be saved and hear the whole world cry?'[3]

The overriding sense of compassion appears very clearly in the *bodhisattva*'s vow:

> However innumerable sentient beings are, I vow to save them!
> However inexhaustible the defilements are, I vow to
>   extinguish them!
> However immeasurable the *dharmas* are, I vow to master them!
> However incomparable enlightenment is, I vow to attain it![4]

It is this strong sense of identity and fellow-feeling in the midst of universal suffering that makes the concept of the *bodhisattva* such a major contribution to the Buddhist understanding of suffering. Yet it should not be regarded as an innovation, for it was founded on deep consideration of the Buddha's own life.

The details of the Buddha's life (in about the sixth century B.C.) which can be historically verified in the strict sense are very few. In fact, it has sometimes been put extremely that they could be listed on a post-card. In very briefest outline, it is known that his name was Siddhattha (Sanskrit Siddhartha) of the family Gotama (Sanskrit Gautama). He was of the warrior (*kshatriya*) class, and lived in great luxury for twenty-nine years. He married and had a son, Rahula, but he found that indulgence of the senses gave no satisfaction. He therefore went apart, and practised great austerities

---

[1] For texts illustrating the six perfections, see E. Conze, *Buddhist Texts*, pp. 135 ff.
[2] This is the 'horizontal awareness' of Aurobindo; see p. 231.
[3] H. P. Blavatsky, *The Voice of Silence*, p. 78.
[4] Trs. Conze, *Buddhist Scriptures*, pp. 183 f.

Development

and self-mortification. In this he resembled the forest-hermits who reacted against the elaboration of Vedic rituals and priestly dominance, and it is possible that his first stumbling attempts to find greater satisfaction were a part of that protest movement.[1] But he found that his austerities led nowhere, so he sat beneath a tree on the banks of the river Naranjana, detached and composed. It was beneath the tree of enlightenment, the Bodhi or Bo tree, that the great awakening took place.[2] After some hesitation he decided to share his enlightened knowledge with any others who wished to hear it, and he spent the rest of his life conversing with various disciples—'the deathless has been found: I instruct, I teach *dharma*'.[3]

The brief outline has been filled in with countless details and stories, whose authenticity is, in the nature of the case, difficult to establish objectively. Yet that does not make them valueless. On the contrary, the stories told of the Buddha were among the most illuminating ways in which subsequent ages could explain and illustrate his teaching. The difficulty of establishing the actual details of the life of the Buddha is an important fact in itself, since it emphasises yet again that the Buddha pointed, not *towards* himself, but *away* from himself, to the truths that he had discovered. Thus as a Buddhist writer has commented on this phenomenon:

The so-called historical facts of the Buddha's life were regarded as of so little importance that, up to the present day, it is impossible to ascertain the exact year of the Buddha's birth. Even the century in which he lived is a matter of controversy between the various Buddhist

[1] See p. 209. The Buddha's estimate of the relative value of sacrifices and ritual can be seen in the following verses of the *Dhammapada*: 'If a man month after month for a hundred years should sacrifice with a thousand (sacrifices), and if he but for one moment pay homage to a man whose self is grounded in knowledge, better is that homage than what is sacrificed for a hundred years...Him who has understood the law as taught by the well-awakened (fully enlightened) one, him should a man worship reverentially, even as the *brahmin* worships the sacrificial fire. Not by matted hair, not by lineage, not by caste does one become a *brahmin*. He is a *brahmin* in whom there are truth and righteousness. He is blessed' (viii. 7 (106), xxvi. 10 f. (392 f.), trs. Radhakrishnan).
[2] 'The origin, the origin (of *dukkha*): thus as I duly reflected on these things unheard before, vision arose, knowledge arose, full knowledge arose, understanding arose, light arose... Cessation, cessation: thus as I duly reflected on these things unheard before, vision arose, knowledge arose, full knowledge arose, understanding arose, light arose.' *Samyutta-nikaya* ii. 10 ff. which summarises the chains of origin and cessation. [3] *Vinaya-pitaka* i. 9.

261

Schools. They do not even agree with regard to the name of Siddhartha's wife, or whether Rahula was born before or after the Bodhisattva left his home. In what they all agree, however, is that the Buddha proclaimed the same eternal Dharma, preached by his spiritual predecessors in this world-cycle (*kalpa*) as well as aeons ago...In other words, more is known and said about the Buddha's spiritual lineage than about his descent, though the fact that he came from a royal (or at least noble) family should have made it easy to record the lineage and the historical background of his forefathers. This shows clearly that his spiritual lineage, which might rightly be called his universal background, was regarded as being far more important than the historical and material one.[1]

The mention of the Buddha's 'spiritual lineage' points to another complicating factor: stories may be told of the Buddha, not simply in his existence in the sixth century, but also in his previous existences, since the process of 'again-becoming' is universal. In fact some of the most moving and famous stories of the Buddha refer, as will be seen, to his previous existences. As Bh. Sangharakshita has described it:

Though the Pali canon contains interesting fragments describing various episodes of his last life on earth, it contains no connected biography of the Master in the modern sense. It does, however, contain the *Buddhavamsa*, in which are set forth the lives of the previous Buddhas, his spiritual ancestors, and it does contain the *Jataka* book, which recounts the story of no less than five hundred and fifty of his own previous lives as a Bodhisattva, during all of which he practised the Ten Perfections (*dasa-paramita*).[2]

Thus what matters about the Buddha is not so much the detail of his life or lives but the universal relevance of his teaching which the stories told about him illustrate. The possibility of enlightenment and of the attainment of *nirvana* is a universal truth.

The important point, in connection with suffering, is that reflection even on the barest outline of Gautama's life establishes the fact of almost infinite compassion. The stories of Gautama as *bodhisattva* and *Buddha* exemplify that compassion, but the basic

---

[1] Lama A. Govinda, 'The Buddha as the Ideal of the Perfect Man and the Embodiment of the Dharma', *Maha Bodhi Journal* (1954). For a convenient collection of material relating to the life of the Buddha, translated into English, see E. H. Brewster, *The Life of Gotama the Buddha, compiled exclusively from the Pali Canon* (London, 1926).   [2] *Survey of Buddhism*, p. 40.

fact is what matters: the enlightened One did not abandon the suffering world, but came to its rescue. Among Buddhists it gives rise to a devotion towards the Buddha of love and gratitude—a devotion which can in fact issue on very simple or even ritualistic levels, with the result that 'popular' Buddhism is often quite different from the Buddhism described in these pages. The compassion of the *bodhisattva* extends beyond human beings to all living creatures, and to the universe itself. The wide-ranging quality of self-sacrificing love is perhaps best illustrated in the famous story of the Bodhisattva and the tigress: three princes, Mahopranada, Mahadeva and Mahasattva, were once walking in a park and saw a hungry tigress:

On seeing her, Mahapranada called out: 'The poor animal suffers from having given birth to the seven cubs only a week ago! If she finds nothing to eat, she will either eat her own young, or die from hunger!' Mahasattva replied: 'How can this poor exhausted creature find food?' Mahapranada said: 'Tigers live on fresh meat and warm blood.' Mahadeva said: 'She is quite exhausted, overcome by hunger and thirst, scarcely alive and very weak. In this state she cannot possibly catch any prey. And who would sacrifice himself to preserve her life?'...

Greatly agitated, the three brothers carefully watched the tigress for some time, and then went towards her. But Mahasattva thought to himself: 'Now the time has come for me to sacrifice myself! For a long time I have served this putrid body and given it beds and clothes, food and drink, and conveyances of all kinds. Yet it is doomed to perish and fall down, and in the end it will break up and be destroyed. How much better to leave this ungrateful body of one's own accord in good time! It cannot subsist for ever, because it is like urine which must come out. Today I will use it for a sublime deed. Then it will act for me as a boat which helps me to cross the ocean of birth and death'...So, his heart filled with boundless compassion, Mahasattva asked his brothers to leave him alone for a while, went to the lair of the tigress, hung his cloak on a bamboo, and made the following vow:

'For the weal of the world I wish to win enlightenment, incomparably wonderful. From deep compassion I now give away my body, so hard to quit, unshaken in my mind. That enlightenment I shall now gain, in which nothing hurts and nothing harms, and which the Jina's sons have praised. Thus shall I cross to the Beyond of the fearful ocean of becoming which fills the triple world!'

The friendly prince then threw himself down in front of the tigress. But she did nothing to him. The Bodhisattva noticed that she was too weak to move. As a merciful man he had taken no sword with him. He therefore cut his throat with a sharp piece of bamboo, and fell down near the tigress. She noticed the Bodhisattva's body all covered with blood, and in no time ate up all the flesh and blood, leaving only the bones.

'It was I, Ananda, who at that time and on that occasion was that prince Mahasattva.'[1]

Although compassion is thus without limits, the *bodhisattva* ideal is usually expressed in relation to those many millions in the world who are caught in the chain of suffering and have no idea how to break out of it. They are all too well aware of the facts of suffering but not of the way to its cessation; the compassion of the *bodhisattva* reaches out to them to give them relief and to show them the way:

He becomes endowed with that kind of wise insight which allows him to see all beings as on the way to their slaughter. Great compassion thereby takes hold of him. With his heavenly eye he surveys countless beings, and what he sees fills him with great agitation: so many carry the burden of a *karma* which will soon be punished in the hells, others have acquired unfortunate rebirths, which keep them away from the Buddha and his teachings, others are doomed soon to be killed, or they are enveloped in the net of false views, or fail to find the path, while others who had gained a rebirth favourable to their emancipation have lost it again.

And he radiates great friendliness and compassion over all those beings, and gives his attention to them, thinking: 'I shall become a saviour to all those beings, I shall release them from all their sufferings!'[2]

The exercise of his compassion is by no means academic: it involves the *bodhisattva* in an agonising identification with those who suffer:

A Bodhisattva resolves: I take upon myself the burden of all suffering. I am resolved to do so, I will endure it. I do not turn or run away, do not tremble, am not terrified, nor afraid, do not turn back or despond. And why? At all costs I must bear the burden of all beings. In that I do not follow my own inclinations. I have made the vow to save all beings. All beings I must set free. The whole world of living beings I must rescue, from the terrors of birth, of old age, of sickness, of death

---

[1] *Suvarnaprabhasa* 206 ff. (trs. Conze).
[2] *Ashtasahasrika* xxii. 402 ff. (trs. Conze).

and rebirth, of all kinds of moral offence, of all states of woe, of the whole cycle of birth-and-death, of the jungle of false views, of the loss of wholesome *dharmas*, of the concomitants of ignorance,—from all these terrors I must rescue all beings...For with the help of the boat of the thought of all-knowledge, I must rescue all these beings from the stream of *samsara*, which is so difficult to cross, I must pull them back from the great precipice, I must free them from all calamities, I must ferry them across the stream of *samsara*.[1] I myself must grapple with the whole mass of suffering of all beings. To the limit of my endurance I will experience in all the states of woe, found in any world system, all the abodes of suffering...And why? Because it is surely better that I alone should be in pain than that all these beings should fall into the states of woe. There I must give myself away as a pawn through which the whole world is redeemed from the terrors of the hells, of animal birth, of the world of Yama,[2] and with this my own body I must experience, for the sake of all beings, the whole mass of all painful feelings.[3]

Both those passages suggest that the emphasis is on sharing intellectual enlightenment—opening the eyes of those bound in the chain of suffering to see the way out. In an important sense that is so, because, as has already been pointed out, individual instances of suffering are contained within the general truth of universal *dukkha*; as a result, it is better to point out the universal condition and the way of its complete cessation than to give relief to particular instances of suffering within that condition. Thus suffering occurs as a problem in Buddhism, not so much in its individual occurrences, but because it is a universal condition which *appears* to be inescapable and unbreakable. The problem is to be met, not by manoeuvres within the condition, but by removal of its causes. But that should not be taken to imply that *bodhisattva* compassion has nothing but an intellectual content and concern. On the contrary, Buddhism implies specific and practical action in relief of suffering. Practice may not always have lived up to theory, but the theory is unequivocally clear. It has already been seen at two points how essential in Buddhism is *sila*, ethical conduct. It appeared as one of the three foundations of Buddhism (p. 255). Nothing could be more central than that, and much Buddhist literature is devoted to the lessons and encouragement of

---

[1] The picture of 'crossing-over' by a raft or boat is particularly famous and frequent in Buddhism. For examples, see E. Conze, *Buddhist Texts*, pp. 82 ff.
[2] See p. 203.   [3] *Sikshasamuccaya*, 280 f. (trs. Conze).

Buddhism

practical morality. One of the most important emphases recovered in the development of Mahayana Buddhism was the place of the layman.[1] Not all Buddhists can become monks, and Mahayana drew out the teaching of the Buddha that enlightenment—and morality—can be pursued in public life. The Buddha preached *ahimsa*, non-violence, but only those can practise it who are in a position to implement the alternative.[2] Whatever is done in the world must be done with detachment, 'using this world as though they use it not',[3] but the quest for *nirvana* does not mean that nothing should be done at all. The *bodhisattva* ideal asserts in Buddhism the unifying and identifying activity of compassion. What that means in practice has been seen repeatedly in the lives of many Buddhists in the past and in the present. In the present, it became dramatically apparent to the world on 11 June 1963, when a Buddhist monk, Thich Quang-Duc, burnt himself to death in Vietnam.

The implications of that and other similar actions formed the basis of Thich Nhat Hanh's intensely moving book, *Vietnam: The Lotus in the Sea of Fire*. The book includes the text of his letter to Martin Luther King, originally published in *Dialogues*. In the letter he tried to convey the underlying meaning of Quang-Duc's action.

The self-burning of Vietnamese Buddhist monks in 1963 is somehow difficult for the Western Christian conscience to understand. The Press spoke then of suicides, but in the essence, it is not. It is not even a protest. What the monks said in the letters they left before burning themselves aimed only at alarming, at moving the hearts of the oppressors and at calling the attention of the world to the suffering endured then by the Vietnamese. To burn oneself by fire is to prove that what one is saying is of the utmost importance. There is nothing more painful than burning oneself. To say something while experiencing this kind of pain is to say it with utmost courage, frankness, determination and sincerity. During the ceremony of ordination, as practised in the Mahayana tradition, the monk candidate is required to

[1] For a summary of the duties and obligations of lay-morality, see particularly the advice to Singala in *Digha-nikaya* iii. 180 ff.
[2] *Ahimsa (avihimsa)* is one of the three elements of right mindfulness in the Eightfold Path, the others being *alobha*, non-greed, and *adosa*, non-hatred: 'The monk Gautama has given up injury to life, he has lost all inclination to it; he has laid aside the cudgel and the sword, and he lives modestly, full of mercy, desiring in compassion the welfare of all things living' *Digha-nikaya* i. 4 (trs. Basham).
[3] Jean Nicholas Grou, *Manual for Interior Souls*, §18 (Orchard ed. p. 72).

burn one, or more, small spots on his body in taking the vow to observe the 250 rules of a bhikshu, to live the life of a monk, to attain enlightenment and to devote his life to the salvation of all beings. One can, of course, say these things while sitting in a comfortable armchair; but when the words are uttered while kneeling before the community of sangha and experiencing this kind of pain, they will express all the seriousness of one's heart and mind, and carry much greater weight.

The Vietnamese monk, by burning himself, says with all his strength and determination that he can endure the greatest of sufferings to protect his people. But why does he have to burn himself to death? The difference between burning oneself and burning oneself to death is only a difference in degree, not in nature. A man who burns himself too much must die. The importance is not to take one's life, but to burn. What he really aims at is the expression of his will and determination, not death. In the Buddhist belief, life is not confined to a period of 60 or 80 or 100 years: life is eternal. Life is not confined to this body: life is universal. To express will by burning oneself, therefore, is not to commit an act of destruction but to perform an act of construction, i.e. to suffer and to die for the sake of one's people. This is not suicide. Suicide is an act of self-destruction, having as causes the following: (1) lack of courage to live and to cope with difficulties; (2) defeat by life and loss of all hope; (3) desire for non-existence (*abhaya*).

This self-destruction is considered by Buddhism as one of the most serious crimes.[1] The monk who burns himself has lost neither courage nor hope; nor does he desire non-existence. On the contrary, he is very courageous and hopeful and aspires for something good in the future. He does not think that he is destroying himself; he believes in the good fruition of his act of self-sacrifice for the sake of others. Like the Buddha in one of his former lives—as told in a story of Jataka—who gave himself to a hungry lioness which was about to devour her own cubs, the monk believes he is practising the doctrine of highest compassion by sacrificing himself in order to call the attention of, and to seek help from, the people of the world.[2]

Alfred Hassler commented on his visit to America:

Thich Nhat Hanh came to the West repeatedly disclaiming the role of political expert. He had come, he said, to tell Americans especially about the terrible suffering and disillusionment of his people and about the meaning of the Buddhist-led demonstrations against the Diem and

---

[1] In fact, various monks are known from the Buddhist scriptures to have committed suicide, but not in the 'defeatist' sense. It represented the renunciation of clinging. See *Samyutta-nikaya* i. 121, iii. 120, *Majjhima-nikaya* 144.

[2] *The Lotus in the Sea of Fire* (London, 1967), pp. 117 ff.

Ky governments. Under his tutelage, the nature of the Buddhist intervention became slowly clearer to those who heard him. The monks who were daring to defy both General Nguyen Cao Ky and his United States protectors were neither dupes of the Communists nor ambitious would-be office holders themselves. (Indeed, monks are forbidden to hold political office.) Rather...they had been driven to take the stand they had by their profound compassion for their suffering people, and by the fact that *there literally was no one else who could speak for the war-weary people and their longing for peace.* Far from being a departure from their religious faith, their actions were impelled by it...He is the authentic voice of the wistful, almost unrecognised aspirations of all men, and most of those who listen to him set aside for a while their longing for the simplicities of full alignment with one combatant or the other to hear with a respect close to reverence one who asks for alignment with humankind itself. There is a voice in every age that speaks to us through the red mists of partisanship and anger, and about the realities of injustice and cruelty, reminding us of the common heritage that is our only hope.

> 'Here is my breast. Aim your gun at it, brother, Shoot!
> Destroy me if you will
> And build from my carrion whatever it is you are
>   dreaming of.
> Who will be left to celebrate a victory made of
>   blood and fire?'[1]

[1] *The Lotus in the Sea of Fire*, pp. 109–11.

7

DUALISM, DUALITY AND THE UNIFICATION OF EXPERIENCE

ZOROASTRIANISM, MANICHAEISM AND JAINISM

At first sight the differences between the Western and Eastern traditions seem considerable. This study has shown incidentally that some of the ways in which the differences have often been described are too generalised to be particularly meaningful—the statement, for example, that the Western is world-affirming and the Eastern world-denying; or, as it was put recently, 'the biggest difference is that Buddhism and Christianity represent two irreconcilable attitudes to evil. Do you aim at being passionless, or do you place the Passion at the centre of life?'[1] But although such generalisations need to be broken down into far greater detail (in the case of the second, for example, by estimating the centrality of *dukkha* in Buddhism and the aim of detachment in Christianity), they do nevertheless point to differences at least of emphasis and priority. It may, therefore, be asked whether they are indeed 'irreconcilable' or whether there is any common ground between them. In the most obvious sense there is certainly the common ground of the facts and experiences of suffering, from which, as it has been seen, all religions start. Yet even on that most obvious level, an issue is raised between religions: who or what is the subject of those experiences? The answers given to that question are, in fact, estimates of the nature of being human, and although the various answers given are nothing like so divergent as once appeared to be the case, it would be rash to say as yet that the different religions do not involve serious, even radical, distinctions of anthropological analysis. It may therefore seem that the search for common ground is illusory—as it certainly would be in the syncretistic sense of picking out elements which seem to be saying the same thing. Yet there is in fact one important area of common

[1] *Frontier* (Autumn, 1967), p. 165.

ground, which is particularly vital in any constructive discussions between the religious and the irreligious developments of each tradition—or, to put it more specifically, between religions and Marxism. It is the recognition that dualism is an extremely attractive way of understanding the experiences of suffering, but that it is ultimately misleading. The common ground lies, not in the consequences, but in the purpose, of unifying the contradictory fragments of experience. In what ways can an adequate account be given of the two sides of experience, light and darkness, happiness and sorrow—which are in fact one, since they appertain to the same organism? It might, of course, be regarded as a false question, since there is perhaps no need to 'account' for something that happens to be the way it is: contradictory experiences happen to be possible in the human organism. Religions would agree that it is a false question if it is conceived to be simply a *theoretical* question. They are as much concerned with the practical assimilation of experience as with theoretical accounts of its meaning, though the latter naturally informs the former. It is precisely on *practical* grounds that the question of how to unify experience arises, and to say that it is not a sensible or meaningful question is to say in effect that no one ought to be alive. The fact, as this book has shown, that suffering occurs as a problem differently in different religions indicates that the methods of unification will differ also, but at least there is a purpose in common: on what grounds, if any, can the unity and integrity of human experience be sustained, the good as well as the ill?

It might be thought that it is not particularly surprising 'common ground', because the extreme form of duality, namely dualism, is not particularly credible, and has not, in any case, ever been seriously stated or worked out. The former statement *may* be true (though it would have to be qualified on grounds of experience, as will be seen below), the latter statement is certainly not true. Dualism has been worked out in at least two great and widely influential systems of thought, Zoroastrianism and Manichaeism.

To discuss Zoroastrianism as though it were a single entity is in fact misleading, because it changed considerably in the course of its history. Furthermore, it is extremely difficult to unravel what Zoroastrianism was at any particular moment, for at least three reasons: the deliberate secrecy of many of its rituals; the uncertain dates of the basic texts (many of which are in any case composite);[1] and the fact that although Zoroastrianism had a profound effect on Judaism (and thence on Christianity and Islam), it was opposed and eventually persecuted, so that in the West it ceased to be a living religion. On the other hand, a remnant of Zoroastrianism found refuge in India, where it survives in the Parsis (or 'Persians', a reference to the land where the prophet Zoroaster[2] lived, and where Zoroastrianism flourished). Thus Zoroastrianism has also been influential in the East.

Whether Zoroaster was himself a dualist in his beliefs is extremely doubtful. R. C. Zaehner quotes two texts which might seem to support the view that he was:

I will speak out concerning the two Spirits of whom, at the beginning of existence, the Holier spoke to him who is Evil: 'Neither our thoughts, nor our teachings, nor our wills, nor our choices, nor our words, nor our deeds, nor our convictions, nor yet our souls agree.'[3]

The second says:

In the beginning the two Spirits who are the well-endowed(?) twins were known as the one good and the other evil in thought, word and deed. Between them the wise choose the good, not so the fools. And when these Spirits met they established in the beginning life and death that in the end the evil should meet with the worst existence, but the just with the Best Mind. Of these two Spirits he who was of the lie

---

[1] The sacred book is the *Avesta*, though only a part of the original has survived. It contains three main parts, the *Yasna*, or liturgy, into which have been inserted the *Gathas*, or hymns; the *Yashts*, or sacrificial hymns, and the *Videvdat*, or 'law against demons', with the emphasis on ritual purification. How much goes back to Zoroaster himself is extremely difficult to determine, but it is usually thought that the *Gathas*, or at least the bulk of them, come from Zoroaster.

[2] The date of Zoroaster is uncertain. Traditionally (that is, according to Zoroastrian tradition) it was 258 years before Alexander. If 'Alexander' means the end of the First Persian Empire, it means a date *c.* 630–550 B.C., i.e. at about the time of the Jewish exile in Babylon; this would help to explain the great influence of these new ideas. R. C. Zaehner has summarised the influence by saying: 'The importance of Zoroastrianism, like that of Judaism, lies not in the number of those who profess it, but rather in the influence it has exercised on other religions, and particularly on Christianity, through the medium of the Jewish exiles in Babylonia who seem to have been thoroughly impregnated with Zoroastrian ideas. Christianity claims to be the heir of the prophets of Israel. If there is any truth in this claim, it is no less heir to the Prophet of ancient Iran, little though most Christians are aware of this fact' (*Concise Encyclopaedia*, p. 209). The comments in this book on Zoroastrianism are necessarily tentative, since detailed knowledge of Zoroastrianism is still at an early stage. For introductions, see Zaehner, *The Teachings of the Magi*; Spuler, ed. *Handbuch der Orientalistik*.

[3] *Yasna* xlv. 2 (trs. Zaehner).

chose to do the worst things; but the Most Holy Spirit, clothed in rugged heaven, (chose) Righteousness (or Truth) as did (all) those who sought with zeal to do the pleasure of the Wise Lord by (doing) good works... Between the two the ancient godlets (*daevas*) did not choose rightly; for, as they deliberated, delusion overcame them so that they chose the Most Evil Mind. Then did they, with one accord, rush headlong into Wrath that they might thereby extinguish(?) the existence of mortal man.[1]

But commenting on those two verses Zaehner questioned whether they are in fact dualist in the strict sense:

Two primeval Spirits meet, the Holy Spirit and the Evil One. Yet they are holy and evil, it appears, by *choice* rather than by nature. The Holy Spirit is the Most Holy Spirit of Ahura Mazdah[2] (*Yasna* xliii. 16), but is not identical with him; indeed we read elsewhere that he is his son (*Yasna* xlvii. 2 f.). This means that both the Holy and the Evil Spirits proceed from Ahura Mazdah, the Wise Lord, who is God. It seems, then, that Zoroaster, the founder of 'Zoroastrianism', which is generally regarded as the classic example of a dualist religion, was not himself a dualist, if by that term we mean one who posits two first principles, not one, and makes the Evil One co-eternal with God and independent of him.[3]

Yet there is no doubt that later Zoroastrianism came close to being dualist, by the simple expedient of identifying the Holy Spirit with Ahura Mazdah to the extent that it became another name for Ahura Mazdah. But since the *Gathas* state that the Holy and Evil Spirits are twins, it follows that Angra Mainyu (the name of the Evil Spirit) is equal with Ahura Mazdah—or, as they later came to be named, Ohrmazd and Ahriman are equal and co-eternal principles. In fact even here the full dualist implication was resisted, by, for example, holding that Ohrmazd and Ahriman were derived from an overriding principle, Infinite Time, *Zurvan i akanarak*, or again by saying that the evil principle was not co-eternal, since it would in the end be destroyed. Nevertheless, a limited dualism was implied by those who regarded the two principles as originally being quite separate, but coming into contact when Ohrmazd, the good principle, created the material and spiritual worlds as a buffer state—an area where battle could be joined. Thus, as Zaehner has put it, 'at one stroke "classical"

---

[1] *Yasna* xxx. 3–6 (trs. Zaehner).   [2] *Ahura Mazdah* is the name of the One God.
[3] *Concise Encyclopaedia*, p. 212. Cf. Gershevitch, 'Zoroaster's Own Contribution'.

Zoroastrianism, Manichaeism and Jainism

Zoroastrian dualism not only solved those two hoary mysteries—the origin of evil and the reason for creation—it drained them of all their mysteriousness.'[1] It may, perhaps, be optimistic to use the word 'solved', and it may be more accurate to say with Duchesne-Guillemin, 'l'Iran n'est pas la Grèce et rien ne permet d'affirmer que les grands problèmes s'y soient posés avec la rigueur logique à laquelle nous ont habitués les Philosophes'[2]—to say, in other words, that the problems were met in the terms in which they occurred. Nevertheless, attempts *were* made to present dualism in coherent terms, one of the most notable being Mardan-Farrukh's *Shikand Gumani Vazar* of the ninth century A.D.:

Another proof that a contrary principle exists is that good and evil are observable in the world, and more parrtcularly in so far as both good (and bad) conduct are definable as such, as are darkness and light, right knowledge and wrong knowledge, fragrance and stench, life and death, sickness and health, justice and injustice, slavery and freedom, and all the other contrary activities which indisputably exist and are visible in every country and land at all times; for no country or land exists, has existed, or ever will exist in which the name of good and evil and what that name signifies has not existed or does not exist. Nor can any time or place be mentioned in which good and evil change their nature essentially.

There are also other contraries whose antagonism is not (one of essence but) one of function, species, or nature. Such is the mutual antagonism of things of like nature as (for example) male and female, (the different) scents, tastes and colours; the Sun, Moon and stars whose dissimilarity is not one of substance but one of function, nature and constitution, each being adapted to its own particular work. But the dissimilarity of good and evil, light, darkness, and other contrary substances is not one of function but one of substance. This can be seen from the fact that their natures cannot combine and are mutually destructive. For where there is good, there cannot possibly be evil. Where light is admitted, darkness is driven away. Similarly with other contraries, the fact that they cannot combine and are mutually destructive is caused by their dissimilarity in substance. This substantial dissimilarity and mutual destructiveness is observable in phenomena in the material world.

Since we have seen that in the material world contrary substances exist and that they are sometimes mutually co-operative and sometimes

[1] *Concise Encyclopaedia*, p. 220.
[2] J. Duchesne-Guillemin, *Ormazd et Ahriman, l'aventure dualiste dans l'Antiquité* (Paris, 1953), p. 2.

mutually destructive, so (must it also be) in the spiritual world which is the cause of the material, and material things are its effects. That this is so is not open to doubt and follows from the very nature of contrary substances. I have shown above that the reason and occasion for the wise activity of the Creator which is exemplified in the creative act is the existence of an Adversary. . .

Now the goodness of the wise Creator can be inferred from the act of creation and from the fact that he cherishes and protects (his creatures), that he ordains and teaches a way and method by which evil can be repelled and sin averted, and that he repels and wards off the Adversary who attacks the body; (it can be inferred too) from the organs and faculties of the body (afflicted as they are) by pain and sickness (which come to them) from outside and (which also are) inside the body. . .

From this we must infer that what is perfect and complete in its goodness cannot produce evil. If it could, then it would not be perfect, for when a thing is described as perfect, there is no room for anything else (in it); and if there is no room for anything else, nothing else can proceed from it. If God is perfect in goodness and knowledge, plainly ignorance and evil cannot proceed from Him; or if it can, then he is not perfect; and if he is not perfect, then he should not be worshipped as God or as perfectly good.

If (on the other hand) both good and evil originate in God, then he is imperfect so far as goodness is concerned. If he is imperfect in respect of goodness, then he is imperfect in respect of right knowledge. And if he is imperfect in respect of right knowledge, then he is imperfect in respect of reason, consciousness, knowledge, wit, and in all the faculties of knowing. And if he is imperfect in reason, consciousness, wit, and knowledge, he must be imperfect in respect of health; and if he is imperfect in respect of health, he must be sick; and if he must be sick, then he is imperfect in respect of life.[1]

Another equally sophisticated system of dualism was that of Mani and the Manichees.[2] Mani was a religious teacher in Mesopotamia who was executed by the Persians in A.D. 276. He left a body of teachings, which were greatly revered but of which, on the whole, only fragments have survived. Much of our present knowledge comes in fact from Augustine, who was at one time a member of one of the lower orders of Manichaeism (a 'Hearer'), but who became disillusioned with its teachings and

[1] M. Eliade, *From Primitives to Zen* (New York, 1967), pp. 618–21 (trs. Zaehner).
[2] For a recent survey of Mani and his religion, see L. J. R. Ort, *Mani, A Religio-historical Description of his Personality* (Leiden, 1967). See also H. C. Puech, *Le Manichéisme* (Paris, 1949).

later bitterly opposed it. The other indirect sources, as, for example, the Arabic,[1] are usually less immediate.

Manichaeism spread very widely and claimed many adherents. It spread as far as the borders of the Chinese empire, and perhaps even beyond, since one important Manichaean treatise has survived in Chinese.[2] It was an eclectic system, which was certainly influenced by Zoroastrianism, even though the two were in opposition. It also drew on Christianity and regarded Christ as a figure of central importance:

> Jesus came, he separated us from the Error of the world, he brought us a mirror, we looked, we saw the Universe in it. When the Holy Spirit came he revealed to us the way of Truth and taught us that there are two Natures, that of Light and that of Darkness, separate...from the beginning.[3]

It has in fact been argued that the Manichaeans were genuinely radical Christians in a way that Gnostics, for example, were not, since whereas Gnostics frequently claimed to have been entrusted with secret teaching that made them superior to other Christians, Manichaeans claimed to have superseded Christianity on the ground that the promised Holy Spirit had been received in the embodied form of Mani.[4]

The central question for Manichaeism was the question of evil: whence did it arise and from what cause do men give expression to it? It seemed self-evident that it could not come from a good principle, or God, since God would surely not have been able to create evil things. The Manichaean argument was frequently built up in a chain, starting with small but admitted evils and leading on to all the rest—beguiling men, as Augustine put it, with flies:

> Let not then anyone beguile you, should you perchance be teased by the flies...A person was once suffering from the annoyance I have

---

[1] The Muslims were much interested in the antecedents of their own religion, and put together several accounts of other religions, of which Manichaeism was one. See A. Abel, 'Les Sources Arabes sur le Manichéisme', *Annuaire de l'Institut de Philologie et d'Histoire Orientales et Slaves*, XVI (1961), pp. 31–73.

[2] A. Chavannes and P. Pelliot, 'Un traité manichéen retrouvé en Chine', *Journal Asiatique*, X (1911), pp. 499–617; XI (1913), pp. 99–199, 261–394.

[3] C. R. C. Allberry, *A Manichaean Psalmbook* (1938), II, p. 9 (ccxxiii. 5 ff.).

[4] As a result many of their arguments were based on scripture: 'They choose out certain passages from the scriptures, which simple men do not understand; and by means of these deceive souls unused to them, inquiring, "Whence is evil?"' (Augustine, *de Agone Christiano*, iv (4)).

mentioned; the flies were teasing him. In this plight a Manichee finds him. The man began to protest that they were an intolerable nuisance, and that he hated them with all his heart. The Manichee immediately put the question, 'Who made them?' The man, annoyed as he was, and out of all patience with his tormentors, did not like to say (though he was a Catholic) God made them. 'If God did not make them', continued the other, 'who did?' 'Truly', replied the man, 'I believe the devil made them.' The Manichee, without a moment's pause, (said), 'If the fly be the workmanship of the devil, as your good sense, I see, leads you to acknowledge, who made the bee, which is a trifle larger?' The Catholic durst not say, 'God made the bee, and did not make the fly'; for the one joined hard upon the other. Well, from the bee he brought him to the locust, from the locust to the lizard, from the lizard to the bird, from the bird to the sheep, thence to the cow, thence to the elephant, and last of all to man: and persuaded him that man was not made by God. Thus the poor wretch, being tormented by the flies, became himself a fly, and so the property of the devil; for Beelzebub, it is said, means Lord of flies.[1]

If, then, evil is separate from God, it must be an invasion of the good by an alien, eternally separate, principle of evil.

The Manichees...assert, that before the world was framed there existed a nation of darkness, which was in rebellion against God; and in this war the wretched men believe that the Almighty God could in no other way succour himself, save only by sending a portion of himself against them. And, as these state, the princes of this nation ate up a portion of God, and were attempered so as that of them the world might be formed. Thus they assert that God attained the victory with great losses and tortures and miseries of his own members; which members they assert were mixed up with the dark entrails of those princes, in order to attemper them, and restrain them from their fury.[2]

The world was thought to be a result of this 'fusion in conflict', with good and evil elements interlocked and intermingled. The whole universe represented a struggle of the good to disentangle itself from the evil: the sun represented the pledge of glory, the waxing and waning of the moon represented literally the pulse of fragments of light escaping from their entanglement on this

---

[1] *Hom. in Iob.* i. 14 (trs. Browne, Lib. of Fathers, p. 13).

[2] Augustine, *de Agone Christiano*, iv (4) (trs. Cornish, Lib. of Fathers, pp. 162 f.). Since evil was an invasion of good, it followed that good was passive and defensive. Hence great emphasis was placed on the suffering of Christ: 'And this is Christ, they say, crucified in the whole universe' (Augustine, *Comm. on Ps. cxli* (*cxl*). *5*, §12).

earth: 'The Light shall return to its place, the Darkness shall fall and not rise again.'[1] What was happening on a cosmic scale was happening also in each individual. The good self was trapped in matter and needed to be released. God was 'a luminous immeasurable body and I a kind of particle from that body.'[2] Consequently Manichaean life was a struggle to emancipate the good element from the body: 'What a man must do first is to distinguish the two Principles (of Good and Evil). Anyone who wishes to enter our religion must realise that the two Principles have natures which are absolutely distinct. If a man is not aware of the distinction, how can he put the teaching into practical effect?'[3]

The way of putting the teaching into effect was to pursue a course of life that would lead to the separation of good and evil in oneself and in the universe—which meant in practice an austere and rigid asceticism, a ruthless detachment from matter. It led to almost absurd extremes, whereby the fully-professed Manichaean was not allowed to pick fruit or other food because it contaminated him and caused suffering to the object from which the food was taken. On the other hand, he was allowed to eat, and Manichees of the lower orders were required to bring him food, because his digestion of the food was the actual process of separating the good and evil elements:

Gradually and inevitably I was drawn to accept every kind of non-sense—as that a fig weeps when it is plucked and its mother tree sheds tears of sap. But provided the fig had been plucked by another man's sin and not his own, some Manichaean saint might eat it, digest it in his stomach and groaning and sighing in prayer breathe out from it angels: nay more, he might breathe out certain particles of the Godhead; and these particles of the true and supreme God would have remained in bondage in the fruit unless set free by the teeth and belly of some holy Elect one.[4]

---

[1] Allberry, *Manichaean Psalmbook*, p. 215 (*Pss. of Thomas* 8). For a fuller description see, e.g., ccxxiii. 30 ff. (p. 10): 'The sun and moon he founded, he set them on high, to purify the Soul. Daily they take up the refined part to the height, but the dregs however they erase.'

[2] Augustine, *Confessions* iv. 16 (trs. Sheed).

[3] *The Chinese Treatise*, Chavannes and Pelliot, *op. cit.* XI, p. 114.

[4] Augustine, *Conf.* iii. 10 (trs. Sheed). Cf. also *Comm. on Ps. cxli* (*cxl*). 5, §12: 'We, they say, forasmuch as we are enlightened by faith in Manes, by our prayers and our Psalms, we cleanse thereby that bread, and transmit it into the treasure-house of the heavens' (trs. Lib. of Fathers).

Dualism, Duality and Unification

Augustine came to reject the Manichaean position, but he did not cease to respect the skill and the coherence with which it was argued, though he noticed that it was more destructive than constructive.[1] However, the real strength of Manichaeism, as of other dualistic systems, was that it corresponded to experience. It picked up the very clear sense that life *is* a struggle, and that it often appears to be the case that suffering is an enemy and that 'the good that we would we do not do'.[2]

In the Eastern tradition dualistic tendencies have appeared most clearly (apart from the continuation of Zoroastrianism among the Parsis) in Jainism, though it would be wrong to describe Jainism strictly as dualist, because it rejects the idea of two warring, co-eternal, principles. Nevertheless, it represents, in the Indian context, an understanding of the self in relation to matter which in some points bears comparison with that of the Manichees. The soul, known as *jiva*, life, is an entity completely enmeshed in matter, and for its salvation it needs to be released. Every single thing in the universe has its soul, divided into five categories according to the number of senses possessed. The highest category has five senses, and includes men and the higher animals (particularly monkeys, horses, elephants, parrots and snakes); the second category has four senses, touch, taste, smell and vision, and includes large insects, such as bees and butterflies; the third category has three senses, and includes small insects; the fourth has two, taste and touch, and includes worms, slugs, leeches and similar creatures; the fifth has only one sense, that of touch, but it includes objects that other systems would regard as inanimate, stones, trees, plants, and in fact every thing in the universe. Thus the universe is 'alive'. Even stones contain a soul tightly locked in matter, so that if a stone is kicked it suffers pain, even though it cannot cry out to show it.

Entanglement with matter is what Jains understand by *karma*. *Karma* is the flow of matter which seeks an entry or hold on *jiva*, somewhat like a parasite. Selfish and cruel acts let *karma* in, good deeds are neutral, but suffering voluntarily undertaken breaks up the accumulation of *karma* and sets the *jiva* free. Until that happens the *jiva* is bound up in rebirth, exposed to suffering even in what

---

[1] See, e.g., *de Util. Cred.* i. 2 (trs. Browne, Lib. of Fathers, pp. 578 f.).
[2] Rom. 7: 15.

Zoroastrianism, Manichaeism and Jainism

are regarded outside Jainism as inanimate objects—in wood on
a carpenter's bench or iron on an anvil:

> From clubs and knives, stakes and maces, breaking up my limbs,
> An infinite number of times I have suffered without hope.
> By keen-edged razors, by knives and shears,
> Many times I have been drawn and quartered, torn apart and skinned.
> Helpless in snares and traps, a deer,
> I have been caught and bound and fastened, and often I have been
>   killed.
> A helpless fish, I have been caught with hooks and nets;
> An infinite number of times I have been killed and scraped, split
>   and gutted.
> A bird, I have been caught by hawks or trapped in nets,
> Or held fast by birdlime, and I have been killed an infinite
>   number of times.
> A tree, with axes and adzes by the carpenters
> An infinite number of times I have been felled, stripped of my
>   bark, cut up and sawn into planks.
> As iron, with hammer and tongs by blacksmiths
> An infinite number of times I have been struck and beaten, split
>   and filed...
> Ever afraid, trembling, in pain and suffering,
> I have felt the utmost sorrow and agony...
> In every kind of existence I have suffered
> Pains which have scarcely known reprieve for a moment.[1]

It will be gathered from that passage that Jainism can be deeply
pessimistic in its understanding of life and of the universe. This
pessimism appears in one of the most familiar passages of Indian
literature, the parable of the man in the well. It appears in several
versions, and it was repeated outside Jainism as well. The following is the version in *Samaradityakatha*:[2]

> A certain man, much oppressed by the woes of poverty,
> Left his own home, and set out for another country.
> He passed through the land, with its villages, cities, and harbours,
> And after a few days he lost his way.

And he came to a forest, thick with trees...and full of wild beasts.
There, while he was stumbling over the rugged paths...a prey to
thirst and hunger, he saw a mad elephant, fiercely trumpeting, charging
him with upraised trunk. At the same time there appeared before him a
most evil demoness, holding a sharp sword, dreadful in face and form,

---

[1] *Uttaradhyayana Sutra*, xix. 61–7, 71, 74 (trs. Basham, in *Sources of Indian Tradition*).
[2] ii. 55–80 (trs. Basham).

and laughing with loud and shrill laughter. Seeing them he trembled in all his limbs with deathly fear, and looked in all directions. There, to the east of him, he saw a great banyan tree...

And he ran quickly, and reached the mighty tree.
But his spirits fell, for it was so high that even the birds
    could not fly over it,
And he could not climb its high unscalable trunk...
All his limbs trembled with terrible fear,
Until, looking round, he saw nearby an old well covered with
    grass.
Afraid of death, craving to live if only a moment longer,
He flung himself into the well at the foot of the banyan tree.
A clump of reeds grew from its deep wall, and to this he clung,
While below him he saw terrible snakes, enraged at the sound of
    his falling;
And at the very bottom, known from the hiss of its breath, was
    a black and mighty python.
With mouth agape, its body thick as the trunk of a heavenly
    elephant, with terrible red eyes.
He thought, 'My life will only last as long as these reeds hold fast,'
And he raised his head; and there, on the clump of reeds, he saw
    two large mice,
One white, one black, their sharp teeth ever gnawing at the roots
    of the reed-clump.
Then up came the wild elephant, and, enraged the more at not
    catching him,
Charged time and again at the trunk of the banyan tree.
At the shock of his charge a honeycomb on a large branch
Which hung over the old well, shook loose and fell.
The man's whole body was stung by a swarm of angry bees,
But, just by chance, a drop of honey fell on his head,
Rolled down his brow, and somehow reached his lips,
And gave him a moment's sweetness. He longed for other drops,
And he thought nothing of the python, the snakes, the elephant,
    the mice, the well, or the bees,
In his excited craving for yet more drops of honey.
This parable is powerful to clear the minds of those on the way
    to freedom.
Now hear its sure interpretation.
The man is the soul, his wandering in the forest the four types
    of existence.[1]
The wild elephant is death, the demoness old age.

[1] Divine, human, animal, demonic.

The banyan tree is salvation, where there is no fear of death,
  the elephant,
But which no sensual man can climb.
The well is human life, the snakes are passions,
Which so overcome a man that he does not know what he should do.
The tuft of reed is man's allotted span, during which the soul
  exists embodied;
The mice which steadily gnaw it are the dark and bright fortnights.[1]
The stinging bees are manifold diseases,
Which torment a man until he has not a moment's joy.
The awful python is hell, seizing the man bemused by sensual pleasure,
Fallen in which the soul suffers pains by the thousand.
The drops of honey are trivial pleasures, terrible at the last.
How can a wise man want them, in the midst of such peril and
  hardship?

In this desperate situation, the only salvation is to disentangle
jiva from matter which holds it in bondage. It can only be done
by avoiding all contact with matter which might cause injury:

One should know what binds the soul, and, knowing, break free
  from bondage.
What bondage did the Hero[2] declare, and what knowledge did
  he teach to remove it?
He who grasps at even a little, whether living or lifeless, or consents
  to another doing so, will never be freed from sorrow.
If a man kills living things, or slays by the hand of another, or
  consents to another slaying, his sin goes on increasing.
The man who cares for his kin and companions is a fool who suffers
  much, for their numbers are ever increasing.
All his wealth and relations cannot save him from sorrow.
Only if he knows the nature of life, will he get rid of karma.[3]

The technique of non-injury was carried to great extremes, and
it is probably the best-known characteristic of the Jains. Great
care is taken that nothing should be killed, even inadvertently.
The Jain monk carries with him a small brush with which to
clear the path before him, lest he tread on some unseen insect and
kill it. He wears a mask across his face, strains all water before he
drinks it, and never lights a fire or lamp—not only because insects

---

[1] I.e. 'time'—time was reckoned in fortnights, following the waxing and waning of
the moon.
[2] The great hero is Mahavira, the founder of Jainism.
[3] *Sutrakritanga* i. 1.1, 1-5 (trs. Basham).

are attracted to the light and are thereby destroyed, but also because fire itself is living:

> The man who lights a fire kills living things,
> While he who puts it out kills the fire;
> Thus a wise man who understands the Law
> Should never light a fire.
> There are lives in earth and lives in water,
> Hopping insects leap into the fire,
> And worms dwell in rotten wood,
> All are burned when a fire is lighted.[1]

The Jain monk walks in the world with fragile and gentle delicacy, sensitive to the sorrow and suffering of all around him, even of the earth itself.[2] Along with extreme care in avoiding injury to other souls, the Jain monk practises great austerity in his own life in order to assist in the disentanglement of *jiva* from matter in himself. It can lead to the great climax of allowing oneself to starve to death. Ideally it is prepared for by a course of progressive fasting, but if sickness occurs unexpectedly, the 'fast unto death' (*itvara* or *sallekhana*) can be undertaken without preparation:

If a monk feels sick, and is unable duly to mortify the flesh, he should regularly diminish his food. Mindful of his body, immovable as a beam, the monk should strive to waste his body away. He should enter a village or town...and beg for straw. Then he should take it and go to an out-of-the-way place. He should carefully inspect and sweep the ground, so that there are no eggs, living beings, sprouts, dew, water, ants, mildew, drops of water, mud, or cobwebs left on it. Thereupon he carries out the final fast...Speaking the truth, the saint who has crossed the stream of transmigration, doing away with all hesitation, knowing all things but himself unknown, leaves his frail body. Overcoming manifold hardships and troubles, with trust in his religion he performs this terrible penance. Thus in due time he puts an end to his existence. This is done by those who have no delusions. This is good; this is joyful and proper; this leads to salvation; this should be followed.[3]

Jainism is thus potentially dualist inasmuch as it sees an inimical relationship between *jiva* and matter. The whole universe is derived from the two eternal, uncreated and independent categories

---

[1] *Sutrakritanga* i. 6 f. (trs. Basham).
[2] See, e.g., *Acaranga Sutra*, i. 1.   [3] *Acaranga Sutra* i. 7, 6 (trs. Basham).

of *jiva* and *ajiva*, the conscious and the non-conscious. And yet the full dualist implication was resisted, because it oversimplifies the phenomena. On theoretical grounds, it was made improbable by the fact that Jain philosophy is not dominated by the logical rule of the excluded middle, either y or not-y. On the contrary, Jainism (and much other Indian philosophy) values the more subtle refinements of 'the rule of manysidedness' (*anekantavada*), which is not congenial to dualism.[1] It is related to the theory of *syadvada*, conditional predication, which asserts that whatever 'reality' may be in itself, it is known by its expression of itself in multiple forms, which means that no absolute predication is possible. On more popular grounds, dualism was excluded because creation was not taken back to a conflict between two co-eternal principles. Indeed, Jainism denies that creation is a consequence of divine will or purpose altogether; natural law is a sufficient explanation, and the existence of evil and suffering rules out a well-disposed creator:

Some foolish men declare that Creator made the world.
The doctrine that the world was created is ill-advised,
    and should be rejected.
If God created the world, where was he before creation?
If you say he was transcendent then, and needed no support,
    where is he now?...
How could God have made the world without any raw material?
If you say he made this first, and then the world, you are
    faced with an endless regression...
If God created the world by an act of his own will, without
    any raw material,
Then it is just his will and nothing else—and who
    will believe this silly stuff?
If he is ever perfect and complete, how could the will
    to create have arisen in him?
If, on the other hand, he is not perfect, he could no more
    create the universe than could a potter...
If out of love for living things and need of them he made the world,
Why did he not make creation wholly blissful, free from misfortune?...
God commits great sin in slaying the children whom he
    himself created.

---

[1] Hence also the popularity of another famous Indian parable, that of the blind men feeling different bits of an elephant and declaring from its trunk that it was a snake, from its leg a tree-trunk, from its tail a rope, etc.

Dualism, Duality and Unification

If you say that he slays only to destroy evil beings, why did
  he create such beings in the first place?...
Know that the world is uncreated, as time itself is,
  without beginning and end...
Uncreated and indestructible, it endures under the compulsion
  of its own nature,
Divided into three sections—hell, earth, and heaven.[1]

Thus Jainism represents an inherent dualism which corresponds
to human experience, but in which the full dualistic position is
resisted. Dualism corresponds to the experience of tension and
conflict, in the observation both of oneself and of external
phenomena. It is in that experiential sense that religions have
recognised the force and attraction of dualism, and yet they have
reacted away from it as being ultimately misleading. They have,
in other words, tried to find ways in which to unify the diverse
phenomena of existence. In the Eastern tradition, Hinduism,
which still gives full reign to the experiential satisfaction of
dualism in popular religion, eventually unified the phenomena in
the view that all reality is an aspect or manifestation of Brahman—
and it is significant, incidentally, that Jainism rejected monism as
firmly as it did theism.[2] Buddhism recognised the attractiveness of
a dualistic understanding of reality, but saw in it the greatest
possible source of delusion, since it represented an attempt to
snatch something permanent from the ceaseless flow of change.
Buddhism unified the phenomena by establishing the universal
truth of *dukkha*.

In the Western tradition, the experiential force of dualism was
recognised by Judaism in its acceptance of the two ways, the
two inclinations (*yazrain*), and the mythological picture of fallen

---

[1] *Mahapurana* iv. 16 ff. (trs. Basham).

[2] See, e.g., *Ganadharavada*, i. 32–9: 'If the soul were only one, like space pervading all
bodies, then it would be of one and the same character in all bodies. But the soul is
not like this. There are many souls, just as there are many pots and other things in
the world—this is evident from the difference of their characteristics...If we
assume the monist hypothesis, since the soul is all-pervading, there can be no
liberation or bondage (for the soul is uniform) like space...Again assuming
monism, there can be no soul enjoying final bliss, for there are many maladies in
the world, and thus the world-soul can only be partly happy...Therefore action
and enjoyment, bondage and release, joy and sorrow, and likewise transmigration
itself, are only possible on the hypothesis that souls are many and infinite' (trs.
Basham). It is interesting to compare with this Ramanuja's criticism of the *advaita
Vedanta* of Shankara, particularly in his view that there must be some distinction
(comparable, *mutatis mutandis*, to Christian trinitarian distinctions) between the self
and the object of its fulfilment.

and warring angels. But even tendencies to turn these into dualistic explanations were resisted, on the grounds of the uncompromisable unity of God—which, indeed, had taken many centuries of often anguished struggle to realise and establish. Christianity stood in much the same position, since it inherited a great deal of its conceptual framework from Judaism; it had only to look at the New Testament to see how readily the experience of living can be expressed in dualistic terms. And yet Christianity, like other religions, turned away. Its rejection of dualism can be epitomised in the change of Augustine from Manichaeism to Christianity.

The essence of Augustine's change of heart was his realisation that dualism is not an explanation; it is an observation enshrined in systematic thought. Augustine had no doubt about the impressive complexity of the Manichaean system, and he recognised the sincerity of their claims to be pursuing the truth of reality; but he also came to recognise that their observations of experience had not penetrated beneath the surface:

The syllables of the names of God the Father and of the Lord Jesus Christ and of the Paraclete, the Holy Ghost, our Comforter...were always on their lips, but only as sounds and tongue noises; for their heart was empty of the true meaning. They cried out 'Truth, truth'; they were forever uttering the word to me, but the thing was nowhere in them; indeed they spoke falsehood not only of you (God), who are truly Truth, but also of the elements of this world, your creatures...O Truth, Truth, how inwardly did the very marrow of my soul pant for you when time and again I heard them sound your name. But it was all words—words spoken, words written in many huge tomes. In these dishes—while I hungered for you—they served me up the sun and the moon,[1] beautiful works of yours, but works of yours all the same and not yourself.[2]

The question, therefore, became for Augustine one of whether Manichaean deductions, drawn from observing the experience of duality, were adequate or correct—whether, that is, they did justice to the phenomena.[3] The essential weakness lay in the

[1] For the Manichaean understanding of the sun and the moon, see p. 276.
[2] Augustine, *Conf.* iii. 6 (trs. Sheed).
[3] This applied as much to objective as to subjective phenomena, as P. Courcelle has emphasised: 'Augustin résiste à leurs arguments; en bon manichéen, il prie les savants de la secte de lui expliquer comment la cosmologie et l'astrologie manichéennes s'accordent avec les données de l'astronomie scientifique.' (*Recherches sur les Confessions de Saint Augustin*, Paris, 1950, p. 76.)

passivity of goodness, which in effect emptied God of significance, and impoverished human experience—by removing the possible value of varied experience in a single, unified subject. Thus one can already see the almost inevitable development in Augustine's thought of evil being understood as *privatio boni*, and at the same time *semen boni*. It is not necessary here to follow the details of Augustine's arguments—though some of them have, of course, appeared in the section on Christianity[1]—nor is it necessary to assess their validity. What is important is to realise the strength of Augustine's conviction—having known the opposite at first hand—that the phenomena of duality must be unified for equality of value to survive. It meant, so far as Augustine was concerned, investigating the unity of God's action and the unity of human experience. As regards the former, he had in fact registered the force of Nebridius' arguments against the fully dualist position of the Manichaeans, long before he detached himself from them;[2] as regards the latter, the unity of human experience was a theme to which Augustine frequently returned. Ultimately it seemed to be a matter of common sense:

If there be as many contrary natures in man as there are wills in conflict with one another, then there are not two natures in us but several. Take the case of a man trying to make up his mind whether he would go to the Manichees' meeting-house or to the theatre. The Manichees would say: 'Here you have two natures, one good, bringing him to the meeting-house, the other evil, taking him away. How else could you have this wavering between two wills pulling against each other?' Now I say that both are bad, the will that would take him to the Manichees and the will that would take him to the theatre. But they hold that the will by which one comes to them is good. Very well! Supposing one of us is trying to decide and wavering between two wills in conflict, whether to go to the theatre or to *our* church, will not the Manichees be in some trouble about an answer? For either they must admit, which they do not want to, that a good will would take a man to our church as they think it is a good will that brings those who are receivers of their sacrament and belong to them in their church; or they must hold that there are two evil natures and two evil wills at conflict in one man, and what they are always saying will not be true—namely, that there is one good will and one evil will. Otherwise, they must be converted to the truth and not deny that when a man is taking a decision there is one soul drawn this way and that by diverse wills...

[1] See pp. 86–92.   [2] See especially Augustine, *Conf.* vii. 2.

286

When eternity attracts the higher faculties and the pleasure of some temporal good holds the lower, it is the one same soul that wills both, but not either with its whole will; and it is therefore torn both ways and deeply troubled while truth shows the one way as better but habit keeps it to the other.[1]

Thus for Augustine the experiential cogency of duality was unified in the overriding unity of God—not a barren unity, but one which set the pattern of relationship; hence the important Trinitarian arguments are not academic but devotional. What remained of importance for Augustine was that the whole work of unifying the diverse phenomena of existence should continue to make sense, without distortion, of the experience of being alive:

'And what is this God?' I asked the earth and it answered: 'I am not he'; and all things that are in the earth made the same confession. I asked the sea and the deeps and the creeping things, and they answered: 'We are not your God; seek higher.' I asked the winds that blow, and the whole air with all that is in it answered: 'Anaximenes was wrong; I am not God.' I asked the heavens, the sun, the moon, the stars, and they answered: 'Neither are we God whom you seek.' And I said to all the things that throng about the gateways of the senses: 'Tell me of my God, since you are not he. Tell me something of him.' And they cried out in a great voice: 'He made us.' My question was my gazing upon them, and their answer was their beauty. And I turned to myself and said: 'And you, who are you?' And I answered: 'A man.' Now clearly there is a body and a soul in me, one exterior, one interior. From which of these two should I have enquired of my God? I had already sought him by my body, from earth to heaven, as far as my eye could send its beams on the quest. But the interior part is the better, seeing that all my body's messengers delivered to it, as ruler and judge, the answers that heaven and earth and all things in them made when they said: 'We are not God,' and, 'He made us.' The inner man knows these things through the ministry of the outer man: I the inner man knew them, I, I the soul, through the senses of the body. I asked the whole frame of the universe about my God and it answered me: 'I am not he, but he made me.'[2]

The quest for Augustine was eventually reduced to extremely simple terms:

> *Aug.* Deum et animam scire cupio.
> *Ratio.* Nihilne plus?
> *Aug.* Nihil omnino.[3]

---

[1] *Conf.* viii. 10. [2] *Conf.* x. 6.
[3] *Soliloquia* ii. 7, in a section appropriately headed, *Quid amandum.*

Dualism, Duality and Unification

The search for ways of adequately unifying the diverse phenomena of existence, which on a superficial level suggest the experience of duality, represents important 'common ground' between the religions. It certainly represents one of the few points of real contact between religions and Marxism, though in Marxism the experience of duality is expressed slightly differently, in terms of alienation.[1] Nevertheless, Marxism also points to the importance of reducing the tensions of duality by finding adequate grounds for eliminating the causes that give rise to it, and it does so, like other religions, by looking for ways in which the phenomena can be adequately unified.[2] In a way, the quest for the unification of experience is roughly analogous to the attempt to give a unified description to other observational dualities, as, for example, to the duality of physical, or statistical, phenomena: duality is a good way of describing the phenomena as observed, but is it an adequate way? Thus A. Landé, in a book entitled appropriately *From Dualism to Unity in Quantum Physics*, wrote:

The most striking feature of quantum physics is the wave-like periodic relation between coordinates q and momenta p, and between energy E and time t, best known from the rules of Planck, $E = hv$, de Broglie, $p = h/\lambda$, and Bohr, $v = (E_1 - E_2)/h$... The earlier and now the modern quantum rules were introduced as *ad hoc* theorems in order to fit the observed facts. Shall we accept them because they 'work' so well, or should they perhaps be understood on the grounds of less sophisticated elementary postulates?

The traditional answer to this question has been most unsatisfactory. For the last thirty years the wave function has been regarded as evidence of a dominant principle of nature according to which, using Newton's language, matter (and light) is 'endowed with an occult and specifick quality by which it acts and produces manifest effects', namely, a dualistic interplay of wave and corpuscular qualities, attenuated by as fundamental complementarity. And after so many years it is not even felt as problematic any more that matter sometimes displays particle, sometimes wave features. We are told that clicks in Geiger counters and Compton recoil effects can be explained only in corpuscular terms, whereas interference fringes in diffraction experiments can be accounted for only by wave theory. To quote from an otherwise excellent textbook:

'Electrons, instead of having laws similar to classical laws, obey the

---

[1] It is also different because of the Hegelian background of thesis and antithesis.
[2] But, like some forms of Humanism, it does so by imposing a limited and reductionist anthropology; see, further, the conclusion on p. 290.

laws of wave motion... and light is corpuscular in nature, at least when it interacts with matter.' It really looks like waves on Monday, Wednesday, and Friday, and like particles the rest of the week (Bragg). Only a few independent spirits, among them Einstein, Schrödinger, and de Broglie, have steadfastly refused to accept this 'quantum mess' as final.

The situation has hardly been clarified by the introduction of descriptive phrases such as 'duality'. With reference to Planck's and other quantum rules, von Weizsacker writes: 'We know today that $(E = hv)$ is a consequence of a basic fact of all atomic events, the dualism of the wave picture and the particle picture.'[1]

Landé's response was robust:

Neutrality toward the wave–particle paradox, elevated by Niels Bohr and Heisenberg to a 'fundamental principle' of duality inherent in all matter (and fields) is diametrically opposed to the *realism* of Einstein to whom 'the concepts of physics refer to a real world, to things which claim real existence independent of perceiving subjects'. At heart all physicists are realists in Einstein's sense to whom there could only be *either* discrete particles *or* continuous waves of matter, rather than 'whole peas and pea soup at the same time', even if the two 'pictures' might be complementary.[2] Physical questions of the either–or type are not solved by tranquillizing pills dressed in philosophical language. Using the age-old scepticism of philosophers as to the reality of the external world to serve as a cover for our temporary ignorance and indecision, is the policy of 'if you can't explain it, call it a principle, then look down on those who still search for an explanation as unenlightened'.[3]

The importance of this is not whether Landé's proposals are or are not acceptable, but that he recognised that there might be important ground to be gained by continuing to look for a unifying 'explanation', or what he called 'the ultimate bottom of insight'.[4] In that respect, it is analogous to the quest for a unifying 'explanation' of (or insight into) the human experience of duality.

[1] A. Landé, *From Dualism to Unity in Quantum Physics* (Cambridge, 1960), pp. 55 f.
[2] 'There is a duality in the nature of all quantum-mechanic entities, whether we call them electrons, for preference, in one case, or electro-magnetic waves, for preference, in the other. Niels Bohr has coined the word *complementarity* to describe this situation and has thereby stressed that the circumstances in which one or other view is natural are always quite different, so that a conflict between the two descriptions need never arise.' N. Kemmer, 'Waves and Probability', in *Quanta and Reality* (London, 1962), pp. 43 f.
[3] A. Landé, *op. cit.* pp. 97 f.   [4] A. Landé, *op. cit.* p. 104.

Dualism, Duality and Unification

It is not that the explanation 'is' the phenomena, but rather that it is of indispensable assistance in organising and understanding experience, and it is, as a result, programmatically helpful. Above all, the quest is in itself a way of insisting that justice be done to the phenomena *in their diversity*:

> This life is not good but in danger and in joy.[1]

Religions agree in accepting the worthwhileness of the quest; dualistic accounts, whether religious or humanistic, run the risk of undervaluing or seriously diminishing the possibilities of experience. Where religions differ is in the account they give, not only of what constitutes danger, but also of what constitutes joy. Although the points of contact in these accounts are considerable, nevertheless they conceive differently the nature of the joy attainable by men. For this reason, they give different accounts of human nature—that is, of what men *are* in themselves. To recognise how profound are the effects of these differences in the varied cultures and nations of the world is as much politically as spiritually important—though few politicians seem aware of this.

For all religions, there remains the unremitting question of their credibility—that is, of the credibility of their account of existence and of human nature. Fundamentally, this is a question of truth, but it is posed, in practice, as a question of coherence. It is a question of the extent to which religious accounts are, or are not, coherent with each other, and whether they are coherent with other ways (as, for example, the scientific) of observing the universe and of living within it. The exploration of the principle of coherence is perhaps the most urgent task before us in the attempt to understand the relationship, not simply between religions themselves, but also between religious and secular accounts of existence.

In their different ways religions have endeavoured to safeguard the spiritual capacities of the material organism, man; what they have attempted to safeguard is not necessarily exhausted in their ways of trying to explain it—that is to say, what is being explained does not necessarily perish when a particular explanation is shown to be inadequate. For there is certainly the experience of being 'a moving mist', a creature of growth and decay; but there is also

---

[1] J. C. Ransom, 'Old Man Playing With Children', quoted from *Anthology of Modern Poetry*, ed. J. Wain (London, 1963), p. 130.

the experience of spiritual discovery and growth. This is the duality which religions have recognised, but which at the same time they have endeavoured to unify. As Henry Vaughan put in the language of his own tradition,

> False life! a foil and no more, when
>   Wilt thou be gone?...
> Thou art a toylsom Mole, or less
>   A moving mist.
> But life is, what none can express,
> A quickness, which my God hath kist.

The question (to which our lives are, in a sense, our answer) is not simply whether we are 'a quickness', but whether also we are 'a quickness which my God hath kist'; whether, that is, the experience of God is as much to be taken into account as the experience of death. And that *cannot* be known if only a limited part of human experience is accepted as the total truth:

> The skinne and shell of things,
> Though faire,
> are not
> Thy wish, nor Pray'r,
> but got
> By meere Despaire
> of wings.[1]

---

[1] Henry Vaughan, *Silex Scintillans*, 'The Search'.

BIBLIOGRAPHY

(Only those books are included to which reference is made or from which quotations have been taken.)

Abel, A., 'Les Sources Arabes sur le Manichéisme', *A.I.P.H.O.S.* xvi, 1961, pp. 31–73.

Allberry, C. R. C., *A Manichaean Psalmbook*, Stuttgart, 1938.

Allen, J. W., *A History of Political Thought in the 16th Century*, London, 1951.

Ambekar, G. V. and Divekar, V. D., edd., *Documents on China's Relations with South and South-East Asia, 1949–1962*, Bombay, 1964.

Andrews, C. F., ed., *Letters to a Friend*, London, 1928.

Arberry, A. J., trs., *The Doctrine of the Sufis*, Cambridge, 1935.
Sufism, London, 1950.
The Mysteries of Selflessness (M. Iqbal), London, 1953.

Aurobindo, Sri, *The Life Divine*, Calcutta, 1947.

Barrett, C. K., *The Gospel According to St John*, London, 1956.

Barth, K., *The Epistle to the Romans* (trs. E. C. Hoskyns), Oxford, 1933.

Bary, W. T. de, ed. *Sources of Indian Tradition*, Columbia, 1958.

Basham, A. L., contr., *Sources of Indian Tradition* (ed. W. T. de Bary), Columbia, 1958.

Beausobre, Iulia de, *Creative Suffering* (Dacre Paper 4), London, 1940.

Beauvoir, S. de, *A Very Easy Death*, London, 1966.

Berdyaev, N., *Spirit and Reality*, London, 1939.

Birkenhead, Earl of, ed., *The Five Hundred Best English Letters*, London, 1931.

Blackburn, E. A., *A Treasury of the Kingdom*, Oxford, 1954.

Blakney, R. B., ed., *Meister Eckhart*, New York, 1941.

Bonhoeffer, D., *Letters and Papers from Prison*, London, 1963.

Bottomore, T. B. and Rubel, M., edd., *Karl Marx: Selected Writings in Sociology...*, London, 1963.

Bowie, R. R. and Fairbank, J. K., edd., *Communist China (1955–9); Policy Documents with Analysis*, Harvard, 1962.

Bowker, J. W., 'The Origin and Purpose of St John's Gospel', *N.T.S.* xi, 1965, pp. 398–408.
'Intercession in the Quran and the Jewish Tradition', *J.S.S.* xi, 1966, pp. 69–82.
Targums and Rabbinic Literature: an Introduction to Jewish Interpretations of Scripture, Cambridge, 1969.

Brandt, C., *Stalin's Failure in China, 1924–1927*, Harvard, 1958.

Braunsberger, O., ed., *Petri Canisii Epistulae et Acta*, Freiburg, 1896–1923.

Bibliography

Brewster, E. H., *The Life of Gotama the Buddha*, London, 1926.

Bühler, G., *The Laws of Manu*, Oxford, 1886.

Chalmers, Lord, *Further Dialogues of the Buddha*, Oxford, 1927.

Charles, R. H., *Apocrypha and Pseudepigrapha of the Old Testament in English*, Oxford, 1913.

Chavannes, A. and Pelliot, P., 'Un traité manichéen retrouvé en Chine', *Journal Asiatique*, x, 1911, pp. 499–617; XI, 1913, pp. 99–199, 261–394.

Ch'en, J., *Mao and the Chinese Revolution*, Oxford, 1965.

Collingwood, R. G., *An Autobiography*, London, 1944.

Compton, B., *Mao's China, Party Reform Documents, 1942–4*, Seattle, 1952.

Conze, E., ed., *Buddhist Texts Through the Ages*, Oxford, 1954. *Buddhist Scriptures*, London, 1959.

Courcelle, P., *Recherches sur les Confessions de Saint Augustin*, Paris, 1950.

Cragg, K., *The Call of the Minaret*, Oxford. 1956.

Daniélou, A., *Hindu Polytheism*, London, 1964.

Davids, T. W. R., *Early Buddhism*, London, 1910.

Donne, J., *Complete Poetry and Selected Prose* (ed. J. Hayward), London, 1962.

Dostoevsky, F., *The Brothers Karamazov* (trs. D. Magarshack), Penguin, 1958.

Duchesne-Guillemin, J., *Ormazd et Ahriman, l'aventure dualiste dans l'Antiquité*, Paris, 1953.

Einhorn, M., *Wolkovisker Yizkor Book*, New York, 1949.

Eliade, M., ed., *From Primitives to Zen*, New York, 1967.

Engels, F., *The Condition of the Working Class in England*, included in Marx and Engels, *On Britain*, Moscow, 1962.
'Die Kommunisten und Karl Heinzen', in *Marx/Engels Werke*, IV.

d'Entrèves, A. P., ed., *Aquinas: Selected Political Writings*, Oxford, 1965.

Evans, E., trs., *Enchiridion*, London, 1953.

Flew, A., ed., *New Essays in Philosophical Theology*, London, 1955.

Freedman, R., ed., *Marx on Economics*, London, 1961.

Freud, S., *New Introductory Lectures on Psycho-Analysis*, London, 1933.

Friedlander, M., trs., *The Guide for the Perplexed* (M. Maimonides), London, 1904.

Fromm, E., ed., *Socialist Humanism*, London, 1967.

Frost, R., *The Collected Poems*, London, 1967.

Gandhi, M. K., *Non-Violence in Peace and War*, 2 vols., Ahmedabad, 1948, 1949.

Gershevitch, I., 'Zoroaster's Own Contribution', *J.N.E.S.* XXIII, 1964, pp. 12–38.
contr., *Handbuch der Orientalistik, Iranistik-Bande, Literatur I* (ed. B. Spuler), Leiden, 1968.

Bibliography

Giles, H. A., *Gems of Chinese Literature*, London, 1923.
Govinda, A., *The Psychological Attitude of Early Buddhist Philosophy*, London, 1961.
Griffith, R. T. H., trs., *The Hymns of the Rigveda*, Benares, 1920–6.
Griffith, S. B., trs., *Sun Wu: The Art of War*, Oxford, 1963.
Grou, J. N., *Manual for Interior Souls*, London, 1955.
Haithcox, J. P., 'The Roy-Lenin Debate on Colonial Policy: a New Interpretation', *Journal of Asian Studies*, XXIII, 1963, pp. 93–101.
Hargreaves, J. D., 'Lord Salisbury, British Isolation and the Yangtze Valley, June–September, 1900', *B.I.H.R.* xxx, 1957.
Hastings, J., ed., *Encyclopaedia of Religion and Ethics*, Edinburgh, 1908–26.
Hay, M., *The Foot of Pride*, Boston, 1950 (original title, *Europe and the Jews*).
Hick, J., *Evil and the God of Love*, London, 1966.
Horner, I. B., contr., *Buddhist Texts* (ed. E. Conze), Oxford, 1954.
trs., *Milinda's Questions (Milindapanha)*, London, 1963–4.
Hoskyns, E. C., *The Fourth Gospel*, London, 1956.
Hume, R. E., *The Thirteen Principal Upanishads*, Oxford, 1921.
Hyams, E., ed., *Newstatesmanship*, London, 1963.
Iqbal, M., *The Mysteries of Selflessness* (trs. A. J. Arberry), London, 1953.
Jamali, M. F., *Letters on Islam*, Oxford, 1965.
Kaufmann, W., ed., *Religion from Tolstoy to Camus*, New York, 1964.
Kelly, J. N. D., *Early Christian Doctrine*, London, 1958.
Kemmer, N., contr., *Quanta and Reality, a Symposium*, London, 1962.
à Kempis, T., *The Imitation of Christ*,
Klein, W. C., trs., *Ibana*, New Haven, 1940.
Kolakowski, L., *Der Mensch ohne Alternative*, Munich, 1960.
Traktat über die Sterblichkeit der Vernunft..., Stuttgart, 1967.
Kwok, D. W. Y., *Scientism in Chinese Thought, 1900–1950*, Yale, 1965.
Lancaster, L., *Masters of Political Thought, Hegel to Dewey*, London, 1959.
Landé, A., *From Dualism to Unity in Quantum Physics*, Cambridge, 1960.
Lecler, J., *Toleration and the Reformation*, London, 1960.
Lenin, V. I., *Collected Works*, 30 vols., Moscow, 1927–32; 52 vols., Moscow, 1958–65.
Lewy, G., *The Catholic Church and Nazi Germany*, London, 1964.
Li Jui, *Mao Tse-tung*..., Peking, 1957.
Macdonell, A. A., *Hymns from the Rig-Veda*, Oxford, 1923.
Mao Tse-tung, *Selected Works*, I–IV, Peking, 1961.
Quotations from Chairman Mao Tse-tung, Peking, 1966.
Marx, K., *Contribution to the Critique of Hegel's Philosophy of Right*, in *Marx and Engels on Religion*, Moscow, n.d.

Bibliography

Marx, K., *Das Kapital*, Chicago, 1963.

Economic and Political Manuscripts, in D. Rjazanov and V. Adoratski, edd., *Historisch-Kritische Gesamtausgabe*, III, Berlin, 1932; trs. M. Milligan in D. J. Struik, ed., *Economic and Political Manuscripts*, New York, 1964.

'Erster Entwurf zum "Bürgerkrieg in Frankreich"', *Marx/Engels Werke*, IV.

'First International Review', in *On Colonialism*, Moscow, 1962.

Marx, K. and Engels, F., *The Communist Manifesto*, Chicago, 1963.

The German Ideology, Moscow, 1962.

On Britain, Moscow, 1962.

On Colonialism, Moscow, 1962.

Mascall, E. L., *Grace and Glory*, London, 1961.

McCarthy, D. J., *Treaty and Covenant*, Rome, 1963.

Mei: *see* Yi-pao Mei.

Mendenhall, G. E., *Law and Covenant*, Pittsburgh, 1955.

Moore, C. A. and Radhakrishnan, S., *A Source Book in Indian Philosophy*, Princeton, 1957.

Moore, H., *The Christian Faith in Japan*, London, 1904.

Nehru, J. L., *The Discovery of India*, London, 1946.

Nhat Hanh, Th., *Vietnam: The Lotus in the Sea of Fire*, London, 1967.

Nicholson, R. A., *Rumi*, London, 1950.

Nickle, K. F., *The Collection*, London, 1966.

Niebuhr, R., *Beyond Tragedy*, London, 1947.

Ort, L. J. R., *Mani, A Religio-historical Description of his Personality*, Leiden, 1967.

Pelly, L., *The Miracle Play of Hasan and Husain*, London, 1879.

Plekhanov, G. V., *Selected Philosophical Works*, London, 1961.

Prabhu, P. H., *Hindu Social Organization*, Bombay, 1963.

Prasada, R., trs., *The Yoga Sutras of Patanjali*, Allahabad, 1924.

Puech, H. C., *Le Manichéisme*, Paris, 1949.

Radek, K., *Portraits and Pamphlets*, London, 1935.

Radhakrishnan, S., *The Bhagavadgita*, New York, 1948.

The Principal Upanishads, London, 1953.

The Dhammapada, Oxford, 1954.

East and West, the End of their Separation, New York, 1954.

Radhakrishnan, S. and Moore, C. A., edd., *A Source Book in Indian Philosophy*, Princeton, 1957.

Raghavan, V., *The Indian Heritage: an Anthology of Sanskrit Literature*, Bangalore, 1958.

Rahula, W., *What the Buddha Taught*, Bedford, 1967.

Ray, R. C., trs., *The Mahabharata*, Calcutta, 1890.

Redgrave, A., *Reports of Inspectors of Factories*, 1858.

Richardson, C. C., ed., *Early Christian Fathers*, London, 1953.

Bibliography

Saddhatissa, Th., *Mahavagga of the Vinaya*, Alutgama, 1922.
Sangharakshita, Bh., *A Survey of Buddhism*, Bangalore, 1966.
Schram, S., *Mao Tse-tung*, London, 1966.
Schwartz, B. I., *Chinese Communism and the Rise of Mao*, Harvard, 1951.
Seale, M. S., *Muslim Theology*, London, 1964.
Sen, K. M., *Hinduism*, London, 1963.
Sharma, C., *A Critical Survey of Indian Philosophy*, London, 1960.
Sheed, F. J., trs., *The Confessions of Augustine*, London, 1954.
Skolimovski, H., 'Creative Developments in Polish Marxism', *Cambridge Review*, 1967, pp. 255–60.
Spitta, W., *Zur Geschichte abulHasan alAshari*, Leipzig, 1876.
Spuler, B., ed., *Handbuch der Orientalistik, Iranistik-Bande, Literatur I*, Leiden, 1968.
Struik, D. J., ed., *Economic and Political Manuscripts* (K. Marx), New York, 1964.
Thomas, E. J., *The Life of the Buddha as Legend and History*, New York, 1927.
Tissot, J., ed., *The Interior Life*, London, 1961.
Trenckner, V., ed., *Milindapanha*, London, 1880.
Tritton, A. S., *Muslim Theology*, London, 1947.
Trotsky, L., *Lenin*, London, 1925.
Tucker, R. C., *Philosophy and Myth in Karl Marx*, Cambridge, 1961.
Valiuddin, M., *The Quranic Sufism*, Delhi, 1959.
Swami Virekananda, *Complete Works*, Almora, 1924–32.
Wain, J., ed., *Anthology of Modern Poetry*, London, 1963.
Wallenrod, R., *The Literature of Modern Israel*, New York, 1956.
Warren, H. C., *Buddhism in Translations*, Harvard, 1915.
Watson, B., ed., *Mo Tzu: Basic Writings*, Columbia, 1963.
Watt, W. M., *Freewill and Predestination in Early Islam*, London, 1948.
Wensinck, A. J., *The Muslim Creed*, Cambridge, 1932.
Wesley, J., *An Earnest Appeal to Men of Reason and Religion*, 1806 (8th edn.).
Whitman, W., *Complete Poetry and Selected Prose and Letters*, London, 1964.
Williams, J. A., *Islam*, New York, 1961.
Yi-pao Mei, *The Ethical and Political Works of Motse*, London, 1929.
Zaehner, R. C., ed., *The Teaching of the Magi; a Compendium of Zoroastrian Beliefs*, London, 1956.
The Concise Encyclopaedia of Living Faiths, London, 1959.

INDEX OF REFERENCES

BIBLICAL (IN ORDER OF ENGLISH BIBLE)

Old Testament

Genesis

1: 2	13
1: 31	7, 34, 81
2: 17	88
4: 9	120
6: 1–4	81
12: 1f.	8
18: 16–33	18
22: 1–19	16

Exodus

9: 16	70
15: 1ff.	6
22: 21	5
23: 9	5
33: 19	69
33: 22	61

Leviticus

19: 33f.	5

Numbers

16: 26	15

Deuteronomy

4: 20	9
5: 21	61
6: 4	36
10: 19	5
24: 17	5

1 Samuel

chs. 27–9	180

2 Samuel

12: 7	18
24: 1ff.	18

1 Kings

8: 11	61

2 Kings

21: 5f., 10–13	12

1 Chronicles

21: 1ff.	18, 51

Job

1: 1	19
1: 6–12	19, 51
1: 8	19
5: 9–12	9
14: 7–12	23
19: 25f.	22
32: 2	19
38: 1	21
38: 4f.	21
40: 4	22
42: 2f., 6	22
42: 10	19

Psalms

6: 5	26
37	15
51: 1–5	84
101: 2–4, 6, 8	15
105: 42–5	7

Proverbs

3: 11	16, 78
10: 27	12
24: 19f.	15

Ecclesiastes

2: 24	17
3: 1f.	18
3: 9–14	18
3: 11	21
5: 14	23
7: 29	17
8: 10–14	16
9: 2f.	17
9: 4	17
9: 5f.	23
9: 9	17
9: 11	17
12: 5	17
12: 5–7	24

Isaiah

3: 10f.	11
4: 23	13

Index of References

New Testament

Index of References

Index of References

RABBINIC SOURCES

PATRISTIC WRITERS

Index of References

QURAN

Index of References

HADITH

MUSLIM WRITERS

Index of References

Index of References

Index of References

Index of References

JAINISM

Acaranga Sutra
   i. 7. 6   282

Mahapurana
   iv. 16 ff.   284

Samaradikyakatha
   ii. 55–80   279

Sutrakritanga
   i. 1. 1 ff.   281 f.

Uttaradhyayana Sutra
   xix. 61 ff.   279

ZOROASTRIANISM

Yasna
   xxx. 3–6   272
   xliii. 16   272
   xlv. 2   271
   xlvii. 2 f.   272

MANICHAEISM

Manichaean Psalmbook
   ccxxiii. 5 ff.   275
   ccxxiii. 30   277

Pss. of Thomas
   8   277

Chinese Treatise
   xi (114)   277

INDEX OF MEDIEVAL AND
MODERN AUTHORS

(N.B. This index refers only to actual quotations; for general references and for writers discussed but not quoted, see the General Index.)

Aquinas, T., 94f.
Aurobindo, Sri, 230f., 260

Barrett, C. K., 61f.
Barth, K., 71
Beauvoir, Simone de, 25
Bentley, R., 39
Bonhoeffer, D., 134–6

Calvin, J., 95
Canisius, P., 94f.
Charlton, B., 138f.
Ch'en, J., 187
Ch'en Tu-hsiu, 172
Courcelle, P., 285
Cragg, K., 122
Cummings, A. J., 155f., 159

Deutscher, I., 155
Donne, J., 1
Dostoevsky, F., 53
Duchesne-Guillemin, J., 273

Eckhart, Meister, 162
Einhorn, M., 39f.

Flew, A., 91f.
Freud, S., 1f.
Frost, R., 22

Gandhi, M. K., 234f.
Govinda, A., 237, 251, 261f.
Graham, A. C., 181
Grou, J. N., 266

Hampeté Ba, 128
alHasan alBasri, 129
Hassler, A., 267f.
Hay, M., 37f.
Heath, A. G., 91
Hick, J., 84f.
Hoskyns, E. C., 60
Huang Hsing, 170
Hu Yin, 181f.

Iqbal, M., 122

Jamali, M. F., 133–6

Kelly, J. N. D., 82–4
Kemmer, N., 289
Kilpatrick, T. P., 57
Kovenski, E., 39f.

Lancaster, L., 139
Landé, A., 288f.
Lewy, G., 39
Liang Ch'i Ch'ao, 167f.

Maimonides, 32f.
Mardan-Farrukh, 273f.
Mascall, E. L., 93f.
Mo Tzu, 181f.

Nehru, J. L., 232f.
Nhat Hanh, Th., 266–8
Niebuhr, R., 64

Patanjali, 233
Pelly, L., 131–3
Prabhu, P. H., 219

Radek, K., 156–8
Radhakrishnan, S., 194, 195, 203
Ramanuja, 228
Ransom, J. C., 290

Sangharakshita, Bh., 247f., 253, 262
Sartre, J.-P., 147
Schaff, A., 162–4
Schram, S., 167, 189f.
Schwartz, B. I., 173
Seale, M. S., 124
Sen, K. M., 194
Shalom, Sh., 41
Shankara, 203, 218
Skolimovski, H., 160

Tagore, R., 235f.

Index of Medieval and Modern Authors

GENERAL INDEX

General Index

General Index

Hari, 229
Hasan, 130 ff.
Heaven, 24, 29, 101, 116, 126, 132 f., 147, 181, 252
Hebrews, Letter to, 78 f.
Hegel, G. W. F., 137, 165, 185
Hell, 24, 29, 101, 116, 126
Hellenisation, 27
Heresy, 94 f.
Hermogenes, 83
Hijra, 107, 122
Hinduism, 218 f., 234 f., 284; *advaita*, 227; appearance in, 197, 211 ff., 229, 230–1; and asceticism, 207, 128 f., 229 f., 232; diversity in, 193 ff., 203, 225; incarnation in, 195, 228 f.; literature of described, 198–200, 208 f., 220; polytheism in, 199 ff., 207; Scripture in, 198, 209, 219 f.; the Self in, 196, 215, 226; tolerance in, 194
Hisda, 34
History, 5 ff., 9, 21, 32, 42, 64, 70, 106 f., 110, 122, 133, 153, 160; Deuteronomic theory of, 11 f, 22
Hitler, 37 f.
Hittites, 7
Hudaibiya, Treaty of, 109
Huna, 35
Hunan, 170 f.
Hunan Report, the, 177 f., 186
Hundred Flowers Campaign, 176, 189
Husain, 130 ff.

Iblis, 105, 114, 119
Iktisab, 125
Inclinations, Two, 36, 52
Indra, 199, 216, 229, 253
Industrial Revolution, 140
Inquisition, 155
Irenaeus, 33, 84–6, 89
Isaac, sacrifice of, 16
Ishmael, 35
Islam, 99, 108, 111, 116, 128, 133 ff., 160; meaning of, 105
Israel, land of, 34, 37, 40; religion of, 5 ff., 9, 18, 42 f.
Itvara, 282

Jacob, 69 f.
Jainism, 209, 222, 223, 278–84; many-sidedness in, 193, 283; and non-violence, 281; soul in, 278
Jairus, daughter of, 49
James, Letter of, 78

Jeremiah, 12–15, 29, 70
Jerome, 95
Jerusalem, fall of, 8, 11, 12, 20, 29 ff.
Jesus, 42, 76, 80, 81, 86, 92 ff., 96, 100, 135; ascension of, 61, 72, 92; authority of, 48 ff.; compassion of, 50, 58, 63; death of, 60 f., 64 ff., 71, 92; foreknowledge of, 46 ff.; fulfilment of Scripture, 69, 76; imitation of, 68, 74 f., 77 f., 80, 94, 97, 135; as interpretation of Judaism, 44 f., 53; as light, 59 ff.; practical response of, 48 ff., 54, 57; in Quran, 121 f.; relationship with God, 44 f., 48 ff., 54, 56 f., 59 ff., 65 f., 80, 89; resurrection shared, 66 ff., 72 f., 76; sayings of, 77, 135; as second Adam, 72, silence of, 49; temptations of, 50, 52 f.; as Victim, 82, 89; as Victor, 82
See also Crucifixion, Resurrection, Victory
Jews, persecution of, 27 ff., 37 f.
Jibril, 132
Jihad, 117
Jiva, 196, 278, 282
Job, 19–23, 25, 27, 30, 34, 57, 109, 215
Johanan, 35
John of Damascus, 123
Jonah, 35
Jose, 35
Joseph, story of, 16
Judaism, 42 ff., 284 f.; rabbinic, 31 ff.
Judas, 59, 61
Justice, 35, 69 f., 81, 195
Justification, 84

Kalam, 125, 127
Kali, 204, 206
Kalpa, 262
Kama, 219
Karbala, 131
Karma, 201 f., 207, 213 ff., 218, 220 f., 223, 229; in Buddhism, 248 f.; in Jainism, 278 ff.; meaning of, 195
Karmayoga, 227
Kasb, 125
Kautsky, 152
Khandha, 244
Kharijites, 131
Khawarij, 109, 131
Khrushchev, N., 167 f.
Kolakowski, L., 160–2
Krishna, 209, 225–8; as incarnation, 225, 228 f.

General Index

General Index

Paul, 13, 30, 68–76, 81, 84, 94, 97;
visions of, 68
Pedersen, J., 24
Pen, the, 124
Persia, 52, 125, 271
Peter, 1st Letter of, 77f.
Pharaoh, 6, 69f., 106
Pharisees, 31f., 44, 49, 65
Pilate, Pontius, 54
Polycarp, 96
Polytheism, 199, 201ff.
Potter, image of, 13
Poverty, 37
Prajapati, 208, 210, 216, 253
Prayer, 34, 45, 97, 135f., 207
Predestination, 123ff., 130, 134
Profit, 140, 142–5
Proletariat, 140; dictatorship of, 150, 153
Prophets, 10, 18, 69, 79, 100, 107, 129, 140
Psalms, suffering in, 9
Punabbhava, 247

Qadar, 123ff.
Qadariyya, 124f.
Qadir, 102
Quality (and quantity), 17, 89, 91
Quang-Duc, Th., 266
Quran, 99–122, 124, 126f., 128, 133f.;
created or uncreated, 99; Jesus in,
121f.; problem of suffering in,
101ff.; revelation in, 99f.; social
teaching of, 117

Raba, 34
Rabbinic Judaism, *see* Judaism, Rabbinic
Radek, K., 155–9
Rahula, 260, 262
Ramanuja, 196, 228
Ravana, 223
Rebirth, 195, 213, 218, 221, 226, 228,
239, 246f., 248f.
Redemption, 10, 19–21, 33, 71, 82, 87
Religion, importance of suffering in, 1, 93
Resurrection, 46, 57, 61, 63, 66f., 70,
72, 76, 81, 92, 96, 98, 121f.
Revelation, 5, 7, 14, 28f., 99, 127, 133
Revelation, Book of, 79f.
Revolution, Russian, 151ff.
Robinson Crusoe, 164
Roy, M. N., 180
Rudra, 201, 204, 206
Rumi, 130
Russell, B., 156f.

Sabaeans, the, 100
Sabr, 114
Sacrifice, 28, 34, 36, 71, 75, 82, 89, 191,
199, 200f., 209, 261
Sadducees, 34, 43, 79
Saints, imitation of, 35
Saivism, 204
Samadhi, 255
Samkhara-dukkha, 241
Samkharakhandha, 245
Samsara, 207, 213f., 218, 220f.; in
Buddhism, 249, 265; meaning of,
195ff.
Sanctification, 84
Sariputta, 250, 252, 255, 257
Sartre, J.-P., 147, 162
Sastra, 220, 224
Satan, 51ff., 82, 105, 119
Satyagraha, 235
Schaff, A., 162–4
Scripture, interpretation of, 43f.
Self-change, 148, 155, 190
Senility, 104
Sermon on the Mount, 54ff.
Sermon on the Plain, 54ff.
Serpent, the, 52, 81
Servant, the, 20
Servetus, 95
Shankara, 196, 200, 227
Sheep and Goats, parable of, 58
Shema, 36
Sheol, 24, 26
Shiism, 130
Shubbiha lahum, 121
Sila, 255, 265
Siloam, Tower of, 54, 63
Simeon b. Yohai, 34
Sin, 28, 32, 33, 35, 51, 59, 64, 68, 71, 78,
82, 88, 93, 109, 132, 202; *see also*
Original Sin
Sinification, 165ff.
Sita, 223
Siva, 204, 206
Slavery, 138f.
Smriti, 220, 223f.
Sodom, plea for, 18
Solon, 39
Soul, 83, 89, 207, 228, 230, 241ff., 278,
287
Sruti, 198
Stalin, J., 152, 154–9, 167, 175, 180,
188f.
Stephen, 76
Stoicism, 83

317

General Index

Suffering of animals, 37, 125, 127; as a blessing, 34ff., 207; of children, 125f., 138; consequence of *karma*, 201, 215, 221, 223, 248f.; distribution of, 9, 10, 12f., 14, 16, 19, 54, 63, 101, 108, 215; equation of, 143ff.; and the gods, 201ff., 205; infliction of on others, 49, 221f., 223, 225, 233; of innocent, 7, 15, 19ff., 26, 108, 131; instrumental view of, 3, 35, 37, 78f., 94f., 106ff., 113, 123, 125, 130, 149f., 152ff., 159f., 187ff., 191, 207; practical response to, 18, 46f., 48ff., 54, 56, 67f., 73, 75f., 81, 93, 116ff., 137, 146ff., 149, 163f., 169, 173, 178, 185, 223f., 264, 266, 270; problem of, 1ff., 7, 15, 27, 31, 57, 68, 69, 80, 81, 101ff., 108, 115, 225, 235, 265; as punishment, 11ff., 15f., 19, 22, 24, 27, 29, 32, 33ff., 51, 69, 78f., 85, 106, 108, 129f.; purposeful, 105ff., 201; as redemptive, 21, 28, 36f., 57, 59, 63, 65f., 82, 234f.; as sacrifice, 28, 71, 75, 200f., 205; and sovereignty, 80; as a test, 34, 109ff., 129f.; transience of, 90, 212ff., 240ff.
Suffering Servant, 20
Sufism, 128–30
Suicide, 266f.
Sukha, 240, 250
Sumferei, 64
Syadvada, 283
Synoptics, 58; meaning of term, 46

Tafwid, 125
Tagore, R., 234–6
Tanha, 250–2
Tanhakkhaya, 252
T'ao Ch'ien, 168f.
Taoism, 173, 181
Tathagata, 238
Ta'ziya, 131ff.
Temple, 31, 36
Temple, W., 97
Temptations, the, 50, 52f.
Tertullian, 83f.
Thamud, 100, 107
Theism, verification of, 57, 68, 91f.
Theodicy, problem of, 81, 85, 102

Theravada, 258
Tibet, 188
Time, 17, 206
Tohu wabohu, 13
Torah, 18, 27, 29, 34, 37, 42f.; meaning of, 7, 43
Tragedy, 120f.
Transfiguration, the, 62
Trinity, the, 58, 68, 86, 87, 287
Trotsky, L., 151, 153, 180

Ubada b. asSamat, 124
Udgitha, 210
Uhud, 102, 107f.
Upanishads, 198, 200, 208–18; and Vedas, 208f.
Utopia, 146

Varuna, 201f.
Vedanta, 195, 200, 208
Vedas, 195, 197f., 198–208; Four, 199
Verification, 57, 68, 91f.
Victory, 46, 53, 57f., 62, 66, 72ff., 80, 82, 98, 119, 122
Vietnam, 266–8
Violence, 49, 117, 187–90
Viparinama-dukkha, 240
Vishishtadvaita, 228
Vishnu, 225, 229

Well, Parable of the, 279ff.
Wells, H. G., 154f.
Wesley, J., 92f., 98
Woes, Messianic, *see* Messianic woes
Wolkovisk, 39f.
Woods, parable of the, 30
Wu Chih-hui, 173f.

Yahweh, 5, 9, 11ff., 14ff., 20f., 26
Yama, 203, 205f., 264
Yang Ch'ang-chi, 168
Yezer, 36, 52, 284
Yoga, 227

Zakat, 117
Zekuth, 36
Zion, 21, 29, 41
Zoroaster, 1, 8, 271f.
Zoroastrianism, 8, 52, 125, 270–4